GATEWAYS TO DOGMATICS

GATEWAYS TO DOGMATICS

Reasoning Theologically for the Life of the Church

GERHARD SAUTER

WILLIAM B. EERDMANS PUBLISHING COMPANY
GRAND RAPIDS, MICHIGAN / CAMBRIDGE, U.K.

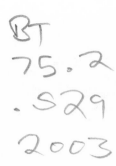

BT
75.2
.S29
2003

© 2003 Wm. B. Eerdmans Publishing Co.
255 Jefferson Ave. S.E., Grand Rapids, Michigan 49503 /
P.O. Box 163, Cambridge CB3 9PU U.K.

Printed in the United States of America

07 06 05 04 03   7 6 5 4 3 2 1

Library of Congress Cataloging-in-Publication Data

Sauter, Gerhard.
    Gateways to dogmatics: reasoning theologically for the life of the church /
    Gerhard Sauter.
        p.   cm.
    Include bibliographical references and index.
    ISBN 0-8028-4700-5 (pbk.: alk. paper)
    1. Theology, Doctrinal. I. Title

    BT75.2.S29 2003
    230 — dc21

                                                 00-026489

www.eerdmans.com

For my grandchildren

Samuel †

Daniel Benjamin

Alina Beate †

Richard Léon

Adrian David

Contents

Indexes

Abbreviations

ANFa	The Ante-Nicene Fathers (Roberts and Donaldson)
APTh	Arbeiten zur Pastoraltheologie
AUU.SDCU	Acta Universitatis Upsaliensis. Studia doctrinae Christianae Upsaliensia
AzTh	Arbeiten zur Theologie
BDS	Bonner dogmatische Studien
BEvTh	Beiträge zur evangelischen Theologie
BFChTh	Beiträge zur Förderung christlicher Theologie
BSTh	Beiträge zur systematischen Theologie
BZNW	Beiheft zur Zeitschrift für die neutestamentliche Wissenschaft
CA	Augsburg Confession
CC	*Creeds of the Church,* ed. John H. Leith, 3rd ed. (Louisville, 1982)
CSEL	Corpus Scriptorum Ecclesiasticorum Latinorum
DBW	*Dietrich Bonhoeffer's Works*
EK	*Evangelische Kommentare*
ET	English translation
EvTh	*Evangelische Theologie*
FKDG	Forschungen zur Kirchen- und Dogmengeschichte
FSÖTh	Forschungen zur systematischen und ökumenischen Theologie
GlLern	*Glaube und Lernen*
GT	German translation
HST	Handbuch systematischer Theologie
HUTh	Hermeneutische Untersuchungen zur Theologie
KuD	*Kerygma und Dogma*

KVR	Kleine Vandenhoeck-Reihe
KZG	*Kirchliche Zeitgeschichte*
LM	*Lutherische Monatshefte*
LW	*Luther's Works* (Pelikan and Lehmann)
NPNF	A Select Library of the Nicene and Post-Nicene Fathers of the Christian Church (Schaff)
NT	New Testament
NZM.S	Neue Zeitschrift für Missionswissenschaft. Supplementa
NZSTh	*Neue Zeitschrift für systematische Theologie und Religionsphilosophie*
ÖR	Ökumenische Rundschau
ÖR.B	Ökumenische Rundschau. Beiheft
OT	Old Testament
PG	Patrologia Graeca (Migne)
PL	Patrologia Latina (Migne)
PSB	*Princeton Seminary Bulletin*
SC	Sources Chrétiennes
SIGC	Studien zur interkulturellen Geschichte des Christentums
SLAG	Schriften der Martin-Luther-Gesellschaft (in Finland)
TB	Theologische Bücherei
TEH	Theologische Existenz heute
ThGl	*Theologie und Glaube*
ThPr	*Theologia practica*
ThW	Theologische Wissenschaft
TRE	*Theologische Realenzyklopädie*
VF	*Verkündigung und Forschung*
WA	*Martin Luther, Kritische Gesamtausgabe* ("Weimar Edition")
ZDPV	*Zeitschrift des deutschen Palästina-Vereins*
ZEE	*Zeitschrift für evangelische Ethik*
ZKTh	*Zeitschrift für katholische Theologie*
ZThK	*Zeitschrift für Theologie und Kirche*

Introduction

1. An Invitation

You are invited to come into a workshop in dogmatics. If questions of Christian faith concern or trouble or distress you, you will find that you have, perhaps unwittingly, been long since engaged in dogmatics. I want to show you what dogmatics involves, to make you acquainted with its rules, and I hope that you will once again take notice of how much this is your own affair. You will not be content to make an occasional visit or to treat dogmatics as work viewed by you but done by those who seem to be much more productive, whereas you yourselves perhaps find it only toilsome or find evidence of blindness in this whole area.

Perhaps you expected something different from the title of this book. You were perhaps looking for a foundation for the Christian faith, for pillars to be sunk deep into insecure ground and supports to be laid (or explored) which would hold out promise of a convincing presentation of the Christian faith. After all, the very meaning of "Christianity" or "Christian faith" is often laid open to question. Considerable effort seems to be needed to make this faith credible and to show that it has a right to exist. Such a foundation would perhaps demonstrate how irreplaceable the loss would be if this faith were to fade from the historical and cultural scene. But our presentation will not take this course, at least not at first. We will have to take up such themes only in chapter IV when dealing with dogmatic crises.

Perhaps you are not so skeptical about the dogmatic enterprise. Perhaps you do not regard it as an occupation that unquestionably handles outdated products. But you have long since lost touch with it except as you are questioned by diehards who are behind the times. You might still have a desire, however, to take up dogmatics again without presuppositions, to start at the beginning and advance by very small steps, on guard lest anyone see that you are engaging in a change of position. It may be that you first need to have the conditions presented to you under which dogmatics is at all possible. Then you will need a new exploration with the newest critical instruments in order that the materials of existing dogmatics might be reconstructed along new and surer grounds, with a steel structure to ensure the brickwork against collapse. We will not begin, however, with these restorative measures. We will deal with them only in IV.1 and IV.2.

I want us to look at some really elementary things first. What is elementary is neither factually nor critically a "nothing." It means beginning where we are. This can involve much toil and conflict, but it will also involve an effort to achieve clarity.

You might perhaps find that I speak too theologically, too directly, going at things like a bull at a gate. My excuse must be that the exposition demands this. But I want to warn you in advance. The truth is that the theme itself causes this procedure. We can come to grips with dogmatics, and even with its probing questions, only if we are ready to face what it has to say to us. Even basic questions cannot be discussed unless we try at least to take them seriously as a part of dogmatic thinking, and not just as a substructure into which any unguarded cellar key can give us access. This is why I want first to describe and reflect upon these matters as I formulate theological statements, and do so rather assertively.

The students who can best adjust to this preliminary work, and take the steps indicated, are those who are used to wrestling with other questions that concern them. These questions will not just be those that relate in familiar or problematic ways to God, faith, religion, or church. Rather, these students have wanted to find out by questioning how well founded are all the things they see and hear in the church and what it says and does, or in the wider sphere of Christianity. To what does this truly point us? Nor should we forget the young theologians of Asian and African churches whose theological instruction has not acquainted them with truth criteria, and who for this reason note that what the church says and does ties them in knots! Are we any better off in our own countries?

To prepare the way for an encounter with dogmatics, we need an adequate knowledge of where it appears and how it comes about. I will thus begin by sketching some of its features. Illustrations should show us what it looks like, and will, I hope, help us to see into what type of thinking we shall be involuntarily drawn. This will happen when we learn to ask the questions that the existence of the church raises, and to put them in a way that causes astonishment at its existence as we try to understand its basis a little better. This existence is indeed not so much irritating and questionable as wonderful and incomprehensible.

We encounter dogmatics when we ask what the church means and deal with the many questions it poses. We need to explore which of those questions lead *in medias res,* into the very heart of what is real.

We can best achieve a living picture of dogmatics if we approach it from different angles and thus get to know it as fully as possible. This book is not structured so as to deal with its theme from beginning to end, or to build up the edifice stone by stone. We shall look at elementary things from different angles or progress from a complex impression to a discussion of the elementary things. It is my hope that in this way dogmatics will be given an increasingly plastic character.

Workshops are not for instruction but for gaining experience. Textbooks come at the end of the learning process, which involves participation in a growing series of tasks which enable us to see how things fit together as we study them (cf. Thomas S. Kuhn, *The Structure of Scientific Revolutions* [Chicago, 1962]).

The first reading experiences of my student assistants have shown that beginners do best to begin with chapter II. A friend has even recommended that the final chapter be read first. The sequence of chapters is not arbitrary, but the fact that different approaches are possible, and even desirable, reflects the diversity of all the paths to dogmatics — and reflects the changing perspectives taken up in this book.

2. The Origin of the Book

This introduction to dogmatics has a long history. Something should be said about this history if its background and its unavoidable distinctives are to be understood.

The starting point was my encyclopedic survey of dogmatics and report on the current state of dogmatics in Germany and German-speaking countries, "Dogmatik I," composed for *Theologische Realenzyklopädie,* vol. 9 (Berlin and New York, 1982), pp. 41-77. Frederick Herzog of Duke Divinity School (Durham, North Carolina), who wrote "Dogmatics in the United States," instigated a translation of my survey in order to promote theological discussion in the English-speaking world. But unfortunately, legal problems opposed its publication. I thus resolved to undertake a new version.

Many insights favored this expansion — first of all, insights I had gained when teaching theology at various places in the United States and at the Christian Theological Academy of Warsaw, not to speak of regular exchanges with colleagues in Oxford and Budapest. These drew attention to the ecumenical character of dogmatics.

This ecumenical approach cannot be recognized simply by going back to the great, common, historical traditions which the churches shared and which are still alive, rudimentary though they may be. That the churches have something basic in common emerged from ongoing conversations in which such things were seen to be supporting elements even though they were not viewed as edicts and could not be reduced to a common denominator. Is it not one of the signs of the truth of theology that in conversations in which there is true hearing a true mutuality comes to light even though it cannot be explained historically, sociopsychologically, or in any other way? Sooner or later dogmatic encounters will lead to a surprising unity even across many frontiers and barriers.

My stays in England and the United States and talks with friends in Poland and Hungary then made me aware of regional distinctives, and these caused me to ask on what basic texts a dogmatics really rests in every place — or ought to rest when we have to appeal to it in cases of doubt or crises of decision. I suggest that such a text should include the direction-pointing formulas of the early church and Reformation theology (I.3.3) and the Barmen Declaration of 1934, whose teaching is outlined in I.4.1 and whose articles are adduced in I.3 and II.8. It is on these statements that I have "positioned" myself initially for my statements. We should not abandon this position in favor of a survey, yet it is significant only as a background for the specific experiences in thinking that point us beyond it. Some of the things I have said may be put in parentheses. They are of only regional interest, at least for now. Parts of chapters III and IV may be treated thus. At a pinch you might omit them altogether, though they are important if you are to capture the whole picture.

Finally I received further impetus from many talks with philosophers, natural scientists, and theologians who have a scientific interest at the Center of Theological Inquiry at Princeton, New Jersey, where I was several times a member, made possible on two occasions by a grant from the Volkswagen Foundation, to which I express my thanks. From exchanges of views it emerged that one of the problems in achieving mutual understanding is that too little is known about the structure and appearance of theology. It is usually used by philosophers and scientists in the form of products that are ready-made or half ready-made. Subjects are chosen — for example, "creation and world contingency," or "indeterminism and freedom" — that appear to lend themselves to a comparison of views in areas of common interest. Theoretical elements, for example, in cosmology, are projected onto theological presuppositions. All-embracing explanations of the world are offered, though it is not clear what precise agreement there is, if any, between the speaker's faith and his subject. Theology is often cut up into specific themes that are used like sets in a theater.

What is meant by theological inquiry? We cannot reply to this question simply by pointing to historical investigations in theology, no matter how imposing. Leading on from the question of theological inquiry, and especially of research into the basis of theology, my concern in previous articles has been to achieve a theory of theology, which I will now try to develop further. Preliminary work on many sections of this book has been done in various essays. Clarification has come through subsequent conversations on them, and I must thank all those who, through suggestions and criticism, have helped to weave these portions (listed in an appendix) into a pattern. In those essays, I have often referred more comprehensively to the state of discussion or to relevant literature. Here I limit myself to the most important examples. Other books can be found in the bibliographies at the end of the book. I make only occasional use of notes. Above all things, I did not want to leave the impression that dogmatics is built on much-worked-over land.

I regard an encounter with dogmatics, in the form of developing theological judgment, as necessary not least because for many decades it has not been clear how theology can approach the intellectual disasters and turbulent understandings that are reactions against the massive changes in reality and their hardly foreseeable ramifications, in other words, how dogmatics is to see itself historically. It has been the custom to adduce philosophical concepts or all-inclusive theories relating to the constitution of reality, or to participate in their development, in order that theology can speak afresh in the new setting. The aim is to prevent theology from being tossed about in the flux of things, even if it is hardly possible (or desirable) to give it a stable footing in this flux anymore. The anxious concern is that the faith cannot be presented with old-fashioned means of thought. If dogmatics is seen as simply part of the tradition, then it can seemingly be replaced even if only by different thinking on traditions.

I must not anticipate what I hope to say and show later. But I must take up the point that if dogmatics can demonstrate that it is truly a movement of thought, then it carries within it an astonishing power of renewal. This power is not just the seemingly dynamic force of an incalculable ability to adjust. It has at least something of the "renewing of the mind" which Paul mentions in Romans 12:2. It is created by the unfathomable acts of God's boundless mercy. From the expectation which is based on this action, theology can develop a sensitivity to everything that has occurred and does occur. In order for this to happen, of course, it must lay itself open to God's action. For this reason, and not because of any desire for self-assertion, theologians must not try to master existence. In memory and expectation of God's action, the theological perception of events will be formed. What Christians say about God implies a specific view of time, and theologians have learned thereby how to speak about the past, the present, and the future in a way that does not connect them as a stretch of time, as if what is past is perishable and has long since gone and what is future does not yet exist.

My hope is that these approaches to dogmatics, and encounters with it, will not just serve as an introduction to theological students but will also act as a stimulus to pastors and those who are involved in Christian education to find in dogmatics a part of their calling.

The biblical references in most cases are taken from the New Revised Standard Version.

I owe many thanks to Michael Beintker of Münster, Hinrich Stoevesandt of Basel, Hans G. Ulrich of Erlangen, Rowan Williams of the University of Oxford (of which I am an external member) and now archbishop of Canterbury, to Diogenes Allen and Daniel L. Migliore of Princeton Theological Seminary for their insights and suggestions for improvements, and to Wallace M. Alston Jr., Director of the Center of Theological Inquiry at Princeton, as well as Don S. Browning and William H. Lazareth, the Directors of Research, for their support. Support has also been found in the suggestions and constructive criticism of past and present colleagues, especially Heinrich Assel, Rainer Fischer, Ernstpeter Maurer, and, in particular, Caroline Schröder. Henning Theißen prepared the indexes.

Thanks are also owed to the friends who helped this book on its way and contributed to the shaping or clarification of certain sections, but who did not live to see its completion: Paul Lehmann of New York, Harold Nebelsick of Louisville and Princeton, Hellmut Traub of Bietigheim, and Ervin Vályi-Nagy of Budapest. With them I experienced the *mutuum colloquium* that dogmatics brings with it.

The German version of the book was finished at Princeton in February 1998 and published in late fall 1998. I am very grateful to Geoffrey W. Bromiley, who translated it, and to my wife, Annegrete, Steffan Davies (Oxford), Mary and Paul D. Matheny (Conroe, Texas), and Jochen Schmidt (Bonn), who helped me to revise several parts of the translation and to complete the bibliographical references. Reinhard Hütter of Duke Divinity School contributed to the proper translation of basic terms that are characteristic of this book.

Bonn, July 2002   GERHARD SAUTER

I. Dogmatics as a Phenomenon

I.1. Why Dogmatics?

I.1.1. Dogmatics from an Outside Perspective:
The Church Steering Itself

Dogmatics is not to be found always and everywhere in the Christian world. It is a discipline in the Roman Catholic Church, a discipline in both the educational and the disciplinary sense. As a sphere of teaching and learning, it also has an acknowledged place in Protestant theology. It is a full field of study only in continental Europe, and even there religious studies have replaced it to a large extent in some Swedish universities. In Scotland and outside Europe, Lutheran, Reformed, and other confessional churches find a place for it in their theological seminaries. Usually in England and North America instruction is given in "systematic theology" or simply "theology." In III.1 we shall have to ask whether and how far these overlap with or at least touch on dogmatics. Many churches and Christian associations completely avoid it. Or do they just avoid using the name?

To see dogmatics without the widespread reservations or even prejudices about it, we do well to take a distant view of the role dogmatics has played in theology and its history. The perspective of an outside spectator can help us grasp the vitality of religion, of religion as a social phenomenon.

By dogmatics in the broadest sense we understand the concepts of thought with which the basic materials of religious experiences and sit-

1

uational interpretations are discerned, worked over academically, checked for errors, and systematized.

This was how the theorist of social systems Niklas Luhmann defined religious dogmatics. It was for him a phenomenon that sociology could explain (*Funktion der Religion* [Frankfurt am Main, 1977], p. 126). Asking what dogmatics does, Luhmann replied that it shows how a "system" or social construct looks at reality. It gives evidence of its vitality. A common religious conviction or lifestyle that binds people together and commits them to one another needs to be regulated. This regulating is not the same thing as external regimentation. It rests on religious experiences and attempts to express their content. It thus needs to be "systematized" in order that contradictions may be excluded and connections of thought established. Only in this way can a total view achieve unity and not become diffuse or disorientating. If it moved in different directions and contradicted itself in principle, it would get in its own way and only cause confusion. The balance between the basic materials of religious experiences and situational interpretations must be preserved. Experiences must be expounded in the light of the existing situation of the adherents of the religion so that they can see how they relate to the adherents' world. If dogmatics focuses on the first religious experiences, which have usually been handed down in spoken form, it runs into the danger of passing on too rigidly what was authenticated in the past and is now thought to be valid. If, however, religious interest shifts to situational interpretations, there is a tendency to base experiences only on the significance of a given moment; a simple flexibility destroys the center of the power of conviction, making it a football bandied about according to the affairs of the day.

Why dogmatics? From a sociological angle it offers a guarantee that a religious fellowship will maintain its vitality as it steers its own course in constant interaction with the surrounding world. A balance sheet must be kept of this interaction if it is to continue. If dogmatics can achieve this result, it will prove itself to be a means by which social systems of a religious origin can steer their course. We must also say that dogmatics is vitally important and even necessary, more so today than ever, if religion is not to become a matter of optional private convictions and thus fade out of the social scene. For this reason it is to be regretted that dogmatics today has taken on so shadowy an existence. We might compare churches and religious groups often enough to ships that are tossed about in storms of impressions, tasks, and values, not holding fast to any one course, and even foundering, because their navigation is so disorderly or their steering is broken. We need more dogmatics, a functional dogmatics, of course, in keeping with the above definition. Whether that which theology calls dogmatics really deserves the name is something we shall have to investigate.

Luhmann's description of dogmatics can help us to look more closely at how religious fellowships are able to steer themselves. It is another question, and need not concern us here, whether it applies to all religions, those that use "thought concepts" and those that do not. Luhmann did not fix on that definition in the void. It clearly rested on systematizations that typify Western culture. For example, we have a dogmatics of law that controls and helps to develop our positive legal systems. The dogmatics of law is the systematics of positive law. Legal texts must be related to one another so as to demonstrate their inner integration. Only then can they be applied consistently to new cases. If contradictions come to light, the sources of error must be found and eliminated by coordination into the total structure.

The definition of a functional dogmatics is broad enough to embrace various forms of community self-regulation by means of thought concepts. The spectrum here is clearly much bigger than what dogmatics usually means in the Christian world.

Eastern Orthodoxy has embodied its tradition in the orderliness of the service and the liturgy. Here its riches are preserved. The unity of the liturgy might be expounded as a "theology." Individual themes that find expression in the liturgy have been commented upon by outstanding theologians, and their thoughts are assembled and find further elucidation. But we can hardly call this dogmatics, nor contrast it with the liturgy as an alternative textual construction.[1]

The Anglican Church often uses the liturgy as a theological guide or even more.[2] Liturgical changes are the fulfillment of theological changes. Accordingly, such theological changes either are fiercely debated or remain peripheral phenomena that are of little more than intellectual interest, even though they might seem to be radical. Theology consists essentially of the received tradition that received its shape from the great achievements of the early fathers and the scholastic theologians.

1. The *Orthodoxe Dogmatik* of the Romanian Dumitru Staniloae (3 vols. [Zurich, Einsiedeln, Cologne, and Gütersloh, 1985-95]) is an exception that proves the rule. This work is an attempt to bridge the gap between Greek and Russian theology on the one hand and Western theology on the other. Liturgy as the source of theology is best seen in *Die orthodoxe Theologie der Gegenwart* (Darmstadt, 1990), by Karl Christian Felmy.

2. See the comprehensive depiction by Horton Davies, *Worship and Theology in England*, 5 vols. (Princeton, 1961-75); 2nd ed., 3 vols. (Grand Rapids, 1996).

Other churches and fellowships of faith that for different reasons do not wish to be called churches find theology in their hymns, their prayers, their education, their lifestyle, and not least their ethos. We find this pattern in the medieval movements that were critical of the church, in the "lower churches," the Methodists and Baptists, in England, known as the Free Churches in Germany, and in the many denominations that have promoted Protestantism in the United States, and that by their missionary work have taken their message to other lands. If systematic presentations occur in Methodism, then these are closely related to the liturgical life,[3] or consist of directions for lifestyle,[4] or, like Anglican theology, give heed to the voices of the early church, drawing on these early sources in a theologically needy time.[5] What we find here is an openness to the thinking experiences of other churches, and especially to the theological traditions that might be called ecumenical, above all those that proceed from the development of dogmas that took place in the first five centuries of Christian history. But is all this really original dogmatic work? Is it not a borrowing from what was produced by other workshops in dogmatics? A loan made from the museum of dogmatic history which can be put to use only with much toil and much straining of historical understanding?

Another motivation for dogmatics as it has been described so far is the need to give constructive validity to the principles of a Christian lifestyle. How will a fellowship of faith define the guidelines for a good life? How can its perspectives of action be determined in a way that is as broad as possible but will still be binding on the community? An ethical starting point is typical of the contributions of Mennonite or Anabaptist theologians who have had such dreadful experiences in history with the dogmatic principles of the churches.[6] Along these lines a fellowship can make its theology plain in contrast to that of others.

Very broadly all these efforts fall in with Luhmann's definition and

3. Geoffrey Wainwright, *Doxology: The Praise of God in Worship, Doctrine, and Life: A Systematic Theology* (New York, 1980).

4. Walter Klaiber and Manfred Marquardt, *Gelebte Gnade. Grundriss einer Theologie der Evangelisch-methodistischen Kirche* (Stuttgart, 1993).

5. Thomas C. Oden, *Systematic Theology*, vol. 1, *The Living God*; vol. 2, *The Word of Life*; vol. 3, *Life in the Spirit* (San Francisco, 1992).

6. *Explorations of Systematic Theology from Mennonite Perspectives*, ed. Willard M. Swartley, Occasional Papers No. 7 (Elkhart, Ind.: Institute of Mennonite Studies, 1984); James W. McClendon, *Systematic Theology*, vol. 1, *Ethics* (Nashville, 1986). McClendon is a Mennonite, but the preface tells us that he was inspired to engage in this presentation when he taught at Notre Dame and cooperated with his colleagues there.

can be subsumed under it. They are all forms of regulation. They can be compared with one another. They show clearly, notwithstanding institutional differences, what is common to them all. Nevertheless, this is only an outside perspective. For this look dogmatics, or what functions as dogmatics, resembles a test tube carrying different mixtures. The substances are the same, the mixtures of them differ.

True for this outward perspective is the fact that

1. Dogmatics resembles a reference system for expressions of faith, showing how these expressions converge.

We need dogmatics if any operation, any train of thought, any statement, any form of action is to be accomplished, for it can have neither goal nor direction without a reference system. The meaning of any action or train of thought or statement must be found in a structure of the common binding dimensions and horizons. Without such a structure the themes cannot mesh. We can neither expand them nor give them precision. We are left with a chaotic field that does not permit any understanding. Religious experience falls apart. Religion can be only an optional or private matter. We need dogmatics, for it offers directions by which to orient our common speech and action and thereby to achieve a nexus of experience that is formative for the fellowship. Only by way of these directions do structures arise to which all the participants adhere in order to gain a criterion of what they think and do. In this way alone a transparency is opened up which enables us to connect our own convictions, even those that are relatively aberrant.

This is one way of looking at dogmatics. But dogmatics cannot view itself in this way alone. If it does, it ceases to be dogmatics, or at least a dogmatics that deserves to be called theological.

I.1.2. "What Christians Believe": A Shift of Perspective

To make such statements we must take a different perspective.

We are motivated to do this by what we found in the observations we outlined above. A closer look at many churches and Christian fellowships discloses an implicit dogmatics, that is, a structure of religious experiences based on various statements and then developed and systematized. This forms a subtext for texts that play a leading role in the forms of life that characterize the church or the fellowship. Other churches, on the

5

other hand, have an explicit dogmatics which bears this name and confronts their forms of church life. It may have different features. For Roman Catholics it is disciplinary as well as educational and theological. For Protestants it bears a relation to the church (depicted in I.1.5) as an "institution" that has its own ranking.

In some sense dogmatics stands alone. This does not mean that it distances itself from liturgy, prayer, proclamation, pastoral ministry, or other church activities or experiences. It does stand aloof from them, but avoids thinking of itself as elevated to higher spheres. A free-floating dogmatics would be a contradiction in terms. It cannot systematize only the underlying material of religious experience, in any case not without losing the substance of its subject matter.

Confronting the church, dogmatics is not something that regulates a church. It does not lay down statutes for its ministry which the church must observe and to which it is subject. Statutes of that kind would confront the church, but in a way that demands submission. Fear of such confrontations, of any kind of religious prescriptions, can easily lead to the rejection of all rules that should guide the churches' judgment. A dogmatics that stands on its own feet can at least help to guard against this fear.

We must now take a further step, one that is decisive for a real encounter with dogmatics. Does not confrontation cut both ways? Is not dogmatics also confronted? That depends, of course, on its orientation. When it confronts us linguistically, it can be a sign that religious experience, and what a fellowship of faith has to say about it, depends on "something" that is outside itself, that encounters it. It points to this something, for what it says is based upon it. In the linguistic confrontation we note also an essential confrontation.

To be able to say this precisely and adequately, we have to speak dogmatically and not just talk about dogmatics.

2. Dogmatics in a truly theological sense says what must be said as credible unconditionally and under all circumstances. God has revealed to us who he is. He has given himself expression by the pledge of his action. This pledge sets free the power of human judgment so that it perceives the reality God has promised. It issues a summons to faith, to faith as the work of God and yet also as human acceptance of what God does. God's promise confronts the church by summoning us to this faith.

In a pillar of cloud and of fire God led his people out of slavery in Egypt through the wilderness and on to the Promised Land (Exod. 13:21). This is a parable of the promise of God that confronts God's wandering people.

Dogmatics, pointing to this concealed yet sufficiently plain presence, can then point the way itself, if in a subordinate role.

Admittedly, we have here a clenched invitation that makes big demands on us. But as I have tried to show, we are not to read this as an obligatory definition. It is more an outline whose contours we will bring out in further encounters. In the first instance I must limit myself to describing the complexity of what is involved.

First of all, dogmatic statements are essentially made in the church precisely when dogmatics confronts the church. Dogmatics does not adopt any standpoint outside the church, as though gradually to draw closer to the church and then to enter it. Sooner or later it has to deal with the church's tradition as it is. This is its subject matter or material. From the outset it takes seriously the fact that it relates to what is said specifically about God, to what is said by the church. Dogmatics has to ask precisely whether what the church says really says what has to be said, whether all that it says and does and thinks keeps in view the promise of God that confronts it. For this reason dogmatics must from time to time oppose a church that keeps silent about this message or threatens to forget it. But it must not conduct itself as a constant critic of the church.

I will leave unanswered a question that might be raised by my second thesis; namely, whether we can speak this strongly of "the" church. I may make the provisional remark that God's promise confronts the particularity of every dogmatics, preventing it from giving its attention only to the boundaries of its own church. For the same reason we can speak quite freely of "the" dogmatics, not the dogmatics of any particular church. Each specific dogmatics will always seek that which is common to all dogmatics as this is confronted by the promise of God which opposes all peculiarities.

To speak dogmatically is to speak from within something. Nevertheless, it is not only to speak from within a religious social construct. That would only give an internal understanding. It is to speak with an orientation that clearly points *beyond* this structure, though the structure is not left behind and does not become superfluous. This orientation is not attained either by a transcendent flight, an ecstatic outbreak, or a profound exploration. It also breaks through the "basic material of religious experiences" (Luhmann). It not only opens up in depth what is the innermost basis of this experience, but is caught up and set in a movement that imparts certain perceptions.

Christianity has called the unity of such perceptions *faith*. Faith has a twofold sense. It denotes what is perceived, but it also denotes the perceiving. This perceiving drops anchor, as it were, in what is perceived. In what follows I will call this point of reference of dogmatics *externality* *(Externität)*. I am adopting a basic saying of Martin Luther. Dealing with the theme of assurance of faith, Luther left the level of concern about how religious fellowship is possible and discussed how fellowship with God comes to us.

> And this is our foundation: The Gospel commands us to look, not on our own good deeds or perfection but at God Himself as He promises, and at Christ Himself, the Mediator.
>
> And this is the reason why our theology is certain: it snatches us away from ourselves and places us outside ourselves, so that we not depend on our own strength, conscience, experience, person, or works but depend on which is outside ourselves [*extra nos*], that is, on the promise and truth of God who cannot deceive. (Martin Luther, *Lectures on Galatians* [1535], trans. Jaroslav Pelikan, *LW*, 26:387)

The externality of faith is that the truth of God is "outside ourselves" *(extra nos)*. This truth carries within it the promise that it incorporates, sustains, and accepts us. God being "outside" us no longer means "without" us or "against" us but comes to mean "with" us.

Dogmatics supports and strengthens this power of faith to judge. It does not embellish the faithful confidence of a few, no matter how that came into being. Instead it helps to give clarity to the common faith as an object and a movement. Dogmatics serves both the perceiving of faith and faith as the perceiving of the reality promised by God (see I.5 and III.3).

Finally, I need to draw attention to the phrase "unconditionally and under all circumstances" stated in my second thesis. Unconditionality means that what dogmatics has to say can be subjected to no other conditions than the one reason which makes possible what it says. Dogmatics does, of course, speak under specific conditions, in an existing situation, historical, cultural, and possibly social. But these things must not determine what it has to say (cf. III.1 and IV.2).

"Unconditional" is a term often used by Paul Tillich. He uses it to indicate the existential point of the Christian message:

> The religious concern is ultimate; it excludes all other concerns . . . it makes them preliminary. The unconditional concern is total . . . there is no place to flee from it.
>
> The word "concern" points to the existential character of religious

8

experience. That which is ultimate gives itself only to the attitude of ultimate concern. . . . It is a matter of infinite passion. (*Systematic Theology,* vol. 1 [Chicago, 1951], pp. 11-12)

I am not now concerned with what applies to us unconditionally, but with the fact that what dogmatics says is unconditional. What it says does, of course, concern us. We can never treat it with disinterest or indifference. But it tells us what must be said as coming from God rather than giving expression to our concern. In this way dogmatics differs from mere reflection on religious experience or the inward supervising of a religious worldview. To this extent the title "dogmatics" denotes a program, or better, the indication of a task, of a specific task that we have not chosen for ourselves.

Stating these things has pushed us well ahead. We seem to have taken a giant step forward, a step into dogmatics itself, into the center of the Christian faith. It is bound up with a shift in our way of talking, a shift that characterizes theological dogmatics. It is impossible now not to say "we" as an invitation is given to participate in this movement, and thus to abandon a comparative standpoint and the perspective of a mere spectator. Dogmatics is what is said *within* the church, dealing first with all that God has done and will do — even outside the church. We might *unwittingly* think we are talking only about *ourselves.* The "we" does not mean that dogmatics is only for those who belong to the church. Nor is it only for all those who are rhetorically taken to be addressed (II.9). Again, our different manner of speech does not mean that all imaginable unrestrained descriptions may pass as mere statements that have to be accepted. Naturally a theological dogmatics has to offer descriptions, but it does so in such a way that we can follow the train of thought. We can understand what is said even though for different reasons we may not agree with it. Thus a shift in perspective can be necessary, for it belongs to the inner versatility of dogmatics.

This versatility is considerably restricted, however, if dogmatics has to tell us only what Christians believe. This desire arouses expectation for many people. Perhaps they wish to identify themselves with what they have taken Christian faith to mean. Perhaps they wish to experience what belief involves, the whole range of it, all of it, in truth, from beginning to end. Many works on dogmatics do in fact offer an inventory of the Christian faith, a summary depiction of what authentic belief is. Even they avoid an encounter with dogmatics, nourishing the prejudice that dogmatics is merely a transmission of the tradition.

Nevertheless, we cannot ignore the question of what Christians believe. The "what" will decide whether those who call themselves Christians see something that is not only worthwhile saying but something that they cannot avoid saying because it is true. That explains the formulation in the second thesis: "What must be said under all circumstances in a credible and unconditioned way."

But how does this manifest itself? How does it find expression in speech?

We must pursue this question. We will have to turn to the New Testament, for at this point we still lack dogmatic texts. Yet what we say will at least impinge on our previous description of dogmatics.

I.1.3. The Language of Faith and Hope

In 1 Corinthians Paul shows in exemplary fashion how a statement of faith can become a point of crystallization in a dialogue, in a turbulent exchange that involves many threatening breaks and pauses. The debate leads up to this decisive point and can then take a new path, and in such a way that the disagreement with all that the Corinthians had taken for granted, or regarded as indifferent, now moves on to a new consensus growing out of acceptance of the promise of God rather than out of a shared conviction.

In the process Paul appeals to tradition (1 Cor. 15:3-4), to something already given a primary status. He stands on that which others have bindingly stated. They are guarantors of its reliability and are able to pass it on. But this recourse to tradition, no matter how authoritative, does not form a true theological justification for what he must say unconditionally in a situation of conflict. The tradition itself points to the fact that Jesus Christ lives in virtue of God's action, and that he does so in such a way that our hope of life with God has its basis with him and by him.

The theological argument, then, points to *God's action that is full of promise: what God has done in such a way as to give promise of his further action and presence.* This is what stands "behind" the theological sequence of 1 Corinthians 15. Yet it does not stand behind the text in such a way that we would have to reconstruct it historically as the condition for the genesis of the text and in order to produce the text over again when we have seen what lay behind it. Rather, "God's work so full of promise" is the theological basis of all that Paul says here in detail. We can see it at the different stages of the argument. It gives these stages their unity. It is the unity of what may be said "in faith," that is, in acceptance and appreciation of this act, and also "in hope," that is, in reaching out to this promise. To this extent, the basis does not lie behind the text; it is in the text, though not directly in Paul's words. Yet it also stands over against the text. The text does not imprison or enclose it. It may be stated separately, and stand behind other texts. It becomes the seed of dogmatic statements which say the same thing, speaking separately, yet not in isolation.

This confrontation, and the arguments that give it the space needed, radically call into question "religious experience as a basis" (Luhmann). It might be an experience of freedom, but a closer look shows this to be reckless and loveless even though it sees itself as without limits. Paul has contrasted with it the hope of life in God, so that hope and freedom are set in the context of the act of God in Jesus Christ. God has demonstrated here who he is. The basis and extent of hope is thus the same as trust in this God. This is what must be stated under all circumstances in a credible and unconditioned way. It must always be asserted in all circumstances. When circumstances change, this specific hope may be unfolded in other ways. But it will always be the same hope if it is real trust in God. The fact that this hope is always the same is shown by its relation to the resurrection of Jesus Christ, a relation about which there is much more to be said.

This might, of course, still be a mental concept enabling us to view and systematize the basic material of religious experiences and situation-related interpretations. The decisive difference, however, is the fact that we can speak about the basis of hope only in a way that is perceptible as the promise of God. Only this basis points unmistakably to God, to the God who has revealed himself in his acts and promises. It proves to be the basis and reason for belief. It does not rest on religious experience. It is pronounced to us and thus experienced. It is not embodied in experience. It tells us itself *why* we believe, *when* we believe *what* we believe. What sounds like a tautological sequence may sound offensive, but for this reason it is well adapted to point us to the inner nexus of the language of faith that includes grounding, condition, and content. Only a statement which compresses all these things can tell us why and how, in trusting in God, we no longer depend on ourselves, but trust in him alone. For this reason the language of faith is so inwardly rich in postulates.

Statements of faith encircle faith like watchmen protecting it, so that faith can develop under their protection. These watchmen are not like prison warders. They do not eye it mistrustfully. They are not preventing its escape. They are faithful companions.

In all that I have just said, I have been following the line of argument in 1 Corinthians 15 and its profound structure. But how does this bring us closer to dogmatics? Paul bursts his way through the thicket of modes of action and the convictions that accompany them. He reduces the confusion to the basic structure in which he formulates one life-and-death question, the question that summons us to faith and hope and love (cf. 1 Cor. 13:13). The answer to this question points us to the nexus which stands behind all interrelated human actions and mastery of them in thought, but which can be perceived only with the aid of specific statements about the reality of God and all that pertains to it. We may, in short, call these statements *statements of faith*. But this is a misleading term. The statements do not presuppose faith as a religious attitude, nor do they reflect such an attitude. They are statements that are spoken *in faith and in hope*. They point to God himself, to the God who has entered into a relationship with us, namely as judge and savior. They have to proclaim this. The language of theology has its truth claim here. And here we encounter dogmatics.

In 1 Corinthians Paul confronted various causes of division which threatened to destroy the community. Groups had arisen who saw their allegiance to this or that party chief as more important than the fellowship of all members of the community with Jesus Christ. Were marriage and celibacy of equal ranking in this difficult time? Was it an indifferent matter, or was it decisive (for or against fellowship with God), what food or drink to partake of or what body controlled the means of life? Could the Lord's Supper be made into a religious party for like-minded people to celebrate themselves, or what is the meaning of fellowship with the body and blood of Christ bringing together the well fed and the hungry? Did the various charismata fall into a hierarchy, and what was their true purpose?

The apostle did not issue orders on these and other questions. He sought to get to the bottom of them and to show that all must decide individually what weight and importance to attach to each of them. This applied even to the scandalous feasting at the Lord's Supper, more than offensive though this essentially was. Paul made it plain that at this feast we meet with God himself. On other issues such as eating flesh offered to idols, he avoided a shortsighted either/or and revealed the "inner tension" of faith. Everywhere his line of argument led back to the gospel which he preached, which the congregation had received, and wherein they stood (15:1): the death and resurrection of Jesus Christ. To give force to the Easter message Paul appealed to tradition, but the decisive point is that "if the dead are not raised, then Christ has not been raised. If Christ has not been raised, your faith is futile and you are still in your sins. Then those also who have died in Christ have perished. If for this life only we have hoped in Christ, we are of all people the most to be pitied" (15:16-19).

The sequence is theological. It does not build upon ideas of a life after death or of the eternal character of an authentic life, ideas that might have been confirmed by a credibly attested event. Instead, it raises the question of faith: In whom can our trust always be placed? Not: Who was the one about whom you learned? But: Who *is now*, and who *will be* forever, the one in whom we trust in life and in death? The question of what Christians believe is unexpectedly radicalized. Obviously all Corinthian Christians shared the religious belief that the Christ whom they worshiped was exalted over death. This surely carried with it, however, the conviction that the destiny of every believer was decided already. This was realized in a completely new and unconditioned experience of freedom.

The apostle, then, cannot just give a sharper edge to a statement of faith that he solemnly repeats each Sunday and bring out its practical ramifications. Naturally he makes very plain to members of the church what they are celebrating in worship and what they think they experience. But he also asks how far what they say about Jesus Christ really reaches. Through this question, he establishes that this core of the gospel has in fact been hopelessly hidden in most of them. With their hope "in Christ for this life only" (15:19), they have reconciled themselves with their own deaths. But this means that all other things have really become indifferent to them and they are negating the true character of that hope.

Paul utilizes a most expansive chapter and many involved lines of argument to correct this emphasis, and to show how far their hope should reach. The basis of our hope is not the credibly attested fact of the resurrection of Jesus. It is the act of *God* that brought this event to pass. On this ground the resurrection of Jesus Christ means that we can live in hope of our own resurrection. Moreover, risen from the dead, Jesus Christ is the hope for both the dead and the living. We would be false witnesses if we were to contradict the witness of God, namely, that he did raise up Christ. He has not really raised him up if the dead are not also raised (15:15). Then even "those who have died in Christ have perished" (v. 18). Verses 15-16 and 17 point out that the humanity of Jesus is not the reason why our destiny depends on his. Instead, God has reached beyond the frontier of death. Death is no longer the horizon of our expectation, not even in the sense that a life hereafter begins with death. The resurrection of Jesus Christ opens up a new horizon. It is the first step of the new history that is sketched in verses 23-28.

The theological reference to the act of the living God makes it plain that death itself cannot finally put up any resistance to God. God will be "all in all" (15:28). Finally, Paul uses tension-filled metaphors to speak about the mystery of the transfiguration that will make each of us at the moment of resurrection fully "transparent" for God. The chapter closes with a shout of praise to the God "who gives us the victory through our Lord Jesus Christ" (v. 57).

Looking at the letter up to this passage, we can see that Paul relates every decision to the question of the basis and extent of our hope. The complex discussion of the relation between the strong and the weak, for example, is very effective when seen from the angle of 1 Corinthians 15. Christians were afraid that they would be infected with idolatry if they ate flesh that had been "sanctified" by sacrifice. Their weak consciences thus led them to an aloofness from others in whom they feared such ungodly thoughtlessness. But those who knew that God is Lord over all things felt themselves to be immune against the misuses which the judgment of their stronger consciences told them could rest only on errors. They could freely decide what they should eat and with whom they should drink, thus unwittingly betraying the basis of their common hope.

Paul says that this is the decisive question of faith. In answering it, people will recognize that this question is a key to decisions and know what it includes, excludes, or even leaves open. Yet the content of the answer is not left to our own freedom or disposing. Those who truly answer must accept what God has done for him who was crucified. Otherwise they are contradicting God himself.

3. Dogmatics is built up as a structure of answers to the threefold question concerning why we believe, when we believe what we believe.

Faith is not at all the same thing as knowing "what we have to believe" and "what can only be believed." When we ask *what* Christians believe, we are also asking *why* they believe *when* they believe. Our never-ending question shows us that the language of faith goes up in stages. It does not allow us to stop at the answer to any one of these questions. We cannot answer one unless we also answer the others. They point to one another, and the answers form a living nexus that cannot finally be tied down. They thus give expression to the dynamic of an *inner* controversy. Hence the church does not need to abandon its own vocabulary or relate to other things in order to be stimulated to give an account of what it says and does. It receives its first and decisive impulse from within. Nat-

14

urally it is the case that the threefold question motivates us, at least in the form of appropriation, so that we know how to put these elementary questions.

I.1.4. Dogmatics as the Sibling of the Canon

The nexus of statements of faith such as we find, for example, in Paul has achieved autonomy, developed according to its inner dynamic, and is still forming itself. Would it not have been more natural to create a systematics of Scripture which Christians could regard as sacred? Would not this have set up a common denominator which could act as a key to open them like the doors of a splendid palace that the many who have left their traces behind were building, that would last through the years, not of a single style, but following a general plan, with the help of which you can find your way through the many rooms and even feel at home there. Many people have tried to take this course in the history of Christian theology, for they have created such a systematics out of sacred Scripture (the Bible) with, at best, the help of some basic theology toward which they were all striving and to which they returned with many variations. During the course of the interpretation of Scripture, many situation-related expansions could have been added to this systematics which would have enriched it and integratively established it.

In the early church we find a fascinating but terrifying example of one such systematics: Marcion's (ca. 85-160) view of salvation. We have only fragments of his system of thought, and we have these only from his theological opponents. Nevertheless, its outlines are clear, consistent, and free of contradictions, and they carry a fatal fascination. Friedrich Nietzsche gave one of his declarations of war on the philosophical tradition the title *Götzendämmerung, oder: Wie man mit dem Hammer philosophiert* (1889), proposing to do philosophy with a hammer. In a similar way, Marcion's program could carry the title, "Salvation from a perversely created world, or doing theology with a razor blade."

Marcion wanted to focus only on the "Christ of the good God" who would bring salvation to a world that had come under the sway of the "creator god." As with a big bang, a completely new history now begins. The world that was subject to a merciless god of power is liberated by the heavenly Redeemer, who had triumphed despite his sufferings in a world of oppression. This radical messianic systematics rests on an experience of redemption and promises to unlock the secret of the world, to shed light on all aspects of life, to separate the old and the new in history, and to lead the redeemed to their heavenly destiny. Marcion could also apply this systematics in a way of textual criticism. His concept of redemption gave him a sharply edged instrument with which he could detach the healthy substance of the Christian doctrine of salvation from alien tissue. From the traditional texts he took out the statements that were true because they were liberating, which, he claimed, had been overgrown by erroneous convictions about God and the world, based on a disastrous respect for the tyrannical creator god. The whole story of creation thus fell victim to Marcion's critical razor blade, but so, too, did many parts of the Jesus tradition and the epistolary corpus.

Marcion's uncannily logical systematics is still fascinating, especially in dark times when the world shows a fearful face.[7] The debate raised by this theology and variations upon it has not yet been concluded. It is like a smoldering fire that can very quickly flame up again.

At that time the church mounted the apostolic tradition against Marcion and began to assemble the canon of Holy Scripture. The rule of faith *(regula fidei)* arose around the same time, in different forms. The concurrence of the two was not accidental. The rule of faith was meant as an introduction to the study of the Bible. It showed God's action from creation to the end and consummation of all things. In order that this could be said in all dimensions, from God to the world and back again to God, Scripture was needed to bring out the tension of the divine work and thus prevent it from being reduced to a common denominator.

In the canon and the rule of faith the church confessed *God's ultimate act in Jesus Christ as the externality of the language of faith and hope.* God's act precedes this language, stands over against it, and can never be repeated or even embodied in human speech. That is why it is external to us. It is "the other" of human speech, but it is expressed *in* that speech, an outside on the inside, not the outside or the opposite.

In this respect, the Bible and the rule of faith are both of the same origin, even though they had different outward causes. Historically speaking, dogmatics can even be called the sibling of the biblical canon, though it has not borne this name yet. The biblical canon is a fruit of the confession of Christ. It cannot be conceived without dogmatics be-

---

7. Adolf von Harnack's *Marcion, das Evangelium vom fremden Gott. Neue Studien zu Marcion* (Leipzig, 1923-24; ET, *Marcion: The Gospel of the Alien God,* trans. John Steely and Lyle D. Bierma [Durham, N.C., 1990]) was stimulated by the catastrophes of the First World War.

cause it is dogmatics that tells us what to read in church — and what not to read. Dogmatics is essential if we are to read in the Bible what it has to tell us.

The inner defining of boundaries by the church proved to be a far-ranging decision, far richer in consequences and perspectives than was first thought. The church separated itself from "erroneous" convictions and called them heresies that would lead people away from accepting the work of God and hence from salvation. The church itself did not choose these boundaries. They were the boundaries of faith and hope that had been assigned to the church. Its territory was that of the whole corpus of Scripture. The church recognized by the assembling of the canon what this corpus was. The rule of faith gave it as clear and concise an expression as possible. It did not allow the church to lose sight of what is external — what stands "behind" Scripture and what is to be found only "within" it.

The church supported its delimitation of the canon by asserting the dignity of Scripture and stressing its age and origin. These were respectable criteria, though difficult to grasp in detail and leaving more questions open than Marcion's single doctrine of salvation promised to do, with its appeal directly to Christ and to Christ alone. A correspondingly high price had to be paid for the canon. The sayings of Jesus were not to reduce to a common denominator. There was tension (noted already by Marcion) between Paul and James. The law and the prophets, moreover, to which both Jesus and the apostles had referred, were included by the church. Did not this seem to be a usurping of the Jewish Bible (only then canonized in this entirety, in a counterthrust)? Or did it expose the church to Judaism? Undoubtedly the inclusion of the "Old Testament" as a part of Scripture occasioned new conflicts concerning the God of Abraham, Isaac, and Jacob, for the church invoked him as the Father of Jesus Christ who had raised the Crucified from the dead — "a stumbling block to Jews and foolishness to Gentiles" (1 Cor. 1:23)! Could not the church have avoided these conflicts at a stroke with a relatively simple religious logic, initiating a globally attractive new age movement that linked faith in Jesus to the experience of a much improved world, and treating that which did not give access to this experience as the legacy of the depraved world of an antiquated deity?

The church intentionally did not take this path. It chose instead to have its path marked out by the God whom Jesus has called the "God of the living" (Matt. 22:32). It heard his promises and his commands in fidelity to the preaching and prayer of Jesus. Following him, it found God's

17

promises and commands in the law and the prophets, and, above all, in the promises given there, it heard the "Yes" and "Amen" of God in Jesus Christ (2 Cor. 1:20) confessed by the apostles. It found here the totality of the Bible, and thus recognized it to be the canon.

By defining the canon, did the church reach a hard-and-fast decision? From a historical-critical point of view, this decision is open to question at more than one point. We should note, however, that behind such standards as the age of the writings or the authority of the authors lies a basically different view, that of the totality of the truth of faith, and indeed of the character of faith.

For that reason, it was no accident that the formulation of the rule of faith accompanied the fixing of the canon. The words were different, but in agreement with the totality of the Bible the rule stated as concisely and pertinently as possible what it means to believe, not statistically, but in commitment; "what Christians believe" means, when they really believe and what they have to believe. This is the birth of dogmatics, but it never cut the umbilical cord to the Bible! These binding texts would always stand alongside the Bible from now on, showing clearly that the church itself stands by the Bible, and how it does so.

4. It is the task of dogmatics to express the deep-lying structure and scope of the truth of faith in Jesus Christ, but not in the way that a systematic exposition of Scripture can achieve. Dogmatics opens up a complex nexus of statements of faith, a "context of justification" (Begründungszusammenhang — context of validation or substantiation) that relate to one another, illuminate one another, and explain one another.

Our third thesis showed the complexity of elementary questions answered by statements of faith. The same applies to the contents of dogmatics, to what it has to say both in detail and in its authentic interrelationship, in a system (III.1.3). The formulation of "why we believe, when we believe what we believe" points to an inner inter-reference on a syntactical level, and along the same lines the propositions or statements form a system whose inner structure is a nexus of references, too.

Dogmatics is not a list of statements of faith that are arranged hierarchically or chronologically and has to be worked through step-by-step. No, dogmatics has to give transparency to the whole nexus of statements, to bring out its structure(s), to follow the references and sequences, and in this way to assess new connections, testing whether they can be said "in faith and hope."

18

"Faith" is an entirety of propositions that is so rich in presuppositions that we can only begin with one of them at a time. But we are not to think that faith begins only when we can prove the truth of a number of propositions.

All those who would speak in faith and hope share a responsibility. They must safeguard the dialogue of faith (v. 3) that is their portion, take an interest in observing it, draw from it new insights that give it precision or reduce it to the essential marrow, cut out wilder growth, and give it room for development when weeds or alien tendrils threaten to choke it. The nexus of dogmatic references should help us to speak responsibly about God, about God's reality, and about everything pertaining to it. So far as humanly possible, it should see to it that the fullness of God comes to expression, that we do not reduce it to limited functions of God, or that it is not merely fitted into our human language — a frightful thought but only too often a realistic one! At best the complexity of dogmatics can simply reflect the wealth of what must be said in faith and in hope. As such, it will never have an end, no matter how full or how nuanced our expositions of Scripture may be!

Giving a *full* expression to the truth of faith cannot amount to the same thing as putting it behind us and thus betraying hope and recollection. We observed this illusion in Paul's opponents in Corinth. Dogmatics can approach the fulfillment of its task only by formulating statements which in different situations lead and invite us to expand the reach of faith.

As the church's canon or standard, the Bible first arose in the struggle for a correct understanding of Scripture as a whole. Two issues were involved. First, how was the Bible to be used? What is the proper understanding of individual texts within the totality of Scripture? Second, is the same sense to be given to texts which tell us in different ways what the Bible proclaims?

An example of Christian teaching which is simply an introduction to the study of the Bible is Augustine's *De doctrina christiana* (397-426; ET, *On Christian Doctrine*, NPNF, 2:519ff.; ET, trans. Sister Thérèse Sullivan [Washington, D.C., 1930]). It deals first with the basic questions of faith, then handles in detail questions of biblical exposition, and closes with directions for preaching. Augustine thus answers our first question ("What do Christians believe?") by pointing to the declared faith of the church, relating this to the Bible, showing how the Bible is to be understood as the source of faith, dealing with the difficulties which this presents, and demonstrating how they can be mastered. This hermeneutical part is the core of the book. It includes a theory of the way the speech of the Bible *(signum)* relates to its reality *(res)*.

Augustine is thus striving for a total view of God, humanity, and the world, and this raises the question whether what is said in the individual biblical texts is to be found already in this total view. In this case listening to the Bible is replaced by a biblical systematics. The exposition of the biblical texts illustrates what theology already knows, even though this is taken from the Bible itself. If we know already what the Bible has to say, then exposition is needed only to confirm it.

But Augustine, even if he seems to succumb to this danger himself, passionately contends against the intransigence of this view. He sees contemporaries who (like our modern fundamentalists) take the Bible literally and thus fail to see what the words are imparting, or who are motivated by their own spiritual experience (like our modern spiritualizers) and thus claim to have a personal relation to God's Spirit which enables them to measure both the Bible and the traditional confession by their own immediacy to God. Such people regard preaching as superfluous unless it simply confirms what they feel in themselves. In both these views Augustine finds a contempt for the reality *(res)* that is expressed in the Bible, though it is not identical with it.

Augustine also gave us one of the earliest examples of dogmatics as a structured presentation of the Christian faith. We refer to his *Enchiridion de fide, spe, et caritate* (ET, *The Enchiridion, Being a Treatise on Faith, Hope and Love*, NPNF, 3:237ff.; ET, *The Enchiridion on Faith, Hope and Love*, ed. Thomas A. Hibbs [Washington, D.C., 1961, 1996]), written between 421 and 424. The handbook was not merely meant to be "handy." It would also take Christians by the "hand" as they sought orientation concerning the origin, nature, and direction of their lives. The title is clearly based on 1 Corinthians 13:13. This text does not really deal with faith, hope, and love as they were later understood as the cardinal theological virtues. Augustine unfolds the whole of what Christians believe, hope, and love, always orientated to the triune God, Father, Son, and Spirit. This elementary book also has the aim of directing and accompanying Christians when they call upon God. They should remember what he has done, perceive his saving presence, and trust in the future that he has ordained. Augustine shows that talking of God extends from the first things to the last. He addresses also the fullness of God, which is revealed in the work of Father, Son, and Spirit and yet maintains its secret. The thinking that seeks to understand this must follow the spectrum of our talk about God. It cannot stop at any one point but must still hold to a fixed course. It moves within a specific area, the area denoted by God's work. Its depth is thus also limited, for only from God himself can we learn who he is and how he reveals himself.

Augustine imparts a particular form of theological presentation whose basic structure has persisted up to our own time. It is distinct from the collections of different sources of the Christian tradition that try to give us the "true faith" or belief as completely as possible. A good representative of this type of dogmatics is John of Damascus (ca. 670-750), who gave the Eastern Orthodox churches a normative collection of doctrinal texts in his *Exact Exposition of the Orthodox Faith* (*Ekdosis tēs orthodoxou pisteōs*; NPNF, 2nd series, 9). In some sense this is a textbook of doctrine for the church, but without being a theology that offers arguments or accounts for its basis. John simply assembles what had been handed down. He follows an essentially trinitarian structure but does not care for thematic balance or other particular orientation. He expands what the tradition had expressly treated and mentions only briefly what had not met with opposition.

We reach a theological crossroads at this point. On the one hand theology can go in the direction of a developing tradition of faith that will come to expression in the life of the church, and especially in the liturgy and the catechism (cf. I.1.1). We can associate such expressions even though they do not form a unity.

Or, on the other hand, theology can be systematized (though without systematization). Though it will not be detached from liturgical rites and other forms of church life (at least not at first), it will develop independently and its task will not only be to accompany worship, education, and piety. It must not only preserve and correct *what* Christians believe, but it must also tell them *why* we can believe. This can be done (as in Augustine) by reflecting on the unity of God in the full text of his works.

I.1.5. No Fear of Dogmas!

The question, "Why can we believe?" can also open access to the basics of the faith and cause us to ask about its structure, the whys and wherefores of theological thinking.

The Western Church took this path, nor did the sixteenth-century crisis that brought division do much to change it. Even though dialogue between the Reformation churches and the Roman Catholic Church brought lengthy controversies about what divided them, we constantly encounter one common purpose.

5. Dogmatics is an attempt to express the finality and fullness of God's action that does not bring human history to an end but promises it its future, the future of fulfilled fellowship between God and us that is already proclaimed when the Spirit of God links us to God and to one another.

The church must move forward into the future of the divine promise. Yet it should not be indifferent to what is contemporary or to what the years bring. To keep a steady course it needs a compass: dogmatics. Dogmatics should not say *everything*. It does not wish to say everything. But it is enabled to say what is *new*. How is this possible?

Our answer finds support in the second and fourth theses. The element of dogmatics is what must be said under all circumstances in a credible and unconditioned way: the finality and fullness of the revelation of God as a promise to humankind. We can say this only as we trust in God and in what he has promised us. This points us to the scope, for we now have to talk about the essence of God as Father, Son, and Spirit, and also about his acts in creation, reconciliation, redemption, and consummation. (Eastern theology stresses the triad creation, redemption, and consummation, Western puts reconciliation in the center. Different but complementary ways of looking at the work of God underlie the conceptions. In what follows I will refer to both series alternatively.)

Here, then, is what Christians believe, not because it is prescribed, but because we accept what God has done in fulfillment of his promise. This determines their expectation and makes possible love as devotion to others. In this way, they can believe.

It is precisely the finality and fullness of revelation that discloses the future. We are thus led back to our second thesis. Formulating its highest common denominator cannot express the truth of faith. We have seen already that when Paul spoke of the resurrection of Jesus, he had also to keep in view God's action, the creative work of God which robs death of its power. The transformation into a spiritual body (1 Cor. 15:44) also points to the church as the Spirit-created body of Christ (1 Cor. 12) in which even the creatureliness of Christians is established in a new way (1 Cor. 6–10). Any attempt to reduce this nexus to one of its constituent elements will congeal our expectation of the presence of God. It was no accident, then, that the early church confessions saw the work of God as expanding from creation to reconciliation, redemption, and consummation and tried to deal with God himself as the living unity of Father, Son, and Spirit. We cannot exhaust the fullness of revelation, but we can give it the trinitarian structure which has been normative for dogmatics even up to this day.

The statements which express the fullness of revelation I have preliminarily called the statements of faith. Why did I not call them dogmatic statements or dogmas? Because it is not at all easy to give a valid explanation of how the term "dogmas" can be used without misunderstanding, especially when we keep in mind in what situation and in what senses it was introduced.

Let us recall the reservations made about the terms "dogmatics" and "dogmatic." These terms are not attractive to those who fear they will be overwhelmed by assertions that are simply posited in the world and that demand our adherence through thick and thin. Those who speak dogmatically, whether in theology, politics, or some other sphere of debate, are regarded as intolerant. They are suspected of refusing to hear arguments and criticism. To be dogmatic is to tolerate no opposition. It is to be immovable, static, paralyzed, even dead. What is dogmatic is fixed and settled, and it makes us settled too. (A printer once read *lehrhaft* [doctrinal] as *lebhaft* [lively] — something dogmaticians dream about.) "Dogmatic" suggests obstinacy and even arrogance. How did it acquire this bad reputation?

In theology, the reservations rest upon a traditional integration of "dogmatics" and "church authority." Furthermore, dogmatics looks back to a long-lasting church tradition and often advocates traditionalism. When these things converge, dogmatics seems to be a traditionalist instrument of power with which the church ruthlessly threatens to eliminate any new, unusual, and critically radical forms of expression. At any rate, this is a common enough experience in dogmatics. The liberation of Christian communities from the mainline churches and their regulations has often gone hand in hand with a liberation from dogmatics. Even where theological scholarship might give it a place, dogmatics is rated poorly. It seems to restrict free research and to hobble the critical spirit. It functions like a rod with which the "official church" wants to govern the theological faculties. Or it is like a bulldozer which, with the help of dogmas, of brazen and divinely guaranteed basic principles, shatters the independent theological thinking that, unfettered from without, whether by the church or by devotional needs, would pursue the question of truth and the perceiving of reality.

This was the lament of Albert Schweitzer. Jesus, he said,

is walled up in the churches. The churches have set up dogmas concerning him. As a historian I would indeed say that they had to do this. They had no option. But because we really have to do with that which *is,* the churches had adjusted a living individual to a structure of dogmas, had eliminated his simple and vital humanity, and had isolated him from all who were not inside the structure. ("Jesus und wir," unpublished lecture at Strassburg, January 22, 1906)

We might add to Schweitzer's remarks by stressing that the dogmatic walling up of Jesus really buried him alive and made the church not only the guardian of this mausoleum but also the usurper of his life.

On this view dogmatics is the hereditary enemy of living history and indeed of vitality as a whole. In this sense, polemicizing against dogmatics is part of the agenda of historical research into theology and its ramifications in daily life and practice. How often do we read or hear that the prophets and apostles were not dogmaticians. That is true enough! Yet neither were they practitioners of historical and practical theology. We are not, of course, condemning these disciplines. We are asking that room be left for the question: In what sense can we ever encounter dogmatics if it is not (or not yet) seen to be a discipline or system?

Prejudice tells us that dogmas are principles which can no longer be questioned. We might dispute this point, but it is not worthwhile. We will never be able to change things.

Perhaps the fear aroused by the word "dogma" is lessened when we recall that this fear was shared by many of the theologians who introduced the term into the church's vocabulary. It was only with misgivings and restrictions, and not with uniform, uninterrupted use, that the church adopted the term from the second century.

The word "dogma" had a very great breadth of meaning then. It included both simple subjective conviction and the exact opposite, that is, a philosophical opinion that could withstand skeptical objections. It included authoritative statements, but also their no less adamantly supported antitheses. "Dogma" could denote a political, philosophical, cultural, or even theological principle upon which further statements could be built. Those who proposed or supported dogmas had still to vouch for them. "Dogma" could also be used for an imperial edict that all had to recognize. In such cases there could be no questioning of its validity. The early church, however, was not ready to submit unwittingly to that kind of use.

Basil of Caesarea used "kerygma" for the truth that is openly proclaimed in the church and reserved "dogma" for the tradition of the mysteries of faith that the monks preserve in their lonely spiritual lives (*De spiritu sancto* 66 [SC 17:232-33]). Dogmas are not the concern of everyone — but they are not secret knowledge either. Nevertheless, it was not fitting that they should be marketed around or exposed in the forum of the public square where only their social value would be rated. As Basil saw it, even the truth of the Bible should not be open on public display. The Bible was open only to spiritual understanding. Hence a direct divine illumination is needed. A specific lifestyle must prepare the ground for it. Dogmas must not be blazoned forth. They were part of an arcane discipline, the inner core of the church's understanding through which Christians could give account of their faith both to themselves and to one another. Only those who were called could judge here according to the criteria of faith, and they would not speak out of any other need to communicate.

Dogma would undergo a change of character when it was used publicly to portray the Christian faith. It had been a free-floating term, but now theologians used it to denote a firmly established opinion or proposition that the church had adopted in a specific sense. Dogma had become a self-evident statement of faith that was so infallibly clear that the church could cling to it and base all that it said and did upon it. Dogmas did not need any further explanation or support.

Another change of meaning only came later which involved some retreat from what had become the usual sense. Dogma was now defined as a statement of faith that through conciliar decisions, or later through papal decrees, the church had expressly established and sanctioned. Dogmas no longer had to be self-evident. They were authoritative pronouncements that the church had made with the powers at its disposal. Those who wished to belong to the church, and to avoid excommunication, had to accept them as a whole. This usage developed in the fourth century when the decisions of the councils made it clear that the church was now an imperial church that was part of the legal system of the later Roman Empire. A combination not without dangers!

Dogma now sounded like regulation and discipline. *What* Christians had to believe — was not this prescribed? *How* Christians had to believe — was not even this also prescribed? With no "if's" and "but's," they must keep to the established faith. They must believe it without raising any question of why. If the question was raised, the answer was that the church had pronounced it. It was the faith of the church.

We ourselves must ask the questions: Why is it the faith of the church? Why had the church to say this and not something else? Those who try to answer these questions instead of being satisfied with the church's declaration must distinguish between the facticity of a dogma and its justification. The reason behind this distinction is the conviction that the church recognizes dogmas because they are true. The truth of dogmas does not depend on the fact that the church maintains them. But is this really so? This is an abiding question, and dogmatics must always leave it open!

Since this distinctive relation between truth and validity needs constant investigation and clarification, we need dogmatics as a warranty of the church's statements of faith. A more inviting but less precise way that is often preferred is the description of dogmatics as reflection on the faith of the church. Reflection is necessary in order to imagine and demonstrate, as far as possible, the reasons why the church has made some things obligatory, and why it has said certain things and not others. We must remember at this point, however, that dogmatics does not come about only when the church decides its binding statements of faith, and that it does not end with the attempt to make such statements plausible. This is how only Roman Catholic theology defines dogmatics. In the words of Karl Rahner, dogmatics is "the academic discipline of church dogma. It is methodical reflection on dogma of the church which is undertaken according to appropriate principles and which systematically embraces a subject on every possible side. Both in method and content, it is necessary and demanded if we are to understand dogma" ("Dogmatics," in *Sacramentum mundi* [Freiburg, 1967], 1:917). Dogma here signifies the totality of statements of faith that have thus far been defined by the church. This totality is more than the sum of its parts, that is, of the dogmas that have been solemnly pronounced over the centuries. These parts have been collected in a manual of doctrinal decisions, and this enchiridion still forms the textual basis of Roman Catholic dogmatics.

Not only must Roman Catholic dogmatics prove the consistency of doctrine that has developed historically. Protestant theology shares the same task! Traditional Catholic dogmatics must also discuss the decisions of the teaching office *(magisterium)* in such a way that it is no longer necessary to radically question their agreement with the Bible but that it needs to confirm once again this agreement.

Reformation theology sharpened and often dramatized the difference between the justification of dogma and its facticity. It, too, accepted the decisions of the early church councils, especially those that dealt with the triunity of God and the unity of Jesus Christ with God. But it rejected other doctrinal statements, for example, the eucharistic transforming of bread and wine into Christ's body and blood (the doctrine of transubstantiation, set in train in 1215). It also followed the Western Church in ignoring the decision of Nicaea II (787) concerning the worship of images, which has always been of very great importance for Orthodox piety and theology.

Reformation theology expressly raised the question of justification, which it answered by examining whether the statements recognized by the church are really in accord with the Bible. This issue will occupy us in III.2. It does not allow us to speak too easily of the "dogma of the church" if we equate "dogma" with the truth of faith. The church does not possess the truth. It relates to it as it points to God and to all that he says and does. It *stands* in the truth, or *abides* in it.

We note that our linguistic usage becomes complex if we try to bring many intentions under a single common denominator. When we define "dogma" as a statement of faith that the church has declared as such, we then have to take into account a specific number of dogmas, which can be increased. This is the official Roman Catholic position. Yet even this is relativized (as we see from Rahner's definition) if the totality of the church's faith is "dogma." Underlying this concept is the belief that this totality will be unfolded as history takes its course, so that dogmatics can contribute to dogma. The concept is still committed, however, to defined dogmas.

The usage becomes unclear, however, if we borrow from the Roman Catholic definition but do not adopt the Roman Catholic understanding of the church. How we see the comprehension of church is directly affected. In fact, the church is not institutionally structured in such a way that it can define — no matter who the head is — what has validity as a statement of faith. The church is itself defined by agreement with the truth, that is, by subjecting itself to what can be stated unconditionally in faith, no more and also no less. It is important to add "no less," for "no less" is encircled by a linguistic nexus and stakes out an area of speech in which we always already move when we speak in faith and with a view to faith. Protestant dogmatics attempts to pace off this area and to give an account of the steps taken in it.

Protestant dogmatics must stand by this position, pointing only to that which is entrusted to the church, to that which it lives out, and to that which it must communicate.

This was not a relic of Catholic teaching that the Reformers could not wholly shake off (it being left for later generations to discover an "undogmatic Christianity"). Such a criticism is wide of the mark, for dogmatics cannot be an institutionalized monologue of the church. By

27

its questioning it is both critical of the church and yet in solidarity with it. It does not have to watch over the church's faith and protect it. Rather, it serves the church by offering it assistance when it seeks to speak the truth and to reflect on it instead of merely functioning efficiently. If dogmatics exists at all, it does so in the church. It relates to the church, and to that extent stands over against it. When the fellowship of faith speaks about what we can rely on in both life and death, this takes us beyond the given boundaries of the church. For this reason dogmatics is relatively independent of the church, and in this way it helps us to see what the church really is.

I.2. Linguistic Elements of Dogmatics

This second section will bring to light the typical linguistic structure of dogmatics, the bones and muscles that give it structure to make its movement possible, not stones that are the foundation upon which a building is erected. This structure gives form to the basic distinctions, the path-forming rules, and the far-reaching interconnections that we will become acquainted with in I.3.

Perhaps this section and what will follow in this chapter may appear too dry, as if we were invited to practice swimming where there is no water. If so, you might perhaps omit I.2-5, first read II and perhaps IV.1, and then return to these sections. Or you might first examine some dogmatic text and take note of the linguistic structure and the way theological judgments are formed. Doing this would make you more familiar with the theory (I.2 and 3) and the context (I.4 and 5). The examples that I use are taken from basic dogmatic texts and are not mere illustrations. They will help us to see what is normative for the structure of dogmatics.

I.2.1. Speech of Consent

The first type of language that must be mentioned when we speak of the way dogmatic material is communicated is the speech of consent. It is called "homology" in the theological sense of the term. Homology here is language that gives a simple and unrestricted Yes to God's action and therefore must be unconditionally and under all circumstances affirmed. This Yes consents to "what really is" and is not limited to a murmur of agreement or an applauding interjection.

This Yes denotes the original moment when the mist of illusions and lies about life is suddenly dissipated by light and we perceive abruptly that all the "ifs and buts" are redundant, collapsing the foggy spiral of reflection on itself. This Yes makes known the presupposition upon which theology can develop. It is the Yes that gives expression to the fact that God has made himself perceptible, and how he has made himself perceptible. For this reason it is an adequate basis for what can be said in faith and hope. There is no other presupposition for speaking about God apart from this action. We must always begin with this Yes and can never leave it behind us. If we take a different approach and try something different, sooner or later we will have to return to this starting point.

When God tells us definitively who *he* is, then the question must be asked who *I* am when I consent and say yes. When God's promise is heard, a light falls on me in which I now see myself differently from the way I thought I knew myself, shockingly differently. This light enables me to say "I" when God tells me: "you" are lost, and yet to you my promise holds, as it is said in the doctrine of justification: "you" are both sinner and righteous at the same time (III.2.1). For this reason God's promise can be accepted only in faith, in faith which follows and does not precede the promise, in faith which is created along with its perception. Hence the illuminating moment of consent is not an intuitive insight, a vision that carries its own evidence. The consent is the strangely different word of faith assaulted, which can never speak of itself.

The Greek word *homologein* means theologically to declare things that all can hear, to declare what is binding, and at the same time to declare one's own acceptance of what is said, to agree to it, to consent, to confess. Declaration here does not mean stating an opinion that has a supporting proof to which it may be referred back. What is homological is sufficient referring to God's promise and action but has to be explained and confessed. It speaks for itself. It characterizes the relation of those who speak to what is said as one of commitment. They cannot go behind what they say. By it they declare what they have received. In human terms homology marks the point at which the language of commitment arises, which cannot acknowledge any other underlying presupposition as the basic condition of understanding.

Christian homology knows only one condition and mentions it itself in all it says. The condition is that God has acted in the story of Jesus Christ. Here he has done and promised specific things. This is the basic condition. It constitutes what Christians say. It is the implicit and inward condition of everything said and done (and suffered) in faith.

We can formulate this condition in either limited or explicit terms. Paul refers to it briefly in Romans 10:9-10: "If you confess with your lips that Jesus is Lord and believe in your heart that God raised him from the dead, you will be saved. For one believes with the heart and so is justified, and one confesses with the mouth and so is saved." Here confession and faith are inseparably bound: raising Jesus from the dead, God made him the Lord of the living. Those belong to him who name him Lord (Kyrios). Those who confess him as such are certain of his victory over death. Paul stresses that we must say this and not just feel it or symbolize it or make it ours in some other way. It must be stated. Why? Does not confession mean much more? Does it not mean coming out publicly so as to show clearly that we are confessors? Does it not mean declaring and communicating our assurance? In some cases might it not mean the surrender of our lives? Paul does not exclude such things. Yet for him they are not the rule. For Paul it depends upon whether one *can* say something specific and *can* say exactly this and not something else.

6. Homology tells us what is self-evident according to faith. It thus makes it plain how it can come to a confessing faith. By confessing we unreservedly place ourselves into what God has done and promised. We confess these things because we here find ourselves in the presence of God. To speak homologically is to stand upon what is received through God's action. Homology tells us where to begin when speaking in faith and hope.

What is really self-evident in theology? Something that believers themselves cannot show. Something with which they point *away* from themselves because they see that they are known by it. They would take a different course if they referred to themselves or immersed themselves in what they discovered in the depths of self-reflection or in what they linked to their own or others' subsoil. That which makes faith possible can only be confessed. Confession means consent to something specific. This something confronts those who state it. We shall have to be more precise about this when we become acquainted with theological statements and the subject matter of dogmatics. When people do not demonstrate themselves but consent to what God has promised them, when they do not express their readiness to believe, they point to the hope of faith and, if God so pleases, to the opening up of others to faith.

Homology asserts what must be said in the full freedom of faith. We cannot say anything else. We cannot say what is contradictory; i.e. we cannot contradict it without falling into radical self-contradiction. That which is self-evident in this profound but very simple sense is often much harder to say. Problematic themes are often much easier to discuss. When it is a matter of drawing or inspiring others, here a few enthusiastic words will often suffice. They will merely have to be drummed home to them.

I speak of homology because the term "confession" has undergone a shift of meaning. Nowadays, we use the term for demonstrative texts. We expect that confessing will show where confessors stand, where they will be found without question on the vast terrain of religious, social, or political debate. Individual Christians or the church must now give unambiguous answers that will show what position they take. Behind these expectations stands an understandable need for clarification. But can the nonambivalence that reduces problems to a single point of decision, and admits of no alternative, serve as a response to complex issues? The surprising thing is that a negative reply is usually given to this type of confessing. We find it easier to have reservations than to give whole-hearted agreement. A negative reply seems to avoid the burden of uncertainty induced by multiple and highly involved challenges and tasks. This kind of use hardly fits in with the Christian tradition that equates confession with homology and thus primarily attempts to say "Yes" to faith and to hope. That tradition is more open to those who have a different view of things.

A different concept of confession established itself because the location of confessing changed. In early Christianity homology was rooted in baptismal practice. The candidates for baptism stated their belief in the basics of the faith, and thus placed themselves in the fellowship of the faith. External pressures changed this practice, although the same words were used at unforced confession. Those who meant to confess Jesus Christ, whether by martyrdom or by taking a stand in controversies within the church, had now to make it clear to whom they belonged. Confession was now understood in terms of the act of confessing which clarified the position of the confessors confronting others. Confession could still have a homological character. If someone under extreme pressure still confesses and says nothing more, confession itself was the last resort. Those who are not relying on others but who see even their own right to exist contested, will say what is the final ground of their being, without regard to the views or the consent of others.

Increasingly, however, formulas were regarded by the church and the empire as important, and agreement with these formulas became normative. Confession became a symbol of recognition. It now seemed as though a prior achievement was demanded if someone was to be able to believe.

Whoever did not accept the faith in full and without the slightest hesitation was lost.

Confession became a kind of ticket that one had to produce to gain admission to heavenly bliss. This, at least, is how the Athanasian Creed was regarded from the fifth or sixth century onward. The initial statement of the *Symbolum quicunque* is that "whosoever will be saved, before all things it is necessary that he hold the Catholic Faith," and what follows is a summary of the theological development that took place from the ecumenical councils of Constantinople (381) to those of Ephesus (431) and Chalcedon (451). The conclusion repeats the initial warning: "This is the Catholic Faith, which except a man believe faithfully, he cannot be saved."

We must recall what Paul says in Romans 10:9: "If you confess with your lips that Jesus is Lord and believe in your heart that God raised him from the dead, you will be saved." But if this text is sung in the liturgy, will it not give rise to the feeling that we are the exceptions and that we can claim ownership? Nevertheless, this text provides the basis of faith, a basis which is inalienable for those who undertake to say: "I believe." The inner basis of faith is always the same as in Romans 10:9-10, though perhaps more broadly stated. Confession, however, is not something that we must do first. We are not to say that only those who believe, that is, who repeat things literally, will then be saved. This would be a fateful sequence: first this or that must be said, then faith becomes possible. No, confession and faith form a unity, as lips and heart do in Romans 10:9-10. They can be torn apart only at the cost of self-mutilation.

A question does, of course, arise (to be answered in my view in the negative) whether the inner condition of faith might not be put in a clause that sounds very much like the introductory and concluding formulas of the Athanasian Creed, and that excludes all those that think and speak differently. All the same, the fact is clear that this symbol, like the prior confessions, seeks to tighten up things. Those who say something substantially different say things that are not really to be believed unless we are ready to be plunged into profound disagreements. Those who are asked, or who ask themselves, *whom* they believe and *why* they believe, must always be ready to say *what* they believe and on what grounds. Rightly understood, the great confessions of the church seek to help us as we thus examine ourselves.

The same applies to the numerous new formulations of the Reformation period which are now documented in church orders or formulas of consensus. These arose out of the intensive theological efforts that were made to come to consent through listening to the Bible, which would clarify the basis of faith. At first glance these texts resemble the traditional confessions. These were either expressly adopted, or their most important statements were reformulated. The Reformation churches had separated from Rome, but they wished to show their allegiance to the early church by these statements and by the liturgy in which they were rooted. They now advanced their own theological reasoning. We can believe because God has justified us, the ungodly. We hear this in his Word that promises us forgiveness for all our sins. All that follows, then, is bracketed by the clause that refers to the work of God. The misunderstanding that human action precedes the divine action is thus avoided. No one can act in this way even when speaking in the name of the church.

The Reformation confessions testified also the confessional state of their adherents and therefore became denominational marks. The churches took separate ways, often influenced by political circumstances and their legal ramifications, but also by their confessions or confessional writings. The *Book of Concord* (1580) stated the Lutheran position. The Reformed were more flexible and often adopted regional views closely linked to church orders. We simply refer to this process because it brings out the confessional significance (i.e., the denominational significance) of the confessions, which threatened to overwhelm their homological character. The validity of such a confession in a church, even if only on paper, is an indication of the confessional tradition to which it belongs. These confessions are then accepted and revised (often pruned and weakened) as need arises when they are exported to the mission fields.

I had to sketch this process lest the accompanying mood might cause irritation. In its origin confession is homology, and it maintains this character. It stresses the inner condition of what must be said in faith, and by what it says in detail (with thematically no limits) it shows us why what is said is credible. This is its theological distinctiveness. It bears the logical structure of homology. It formulates and ties together sentences that we cannot deny unless we renounce faith altogether. Thus displaying the "logic" of faith, it also refers us to the relation between the statements of faith and the basis of faith, but without developing this relation, and without reference to the people of faith and devotion. It is enough if people refer to God, saying nothing else, but stating this clearly. This reference will always carry within it a whole interrelation of extended statements (I.1.4; I.1.5) in which the basis of faith will speak for itself.

Homology uniquely sets forth the "logic" of faith in statements, and by this means shows us what are the necessary conditions. This offers us an opportunity to see and deal with new situations in a different way because the statements of faith have a contour and can be applied to particular ends. Newly disclosed situations provide room for talking about God in a new way, but one that does not part company with homology. Here is stated and in this sense brought forth what is open for faith when we attend to our action and inaction or our relationships to others and to the world in which we live and participate. What is our judgment of things when we speak in faith or with a view to faith? Speaking in faith simply means saying something specific in faith and not saying other things that faith rules out.

In his *Small Catechism* (1529) Luther, for example, stated: "I believe in God the Father almighty, maker of heaven and earth. What does this mean? I believe that God has created me and all that exists" (*CC*, 115). I owe myself to God and I thus stand in fellowship with all creatures. I have not given life to myself, nor do I finally owe it to my parents, my family, my people, my culture. I cannot handle my existence as the subject of my own endeavors (even though I might seek to give meaning to my life, or the reverse, I cannot really do either the one or the other, for as a judge over my life I would get into contradiction with my faith). I can live only within the frontiers of my created being. But these frontiers offer me room and support. I need not wander off to find my destiny. It is found in my creaturehood, in my fellowship with other created beings. In meeting them I come across God the Creator. This confrontation, however, is not the end of the matter. He sets me in a right relationship to himself and to others. It is in this relationship that I have to do with him as the one who protects and upholds all life. How we may understand this protection and upholding in the midst of all the human destruction and self-annihilation in the world is a related question, which can only be raised and studied with confidence from the perspective of faith seeking understanding of God in his person and work.

This is, so to speak, the impetus of the argument into possibly uncharted territory. What is said in this direction, often in a tentative and groping way, must always raise the counterquestion: *Why* can this be said and not something else? At this point we must mention the necessary condition, the credible basis, that permits us to say this and prohibits us from saying the opposite. This basis does not have its source in a deep and silent feeling, in a basic experience, to which reference may always be made. I cannot say, "I believe because I believe . . . ," and then repeat the statement again and again until exhaustion sets in. An answer of that kind tells us nothing. It means that believers simply refer to themselves and believe in themselves. A proper answer is, "I believe that . . . ," and then follows what must be said in faith and not left unsaid. This condition necessary to faith is formulated therefore as a statement of faith or a chain of such statements.

We repeat: we are concerned thereby with theological relations and not with appeals to traditional formulas. Naturally our train of arguments belongs to a story and relates to what has been said before. But that is not yet the decisive point. What matters is that faith "as consent to" what must be believed always must be confessed at the same time. Faith is never speechless or an unexplainable sentimental movement that can then be expressed in speech. Statements of faith are not faith's forms of expression. They are not secondary utterances that are based on a prelinguistic basis for faith that is formed by a personal relation to Christ in the "communion of the Christian with God" (Wilhelm Herrmann, *Der Verkehr des Christen mit Gott. Im Anschluß an Luther dargestellt,* 7th ed. [Tübingen, 1921]; ET, *The Communion of the Christian with God, Described on the Basis of Luther's Statements,* ed. Robert T. Voelkel [Philadelphia, 1971]).

Certainly faith is not exhausted in a language of faith. It is more than a "language game." This is especially true for the human being who struggles with language exactly when he or she wishes to speak in faith and fears that he or she will fail due to the inadequacy of his or her language (I.5.2). Certainly faith is not exhausted in the language of faith because faith must be said and cannot be asserted in any other way. This means that we cannot do without speech. Speech can and should be the means of communication for distinct, discernible, and recognizable contents, and not just a playground for verbal expressions. It is most important, then, to observe logical linguistic relations. Credible terms must be used in an unmistakable way that makes clear what it means to be committed to them and how this commitment relates to other obligations. There is enough room for all that needs to be said — and done — in this regard. It will not be done, however, by using the current words of piety. Specific speech is needed, adapted to specific situations. There must be a sense of what needs to be said in detail, and of the way in which to say it. The grounding does not have to be expressly stated, but it does have to be mentioned. When this happens, what we say is not a vicious circle, for we are permitted to distinguish between presuppositions and conclusions, and to clarify and make more precise the presuppositions, reformulating them if necessary.

I.2.2. Statements Definitive in Dialogue

Basic statements of faith are often formulated as dogmas, i.e., as reliable statements intended to liberate us from illusion and not intended to be straitjackets for our speech and thought. Dogmas are statements of faith from the perspective of faith that must be formulated accurately, clearly, and distinctly. Why?

The function rather than the form of dogmas distinguishes them from homology. They are *experiences in theological thinking.* Like confession, they make mention of the basic conditions, for they say what God has given to us by breaking us open for himself, and so we can accept it and consent to it. Only thus can dogma be a true matter of faith and not the expression of a basic assumption behind which we may not and cannot go. Nor is dogma an external decree. Dogma states that which has unassailable validity. In acknowledging this type of dogma, we say that we are convinced of its truth. For this reason we consent to it. Our consent, then, is not a subsequent act of acclamation on which its validity depends. Reliance on a dogma, and further exploration with its help, is, rightly understood, a mark of modest confidence, of trust in the chance for human knowledge on a basis which no individual, no group, not even the church, could create on its own.

7. An exemplarily "thick" statement of faith can be called a dogma. Our appeal to it demonstrates that we may refer to it in all circumstances as we go forward and wait upon God.

Dogmas are statements to which we can and must refer because they express linguistically the valid and provisionally enduring content of theological knowledge. They initiate and conclude conversations and still leave room for more. They enrich and deepen much-tested and reliable experiences in thinking. We can investigate their grounding and extend their scope. To that extent they are *definitive in dialogue.* They enable us to see the theologically meaningful boundaries of dialogue in faith and open up further dialogue.

Protestant theology likes to speak only of *the* dogma. This is not because there is only one dogma. It is because the basic statements of faith are a unity. They are normative for others and permit us to infer these others. This unity is our knowledge of Christ, so that in the strict sense there is only one dogma. Yet the knowledge of Christ is multi-faceted. We may thus call the basic statements of faith dogmas. The situation is not the same for Roman Catholic theology. It describes as dogmas the unreformable statements that the church or the pope has defined as obligatory. Boundaries are thus set for the church as the fellowship of the faithful. Dogmatic development does, of course, take place, reflecting the growth of the church's historical knowledge.

Why do we rely on dogmas? So as not to neglect the truly essential things. So as not to unthinkingly or arrogantly reject the theological experiences of Christian thought. Through dogmas we enter into experiences in thinking. We strive after knowledge that has found an echo in speech and that can lead on to further knowledge. Dogmas structure that which is to be said in faith and with a view to faith. They answer the basic question: Why should we believe? And the answer is also an act of consent: "I believe . . . ," "We believe in God . . ." We entrust ourselves to him, to who he is, to what he has done and to what he communicates to us.

Dogmas are theological statements that have proved themselves especially reliable. This is because great care went into their formulation. Preceding and recurring controversies brought clarification and helped in the shaping of credible distinctions which are necessary for the faith.

We might take as an example the way the confession of the triune God was made more precise and developed in the Nicene Creed. This creed speaks about God in the unity of his work as creator, redeemer, and consummator. This work embraces us, yet not as one thing, but as an act that is always distinct and different. We begin with this threefold act of God as creator, redeemer, and consummator. The whole Bible speaks of it. This scope has to find expression. We need to answer the question: What does it mean that God acts *in* creation, reconciliation, and redemption? Does God change God's form or appear in different roles? Nicaea had to rule out this misunderstanding. God's action did not involve different modes of encounter, and it was wrong to think that God was, as it were, merged with his action. The controversy contributed to a basic experience in theological thinking. We can describe the unity of God only by saying that the one God has his essence or deity only in intradivine relations.[8] The relation of Father to Son discloses itself as the source of freedom, and in the Holy Spirit this relation is manifest as the love that unites the separated, not in one thing, but in mutual freedom. Faith means living out of this freedom and in this love. The confession of the triune God articulates this experience in thinking the faith.

---

8. Cf. John Calvin, *Institutio christianae religionis* [1559] I 13,6.18-19; ET, *Institutes of the Christian Religion,* ed. John T. McNeill, trans. Ford Lewis Battles [Philadelphia, 1960], 1:128, 142-44.

Another such experience contained in this dogma is bound up with the concept of person. In the language of that time, the concept of "person" meant a being who speaks and acts, or the theatrical mask or role. The latter was not apposite here, for God does not play a role in the world, does not don a mask that conceals his deity. Instead, he acts in the person of the Father, the Son, and the Spirit. Each person relates to the other two. They act together in the care for their creation. Basic to their interconnection is the relation of each of the divine persons to the others. They are not interchangeable. Also important is the irreversible relation of God to the creature. From there, insights about being a human being could grow. As the Bible tells us: God shows his face to the creature. He addresses it in this way. The humans who are thus addressed are also known as persons. We humans are persons because God has taken us up into his work in irreplaceable fashion. Every person is set in a plenitude of relationships and can enter into them. All persons can be affected by them but must not become subject to them or explain themselves by them. The individual sees himself or herself as a person when recognizing his or her own specific identity in gratitude and hope.

The theological concept of person shows us the basis of human personality. It is rooted in the person and work of God himself. These are not self-enclosed or bound, but rather desire "the other" in freedom and bind "the other" with a love that is inexhaustible. God himself is inexhaustible. He constantly meets us afresh and addresses us afresh in unexpected ways. God is free to communicate with us. Basic distinctions meet us here, as well as far-reaching relationships that can be known only by faith and with a view to faith. Along these lines we can measure their depth and breadth. A multidimensional figure of speech is needed here. The movement that begins with "I believe" expands with many twists and turns, but then returns to its starting point. Yet in doing so, it becomes a path that is totally new. It never repeats itself.

How troublesome things would be if we were stuck with the "I" and tried to understand the "I believe" as simply a development of the "I" and to use this as a starting point for all else that follows! This kind of procedure would go along with a concept of the person as a self-subsisting being that relates only to itself. This being might put out feelers on all sides, might possibly taste the whole world, might have dealings with all things, at a distance might even know "God" as the quintessence of all reality. Faith would then perhaps be an unforeseeable process of advance through every sphere of thought, feeling, and volition, and every step would both give satisfaction and yet bring no peace.

Thinking of that kind would not be more profound or radical or original than is the experience in thinking of the trinitarian dogma. But it follows a different path, that of an infinitely reflective self-movement which circles around the "I." In contrast, the trinitarian dogma fixes its attention upon the question of how we are to begin to speak and to think when we seek after God, and when in our talk of God we try to express how distinctive we are in freedom and love, namely, how we are persons. An answer to this question makes it clear that we could not think up this origin by ourselves. Yet, we should know what the basis of our statements is, so this is presented to us in particular statements, in order that we perceive what we rely upon and also to what we may point one another.

Is it possible for this experience of thought to be revised? Why not! It is an experience in thinking. It did not crash upon the earth like a meteor from heaven and leave a giant hole to astonish us. It is a human effort, as one can say, an unheard-of attempt to respond to the task of saying as exactly as possible, without misunderstandings, with far-reaching ramifications, who "God" is upon whom we call, who answers us, to whom we reach out. And at the same time it also becomes visible who we are who give this answer, who ask this question, who are needy, and are able to hope. This attempt, as the history of dogma has shown very often, is an all-too-human, an all-too-churchly, and even an all-too-political affair. The unavoidable debate with the language and thought of late antiquity has left its mark. Why were not many things thought through further? Why did different and better formulations not result?

We must not overlook these questions, but neither can we ignore that even up to our own day the work done on the dogma of the Trinity has never been substantially improved. The problem here is that modern theology has to engage in all kinds of innovative efforts. We must show this in detail, and our investigation must take into account philosophical reflections about the Trinity such as those of Georg Wilhelm Friedrich Hegel and Friedrich Wilhelm Joseph Schelling and the ongoing development of the concept of person. The dogma has more than once been thrown to the scrap heap, but it has proved to be more lasting than many of the alternatives. We must not ignore the richness and openness of the formulations of Nicaea (325) and Constantinople (381). They developed in ways that their authors did not have in mind and that none of them, including popes and emperors, could foresee. No simple development of the doctrine of the triune God could occur. Its structure had to be perceived more and more precisely, and its wealth of relations revealed. Dogmatics had to achieve this through further reflection. The basic theological position came to light in a chain of statements that resulted in a fullness of new insights.

We must not exclude a revision of the dogma of the Trinity. It is also true, however, that a task of dogmatics is to expound and reflect on this dogma as an experience in thinking. Thus far it has proved to be a most reliable dogma. It is so when and because it helps us in particular situations to discover anew who we are in the presence of God. A good example of this is its theologically precise concept of the person.

If we articulate in terms of assertions based upon this dogma our hopes and doubts, our memories and expectations, our action and inaction, and in this regard ask what we might say in faith, that is, unconditionally affirm, we then enjoy the basic attitude of faith. This is so formulated that it invites us into conformity with the work of God that tells us who he is. We need not understand this work. On the basis of that conformity we can say: "We believe," meaning that we share in this knowledge even though our own situations, our personal or common experiences, are so very different. We renew this experience in all circumstances (in keeping with our knowledge), not because a church council has made this decision, nor because a venerable antiquity reached it, nor because tradition established it, nor finally because the liturgy has made it familiar to us, but simply because it was constantly disclosed to us that we referred to this experience. We accepted it because we could agree with it (not the reverse!). We could agree with it because it has proved to be lasting even in stormy ages and in spite of very radical doubts.

For this reason the Augsburg Confession (1530) begins by stating: "We unanimously *(magno consensu)* hold and teach, in accordance with the decree of the Council of Nicaea, that there is one divine essence, which is called and which is truly God, and that there are three persons in this one divine essence" (CC, 67). The decisive point is that consent rests upon the fact that the conciliar decree is true, not that it is old or that a better one has not yet been found. We find here the basic terms in which we are to speak about God. No one can ever achieve something that is more basic. This being so, consent must be given, the consent of faith with which Christians confess God and thereby vindicate the truth of their talk about God both to others and to themselves (see I.4.3).

Primarily, then, dogma relates neither to the church that formulates the statement nor to the list of statements. It relates to its own task, that of serving what must be said about God. Hence it has a different profile. It is a statement, or a chain of statements, which articulates what God has disclosed. With it a corresponding movement in thinking is *in some sense* concluded — I repeat: in some sense, for we can none of us foresee which new statements might arise that will not simply replace the older statements but will also mean a real advance in knowledge. Therefore any profound and far-reaching correction of former theological statements is possible, as long as it does not deny the basis of theological thinking; perhaps this basis comes to light again in the process of such radical questioning. No dogma is formulated for all time or for eternity. If it could be, it would be a definite, i.e., final, statement of truth, but that would anticipate the conclusive judgment of God. We cannot expect this from theology. Theology is a pilgrim theology. It accompanies the people of God on the path of God's history with humanity. The statements that provide dogmatics its starting point and limits are definitive in dialogue. They are the presuppositions of theological discourse (see I.3.2). They help to prevent theology and the church from straying from their allotted path.

I.2.3. Coherence and Complexity

Dogmatics is linguistically complex. It is initiated by the primary account of homology, formed by a network of statements definitive in dialogue and kept in motion by more developed statements.

In relation to its structure, dogmatics appears as a state of theological knowledge that intensively as well as extensively has the unity of the Christian faith as its goal. It is oriented to the extended work of God that constitutes the thinking and hope of the church of Jesus Christ.

Dogmatics has two levels. It recognizes statements controlling other statements. A constitutive example in Protestantism is the doctrine of justification. Everything that we can say about ourselves and the world is oriented to the judgment of God that both saves and condemns (III.2.1). A dense web of statements thus arises. What we say dogmatically is intensive. It depends, not on how much we say, but on what we can say dogmatically. On what can we rely when we ask, or are asked, *why* we believe, *when* we believe *what* we believe?

8. Dogmatics characterizes the state of theological knowledge that has been provisionally achieved. But it permits theological discourse that can rely but not insist on proven questions and answers, being always ready to prove insights to be grounded in dialogue beyond existing limits, so that growth in faith is possible.

41

Many variations, accents and models are possible. That is why we have so many dogmatics. Whether they deserve the name depends on whether they are in constitutional agreement relative to faith's externality (I.1.2).

The development of dogmatics depends on how much time the church has had, what opportunities it has been granted and how it has used them, in order to formulate its knowledge adequately. Ecumenical dialogue, especially in the so-called new churches, is often hindered by the playing off of one state of knowledge against another. Instead, we ought to note and evaluate the implications and consequences of experiences in thinking achieved so far. The perception that leads to dogmatics is also conditioned by the manner and the degree of God's self-discourse. Dogmatics relates finally to the possibilities of knowledge. These may be disrupted by self-seeking, falsified by arrogance, or almost destroyed by self-deception.

Dogmatics is *ecumenically* oriented if and so long as it takes into account the scope of God's action. How far its validity extends we must investigate in a later section (II.9.2).

In virtue of its structure and depth, dogmatics is a systematic discipline. It is mainly an investigation of the basics, a criteriology of theology. It is kept in motion by what must be said unconditionally, by speech that might seem to be incomplete and opaque, but that still achieves a breakthrough. How far does this really attain to the truth in which God sustains us, so that we can say who this God is? Are these simply outbursts of experiences originating in the human, or impressions left by high-flying human longings that have lost contact with the earth, or linguistic excesses fed by deceptive monologues that might also be collective?

Dogmatics is a discipline in the simplest sense of the term. It trains itself in what might be said in faith. It presses forward as statements are demanded. It composes statements that say specific things in a specific and distinctive way and that exclude the contrary. Dogmatics cannot say only that which can be said in faith and with a view to faith. It is also important that what Christians *cannot* say should be clear, and *why* they cannot say it. Dogmatics is a foe of linguistic arbitrariness, especially when we really have to speak. Theology moves in the medium of speech, and hence in a sphere in which "communication" must be on the watch, must not be open to deception, must not be undermined by exhaustive efforts to find proofs. Dogmatics can still arouse confidence. It never disciplines us. Its work is to give clarity to the language of Christian faith by encompassing, within the given state of knowledge, all that can be said on good grounds, namely, in faith.

It must say it as consistently and coherently as possible. Through language, dogmatics joins together statements that rely on each other and are at the same time independent of each other, even when they are related to non-dogmatic statements and forms of speech. It presents an inner structure and in so doing it is self-enclosed, without damaging its historical development and the dialogical process in which it moves. Individual statements can be proved only by what is needed for faith, not by other principles.

What does this state of knowledge include? For Roman Catholics the answer is easy. They rely on all the prior definitions of the teaching office. They reflect on these dogmas. They expound them. So dogmatics has a hermeneutical task. It interprets what the church has decided to be obligatory to faith.

The Reformation churches took a different path. They did, of course, refer to basic dogmatic statements. They did so, however, because they found here the substance of the biblical texts. As we noted in I.1.5, they endorsed the conciliar definitions of trinitarian and christological teaching. But so far as possible they did not treat the "church" as a subject of dogmatics. Two fundamental distinctions were also made.

In the doctrine of justification they consented to the divine act of judgment and salvation that transforms us into God's justice and is therefore totally different from any evaluation of all human achievement. We cannot save ourselves. We must receive salvation in faith alone. This doctrine was formulated as a paraphrase of the biblically attested gospel. The Reformers thus subjected themselves to the message of the free grace of God. They brought under this norm everything that could be said and done in the church as a fellowship of justified sinners.

Their appeal was directly to the Bible, not in order to set aside the tradition of the church, but in order to ask for its legitimacy. The distinction between the Bible and the church corresponds to their insight that the church owes its origin to the Word and Spirit of God with which God is still pursuing his work today. Both the doctrine of justification and the appeal to Scripture alone (III.3) tell us how we may believe the church but must not believe in it.

I.3. Dogmatics as Building Theological Judgments

How is dogmatics constituted? We must now consider its inner construction, the structure itself and the elements that go into it.

Our primary concern now is not the thematic structure of dogmatics. There is, of course, a classical arrangement: God and his creation, Jesus Christ as our Savior, the church of Jesus Christ and the future of humanity and the world. But apart from the fact that other arrangements are possible, this arrangement does not tell us how the themes originated or why they are so inwardly restricted.

When we turn our attention to the structure of dogmatics, it emerges as a living and growing linguistic product. Only in III.1 will we try to set forth the architecture of dogmatics, the way it is constructed, with typical examples from the history of its construction.

The dogmatics into which we are now introducing you is not an unbroken form of alien knowledge with which we have to wrestle and which, after a critical review, we may either reject or accept. If that were so, two things would be needed: first, a standpoint from which to view what is handed down or communicated in some other way, and then a methodology. Again, if dogmatics rested on the statements of religious existence, it would only have to give it linguistic expression and adduce the related linguistic materials. Dogmatics, however, is a process of forming judgments in faith and hope. In this process we either exist in it or are drawn into it even if with different degrees of intensity, with different states of information, and with an ability to form judgments that must still be developed. This is why dogmatic thinking is needed.

I.3.1. Making Distinctions Necessary for Faith

9. Dogmatics starts with necessary distinctions between what must in all circumstances be said in faith and hope, and what must not be said at all.

These distinctions help us to stake off the area in which we can move in faith and in hope. We can begin by thinking and saying many things, but not everything is really possible or well founded in theology. We may use as an illustration the first thesis of the Barmen Declaration of May 31, 1934 ("The Theological Explanation of the Confessional Synod of the German Evangelical Church").

Historically this text came into being at a time when the unity of the German Evangelical Church was under grave threat from outside precisely because it was being brought under ecclesiastical and political pressures. National Socialism had again approached the question of the relation between church and state, and the "German Christians," who were close to the National Socialists, saw an opportunity to bring the territorial churches with their different confessions (Lutheran, Reformed, Union) under the banner of a people's movement and to create a national church. The identity of this church would be found in the mission of Germany that was nurtured by the historical experiences of the German people.

This was the situation. Now to the point. The church leaders and theologians who met at Barmen did not address the situation directly. They advanced a theological explanation, or declaration, containing six theses which focused on what must be said unconditionally and what is credible in all circumstances. Only what must be said in *this* situation and in relation to it? No, it did not say this. The theses are formulated in such a way that it becomes clear that these things *must* be said in *all* circumstances, even though the circumstances might be very different.

A verse or two from the Bible introduce each thesis, not as an edifying adornment, but to show that the thesis is in accord with the biblical testimony. Why and to what degree this accord is decisive is stated by the first thesis, John 14:6 and 10:1, 9 being cited in support.

> "I am the way, and the truth, and the life. No one comes to the Father except through me" (John 14:6). "Very truly, I tell you, anyone who does not enter the sheepfold by the gate is a thief and a bandit. . . . I am the gate. Whoever enters by me will be saved" (John 10:1, 9).
>
> Jesus Christ, as he is testified for us in the Holy Scripture, is the one Word of God whom we are to hear, whom we are to trust and obey in life and in death.
>
> We repudiate the false teaching that the church can and must recognize yet other happenings and powers, images and truths as divine revelation alongside this one Word of God, as a source of her preaching. (*CC*, 520)

The final paragraph, the rejection, best presents the challenge to the church then. It was not to acknowledge, alongside the one and only and indivisible Word of God in the person of Jesus Christ as a source of proclamation and as God's revelation, any other historical facts, figures, movements, or principles. In the existing situation, what was demanded was a people's religion that believed — yes indeed, believed — that it could perceive the voice of God in the blood and soil of Germany, and that could read the will of God from the history of the soul of Germany with all its productive convulsions. Over against this belief the Declaration rules that these things cannot be either revelation or a source of proclamation! The historical events and figures might well have been powerful. Perhaps they carried a meaning that could not be refuted. But they could neither explain nor replace what God had said once and for all in Jesus Christ. Hence the church was not to seek its unity in historical or social units or in political movements of unification.

The delimitation sheds light on the thesis. It clearly reveals its profile. But it does not simply show what it is opposing. It asks the question: Whom are we to trust and why can we believe? It replies: him who has made himself known in Jesus Christ and him alone, so that believing means following, trusting, and obeying Christ in both life and death. For God made himself known in Jesus Christ, in his life, in his death, in his presence as the risen Lord. He has done so in such a way that we can follow him, trust him, and obey him.

These steps are all linked to hearing God's Word. Hearing the promise and command of God breaks into the monologues in which individuals, groups, and peoples reflect themselves. These are all hopelessly caught up in themselves. They cannot get beyond the way they are, their origin, history, and experiences. They cling to whatever gives them meaning. Their monologues are always seeking a basis. The basis is to be found, however, outside themselves in the promise and command of God (I.1.2).

We find out here what must be said unconditionally when it is asked: Whom may we trust, whom or what may we hear, whom may we obey, whom may we follow in life and in death? What must be said, both today and not just today, is drastically perverted if we are silent at this point. We cannot say anything else. We have to say this. That is why it is unconditional. It must be said no matter what the circumstances are under which we speak. While we must not ruthlessly push ourselves forward, we are always under extreme pressure. We must pay no false respect to anyone. And we can always be full of hope. Unconditional also means that we have to speak in every situation or circumstance, and not just in specific ones. We must never say one thing today and another tomorrow. Naturally we must take note of individual situations, but in each and all of them we must speak this word. It is not for occasional use only.

What must be said unconditionally does not arise out of this basic relation, nor is it simply its expression. It is our human answer to the pronouncement of God, to his promise and direction. It is not caused by anything contained in this answer that presses for expression in it (though this is demanded). It waits for something outside itself that will evoke it. This outside thing is the unexpected divine address that is made and demands a hearing. People see that they are called, not only out of the closed conditions of their lives, but also out of the prison of the self, the incurving in upon oneself, as Luther termed our hopeless situation *(homo incurvatus in seipsum)*. What must be said unconditionally does not arise from within oneself, nor does it accord with what others experience in radical self-reflection. It unites people in acceptance of what God has done for them and said to them. Silence in his regard means either a forgetting or an overlooking of this fact.

Here, then, is the focus of the first thesis of the Barmen Declaration. What it says points us to that which the church's proclamation should uphold unconditionally if the church is to be the fellowship of those who hear what God has to say. In this fellowship will be found those who (no less than all others) know that they are already claimed by their social role, by their calling with its duties, by the emergencies that command them, by conditions that are by no means indifferent. But how can these very different people respond in faith in view of the difference in their perspectives, their experiences, their social relations, their attitudes, and their position, which gives them a greater or lesser view of things? They might perhaps acquire a sharper sense of common obligation. They might recognize a more overarching goal of action. They might see that they are bound together by a worldview, by an imperative view of the world, of society, and of history with its perils and opportunities. But such things, according to the anathema of the first thesis, are part of the "events and powers, figures and truths" which we must reject as pure presumptions. They do exist. They can captivate us. We can hardly escape them as we go about in daily life and agree or disagree with others. But one thing they are not. They are not the revelation of God or a source of the church's proclamation.

The whole point of the thesis is to make this distinction. It does, of course, need to be expounded and clarified. Everything is presupposed! "Jesus Christ, as he is testified for us in the Holy Scripture" — can we really say this so baldly when we consider the lack of conformity in the Gospels, the different pictures of Christ that the other New Testament writings give, and the want of uniformity and consistency in the relation between the New Testament and the Old? Ought they not have said, provokingly, "Jesus Christ, the Jew"? One might think that this would at a stroke have shown what position they took up against the inroads of the racial delusions of the National Socialists with their anti-Semitism, and indeed against the long-smoldering anti-Judaism of the Christian churches!

These are just two of the many questions that arise. Only a closer development of the thesis could answer them. We should have to consider the relation between the verses from John's Gospel and the thesis. It must explain the concepts that are used: Jesus Christ as the Word of God; revelation; proclamation; Holy Scripture. Where does the Old Testament fit in? The thesis obviously cannot give an exhaustive account of these terms. For one thing, it has to be short. It has to make a statement, to hold up a banner that will rally the troops. For another, it must restrict itself, forging a distinction that is necessary for faith.

This is the distinction between the hearing of God that calls for trust and obedience and a monologue of greater or lesser degree that causes us to circle around ourselves, to reflect upon ourselves, to see ourselves in the situation in which we are and which lays claim to us. The thesis stresses the point that there is this difference, and thanks God that it exists, for otherwise we would be lost forever in our monologues, and would fail to see that they exhaust us. We have to make this distinction once the events and figures seek to win power over us, claiming that they are the truth and have the last word.

It is not shown how the distinction is to be made in detail, that is, against what events and figures with their pressures and their claims to truth. This could not be said once and for all, for then the thesis would have only one application. Many applications are left open. The thesis limits itself to what is possible for the church on its journey, to what must be said unconditionally in all circumstances, for otherwise a hearing of God would not be possible so far as we are concerned.

We cannot read from the anathema what is to be distinguished. It certainly seems to make possible further applications, for it suggests where the front line was even at that time. If we were to read the thesis in 1934 and the years following, we would see who was meant. But theological judgment will see that if we do note the front line, we must not cite contemporary parallels. This would be easy enough. If a position was wrong then, would it not still be perverted today? We have only to make the appropriate criticism.

Adopting fronts, however, is not the same as making the distinctions that faith requires. It might, in fact, obscure the distinctions. The distinction between what must be said unconditionally and in all circumstances and what may never be said in any circumstances does not and cannot rule out decisions of a different kind. It can never prescribe where, when, and over against whom such decisions must be made. If it did, it would not really give direction. It would not have pioneering force in every situation. It would put blinders on us and seize the reins. Deviation would not be possible. The distinction can rule out only what for the sake of faith must never be said if error is to be avoided and, which is worse, if will-o'-the-wisps are not to be trusted.

Like the other Barmen theses, and all good theological statements, this thesis avoids the common alternative of concrete and abstract. If we understand by "concrete" something tangible confronting us — for example, a given situation or persons who evoke sympathy or antipathy so that we have to take an obvious attitude toward them — then the anathema of the first thesis seems rather theoretical. It is too general, much too remote from historical events, too abstract. The "concrete" here, however, is not the real issue. What is at issue is the making of a judgment.

If the thesis had related only to the National Socialist movement and its supporters, the "German Christians," its scope would have been limited to ecclesiastical politics. We would then have to look today at a right-wing revolution with a Christian tinge, or at a kind of national Christianity, if we wanted to see a contemporary application. But what would then be gained? We can form fronts and adopt positions in the political trenches and the war of worldviews, but in this case the first thesis would be valid only so long as the situation lasts and the debates continue that formed the fronts and thus brought the thesis into operation.

We need to note how far astray this leads us. We replace a distinction that is necessary for faith by a division of the world into friends and foes, into good and evil, and it is already clear on which side the one who makes the judgment stands. In place of theology we would have political strategy, with a fatal conception of politics that knows only supporters and opponents. A thesis of this type could hardly be a call to faith, a call to subject oneself to the judgment of God that applies to all, no matter on what front they stand. A total war would be declared in the name of omnipotent politics. The allegiance of all would be claimed. Unconditional adherence would be demanded. It is precisely against such a view that the first thesis of Barmen is directed.

Were we to derive the thesis from its historical and social context, we could explain it as follows. The thesis arose within the total state of National Socialism and the associated worldview. The events and powers and figures and truths that claim to be God's truth are a sign of a religiously exalted politics or a political religion. This kind of consecration might not be expressly made, yet it lies behind the claim that all life is affected, that everything is made plain both outwardly and inwardly, both theoretically and practically. What does not subject itself is disruptive and must be resisted and excluded by every possible means. This is the way a worldview thinks and acts. It offers views of the world which are inescapable if one is to live prudently; but claiming to be the only possible view, it also tells us about the inner unity of the world and how it can be mastered. The worldview makes a total and all-embracing claim. It sees that it is one with the law of the action under which it has appeared and which will sooner or later permit it to overrule the world. It is itself a power even though it is embodied in certain principalities and is grasped by the powerful. Worldviews reduce the world to a principle, and in the light of it turn the world upside down or right way up, as they see it. They neither know nor acknowledge anything that opposes their claim.

With this sketch I have tried to explain in some sort the worldview that the church was confronting in the Hitler regime. It may be disputed whether it can be generalized in this way. Perhaps we are to equate National Socialism with earlier or later worldviews. Perhaps this was only an incomparably irrational, anachronistic special instance.

We are moving here at the level of a theory of the rise and fall of cultures. Showing what is normal and abnormal, this theory throws insight on the processes of history in the light of their structures. For example, it can point to the fact that these worldviews were part of the age that began in eighteenth- or nineteenth-century Europe. Similarities are also seen, however, with the worldviews of the state religions of antiquity. With one of these, that of the Roman Empire, early Christianity clashed, just as the twentieth-century churches did, with the totalitarian states.

To a limited degree explanations of this kind can be helpful. They show, for example, how various experiences foster political culture. The Barmen Declaration, however, does not rely on this type of analysis or prognosis. It recalls the first commandment: "I am the Lord your God. You shall have no other gods but me" (Exod. 20:2-3; Deut. 5:6-7). It challenges us: Why are we able to speak about this God? Do we really trust him? There can be no compromise between the worship of this God and idolatry. Where do we stand on this field of tension? Where do we draw the line unconditionally and in all circumstances? The Declaration gives an answer. It offers a definitive dogmatic response. It forms a judgment. It invites us to do the same.

I.3.2. Following Rules That Mark Out the Way

10. Theological rules of dialogue constitute the core of dogmatics. Their orientation is to faith and hope. They tell us on what we can rely in all circumstances.

I call this thesis a rule. Rules are not general keys in every situation. They are not the directions for use. They are part of the process whose regularity they depict. They help to constitute the event. The rules of chess limit the inconceivable number of possible moves in a game. But they also permit a limited number that is still incomparably great. The rules of traffic prevent accidents. They are thus limits that make greater freedom of movement possible. The point is that they help us on our way.

These examples might seem out of place when we treat theology. Theology is not a game. It is not a highway code. That is true. But it misses the point of the comparison. For one thing, participants must all observe the rules. Otherwise interaction is impossible. Again, rules are needed so that spectators may know what is really happening. Without them, they cannot understand what is done. They are confronted by a mixture of arbitrary and disconnected elements with which they can have no dealings. They cannot go along because they do not know what is happening or how the game is played. We have to know the rules to be able to take part in the game or follow it as nonparticipants.

Basic and normative theological statements are the rules of thought and knowledge. Theological agreement rests on them. This agreement is a human concern in the search for true knowledge. It is first provisional. It is referred to goal-directed processes of dialogue rather than to an arbitrary exchange of thoughts and opinions. Theology necessarily demands a related dialogue with others in the search for a common perception. It does not arise when theologians spin out a thread of thought that ensnares others.

The basic and normative statements are also the rules of dialogue. They are the rules that govern mutual conversations, the kind of dialogue that we find in letters of Paul, a dialogue into which the readers are invited, so that they can take part in the conversation, or it may be an inward dialogue in which we discuss a matter with ourselves. The theological rules of dialogue deal with matters of faith. They promote conversations about faith which are not just for special occasions but go on continually when it is a matter of clarifying the themes of faith.

Insofar as dogmatics names the rules that govern the formation of theological judgment, and observes them rather than applying them, it does not just administer tradition.

The rules of dialogue determine the course of conversation but do not force it into a fixed schema. They are a core that crystallizes the conversation. They are way-marks that help to generate decision. As in 1 Corinthians (see I.1.3), they show what can be said in faith and what cannot be said in faith. They do not narrow down the conversation. On the contrary, they make it possible. They allow it to be conducted in the full freedom of faith and with a readiness for new insights. The rules of dialogue help the conversation forward by telling us what must be said in any case, whether sooner or later. According to the state of the conversation, the rules will either be there at the beginning or they will emerge as aiming points as the conversation proceeds. What is decisive for faith will finally be known as the paths have to part, that is, when the dialogue cannot proceed without contradictions arising in relation to what must be said in faith.

That was the point of the rule of faith in the early church. This rule formulated for the first time what can be said in faith and what has to be said. The word "rule" did not then, as it does so often now, carry with it the thought of a formal regulation. What was meant by rule was norm. Even that can be misunderstood. It might be thought that the rule of faith is a short and succinct statement of the Christian faith, and that from these few sayings one can deduce what might then be said within the whole sphere of faith. This would be an extensive explication and application, but it would not be true *knowledge,* which can involve definite, contoured, and often surprising perceptions. Knowledge is not indefinite. It does not roam freely. It takes place on paths that lead to a specific terrain. But it does not follow tracks that have been laid down once and for all.

Ludwig Wittgenstein, with his theory of language games, has referred to the regularity of knowledge and of the understanding that aims at this knowledge (*Philosophical Investigations,* trans. G. E. M. Anscombe [Oxford, 1958], e.g., pp. 26-27 [no. 54]). This theory indicates the boundaries within which we must always move when speaking in a specific manner. We cannot transgress these boundaries as long as we use the language in question. What we may perceive or apprehend differently, for example, intuitively, still has to be communicated within these linguistic boundaries. Various language games are possible within the boundaries. We might find the most complex academic theories but also simple forms of everyday speech. But there is no relation between any of them and a capricious manner of speech. The theory of language games seeks to illumine the relation between an understanding that leads to specific knowledge and the rules that have to be followed. It neither can nor seeks to do more than this. But it does a great deal. We shall have to point out, for example, that no one can unexpectedly switch language games without having to follow different rules. A tennis player cannot win by suddenly changing the game to boxing.

But does all this apply to theology? One might automatically resist this conclusion. Yet is not theology a language game in the sense depicted? It is not, of course, mere play. Nor is it a mechanical following of rules that we have only to recall. Yet it is still tied to specific words and their context that carry specific meanings! Think of words like "belief" or "believe." In everyday use these denote subjective attitudes ("I believe that such and such might happen"), the early stages of indefinite opinion or of real knowledge. Yet the words can also be an expression of confidence ("I believe you"). Nevertheless, when we say that we believe that God created us, or that we believe in Jesus Christ, or in the resurrection of the dead, we cannot appeal any longer to the everyday use, not even as a shell into which we can pour new content. A linguistic context has now become the rule. This is not a free invention. We are told here what rule applies when Christians tell us what they believe, whom they believe in, and why they can believe. Those who follow this rule are not propagating subjective convictions that might perhaps help to persuade others. They are stating something specific which others might perhaps adopt as they themselves do. In the process they forget themselves. This language game is a good game. It is serious, but not grim.

The rules of dialogue do not by a long way say everything that can and must be said in detail. If they did, dialogue would be superfluous, or no more than stereotyped repetition. The dogmatic rules within which we set the relations of Father, Son, and Spirit, and their connection to the path trodden by humanity and the world between creation and redemption, open up for us a firm perspective that continuously helps us to find new things. We see from 1 Corinthians that authoritative dictates cannot overcome the problems at Corinth. A sharper dialogue of faith has to be formulated, a dialogue that will set on track specific statements of faith and put them in motion.

The rules of dialogue, of course, prevent us from speaking recklessly even when simply adding to what others have already said. The result will be a conventional conversation. This is a danger which has found abundant testimony in church history. "Our Lord Christ has surnamed Himself Truth, not Custom," as Tertullian remarked (*De virginibus velandis* 1.1; CSEL, 2:1209, 9f.; ET, *On the Veiling of Virgins,* ANFa, 4:27). If this were not so, we would go astray if our conversations did not follow the rules but were based on some authority that told us what we were mechanically to repeat. The rules of dialogue resist the authoritarian thinking that calls for repetition or simple agreement. In such a case there can be no dialogue with thrust and counterthrust leading on to a result. One ram now leads and the herd follows, bleating its assent. The first thesis of Barmen rejected this idea of a faithful following by rejecting the leadership principle and its guarantee of a collective political policy. That principle had momentous consequences for political culture, but how much more so for the church as a fellowship of faith! It could have given the church more cohesion for longer or shorter periods, but at the cost of an inner weakness due to the renouncing of a true dialogue of faith.

For a good illustration we might refer to the decision reached at Chalcedon (451) regarding the proper way to speak about Jesus Christ. The question at Chalcedon was this: "Who is this Jesus Christ upon whom we call, whose coming into the world we remember, whose death we proclaim at each service until his coming again, and whom we await as the hope of life?" This was and is an elementary question. It is posed whenever we invoke him. It has to be answered if we are to say clearly who this Jesus is both in a religious world that knew many gods and god-related heroes, and also in the Jewish world, which taught that there is one God who is infinitely exalted above everything earthly, and which awaited the Messiah that would be the herald and forerunner of the coming world, but which never confused the divine and the human.

In the preceding councils, of Nicaea (325) and Constantinople (381), the church had formulated the confession of the triunity of God as Father, Son, and Spirit. It must now express the unity of Jesus Christ as both God and humankind. This task of thought did not inescapably demand contact with the highly developed linguistic vocabulary of philosophy, as Adolf von Harnack stated: "it becomes clear that dogmatic Christianity (the dogmas) in its conception and in its construction was *the work of the Hellenic spirit upon the Gospel soil*" (*Lehrbuch der Dogmengeschichte*, 4th ed. [Tübingen, 1909], 1:20; ET, *Outlines of the History of Dogma*, trans. Edwin Knox Mitchell [Boston, 1957], p. 5). It demanded reflection both on all that the Bible had to say about God and humanity and also on all that we can properly say about God both as individuals and as a fellowship — the sum total, indeed, of the language of faith.

The Chalcedonian Definition runs as follows:

Following, then, the holy fathers, we unite in teaching all men to confess the one and only Son, our Lord Jesus Christ . . . in two natures, without confusing the two natures, without transmuting one nature into the other, without dividing them into two separate categories, without contrasting them according to area or function. The distinctiveness of each nature is not nullified by the union. Instead, the 'properties' of each nature are conserved and both natures concur in one 'person' and in one *hypostasis*. (CC, 35-36)

Long and serious controversies and many attempts at compromise preceded this formulation. The debates often seemed to be about words and even letters. The definition served as a conclusion. No one could go beyond this point and no one could fall short of it without running into fundamental errors. The statement has always been an important rule of dialogue.

It did not receive the character of an imperial edict even though the emperor wanted unity for political purposes, seeking agreement not only among pugnacious theologians but also among the laity, who were involved willy-nilly. Prayer and worship and understanding of the Bible were all passionately at stake.

Consensus was not achieved also by a sharper definition of philosophical concepts. These could be illuminating if clarified. The terms "nature" and "hypostasis" had always given rise to problems, even more so than the term "person," which had been given a new theological definition. Today we often suspect these concepts of being too static. The fourfold delimitation (without confusion, change, division, or separation) points the way ahead. Four possibilities of thinking of the union are excluded: confusion, change, division, separation. We do best to think of a square in relation to which four possibilities (no more) are ruled out. The mystery of the unity of deity and humanity in the person of Jesus Christ is to be found, linguistically, in the empty space formed by this fourfold delimitation. It defies expression, for it defies comprehension. It is a pure miracle. Yet we can speak of it as long as we unconditionally avoid thinking in terms of a symbiosis or a separation of the deity and humanity.

Precision is here given to what in I.3.1 we called necessary distinctions. The unity of deity and humanity in Jesus Christ embraces not only the mystery of the incarnation of God but also his and our humanity in the world under the curse of "transitoriness." As true God and true man, Jesus Christ redeems all those who are alienated from God by guilt. That is why we can believe even if we do so with a wonder that cannot be expressed. God has taken to himself a hopelessly lost humanity. He reconciled the world to himself in Christ (2 Cor. 5:19) and yet did not surrender his deity. Reconciling does not mean mixing into an undifferentiated oneness. God acts for the world. He is thus distinct from it even though he never separates himself from it.

The distinctions have to be made. They are necessary for faith. They thus become rules of dialogue (I.3.2) because they constantly offer orientation when we ask concerning the relation between God and humanity. They tell us that the two are distinct but not separate. The distinctions relate to the fact that the world has been reconciled and is being reconciled with God. They do not allow us to restrict the reconciliation to individuals or to the soul. Nevertheless, the reconciliation is not yet complete in the sense that it does not already encompass all people no matter whether they accept it or not. Reconciliation goes along with the entreaty "Be reconciled to God" (2 Cor. 5:20). It is, therefore, an incessant summons to faith.

This summons to faith links us to Jesus Christ. It tells us to whom we should listen and how this fellowship is set up. All this finds further exposition in the second Barmen thesis. This thesis arises out of the basic distinction of Chalcedon. It also shows us that the rule is definitive and can be applied to other issues. It runs as follows:

> "Jesus Christ . . . became for us wisdom from God, and righteousness and sanctification and redemption" (1 Cor. 1:30).
>
> Just as Jesus Christ is the pledge of the forgiveness of all our sins, just so — and with the same earnestness — is he also God's mighty claim on our whole life; in him we encounter a joyous liberation from the godless claims of this world to free and thankful service to his creatures.
>
> We repudiate the false teaching that there are areas of our life in which we belong not to Jesus Christ but another lord, areas in which we do not need justification and sanctification through him. (CC, 520)

There are many distinctions in this rule: promise and claim, liberation and bondage, justification and sanctification, indirectly faith and works, above all what God does and what we do. At every point we are referred to God in Jesus Christ. In him we are linked with God. In fellowship with him we are totally liberated and totally claimed.

Promise and claim: Do we have here a real distinction between what God does and what we do? Or does a slight ambiguity arouse the thought that a transition is in process that helps us to evade the problem!

In what direction are we pointed? We seem to be referred to the fact that membership in Jesus Christ results in action corresponding to this fellowship. In Jesus Christ we partake of everything that allows us to stand in the presence of God. Thus our whole life belongs to him. Does not this have to show itself by acts that reflect what Jesus Christ is for us: wisdom, righteousness, sanctification, and redemption? Might not this find demonstration in the forging of right relationships, in the living of a holy life, in a lifestyle that gives further evidence of liberation?

The second thesis of the Barmen Declaration does not take this path. We see this when it relates justification and sanctification only to what Christ did for us. We have need of this act — constant need — if we are really able to act ourselves. Christ himself has been "made" wisdom, righteousness, sanctification, and redemption. He subjected himself to what God is and what God wills. We follow him. We are thus placed under the judgment of God. In no way can we justify ourselves, not even by our works, and especially not by works through which we show what God has done for us. It is equally impossible that we should sanctify ourselves, in our areas of responsibility, by our action or inaction.

There is thus no human possibility that we should first put faith before works but then find in the works that follow faith a demonstration of our faith. There is no sphere of life in which we do not need both justification and sanctification by Jesus Christ. All that we do is corrupt and misguided unless we are always and everywhere referred to Jesus Christ. Nothing should seek to contradict what he is for us. In all our acts we are summoned to faith.

All this enables us to form a judgment within the boundaries depicting the distinction between the lordship of Jesus Christ and human autonomy. Here and now we have to recognize what are the "godless bonds" from which we are freed. We can recognize them only if we see that we and all that we do constantly need justification and sanctification. We have to follow this rule, trusting that liberation for "free, thankful service" will take place for us, and that it will do so in a way that shows that, even in detail, action that serves the creatures of God is possible.

I.3.3. Perceiving Relationships

11. Dogmatics is formed by the interrelation between all theological statements, which is yet open.

Ideally dogmatics is a linguistic context that represents everything that belongs to the Christian faith. But we can only approximate to this ideal. In the first instance the Christian faith is not much more than a label showing us what is at issue, what game we are playing (in terms of our seventh thesis). It is only within that context, that is, dogmatically, that we can show what is really *faith* and really *Christian*. We must accept this fact if we want to speak plainly and relevantly, or credibly according to our second thesis. We give no credibility to faith just by imparting confidence or convincing people suddenly. In these cases attention focuses on the speaker and his or her action, not upon what is said, and said in such a way that in and by itself it leads to faith, to trust in God, upon whom we can rely in both life and death.

Ephesians 3:16-19 marks the scope: "I pray that . . . Christ may dwell in your hearts through faith, as you are being rooted and grounded in love. I pray that you may have the power to comprehend, with all the saints, what is the breadth and length and height and depth, and to know the love of Christ that surpasses knowledge, so that you may be filled with all the fullness of God."

Breadth and length and height and depth suggest a three-dimensional space which has segments both before and behind, both above and below, both to the right and the left. The arrangement helps us to see things in their right places. It points to the relations and interconnections. It makes observation possible. To be sure, the love of Christ as we should know it surpasses human knowledge. Our own knowledge of things cannot grasp this love. Yet even so, even though its fullness is beyond our normal or heightened comprehension, we should perceive this love, and perceiving it means expressing it, even if our words become confused. Our relation to what must be fittingly said here, or rather, the misrelation of our ability to grasp what has laid hold of us, also has a linguistic place even on the outer limits of speech. Dogmatics plunges us, often intensively, into the very depths.

Faith is neither blind nor dumb. It has to make statements about what it perceives through general observation, through specific glances, or through catching the true meaning of individual things. In theses 9 and 10 we referred to distinctions and rules that we must follow. We have to take the paths that lead to the assigned terrain. We thus move in an area that shows us everything related to it, things preceding and things following, though not in the temporal sense of sooner or later. Nearness and distance are involved, intensity and extension, connections and delimitations. We can never see the totality; we can only grow into it.

Clarification may be found in the fifth Barmen thesis, which links the two orders of church and state that so frequently come into conflict. (The italics are my own.)

"Fear God, honor the king!" (1 Pet. 2:17).
The Bible tells us that according to divine arrangement the state has

the responsibility *to provide for justice and peace in the yet unredeemed world,* in which the church also stands, according to the measure of human insight and human possibility, by the threat and use of force.

The church recognizes with thanks and reverence toward God the benevolence of this, his provision. She *reminds* men of *God's Kingdom, God's commandment and righteousness,* and thereby the responsibility of rulers and ruled. She *trusts and obeys the power of the word,* through which God maintains all things.

We repudiate the false teaching that the state can and should expand beyond its special responsibility to become the single and total order of human life, and also thereby fulfill the commission of the church.

We repudiate the false teaching that the church can and should expand beyond its special responsibility to take on the characteristics, functions and dignities of the state, and thereby become itself an organ of the state. (CC, 521-22)

Here a distinction that is necessary for faith is made between church and state. If the two are intermingled, the state threatens to become a totalitarian state and thus to lose its essential character, or else the church finds freedom to posture as a quasi state, as a force that sustains the state, or as a possibly hostile state within the state. Naturally the church may still come to political expression within constitutional bonds, and what it says may be critical. But the distinction remains, and it prepares the ground for new ethical insights and tasks. It is always directed against political totalities that violate the divine appointment. It shows that church and state can helpfully coexist, and it is a sign that both are under the sway of God alone.

Within the necessary distinction some further theological links should be mentioned. These involve new distinctions and differences that help to expand our faith and hope.

We live in an unredeemed world. Not in a corrupt world that we need to turn upside down, completely reshaping it from head to toe! But in a world in which the power of evil has not yet been defeated. Our world is not yet what it ought to be according to God's will. We can say this, of course, only if we know what the will of God is.

This will does not hover over us like an idea or a utopian fancy. We have to be reminded of what the kingdom, command, and righteousness of God are. We get this reminder when we pray for them. Faith and hope are anchored in prayer. Their orientation is to the fact that God upholds all things through his foresight, his providence. We therefore have grounds for hope: "Deliver us from evil" (Matt. 6:13).

By both its prayers and its preaching the church reminds the governing and the governed of their responsibilities. One such responsibility is that of promoting peace and justice, which might be threatened if the kingdom, command, and righteousness of God were given a political connotation. These concepts, however, are not unrelated to political responsibility. The relation lives on in prayer and preaching.

Prayer and preaching are the hinge connecting church and state and individual and society. Faith and hope can never be either a private affair or a political goal.

The connection that faith and hope express is that God rules over the whole world and gives it the promise of redemption. The dogmatic concepts of providence and world redemption offer us eschatological perspectives.

We must uphold this link even if in fact we face a confused situation in which church and state, religion and politics, are intermingled. When we see this link, we are enabled to await an encounter with the same living God to whom the Bible bears witness. For this reason we must give expression to this link, reflecting the fact that we do await this God and will encounter him. Patient thinking and spiritual elasticity are needed lest we be mired in provisional impressions or draw too hasty conclusions. Shortsighted thoughts, simple associations, and rapidly projected insights might well be stimulating, but they do not bode well for dogmatics.

I.4. Reaching Consensus

We now look at a specific *type* of theological texts. They resemble dogmatic texts in many ways, but they are different, though not antithetical. For to an extent, they are conditional upon dogmatic texts; then again they also provide impulses for further theological work. They bring the question sharply into focus: what may a church not say under all circumstances when it speaks in faith and hope? They contribute to the *drawing of the border* which is necessary for faith.

We shall meet the structural moments of dogmatic speech, described in I.3, here again; some linguistic elements of dogmatics (I.2) will also return. Texts of this kind, however, have a different *function* from dogmatics. The task of dogmatics is to develop, as far as possible, the totality of what must be said in faith, hope, and love under all circumstances. In comparison to that, the texts to which we shall turn now are sharper in content. They state what a church sees itself as obligated to say when questions arise about its essential nature and it replies by showing where and how its theology is leading it. They *compress* the account given by a particular church at a particular point in time, usually at a critical moment for the church in question, when the essential nature of the church is at stake.

This obligation finds its plainest expression in an express *commitment* to these texts. They are shown to be binding because they rest on what is binding. Their rank may be compared with that of state constitutions. The distinction is that they do not owe their origin to a union formed by an assembly that gave the state its constitution.

The commitment of the church expresses the fact that it cannot create this theological obligation itself. It sees itself as dependent on what God has done and has promised to do, and also on his presence. The presence of God in its full scope is the subject matter of church teaching. This subject matter stands in opposition to all attempts to overlook or suppress it.

These features characterize theological texts of this kind as church "doctrine," as opposed to false doctrine.

12. Church doctrine expresses what a church lets itself be told unconditionally.

When it is linked to a church and does not have the illusion of floating free in the void, dogmatics always stands related to doctrine, just as doctrine always stands related to dogmatics because it needs the judgment that dogmatics develops.

I have tried to portray doctrine here as it is found in the history of the Protestant church and its theology. Yet it can also be compared meaningfully with the basic texts and statements of other churches, which have a similar effect. Many churches and church fellowships which reject "dogmatic" renouncements (I.1.1) are also opposed to making doctrinal statements. They do uphold and pass on what they regard as necessary to faith, but they do this through their hymns and prayers and ethical norms. What is obligatory for them and unites them finds expression in their liturgies, in the way they use the Bible, in their attitude to the state and public morality and civil religion, but above all in the ethical goals to which they are committed and which bind their members together. Has not this kind of common nondoctrinal commitment now long since caught up with even those churches which can look back to a previous doctrinal tradition?

I.4.1. Development of Doctrine

Let us take a more recent example by way of illustration. The United Church of Christ (UCC), formed in 1957 and now united with the German Evangelical Church (1980), is a fellowship that initially had no confession.[9] The churches that constituted this union were American denominations which had adopted in part the doctrinal traditions of the European churches to which their founders belonged. Christians with a Congregationalist, Reformed, and partly Lutheran background all came together in the United Church. They deliberately chose not to formulate a common confession of faith or to adopt a confessional position. Instead, they put forward a "Statement of Faith" that left room for both differing convictions and also new ones.[10] It quickly became apparent, however, that some obligatory doctrine was needed as they built up the congregations and became immersed in political and social action. Without it they would be wafted about by the changing winds of public opinion or — and there is only one seeming contrast — become institutionalized in discharging the tasks of leadership.

In 1977, twenty years after the union, a doctrinal report came out: "Toward the Task of Sound Teaching in the United Church of Christ" (in Frederick Herzog, *Justice Church: The New Function of the Church in North American Christianity* [Maryknoll, N.Y., 1980], pp. 140-48). The phrase "sound teaching" is taken from the Pastoral Epistles (1 Tim. 1:10; 2 Tim. 4:3; Titus 1:9; 2:1; cf. 1 Tim. 6:3; 2 Tim. 1:13; Titus 2:8). It means true teaching that will be a basis for a true lifestyle, as opposed to all counterfeit and thus confusing philosophies of life. The associations of the English term "sound" carry with them the thought of a lofty and attractive musical note, an orchestral sound or the sound of music. The term "doctrine" is avoided. It is an overloaded term and suggests authoritative instruction. What is wanted is not doctrine but teaching that will help the learners in the doubtful and ambiguous situations of daily life.

The preamble gives us the background to this formation of doctrine. The church is seeking to live out its faith by a Christian presence and by championing the rights of minorities. "Responsive action has tended to

---

9. Cf. Hanns-Peter Keiling, *Die Entstehung der "United Church of Christ" (USA)* (Berlin, 1969); Louis H. Gunnemann, *The Shaping of the United Church of Christ* (New York, 1977); *United and Uniting: The Meaning of an Ecclesial Journey. United Church of Christ 1957-1987* (New York, 1987); Frederick Herzog, "Thesen zum Zusammenführen der Ströme der Reformation," *EvTh* 43 (1983): 548-56.

10. Gunnemann, pp. 69-70.

precede and take precedence over theological reflection. . . . The United Church of Christ also seems to have scattered its energies so frenetically in pursuing many new causes that an enervation of spirit and aimlessness have set in. The United Church of Christ, its people and pastors, worried about institutional maintenance and growth, is caught in the search for identity" (p. 142).

Social psychology almost seems to be what is at issue in this perspective. A church fellowship, like any other social group, needs a demonstrable identity if it is to see and to show others who it really is, and to differentiate itself from comparable formations, especially when it engages in political and social controversies. In fact, however, the need for teaching goes far beyond this. "Times of profound temptation in the church are also times for discerning and claiming God's renewing call to faithful ministry. In this present time the questions of identity, faith, and the place of the ordained ministry are all powerful signs of an awareness that the renewal of the teaching office in the church is an urgent need and opportunity" (p. 142). "Church and society are caught in increasing conflict. In this situation, God calls upon us to give a new account of our hope lest we be 'tossed to and fro and blown about by every wind of doctrine' (Eph. 4:14)" (p. 145).

What is expected of "teaching" is that it will help us in making distinctions. Teaching begins by confessing the triune God in the unity of his action. It then perceives his covenant, which brings the church together and unites it, always in the promise of righteousness, of life, and of the presence of the Spirit (pp. 145-47).

The statement is especially instructive because it proceeds cautiously. It prudently avoids trying to win back the church and its threatened consensus by making an ethical appeal. The political, social, and moral challenges cannot be ignored, but they are not used to line up the whole fellowship and to initiate a forward march. They rather pose the question: Upon what can the church rely if it is to do what it can do without false caution and to leave alone what it must forego?

The leaders of the UCC adopted the statement of faith by resolution. They thus gave it authority as the teaching of the church. Yet they did not really adopt it as part of church doctrine. The process of formulating statements either to undergird a church fellowship or to prepare the ground for it (cf. the Leuenberg Concordat) through a common declaration of theological principles is one of the ways by which Protestant churches might develop their teaching. Yet it is surely exceptional. Normally the development of doctrine involves several stages in which the structural and linguistic elements of dogmatics play a decisive role. The outcome is then declared to be binding because it *has shown itself* to be compelling, not as the result of the declaration itself.

A church on a stricter view can never *posit* doctrine. It can only mark the boundaries it meets when it asks what is the truth of what it says and the credibility of what it does. With the help of doctrine the church can stand up against all claims to power, even its own!

Upon what may the church rely? This is what it confesses in its teaching. It makes an express pledge to say certain specific things and to rule out the opposite. In doing so it follows certain distinctions which it owes to the divine actions. Therefore, in a razor-sharp and hence exclusive manner, doctrine tells us what the church has perceived to be God's promise and God's direction. Doctrine imposes this alien word as an express obligation.

13. Doctrine commits the church to its externality, and its state of knowledge will correspondingly express that which characterizes its power of judgment.

The answer to the question: Upon what does the church rely? is to give an account of "the hope that is in you" (1 Pet. 3:15). This account will show how the church is to be guided. Doctrine is not a mechanism whereby a religious fellowship can direct itself (I.1.1). The account of the hope that is imparted to the church is not produced by probing the inner impulses of a Christian fellowship.

I.4.2. Dogmatic Dynamics of Doctrine

In times of intellectual and spiritual confusion, basic theological distinctions can be reached and delimitations formulated that will relate first and foremost to the critical situation, though always with the purpose of stating clearly what theology must say in all circumstances and unconditionally in this situation.

14. A limited text consisting of theological statements will be seen by its reception to have such weight that a church has to confess and proclaim it as its doctrine, showing that it is definitive in dialogue. Doctrine gives unmistakable precision to the language of faith.

Dogmatics can then build further on doctrine by intensively and extensively developing its statements and exploring their grounding (III.1). The succinctness of its contents differentiates doctrine from dogmatics. Doctrine demands exposition for this very reason. It calls for a more far-reaching and an interconnected explanation that will open up its content and not just repeat it or comment upon it. (Friedrich Schleiermacher's *Christian Faith,* first published in 1821-22, is an example.)

We might also quote the Augsburg Confession (1530) and the Barmen Declaration (1934) as further examples of the Protestant development of doctrine. Both texts were formulated with the intention of establishing delimitations which would set out the scope for possible consensus (I.4.3) and make the language of faith precise with regard to one or more contentious questions. Whether this endeavor has been heard by others and has held good, however, and whether such texts become formative doctrinal documents for a church, is another story and cannot be anticipated by means of their author's intention. But doctrine corresponds to the stated intention to contribute what is humanly possible to church unity, that is, to strive for theological knowledge but not to stand in the way of unity by doing so. The Augsburg and Barmen documents did not arise as doctrinal texts; they became such due to circumstances that were not at first envisioned. Only later did it become apparent that they had succeeded in formulating forceful distinctions to which the Protestant church could constantly return when it became clear that further distinctions were needed. In this reception process we also see the dovetailing of church doctrine and dogmatics.

At the Diet of Augsburg the Protestant "estates," at the command of the emperor, stated plainly both what they believed in common with the "traditionalists" and what they believed to give grounds for separation. The aim of this comparison was agreement. Instead, it led to the confrontation of two religious "parties," divided by opposing and unbridgeable opinions. The signatories and defenders of the Augsburg Confession were forced to establish their own church, and this church found in the Augsburg text its doctrine (or confession) under the pressure of the ecclesiastical politics of the time.

The Barmen Declaration, too, was not originally meant to be a piece of doctrine or a confession, at least not in the confessionalistic sense as the founding document of a new or renewed church. The delegates of the German Protestant churches discussed and accepted it, but at this critical hour their desire was to give an external expression of the Christian faith, committing themselves in a way that would so state the unity of the church that it would become clear that this church was not self-originating and therefore its unity did not rest on a legal enactment but would be found in the fact that the church confessed its basis, and by the way it did so.

This church measures itself by what is binding for it, and by what it sees to be binding. The real theological weight of this Declaration (and its designation reflects the caution used lest theological insights should be made binding!) would show itself only as the years passed. Even today, it is far from being exhausted. This can be seen not only in the German Protestant churches, which took up the Barmen Declaration in their reordering made after 1945 (the United Protestant Church and the churches of Kurhessen-Waldeck and Baden made it a part of the ordination vows), but also outside Germany. It was adopted by the Dutch Hervormde Kerk and by the United Presbyterian Church in the USA; it influenced the Church of South India; and it played a part in the struggle against racism in South Africa and also in the liberation movements in South America and Asia.

In both these confessions it is apparent, though not strictly stated, that one of the marks of Protestant doctrine is that it helps the church to test its own decisions and actions and the ramifications of its actions, decisions, and speech. The church subjects itself and its doctrine to an external examiner. It does not judge itself. In a strict sense the church cannot create its doctrine. It can only set the boundaries that it comes up against when it asks about the truth of what it says and the credibility of what it does. With the help of doctrine the church resists mere claims to power, even its own claims.

A further mark of doctrine, strikingly expressed in the Barmen Declaration, is that it reduces contentious issues in a crisis situation to fundamental questions that can be decided only by the use of distinctions and not by compromises. In some situations what is decisive has to be stated, but in such a way that what is said goes much further than the situation itself. Doctrine, then, cannot be reduced to shortsighted crisis management.

In the Barmen Declaration it is made clear that the externality of faith solidifies in distinctions that prepare the ground for theological and political decisions. A frontier becomes visible, on the far side of which the church can no longer be the church. When the church recognizes this frontier and formulates it expressly, we then have doctrine. The frontier on the far side of which the church can no longer be the church leaves no more space for any other church. Drawing this frontier is the function of doctrine when seen from within. When seen from without, the development of doctrine gives a church its particularity.

I.4.3. The Compelling Nature of Doctrine

Churches are distinguished from one another not only by doctrine but already by their development of doctrine. Dogmatics differs from doctrine along the same lines. It tends to be ecumenical.

15. Doctrine comes into being when dissent is vanquished and consensus is achieved.

A church then says what it has to say in its situation, and also what it must rule out if it is still to be the church. It must not attempt to say everything on each occasion. It has to see what paths can be taken at each time and in each place. Doctrine, then, is not a set of church rules. It marks off a particular path and invites others to take it.

This limited role threatens to be overshadowed by the imposing doctrinal structures that have been set up by the Christianity of central Europe. For a long time these structures have demanded a degree of care and renovation that, quite alone, far outweighs our power to carry them out. Two centuries ago Christians were weighed down by the fullness of what they had to uphold and learn as doctrine. Reference verses were made for the Augsburg Confession in the second half of the eighteenth century, and they ended with a heartfelt sigh: "that is the sum of all doctrine, and may the Lord protect us from any more." Today, of course, many Christians in many churches want more doctrine, but more in quality, not in quantity!

But for this reason doctrine of this sort cannot be *binding* in the sense in which Germans usually are using the term as a kind of expression of a well-intentioned readiness not to offend others by too lofty claims, a readiness to meet them halfway. One has become accustomed to using the term "binding character" in this context. The hardness that is part of "commitment," of binding nature, is thus toned down. But a problem arises here. On the one hand we want to avoid giving the impression of an absolute knowledge that is above time and independent of space, and yet on the other hand we do not want to give way to all manner of opinions. It is best, perhaps, to speak of truth rather than commitment. We must remember at the same time that we can express the truth of faith only by being ready to uphold "sound doctrine"; "false doctrine" will lead us into error. Sound doctrine will then be for us the truth content of what we are committed to say.

When something is binding for us in either speech or action, it is also a boundary of what is not binding. More precisely, it is the boundary of speech and action that is not *binding in faith,* but which is subject to other standards and purposes. This should therefore be called "non-binding," even if it can seem normative or dictated by a norm.

In German, the word *Verbindlichkeit* (binding nature) sounds ambivalent: its range extends from "binding force" to "civility." Used so far to mean what is obligatory, it can also suggest the compromise between the authority of faith and the relationship of trust that is a part of faith. We have difficulty with the biblical statements that make all-surpassing claims to validity. In trying to soften their sharpness, we use a term like *verbindlich* for that which has to go along with faith. This is a kind of palatable iron ration, or emergency supply. In this way the attractive sayings and exemplary attitude of Jesus might easily seem to be *verbindlich:* they invite us and do not put too big a demand on us.

What is binding for faith in the biblical sense, however, makes an abrupt claim to validity. It has none of the heartwarming and sympathetic sounds that usually cling to more courteous sayings. How inflexible are the concluding statements of the last book of the Bible which underline its compelling nature (Rev. 22:18-19)!

We are on the wrong track if we seek the character of what is binding in faith only by contrasting it with the well-intentioned statements that are not binding. We get the sense of what is binding in faith only through using terms like "promise" or "commitment." We regard a thing as binding only when we cannot do other than confess it.

A good illustration is found in 1 Timothy 3:16:

> Without any doubt, the mystery of our religion is great:
>
> > He was revealed in flesh,
> > vindicated in spirit,
> > seen by angels,
> > proclaimed among Gentiles,
> > believed in throughout the world,
> > taken up in glory.

The introductory saying tells us that what is being stated here is so by common judgment. What can be more binding than what is manifested to all people and established by a common verdict? But for Christian readers or hearers, homology, or confession, can be discerned here. The community confesses that which has made itself known to it. It subscribes to the confession of Christ, and thus experiences its truth. It must express it only as a mystery, but it must express it. The church has to say something of this kind, and not merely by way of delimitation. It makes it clear that it cannot say everything, but it has to say what has been presented to it. The church's commitment requires a linguistic medium that will cover what is to be perceived, and nothing different. This medium is the binding church doctrine. *Doctrine points to the frontier beyond which there is no more reliance on faith.* What is unconditioned, what must always be said under all circumstances, confronts us here. Doctrine does not allow us to think about ourselves, or to reflect ourselves when we are asked, or ask ourselves, what is worthy of faith.

But how does doctrine become binding?

On a Protestant view doctrine always mentions the criteria which make it binding. It tells us why it is obligatory: it is because it shows us what makes it binding for itself. An instructive illustration is found in Article VII of the Augsburg Confession, in its doctrine of the unity of the universal church. For true church unity it is enough if we "agree *(consentire)* concerning the doctrine of the gospel and the administration of the sacraments" (Adam Schaff, *Creeds of Christendom* [Grand Rapids, 1985], 3:11-12). Previously the article had defined the church as "the congregation of saints in which the gospel is rightly taught and the sacraments rightly administered (according to the gospel)."

It will pay us to consider the structure of this formulation more closely. The key words are to *agree* concerning the *doctrine* of the *gospel.* We are moving from the outside to the inside in this argument. First, we meet with a human agreement. But this agreement is not arbitrary. It is tied to the doctrine of the gospel, to the gospel as it is proclaimed according to the German version. The doctrine is the same as the content of the proclamation. It tells us what the gospel says and how it is to be communicated, namely, as good news, and not as an enlightenment or as a prescription for a better lifestyle. The doctrine tells us these two things in a way that forces us to decide whether the proclamation is really according to the gospel. The same holds true in relation to the sacraments. If it is, the doctrine of the proclamation will show us what it means to subject ourselves to the gospel and to be directed to it as the message of what God has done, in which God himself imparts himself to us.

The distinctive drift of this formulation should now be plain. In fact, we should now read it in the reverse order: gospel, doctrine, agreement or consensus. The gospel precedes human consensus. However, it does not soar over it, neither does it build upon it. Agreement on what is to be proclaimed is, of course, essential for the fellowship of faith. But the consensus cannot serve as the smallest common denominator for convictions that would otherwise clash with one another. *Consent* to the content of the gospel grows solely out of *assent* to all that must be said in faith in the gospel. This is how doctrine is constructed. It is the bond between the gospel, in which God imparts himself to us, and the church consensus that appears when the gospel is obediently heard. A mark of this bond is the commitment in faith.

This is an interlacing that is worth noting. A movement takes place from God to us, and it is accompanied by our orientation to God. Doctrine occupies the middle spot. It binds us, also being bound, bound to God, who has irrevocably bound himself to humanity and the world in Jesus Christ. Herein lies the compelling nature and binding force *(Verbindlichkeit)* of doctrine, which does not subject us to itself, but frees us for the unanimity of faith. It is a blessing which lifts us up, not a yoke under which we must bow.

This is why the Reformers stressed again and again that their doctrine was not a common opinion of their own, nor a pious arrangement. It was the doctrine that God himself had established, and he had charged them to pass it on, even expounding it to them. With the doctrine he also established the church, and the church must keep only to this doctrine, unconditionally and in all circumstances. Says Luther in 1531:

> Furthermore, it is quite evident that there is a great difference between teaching and life, just as there is a great difference between heaven and earth. Life may well be impure, sinful, and frail, but the teaching must be pure, holy, clear, and steadfast. Life may well be in error and not keep everything which the teaching commands, but the teaching (says Christ) must not lack one tittle or letter, whereas life may perhaps lack a whole word or line of the teaching. The reason is this: The teaching is God's Word and God's truth itself, while life includes our actions also. Therefore the teaching must remain altogether pure. If someone falls short and is frail in life, then God can indeed have patience and forgive, but in the teaching itself, by which one is supposed to live, God can and will tolerate no changing or cancellation, and he ought not tolerate anything of the sort. (*WA*, 30/III:343.23-33; ET, *Commentary on the Alleged Imperial Edict*, trans. Robert R. Heitner, *LW*, 34:77)

The character, not the extent, of doctrine is irrevocable! Naturally, Luther is aware that doctrine has not come down from heaven. We can easily miss this point when we equate doctrine with the Word of God. But note should be taken of the relation between a doctrinal statement and its claim to validity. If the formulation does not point to God's action and judgment, it is an aberration, no matter how comprehensive or systematically perfect it might appear to be! In this respect, doctrine is more endangered, or the dangers facing doctrine are graver, than the deficiencies of life, which is endangered in any case.

If doctrine really is God's Word, in what way does it then differ from the gospel? In fact, doctrine does not say anything different from the gospel, but it says it in a different way. What it states is the truth of God. As an affirmative statement, in a specific linguistic form, it is uttered as a word that binds us, with the certainty in faith, hope, and love, and with this statement the truth of theology is upheld and does not fall. When they are formulated and tested, such statements stand in relation to other forms of Christian speech, words of comfort or of challenge, for example. These words orient themselves to the statements and can follow them. Without statements of this kind, all our speech will sooner or later lack direction. It will be misled by spontaneous fancies and will think only of what it might accomplish or of how it arose.

Theological doctrine has to be inalienable, at least when it involves discussion of the faith that at the decisive points can only lead on to faith.

Nevertheless, doctrine is constantly given a bad reputation. It is suspected of containing only "propositions" which may well be "correct" but, though gilt-edged, are also static and lifeless, and therefore not convincing. They do not summon us to life or illuminate us or propel us forward. This prejudice against doctrine surely rests on bad experiences with theological doctrine and its teachers. But there lies hidden behind it a very different understanding which sees in doctrine a free cultivation of the concepts of faith which occur as we all express ourselves within our own experiences and unite with the utterances of others who are of the same mind. I think, for example, of a consensus that has prevailed for many years in the church and in religious education. By definition the gospel, as good news, makes us glad and liberates us, shaking off every constraint, so that finally, finally, we can come to ourselves and be known to one another. The converse immediately follows. What is salutary and liberating is the gospel. It is what God has in mind. Considered apart, and torn from their theological context, these thoughts are echoes of biblical motifs and theological themes. At best, however, they amount to half-truths. But for the most part they are attempts to define the gospel in terms of what is

71

best for us, and that is false doctrine even though it might be extremely powerful.

The claim that we can develop a new common conviction and bring about agreement at any time can turn this conviction into something tyrannical, more so than a theological doctrine. For when a theological doctrine can be seen for what it is and is not afraid to be called such, it stands in confrontation with every form of opinion building. It does not reject such forms but critically engages in them, asking what criteria they are using, and making distinctions in relation to what can claim true validity.

Theological doctrine expresses "what we believe" in a specific scope and context. It is thus referred back to the word that binds us or releases us. In itself it cannot bind us or release us. Commitment to it grows out of this word and leads back to it. Jesus Christ empowered his followers to bind and to loose (Matt. 18:18). When we are linked to him, we are freed from guilt. We are thus linked to his judgment. By our accepting this judgment, what we say becomes binding.

This means that our word has this binding force. It is a discerning word, a judgment that distinguishes salvation from perdition, truth from falsehood, life from death. Tied to this judgment, we must learn to judge, not least what we ourselves say. This judgment has nothing to do with the condemnation of those who think differently. It is a testing of the spirits "whether they are from God" (1 John 4:1). Jesus is the Christ, the true Messiah. We have to confess this when we ask who God is and who his Son is, and when we ask what the meaning of his "coming in the flesh" is for the promised future, and what we can call "redemption." Confessing Jesus binds us, and so do our understanding of the world and of time, what we say about God, and our perception of history. These things bind us to a decision that God himself made when he revealed himself in the sending of his Son. It is only in this context that we can decide how we are to view Jesus of Nazareth.

The history of Protestant theology has frequently shown that "doctrine" and "decision" are closely connected. Doctrine obliges us to say something *specific* and *decisive*. The decision, however, is not a gesture of decisiveness. Doctrine hems us in, telling us both what we *can* say and what we *must* say in faith. It sets limits, helpful limits, to our imagination. But doctrine does not exclude what may be said in hope and said anew and differently. The specificity of doctrine is connected with the fact that God has *acted* in a specific way. "He was manifested in flesh" (1 Tim. 3:16). He has spoken definitively (Heb. 1:1-2). This opens up doctrine. No bar is set upon it.

There would seem to be little point in protesting against the view that Christian doctrine does not consist of "eternal truths" but needs to be expounded each time afresh in different situations in order to stay alive and moving. We must not treat doctrine as a museum piece, but this depends neither upon arts of exposition nor upon attempts to actualize it. What it requires is that in their different situations, with all that unites and separates them, people may find themselves in the consensus of faith. This consensus, as we noted with reference to Article VII of the Augsburg Confession, is no mere formal agreement that might evaporate with further evaluation of the gospel. It is an agreement between what can be said in faith today and the definitive Word of God.

We are bound, then, by the Word that commits us to faith. This Word establishes fellowship, a unity in the perceiving of the gospel that leaps over frontiers of all kinds, even the wider divisions of time and space.

This unity grows out of the confession of Christ as the one mediator between God and us, Jesus Christ, "who sacrificed himself to win freedom for all mankind" (1 Tim. 2:5-6). We find our fellowship in him. Through the liberation that has come to us we see that we belong together, that we are referred to one another. We become one in faith in him who has redeemed us. We become aware of this unity as we are summoned out of our all-too-human distractions and place ourselves under the judgment of God.

For believers doctrine cannot mean indoctrination, if by this we mean learning to repeat in prayer what has been prescribed. Doctrine involves instruction in the correct way of speaking about God. It enables us to say what is true for us even if we might not say it of our own accord. Only this can then be passed on to others in a way that they can accept it without putting in its place a group opinion of their own insights. A doctrine is shown to be binding when the unity that is sought and expressed lies far beyond the simple unity that guarantees identity and brings people into line. Christians become one by looking to Christ. What they perceive there, each from his or her own angle, is the basis of their consensus and gives it weight and stability. This is one of the happy experiences which doctrine can offer.

Theological doctrine also includes the well-grounded exclusion of what we may not say under any conditions. Christopher Morse, in his book *Not Every Spirit: A Dogmatics of Christian Disbelief* (Valley Forge, Pa., 1994), has offered us an outstanding example of what it means to distinguish between spirits.

I.5. Spirituality and Faith

I.5.1. Theological Speech in Asserting Statements

16. Dogmatic texts are made up of theological statements. These formulate the contents, in a way that puts the question: Are they true or false? The significance of a statement does not depend upon those who formulate it, nor is it linked to those who pass it down.

The "truth value" of a statement is found in its meaning (Gottlob Frege, *Funktion, Begriff, Bedeutung. Fünf logische Studien,* ed. Günter Patzig [Göttingen, 1966]). A statement may be repeated but will still say the same thing even when it is said by different speakers and for different hearers in very different circumstances.

Thus when Paul says in 1 Corinthians 12:3 that "no one can say 'Jesus is Lord!' except by the Holy Spirit," he took the first step in the direction of the dogmatic statement that Jesus Christ is Lord, which the early church would develop under Christology when speaking of Jesus as the Christ, as the one who was crucified and raised again, as the one who sits at the right hand of God, as true God and true man, as the coming judge, as the one who rules the world in complete subjection to God.

Except in 15:20-28, Paul did not work out these themes in 1 Corinthians. He simply referred to the cry "Lord Jesus," probably an ecstatic cry that derived from endowment with the Spirit and immediacy to God, and that the Corinthian believers thought would be given only to a few chosen ones. Paul, however, adopts this cry from the ecstatics and their inspired speech, and says that we can speak in this way only by the Spirit of God. The ecstatics in Corinth seemed to be saying the same thing, but were referring to their own divinely given spiritual power, thus suddenly establishing themselves as being able to call upon Jesus in this special way. The argument of Paul, however, is that this is ruled out. It is ruled out by the presence of the Spirit of God. This presence manifests the lordship of Jesus and alone makes it possible to speak correctly about Jesus Christ. "By the power of the Spirit of God" is not for this reason a proviso. It is not the case that we may speak of Jesus as much as we want, and as loudly as possible, so long as something very special is included, that is, the Spirit of God. Instead, the proclamation of Jesus as Lord is itself the sign of the work of God that sets us before the cross of Christ and helps us to see that the death of Christ is the "word of the cross" (1 Cor. 1:18) and God's verdict upon him, that is, upon him whom God has made "our wisdom, righteousness, sanctification, and redemption" (1 Cor. 1:30). When we say "the Spirit of God," we are describing the theologically necessary condition of our speaking of Jesus as the one to whom God has acted in a life-creating fashion in an action that is full of promise. Here is the imprint of the homological character of that cry, and Paul confirms it by speaking further of the Spirit and his gifts. The calling upon Jesus as Lord, which is hardly understandable as an enthusiastic cry, thus finds an understandable place in the confession of Christ. It is a basic saying repeated by all who accept the lordship of Christ. In the confession of Christ, Christians confess (in short), not a thing or a person, or not just a person; they say who Jesus Christ is.

If Christ is the Lord in the confession of his followers, he is not just the Lord in this confession, that is to say, so long and so far as people accept this and see its ramifications. If that were so, the statement that "Jesus is Lord!" would not be theologically true. As a statement it has its own value, the truth of which needs theological consideration. In his death all death was divinely affected. Our life thus belongs to him, to Jesus Christ, and if we can say honestly no more than *"our* life," then this does not restrict the range of the promise of his life. All these things are included in the meaning of the statement that Jesus Christ is Lord when we accept Paul's definition. But we can say such things only in the power of the Spirit who is from God. Their truth does not depend on how people feel at a given time. This, too, keeps the statement that Jesus Christ is Lord firmly rooted.

The theological statement stands on its own feet even when it is accompanied by other forms of speech, as when Jesus is addressed as Lord in prayer. It has a theological grounding. It cannot be adequately expounded in terms of the traditional history of the word "Kyrios," meaning "Lord." The invocation *"Kyrie eleison,* Lord have mercy upon us," as used in Christian worship, does not simply echo an antique religious ceremonial that became fainter with time and might be replaced now by terms that suggest a nearness to God or a greater native relationship with God that might only have reappeared in Jesus of Nazareth.

The basis of the statement that Jesus Christ is Lord is the presence of God's Spirit. Here is the presupposition of all theological speech. This presupposition can only be formulated theologically and in further statements, statements that make it plain step-by-step that the presence of God's Spirit is one part of God's far-reaching activity that includes much more than enabling us to speak about God.

A mark of this nexus of statements is that theological statements are unique. They cannot be explained by other forms or acts of speech. They cannot be explained in a way that makes them superfluous. They do not originate in ecstatic attitudes, in violent experiences, or in the silence of profound intuitive feeling — though this is not meant to speak against a nondiscursive grasp of the externality of faith or a different way of indicating the coming of the truth of faith! The fact that they have their own origin, however, can find expression only in statements that support their specific truth content by pointing to the sovereignty of God in what he does and in the range of what he does. These statements are irreducible. They speak for themselves. God's action cannot be demonstrated by the act of human speech or even find sufficient expression in such acts. Even an expressive reaching out to the limits of human language cannot represent them, for here attention might be directed away from the expectation that God will act to the human speaker.

For this reason, statements are an inalienable part of theological discourse when it takes place in faith and in hope. Otherwise faith and hope would simply be human attitudes that try to reflect God's action, or to see themselves as effects of this action, without being ready to see and hear what it is that God seeks to achieve. Theological statements, then, are embedded in that which must also be said in their exposition if they are to be distinguishable as theological statements, namely, in the presence of God's Spirit. In this way they display their uniqueness; they are prepared for the activity of God.

We encounter at this point a sustaining dogmatic theme, namely, the Spirit of God, who represents *God* with us and *us* with God. Through him God comes to us and we are set before him. The Spirit represents us as we do not know what to pray for (Rom. 8:26). He gives us the right words at the right time in order that we may unerringly say what is real (Matt. 10:19).

These are characteristics of spiritual life, of *spirituality*. Spirituality needs theological statements because these statements expressly subject themselves to the question of the truth value of Christian discourse. We cannot do without them even if they are not always the final end of wisdom. They are often suspected, even so, of having been torn from living linguistic usage and degraded to lifeless preparations. What they have to say carries no weight, at least in our own day. Even among theologians we find an increasing number who regard such statements as not merely dispensable but as harmful to faith.

An allergy to statements has developed, nurtured by a high sense that they are merely "objective" and therefore irrelevant, impersonal, and alienating. We should investigate this rejection more closely than is possible here. We might mention just two symptoms. The first is the constant equation of speech with action that creates relationships and sustains life. The second is the trust in the saving power of speech when communication is successful.

A shift takes place here. The root of theological speech is cut, namely, the homological harmony with the work of God. In place of this we find measures that create trust because they correspond to the promises of God and even bid fair to ratify it. The result is the uprooting of the obliviousness to ourselves *(Selbstvergessenheit)* of speech "in the Spirit" and of the reference to the presence of God's Spirit. Instead, stress falls on the credibility of faith. We uphold the promises of God by fashioning trust in them and also trust in one another.

All this seems to work in with studies in linguistic theory, especially in Protestant theology that has learned from the Reformers that the promise of God is also the pledge of his saving grace. The promise of God imparts what it says. It accomplishes what it promises. Can we not accept and pass on what it says only in confidence and as mediators of God's promise? "Performative" is the key word to describe this speech that is effective. (Cf. John L. Austin for the distinction between mere statements and performative speech events, *How to Do Things with Words* [Cambridge, 1962].) Is this not a much better term than "informative," for example? A word like that interposes itself between reality and ourselves. It thus deforms our perception rather than transforming it into reality.

God certainly pronounces what he promises. But we should not equate this with our own speech actions. If we ascribe the fulfilling of promises to our own act of speech and thus reduce it to the mere promising, we hopelessly exaggerate what our own speech can perform. Human performative speech can only stand by what it promises if it no longer contains anything of God's faithfulness to his promises. It thus fails to promise in reality, and restlessly seeks to realize what it has affirmed. In doing so, it completely wears out what has been said.

The word "perform" suggests a performance which, if successful, might attract spectators. The criterion of this type of communication is success. By taking up this thought, however, theology would abandon itself to a basic trend that counts only on the active and relational aspects of speech. That which is achieved by information is built up in common and thereby determines the interpretation of what is said (Paul Watzlawick, Janet Helmick Beavin, Don D. Jackson, *Pragmatics of Human Communication: A Study of Interactional Patterns, Pathologies, and Paradoxes* [New York,

1967], esp. pp. 51-54). A performative speech action resembles the magic staff of King Midas which turned everything he touched into gold. Performative speech actions establish relationships. They awaken trust. They are themselves interactions. They meet up with a worldview that sets before us a vast current of actions and interactions and counter-actions. Only successful communication is important here, not *what* is being said.

Theological statements are deflected in this way, and sooner or later dogmatics can suffer as a result. For at its basic core dogmatics consists of statements which deserve to be tested regarding *what they say*. Are these statements true or false? The paths of this testing seem to be very complex, as we saw in I.2.1, I.2.2, I.3.1, and I.3.2. There are old and very rooted prejudices against this form of speech. Theology, it is said, consists of more than statements, and when statements are used, they must be those that allow us to feel something. The insight is both unassailable and also helpful that people must be addressed in different ways and that agreement between them must also be achieved in a vast variety of forms. Precisely because of this variety, statements are necessary to achieve clarity but not to give linguistic control or domination. Statements, and the efforts surrounding them, are necessary so that the haze which language causes is lifted so far as possible.

These reservations about statements may stem from the suspicion that theology seeks to assert claims that it cannot prove. Such statements should be replaced by forms of speech in which people engage themselves for one another and thus stand up for one another. In this way they might form a basis of trust for the promise of God, an unlimited confidence in the God of unconditional peace, of love that has no limits, of righteousness that makes no claims, and of life that cannot be contradicted (Hans-Georg Geyer, "Thesen zu einer kritisch-systematischen Revision des Begriffs der kirchlichen Lehre im Protestantismus," *EvTh* 42 [1982]: 265-70, esp. 269). For "the question regarding the conditions of the possibility of true statements about God is not really the basic question in the doctrine of the church. It should be revised into the question of the conditions of the possibility of the linguistic orientation of a true promise of God that people can give for each other" (p. 268).

The latter question brings into play a new criterion of truth that is much more rigorous than what has previously engaged dogmatics: "the question regarding the conditions of the possibility of *true statements about God.*" It will strain dogmatics to the uttermost if it puts this question ahead of all else that it is entrusted to say. If theology can only give speech actions, then unwittingly the action of God is mistakenly reduced to a speech action, too. The exposition of the Word of God (first under the influence of personalism and dialogical philosophy, and today under that of the theory of speech acts by way of introduction) (John R. Searle, *Speech Acts: Essay in the Philosophy of Language* [Cambridge, 1969]), in terms that relate it to our human constitution, is fully avenged at this point. True speech, it is said, opens up and indeed creates reality by making it possible for us to understand ourselves, to find ourselves, and not to misuse what is to hand but to use it to our own salvation and for the profit of all. Theological speech thus comes under ethical pressure and the pressure of success. The promise of God is to find fulfillment in pledges that are passed on from person to person and thus bring his action to completion in this particular way. The promise no longer draws attention to God's work and causes us to wait upon God. Instead, we are enlisted for the realization of God's promises.

If, however, we focus our speech on God's promise, then our first concern is with what God has said. This Word goes forth as an address to us. It is a pledge that we must hear. Those who have received it bear witness to it as such. God's Word has encountered them as they perceived something definite and clearly contoured that did not originate in what they themselves could see or say. Herein lies the distinction between the promises of God and our own statements. We cannot get behind this distinction. If we were to try to do so, we would be negating everything that has its basis and future in God. The affirmation of the promise with which we sincerely accept God's communication to us is a clinging to that promise and an agreement with it. This affirmation is the faith that God pronounces righteous (Gen. 15:6), that he judges to be faithful to his promise. Faith is transferred into a state of hope. It is "informed" in this sense. Hope awaits the judgment of God that will tell us what is real and on what we can rely. This is the *externality of faith* on which the assurance of theology is grounded. As Luther said, we are assured that we can rely on that "which is outside ourselves, that is, on the promise and truth of God who cannot deceive" (I.1.2).

What Luther says relates very closely to the doctrine of justification, the message of the free grace of God that imparts God's righteousness to us, the righteousness of God that is for us, the righteousness that is outside us which is true as God's righteousness and with which God grants truth to us. As the righteousness of God, not ours, it breaks into our self-enclosed world of thought and speech and action, and causes us to recognize how God acts on our behalf *(pro nobis)* and who he is in this action.

The "outside ourselves" *(extra nos)* becomes apparent when theological statements are supported by statements of promise in which God makes plain to us who he is that thus acts.

We define theology correctly when we see that it rests on the mystery that is solved by confession of the triune God and that is sketched out in the doctrine of the Trinity, the living God in the perichoresis of Father, Son, and Spirit. The deity of God is fulfilled in this movement. The presence of the triune God sustains and encompasses the world and its history. God's inexhaustible deity is revealed in his being for us but is not exhausted in the process: the *extra nos* remains in effect in the *pro nobis*. The doctrine of the Trinity thus states the inner grounding of the faith that is upheld by God, that cleaves to him, and that is prepared for him. Faith means God's intensive immanence in constant encounter with him.

Can this be expressed in the long run with the help of anything other than asserting statements? They promote trust in God's promises. They thus represent a space between God's promises themseves, in which he imparts his presence, and faith, which is aroused and sustained by the promises. Therefore asserting dogmatic statements are a kind of tangible symbol for the intangible reality of God. This is because they denote this reality without ever reifying it and making it an available object.

When we talk in faith, hope, and love, we also swing into the work of God in his self-communication. Human speech is taken up into this movement. Luther depicts this in his exposition of the second and third articles of the Apostles' Creed in the *Small Catechism*:

> I believe in Jesus Christ, his only Son, our Lord. . . .
> What does this mean? Answer:
> I believe that Jesus Christ, true God, begotten of the Father from eternity, and also true man, born of the virgin Mary, is my Lord, who has redeemed me, a lost and condemned creature, delivered me and freed me from all sins. . . . This is most certainly true.
> I believe in the Holy Spirit, one holy Christian church. . . .
> What does this mean? Answer:
> I believe that, by my own reason or strength, I cannot believe in Jesus Christ, my Lord, or come to him; but the Holy Spirit has called me through the Gospel, enlightened me by his gifts, and sanctified and preserved me in true faith. . . . This is most certainly true. (CC, 116)

In expounding the second article, on redemption, Luther insists that reflection cannot help us attain to a relationship with the self in which we can also find a relationship with God. By undertaking to state and declare that we believe in God, we also confess that Jesus Christ is our Lord who has "secured and delivered" us by his life and death, so that we are his. We can learn who we are and what we can do only by reading it off from Christ. But in knowing Christ we see that we are subject to the judgment of life and death, of being or nonbeing. Only in this judgment can we learn to know ourselves.

The exposition of the third article shows that we can say these things only in the power of the Spirit. Luther puts this dialectically: "*I believe* that *I cannot believe,* but the Holy Spirit *has sanctified and preserved me in the true faith.*" Faith cannot explain itself. It refers to that which makes possible what it says. Therefore it does not owe itself to our human powers. We cannot decide what to say or not to say. If we want to say who we are and how we live, we can only say what we have been empowered to say. The reference to the presence of God is the basis of faith. The mystery of God is thus stated with incomparable clarity, a clarity far surpassing all our efforts to demonstrate the plausibility of God's sovereignty and of the wonders of faith by linguistic theory. Luther's exposition of the third article thus takes us back to the opening of all three articles: "I believe." It points us to the path that the creedal statements indicate, a path that we must constantly tread afresh, a path that thus always leads us to new perceptions.

Precisely this strictly theological statement hits what we can express only in a very personal way in full freedom from within. It is not a linguistic crutch that is useful only so long as we cannot formulate our own creed, that is, our own specific convictions that correspond to our own experiences and circumstances. The fact that what is said here is "most certainly true" does not depend on the authority of those from whom the creed derives, nor, of course, on the authority of the Reformation expositor. The statements are valid because they are true. The form of the statements itself points to the structure of their grounding. We can test them by this grounding. This grounding establishes the truth content of everything that follows, making good its claim to credibility, credibility in terms of Christian belief. How could we decide this except by testing by means of dogmatic statements that themselves can offer no final proof but refer themselves to the judgment of God?

17. Dogmatic statements are necessary because theology is relatively independent in relation to its subjects. They represent the externality of the promises of God. The presence of the Spirit of God is their presupposition. They are unique for this reason.

Between the boundaries of the promises of God and the faith they evoke are many things for which we have many names: proclamation, consolations, admonitions, common prayer, signs, symbolic actions of worship, reflection on what we do or fail to do. In a narrower or broader sense these are all parts of theology, but they are not theological statements in a dogmatic sense. Such statements stand over against speech actions insofar as they refer us to the "outside ourselves" on which all the utterances of faith depend.

Today we are more aware than perhaps previous generations were of how limited dogmatic statements are from the standpoint of communication. Expressing the thinking of faith, these statements have their own weight, but they are themselves embedded in other speech actions that are rooted in specific forms of life. Dogmatics, then, must set out the scope of what theology can say in a web of other forms of communication, but without isolating so that it has its own dynamic. Dogmatics is very rich in relationships. We see from this that it does not derive from an individual or collective human reflection of those who address themselves as believers, or from a reflection of what they know about themselves and that which passes between them.

Theology is interpersonal communication. It is one person's speech with someone else. It is thus related to subjects, to those who talk with one another. But what is communicated, what is shared linguistically, derives its life from God's promise to act. For this reason dogmatic statements are relatively independent of their subjects: relatively, for individuals are always involved; but independent, for individuals are addressed, but not in virtue of the ability of others to address them. Only for this reason can dogmatic statements lead on to the free agreement of individuals with the acts of God that concern them all. By nature, culture, nationality, and race, indeed, even by historically developed confessions and church membership, people may be alien to one another. But when they listen in common to that which is real on the far side of society, they experience that which draws them together and is for their common benefit.

Those who have dealings with and are exposed to dogmatic statements can learn from them and from the study of them what it means to become oblivious of ourselves. This obliviousness of ourselves, which in Jesus Christ is imparted to them through others, is a gift of grace. What it means, however, can hardly become plain except through the objectivity of dogmatic statements, an objectivity which does good and brings liberation even though these must not be demanded of them.

82

I.5.2. Practicing the Language of Faith

Dogmatic speech is based on the development of theological concepts. It gives precision to words by relating them to the action of God and to our human experience of this action. It regulates their use. It thus distinguishes itself from the everyday use of words like "faith," "love," "hope," "justice," "peace," "life," "death," even "God." It guides the understanding that Christians share with each other and marks off the way in which their use of such words coincides with or differs from the common usage.

The impression might be given that dogmatic speech gives stability to the meaning of terms and even tells us how we are to think and speak. But that would be a mistake. The more precise theological terms are, the more open they are for us to perceive what takes place between God and us. They offer us a reliable sketch of what we might expect and might therefore recognize. But they can only hold this expectation open; they cannot replace it. If we regard the expectation as superfluous and want to discard it, we will be using theological terms to describe our own encounters, grasping their meaning, introducing them into existing worldviews, and thus taking possession of them. A perception, however, that is promoted and guided by theological concepts will teach us what it is to know a productive and linguistically creative tension, tension between the aspects in which we recognize things familiar to us and all the unhoped-for things that encounter us and that surprisingly encircle and perhaps permeate what is recognized and give it new contours. Often we cannot at first express perceptions of this kind in words. We then have to search for terms in which to put them. We are forced into experimental attempts. When we achieve a happy result, this will often give us an integrative insight into the links and connections of reality that have thus far been hidden from us. When this insight is formed, it can develop into a recognition that brings clarity and thus meets the concern for clarity that is proper to dogmatics.

Theological concepts are not isolated. They are linked to a specific form of speech, the language of faith. They are structured within a movement: in faith and hope. The biblical writings follow this pattern. The movement gives shape to liturgy, to instruction, to pastoral care, and to theological teaching. It thus more fully displays both its clarity and its relational wealth. Faith must always be also a form of speech.

We learn the language of faith when we learn to use it, that is, to speak in faith and hope. In part this involves learning to know the theological significance of basic words. What is the theological meaning, for

83

example, of terms like "promise," or "grace," or "spirit," and how do they relate to one another? We have to learn to use such terms correctly and not mistakenly. This sounds much easier than it really is. For it is not enough simply to know the semantic range of a term. Every term that has found precise theological definition is related to others in a linguistic nexus, and only from this does it derive its reference and "meaning." Only if we find our way into this nexus can we learn the grammar of the language of faith and recognize its *structure of references.* How rich in associations is the theological term "promise," for instance. It carries with it the faithfulness of God. When the promise relates to God's action, it is also the promise of a specific future that brings us into the reality of God and causes us to rely on God. The fulfillment of the promises of God, where possible, will dramatically intersect our own wishes and longings. We can observe it as we await it, and yet it is still unexpected.

To practice the language of faith, or rather, to become practiced in it, means learning to speak in faith, hope, and love and being able to say what faith and hope mean. We can do this by learning the grammar of the language of faith. This grammar helps us to penetrate the dimensions of faith. It thus gives us a firmer faith. It protects what must be said in faith. To this degree the language of faith gives profile to the fellowship of faith. It also has a pragmatic function in its approach to doctrine, excellently dealt with by George A. Lindbeck in his study *The Nature of Doctrine: Religion and Theology in a Postliberal Age* (Philadelphia, 1984). The language of faith is the only possible human place at which an answer can be sought and found to the question of God, and of ourselves in the presence of God.

18. "Faith" stands between the crisis of human self-knowledge and renewed invocation of God.

Faith refers us to God and his work as we find it in Jesus Christ. It refers us to God's prevenient grace. It tells us where grace is to be found and where we can seek it. Faith is an indication of God's gift. It is itself a gift that precedes all that we can expect for ourselves, for others, and for the world. It tells us what we may and should ask from God. It holds this before us. It does not prescribe this for us or tell us so fully that any further words are unnecessary. It teaches, which means that it tells us what can be learned, though lifelong practice will be needed. (Luther gave an example in his morning and evening prayers for God's blessing.)

Faith therefore leads those who ask to renewed calling upon God. It

84

tells us what we need to know in this regard, namely, how to recognize the overflowing fullness of the gift of God (II.5).

Let us use the profound structure of the Apostles' Creed to explain this guidance for faith. The creed deals with the triune God and his acts as creator, as redeeming reconciler, and as life-giver. In doing so it shows where we stand and how we are situated, namely, under the omnipotence of God, under the dominion of Christ as the judge who saves, and within the inbreaking of indestructible life at the side of God. The third article links together some expressive concepts like pearls on a chain. Linked together in this way, they offer a statement of hope even for our own day.

"Faith" therefore introduces us to the scope of God's work, its length and breadth, its height and depth, its concealment and its manifestation. It is thus the aesthetic form of all that we can become aware of in the presence of God. It thus offers a "schema," a loose coordination of all linguistic efforts, associations, notions, and surprises in our spiritual and intellectual perception, and thus also in what we feel and experience. It is a schema, for without such a structure no perception would be possible and certainly could not be communicated. Without a set form our perceptions would degenerate into private impressions. Faith becomes a form for our intellectual retina. It is not a product of our reflection on what we see and note, nor is it an object that we are to gaze at and revere, but also at times to set aside, to manipulate, or to oppose. It has objectivity in the sense of being a resistant force that helpfully breaks into our perspectives. Naturally we must be on guard lest this inalienable schema entice us into schematism. Dogmatics can help us here if we enter it as a movement of speech in faith and hope. For it lets us breathe again, taking away our confusion and enabling us to look around freely.

Dogmatics therefore shares with the language of faith the experiences that go with it. It serves the language of faith by clarifying it, by protecting it against misunderstandings, and by seeing to it that it does not become pious talk. The language of faith and dogmatics need one another. Apart from the language of faith, dogmatics would in the longer or shorter run become sterile and the language of faith would become vague without dogmatics.

The language of faith consists of a specific combination of precise terms which receive their meaning from the way they are combined. The combination, however, leaves many things open. There are many gaps, so that we may adequately cling to it, and with its help we can move forward. Yet it does not resemble a synthetic web that is so dense that it takes away our breath. Its aim is to help us find the right words. We want to express our experiences, comparing them with what has happened to us. We want to test our perceptions. How are we going to say all this in faith and in hope?

The success of this is not in our own power, but it is vitally necessary that it should be possible. What success means is nothing less than that our everyday speech, and the terms it uses, should harmonize with God's address to us, with his responses to our human lamentation, expectation, opposition, resignation, and consent. We can learn this from the book of Job.

The break in what we say about God and about ourselves can be closed only by the presence of God's Spirit. Without this presence the break becomes a cleft into which we plunge headlong. The presence of God's Spirit stands between our perceptions and reality. Its intervention is not perceptible, but it gives life to what we say. It is the source of spiritual life. Spirituality is the nonphenomenological element in God's communication with us and therefore in the faith language in which believers move, understanding one another in faith, in hope, and in love.

If we follow earlier Christian usage and regard "spirituality" as "spiritual life," we come upon the forms that lay their imprint on this life. This life is manifested in these forms. Spirituality means the spiritual life of all Christians, not of elite virtuosos. No one can choose the degree of the complexity of his or her spiritual life. We cannot search for spirituality. It is given like life itself. It is indeed the original form of life with God.

Included in the spiritual life are prayer, the liturgical celebration of the presence of God in worship, and continuous Bible reading (lectio continua). The interlocking of these forms with their rhythms and pauses; their periods of hearing, speech, and silence; and their gestures as we are set before God and face one another in his presence, helps to create a nexus of faith perception that enables us to recognize specific things. This perception is guided by the promises of God which contour his will through his actions. We can recognize God's actions without their being prescribed for us in a way that we have only to follow. Faith is expectation of the coming of God. But it is also awareness that God will fulfill his promises in surprising ways that differ widely from our expectations. The presence of his Spirit, his promise to be with us and in us, can accompany the configuration of fulfillment as the empty spaces are filled and the speech of God gives us a broad view of things — much broader than that of our ordinary vision. We still have the promise of the presence of the Spirit even when we imagine that God has forsaken us, even when words fail us, even when darkness encompasses us, even when we can no longer see, even when we feel that we are perishing. Theology reminds us of this, and it can help us by bearing the fact that the presence of God's Spirit is intangible. In faith and in hope: the two together characterize both the binding nature and yet also the openness of theological statements.

The history of Christian spirituality offers many examples of a fresh and liberated ability to speak from unexpected angles, but also of the painful and unsuccessful search for the right words in which to describe the fact that in the light of the divine promises everything seems to be dark and confused and shadowy.

The tense cooperation of the language of faith and the speech (or silence) of spirituality makes it plain that something is present here which cannot be seen but about which we can talk. We can record it and describe it in outline, but we cannot make it visible. "Faith is our guide, not sight" (2 Cor. 5:7). Otherwise we would already be at the goal.

I.5.3. Dogmatics as a Reminder

In the spiritual life the language of faith constantly enters impassible terrain and new territory. It has to say many things about which it has no certainty. It must make epigrammatic, one-sided, and borderline statements, for it is not on a fixed track from which an error means derailment. Our expressed faith, the creed, is a pointer, too. It helps us to take the right path. Dogmatics gives stability to the experiences in thinking acquired on this path. It does not simply follow the path that leads from the Christian past to an unknown future. Within this time span, it is the path on which we expect God. We must constantly enter this path. Others have gone this way before us, but it will not be the same path for us.

19. Dogmatics is the aid to memory for the spiritual life; it helps us not to forget essential things.

For this reason dogmatics must focus on essential things, on what must be said unconditionally and under all circumstances. It makes distinctions that point the way to faith and gives us rules for speaking in faith and hope that show us the right path. It does not claim, however, that these rules and distinctions are ready-made values. It has assembled many things over its long history, but far from overawing us, its knowledge can encourage us to practice the language of faith and to exercise our vigilance.

In these exercises the trinitarian structure of the creed is a vital help. When we learn to orient ourselves to speaking about the triune God, about Jesus Christ as true God and true man, about life in the Spirit and in the hope of God's coming, we come across a vast number of interconnections and cross-references that will give us the breath we need if we are to find ourselves in the history of God with humanity — a history that exceeds our expectations and that we could not invent out of our own heads. Immersion in the trinitarian structure of the language of faith prevents our language about God, humanity, and the world from ever becoming superficial. It will not let us reduce what we have to say to a few themes and monotonous stereotypes.

By keeping to this structure of the language of faith, dogmatics helps us not to forget anything essential, not to forget the distinctions that point the way to faith (I.3.1) and the rules that show us the true path (I.3.2). These things are, as it were, the basic reserves of the language of faith. Dogmatics lets the language of faith take its own path. It follows it as it expands upon God's actions. It is aware of its wide span which holds together thoughts and expectations. It tells us to what we should refer back if we are to find the right approach. In its profundity it shows us how we are to seek after God and to talk about him.

Dogmatics thus serves to master the language of faith, as a language in which we can express ourselves openly, moving in a nexus of references and seeking agreement with others. Yet this kind of mastery differs from other kinds. It brings us to the very limits of speech itself. Even a master of the language of faith like Paul could say that "we do not really know what we ought to pray" (Rom. 8:26).

Dogmatics has become an aid to the church's memory especially by helping to develop the church year.

We are accustomed to treat Advent, Christmas, Epiphany, Good Friday, Easter, Ascension Day, Pentecost, and Trinity as a series. Early Christianity focused on only one festival, that of the resurrection of Jesus Christ from the dead. This turning point and new beginning fixed the weekly rhythm. The week begins with the day of the Lord, Sunday. In this it differs from the Jewish Sabbath, which closes the week. The Christian community finds the structure of its common life in God's new creation, in its "being in Christ" (2 Cor. 5:17). It orients itself, not to the divine day of rest which stands at the end of the original all-embracing period of divine activity, but to the sign of the promised rest of God. For this reason the Presbyterian church treats Sunday, the Lord's Day, as a day not merely of rest from labor but of joy in God, and a day which has thus remained more important than all the individual Christian festivals noted above.

Other festivals were only gradually added to that of the resurrection. The Christian year thus came into being as a rhythm of Christian memory and Christian hope. This process was closely linked to the development of dogmatics in the early church. If we consider the origins of Christian festivals, their inner basis and not the peripheral historical circumstances, we shall find elements of tension both dogmatically and practically:

The development of feasts relating to Christ is closely connected with the development of christological and trinitarian dogma.

The feasts pertaining to the great acts of God are constitutive for the Christian community as it remembers and awaits Jesus Christ.

The dogmatic formulations express the scope of the work of God which cannot be structured in a purely cyclic way but has a progressive history recorded in narratives.

What God has done, the once-for-allness of the Christ event, is full of promise and cannot be stated either once or once and for all.

A path is indicated for the church and its members that they can follow year by year, always beginning again at the beginning.

Easter is close in time to the Jewish Passover, and originally both took place at the same time. In all probability the early Christian communities in Palestine, especially in Jerusalem, still kept the Passover. They associated it with recollection of the death of Jesus and celebrated it in expectation of his return (Wolfgang Huber, *Passa und Ostern. Untersuchungen zur Osterfeier der alten Kirche,* BZNW 35 [Berlin, 1969], pp. 28-31). They saw in the resurrection of Jesus the Yes of God to our broken lives and their new beginning in communion with God. All this was enclosed in the celebration, and it held open the promise of what we can only await.

The Passover also commemorated redemption and looked forward to it in expectation of God's liberating work at the same time. At first, then, Easter naturally was rooted in the Passover and entered history by means of it. But the more believers sought to say what had really taken place at and with Easter — who encounters us here and how he does so — the clearer it became that this was different from what was represented at the Passover.

A different question now becomes of theological concern. For the Christian church it is a decisive question: Who is Jesus Christ? This question has first to be put as clearly and unmistakably as possible if the underivable answer given by Easter is not to be obstructed by erroneous questionings. We have to give this answer in a way that preserves its character as a message.

We find here the starting point of the doctrines of Christ and the Trinity that were settled by the conciliar decisions of the fourth and fifth centuries. Many other motivations lie behind these formulations, but the link with the Easter message is unmistakable. Constantly using new approaches, the early church theologians tried to say who Christ is for us, and who we are, by saying, not who Jesus Christ once was, but who he is now in his relation to God, and therefore to us and the world. Detailed questions demanded clarification. For example, the New Testament says both that God raised up Jesus and that Christ is risen. How can this be so? How can the object also be the subject? Again, does the communion of Jesus with God begin only with God's action toward the crucified Jesus and at his resurrection? Or did Christ rise up from the world of the dead by his own divine power?

Statements then had also to be made about the economic and the immanent Trinity. These were not speculative sophistries. They were necessary in order to leave space for the presence of Jesus Christ and for encounter with him. They prevent us from thinking of the living Christ as the mere founder of a religion whose gesture of initiation must be represented, or as a figure who symbolizes a deeper penetration into religious life, or as a guiding star that will help us to live a better life. The early church confessions, especially the creed of Constantinople (381) based on the Council of Nicaea (325), help us to pass on the Easter message right. For this reason they have always had a place in the liturgy.

The dating of the Easter festival goes back to the Council of Nicaea. Prior to that there was prolonged controversy between Rome and Asia Minor. Easter is now observed on the Sunday after the full moon that follows the beginning of spring (Huber, pp. 61-88). This arrangement separated Easter from the Passover, which is celebrated on the first full moon of spring (14 Nisan). It seems to be a mere accident that the date of Easter and the dogma of the full deity of Christ were established at the same time. The dating of Easter had led to a division in church politics and a trial of strength between West and East. Communities like the Quartodecimans had previously fasted representatively for the Jews at the time of the Passover, a feast of liberation for the Jews themselves. But this practice was long gone (Bernhard Lohse, *Das Passafest der Quartodezimaner*, BFChTh II,54 [Gütersloh, 1953]; Huber, pp. 12-31). Yet the way in which christological and trinitarian dogma was developed has something very decisive to say indirectly about the relation between the Passover and Easter.

The so-called Nicene Creed of the Council of Constantinople (381), which expands the Roman baptismal symbol, understands the message concerning Christ in the context of *the* work of God as creator, reconciler, and consummator, as Father, Son, and Holy Spirit. In between, stylistically different, is a story of Jesus Christ from his being with the Father to his exaltation to the right hand of God and his position as judge of all people.

The two dogmas sought to establish clarity on why we are to confess Jesus Christ as God. They thus serve, among other things, to unfold the Easter message. In the fourth century a process got under way to structure this message and to initiate further festivals relating to Christ (Georg Kretschmar, "Festkalender und Memorialstätten Jerusalems in altkirchlicher Zeit," *ZDPV* 87 [1971]: 167-205, esp. 187; Huber, pp. 148-208).

He who died on the cross rose again on the third day. The third day prior to Easter thus achieved an importance of its own. Remembering the death of Jesus became an observance in its own right apart from Easter, both chronologically and theologically. Good Friday became independent of Easter. It preceded it and led up to it as the chief Christian festival.

From the middle of the fourth century the coming of the Redeemer into the world was particularly celebrated as the birth of the divine child, that is, Christmas. God became man, and thus from the very first, as well as with his entry into the world, Jesus Christ is true God. The Council of Nicea had stated this in 325, and liturgically it was followed by Christmas as the feast of the theophany. The East, however, chose the day of the baptism, January 6, and to this day it still celebrates the epiphany of God on this day (G. Kretschmar, "Theologische Perspektiven zur Inkarnation und zum Weihnachtsfest," in *Festtage. Zur Praxis der christlichen Rede*, ed. Herbert Breit and Klaus-Dieter Nörenberg [Munich, 1975], pp. 9-33).

Also in the fourth century the feast of the Ascension was introduced, celebrating Christ's exaltation. We see here another element of the Easter acclamation, "Christ is risen." Jesus Christ has been exalted to God and now reigns over the cosmos.

It was no accident that this process developed alongside the fashioning of the dogmas that God is triune and that Christ is true God and true human being. The process is linked to the middle portion, the almost narrative section, of the Nicene Creed. The sequence of festivals relating to the story of Jesus Christ is a liturgical application of the dogmas. Dogmatics is the basis of the church calendar and not vice versa. The inner grounding is that the perception of the presence of God in Jesus Christ was so abundantly rich that it could not be compressed into a single festival. It had to seek further development as the confession itself had done.

But did this development threaten to undermine the unity of the Easter message? Is not that unity lost as we move first to the cross, the resurrection, and the ascension of Christ, then back to his coming into the world (Christmas), and on to the creation of the church by the Holy Spirit (Pentecost)? For Christianity now found it necessary to take this extended path each year, and to celebrate in its feasts the ongoing history that Jesus of Nazareth had once begun, that looks back to the history of the people into which he was born, and that continues as long as humankind carries it on.

Unlike this continued history, however, dogmatics focuses on the Easter message and expands it in its own way. Christianity finds that it is summoned and caught up into the history of God in his dealings with humanity. It is thus freed from having to interpret its own history all the time. The power of this redemption comes from the history of Jesus. It is a redemption that thrusts it into the advancing action of God.

This cannot be symbolized by a linear progression. The scope is theological. It is portrayed dogmatically and develops the faith in which we believe. Faith is, of course, a whole even though linguistically it cannot be given a single focus out of which we may develop it as needed. The whole of faith is not like that of a continuing history. It emerges once we perceive its distinctive sequence. The faith that depends on the Easter message cannot thus be stated in a single sentence or reduced to a single concept. This poses a challenge for many theological conceptions that attempt precisely these things! And because faith in its fullness cannot be believed all at once, it has to be distributed among the different festivals. Far from splitting it up, this fact characterizes in a varied but irreducible way the encounter of Christ with the church.

The message of creation, reconciliation, and consummation thus structures the experience of time. God's history and our human history do not run parallel to each other. God's history is not, as it were, a superhistory. The two do not intersect in the infinite. Nor does God continually invade human history but then let it resume its normal course as the daily routine is again adopted. A view of this kind leads to a fatal misunderstanding of festivals. Whenever we speak about God, we are referring to what he has done and will do. We can only share in the imparted fullness of God by speaking of it one thing at a time.

Here, then, is the inner grounding why we celebrate the faith in which we believe step by step. The feasts are not separate from everyday life. They do not suppress this life or even annihilate it. They often lose their point today because they are thought to hold out before us all the things we miss in daily life, all the things we hope for, all the things that ought to be, and yet both before and after the feasts we find no reality in these things. How frequently, for example, is Christmas burdened with the expectation that it will make up for everything and accomplish good things for the family. The very expectation leaves behind a flat aftertaste. The festival is made a substitute and gives no festal joy.

When celebrated with faith, a feast lifts us out of ourselves. It sets us in the history of Christ: "Lift up your hearts. We lift them up unto the Lord." Thus it is decisive for the feast who is proclaimed in it and what is said by him, and all this in a salutary way that is caught up in a history that we "have" and that we imagine to have "with God." Commemoration and expectation are constituted in this way. We can look both backward and forward, though not to our own acts and omissions, in an effort to sum up what we can or must still achieve. Our glance falls rather on Christ, the First, the Last, the Living One (Rev. 1:17-18).

With its variety the church year, as the year of Jesus Christ, is an aid to the church's memory, the aid that carries hope and helps the church not to forget from where it might set out and what it might expect. We notice here the link between dogmatics and the life of the church. We shall go on to give some striking examples.

II. Dogmatics in the Church

II.1. Dogmatic Statements, the Inner Grounding of Church Life

In the church we find preaching, praying, confessing, blessing, counseling, admonishing, criticizing, and comforting. Commentaries are given on events of the time, and emergencies are dealt with. Sides are taken. There is much talk and reflection on whether the church is still needed and why. There is a variety of external reasons for all this activity. Motivations such as the preserving of traditions, inherited responsibilities, needs of various kinds, and challenges that demand answers.

Our precise question is: What makes possible, or better, what is the basis of what the church does? What actions are necessary under all conditions? What are their features? Why can they not be confused with the work of any other body?

We are shifting perspectives here once again by plunging into the middle of church actions. We need to discover why we must inevitably ask: "What is the reason for this? Why does it take place as it does?" As things are done or said, the question has to be asked: "What is their basis?"

Church work takes many forms, and therefore dogmatics cannot be reduced to a single manifestation. There have been, of course, impressive illustrations of the effort to trace back dogmatics to a "primal situation," to connect it with an all-embracing activity of the church, and thus to create for theology a unity which is threatened by divisions in the methods and goals of theology. Friedrich Schleiermacher defined the single aim of theology as church leadership as establishing harmony between divergent theological orientations and beliefs and stabilizing centripetal and centrifugal forces (II.8). For Karl Barth, dogmatics served as a criterion for preaching, for preaching in the broadest sense as proclamation of the Word of God. Beginning with proclamation, we have to ask what can soundly be said. The answer is not to be found in a normative collection of themes, but in a questioning of what is said in the church, of its theological validity, that is, of its being based on what God has said, and its dependence on whether or not it is confirmed by God (II.4). Paul Tillich regarded pastoral care the true source of theology, for it imparts meaning to life (II.6).

Obviously a dogmatics that is shaped by one such concept of the church's action cannot be reconciled with other dogmatic models. These essential distinctions explain some of the many divergent theological trends and "schools." They force students to decide for one or the other functional definition instead of helping them to discover the ecumenical relation of dogmatics to the church and to discover themselves in the church, so that they cannot merely have the role of spectators who either criticize or applaud. We must avoid at all costs the impression that dogmatics is uniform even if it does promise to offer us an impressive systematic totality. We will attempt here to look at various modes of action and see whether their grounding *(Begründung)* forms a consistent context.

20. When we ask what is the basis of what the church does, the inner grounding, the answer has to be formulated in the context of theological justification, and hence dogmatically.

The question of the inner grounding of what the church is doing offers us a distinctive approach, for we can move on from the church's action to that which confronts the church with its reason to be. This encounter takes place when the question of the inner grounding is posed. This question is often suppressed nowadays, and the result is that the relation between the church and dogmatics has become a neuralgic point in theological education.

Students often say, "I believe this, but I speak only for myself." They have no wish to be aggressive. They do not want to thrust their beliefs upon others. They feel they can say no more than that unless they add, in the same breath, that this or that is true only for them. They might invite others to share their convictions, but they make no demands on them. They make no claims for what is true only for them. The cause of this timidity may be a questioning of the claim of dogmatics to make binding statements (I.5.1). Objectivity is lacking. Therefore all we can do it seems, is to express ourselves in the performative communication of our own convictions. But this leads to a renunciation of language and makes us unable to say what must be said unconditionally and in all circumstances without a know-all manner or any authoritative claims and without constant reflection on how theologians relate to others or on whether they make unreasonable demands on them. People who always think in these directions see the church as a social structure which leaves room for people to express themselves according to their innermost moods, to state their feelings as they judge best, to be able to say what they themselves think, to state their own opinions. Education in dogmatics, however, needs to be clear and open about what is to be said to the church and about what is entrusted to it. It has to know without doubt what has to be done and said unconditionally. It thus needs to have a basic understanding of the inner grounding for what the church does.

This is not possible if we simply relate the methods to the meeting of needs. An orientation to needs makes for lasting alienation from the question of the inner basis of the church's being. The opinion might be voiced, for example, that the church is an enterprise that over hundreds of years has not improved its product, let alone basically changed it. Has not the demand for its product obviously declined over the years, and since it sells so little, should it not be withdrawn from the market?

Why do we bristle when we hear views of this kind? Because market strategies and their justification conceal the necessary question of the inner grounding and do not allow it to be put. Purely functional explanations are offered: for instance, "The church is here to achieve this or that (perhaps even to usher in the kingdom of God!)." In contrast, the inner grounding tells us what has to be said to the church, what actions are entrusted to it, and all this in such a way that it is not free to decide whether it can continue to say or do this or not. It is not free to decide this because it instinctively points beyond itself. If we no longer ask about this basis, or if it is no longer debated among us — and this is now the case, or very often the case, in many church communities and institutions, even among their leaders! — but allow other issues of the day, for example, contentious ethical or organizational issues, to dominate the conversation, then there is a clear demand for dogmatics, especially in order to arouse a sense of priorities, instead of drumming in instructions to act. Dogmatics makes us aware of what has to be said and done unconditionally and in all circumstances. It does not compete with the many extensive tasks that the

97

churches undertake. It cooperates with them, defining them by relating these tasks to the inner grounding for them.

The church is thinking about what it does when it asks about the source of its life. To what is it referred? It thus avoids making itself the subject. The church has not selected for itself what it must do unconditionally. After all, it has not selected itself.

We must ask concerning the distinctness of what the church does. Without any claim to completeness, a sphere of phenomena and a place of encounter must be described. The grounding must thus become apparent. The church is confronted with itself.

By its origin in God's Word and Spirit, the church is called to specific actions in order that it may be manifested as a church, as a *hidden* church, however, that points to its basis in the acting of God. Through what it says and does, acts and calls, the church points to this action, calls to attention that it does not talk from itself and that it can bring forth neither itself nor the aims of its actions. These references are signs, the marks of the church, the signs of its being as the church.

We can speak of the church only in faith and hope. This is true of the so-called visible and perceptible church in particular. This church is characterized by marks that do not simply tell us where the church "is to be found" like other social constructs. They tell us how we can recognize it as the church.

This was the way Luther was thinking when he adduced as "marks of the church" baptism, the Lord's Supper, the gospel,[1] the forgiveness of sins, mutual conversation and the comfort it gives,[2] the office of preaching, prayer and confession, the cross and suffering,[3] the acknowledgment of marriage and of the political order, the sufferings of the church in the world, and the renunciation of retaliation.[4] Obviously these features are on different levels. Nor is this an exhaustive list. We cannot check off each

---

1. *Ad librum . . . Ambrosii Catharini* (1521), *WA*, 7:720.32–721.1.

2. *Schmalkaldic Articles* (1537), *WA*, 50:241.2-3. These are not marks of the church but are mentioned along with the preaching of the gospel, baptism, and the power of the keys, i.e., the authority to bind or to loose those who need forgiveness (*The Book of Concord: The Confessions of the Evangelical Lutheran Church*, ed. Theodore G. Tappert [Philadelphia, 1959], p. 310).

3. *Von den Konzilien und Kirchen* (1539), *WA*, 50:628.29-30; 630.21-22; 631.6-7; 632.35–633.11; 641.20-21; 641.35–642.7; ET, *On the Councils and the Church*, trans. Charles W. Jacobs, *LW*, 41:148, 151-54, 164-65.

4. *Wider Hans Worst* (1541), *WA*, 51:479.4–485.7; ET, *Against Hanswurst*, trans. Eric W. Gritsch, *LW*, 41:194-98.

item and then say at the end whether the church is present or not. Even together they do not present anything like an outward side of the church that is visible to all, as opposed to an inward side which can be spoken of only by those who belong to it. The marks of the church are connected only because they point to the origin of the church, where its life comes from and what is entrusted to it. In different ways and places all the signs point to this character, and they display it by referring to one another.

The marks and symbolic actions point us strongly to the inner grounding of the church's being. They are meaningful only insofar as they make clear what is the connection between the empirical and visible church and that which the church cannot represent but can only point out. These marks constantly tell us new things both to say and to do, for they point beyond themselves and do not direct attention to themselves. By pointing above and away from themselves, they are the optimum of the church's visibility. Looking beyond the church is both possible and open to us. The marks show us the link between the church and its origin. But taken together they do not present the whole picture. The factual existence of the church, its actual presence, is of such a sort that the question forces itself upon us what the church truly is, not in an ideal form, but in reality. When we speak about the marks of the church, this question is kept alive, for the answer is unfolded. For the notes of the church are steps leading to its inner grounding. This grounding points us beyond the church. For example, the ministry of the Word and of the sacraments follow the inner grounding. They move in a sphere in which the phenomenon "church" is more than the factual church. Only in this grounding is it the true church. This reference to the inner basis must be both seen and heard. Otherwise the church will have no definition. Its contours will be blurred. A diffuse and confusing picture will emerge, no matter how forceful and attractive "church" might seem to be. Clarity is found when there is reference to that which is real outside it, and to that which confronts it, namely, its externality, God's action (I.1.1).

But how can this externality be made clear? We may think of preaching, baptism, the Eucharist, confession of sin, prayer for forgiveness, liturgy, catechesis, church leadership, diaconate, and mission, not to forget the life of the church year, but these are not to be considered spheres of action here. It cannot be contested that they are also such spheres, but in this context we have to question them as to the clarity of the external form.

Do they, as marks and symbolic actions, really refer us to the *prevenient action of God*? Do they point us to the source of the church's life, to what God has entrusted to it in what it says and does, to what it thus can-

99

not say about itself or ascribe to itself or claim for itself, to what it also must not fail both to say and to do? The inner grounding calls for statement, and this brings us back to dogmatics in an elementary form. The nature of the church as a church is at issue, its faithfulness to its origin in God's Word and Spirit.

The externality of the promise of God links the various forms of speech and shines through the different forms of the church's life and activity. It gives coherence to dogmatics. It is a hidden unity that manifests itself in the theological context of justification, though no comprehensive systematics or conclusive theological concept can either attain to it or present it.

The signs of the church are thus part of its concealment. They are signs of God's own self-asserting work. We can bear witness to their existence as such. The notes of the church are like joints connecting what God does in his own way and what may be seen by us. Those who are touched by what is the source of the church — who suffer, who speak about God in all temptation, who confess their guilt to God — they do not see the church in the first place but they see the promises of God in all they do and suffer, and they therefore do all things in faith, in hope, and in love. This can be expressed as follows: "We can do these things and suffer these things because . . ." This "because" stands in a theological context. We pray, for example, because we stretch out our hands to God on behalf of ourselves and others, and our intercession links up with prayer as speaking to God, which has to be defined more precisely as speaking *of* God and thus leads to speaking *about* God, which answers the question of who God is. All dogmatic statements are interconnected. Together they yield a theological context of justification that in its totality confronts the church and displays the complex of its inner grounding. The reference to the "because" and its range are the substance of dogmatics. Dogmatics develops the inner grounding of what the church does. Therefore it is not a theory of church practice. It is not an outline or ideal or set of obligations that the church must put into practice. Rather, it reminds the church again and again of who is really at work here.

According to the rule of Chalcedon (I.3.2), God's action and our action may neither be mixed up nor be torn apart here, especially in respect of the *sacraments*. The sacraments are actions in which the relation between what God does and what we do is expressly delineated. We baptize people on the commission of Christ. They are placed under the lordship of God and freed from false ties. Their sins are remitted in the name of Christ. God has made their past his own concern. The memory of Christ is celebrated in the proclamation of his death until he comes, and we are thus given a place in God's new creation. Do we act here on behalf of God? Are we his substitutes? Or are these acts specifically authorized and sanctified in themselves? No. What characterizes these acts is that on the commission of God we do what we could and might never do on our own account, and in so doing we point to the work of God, the basis of the church's ministry and service.

If the work of God and our human work are not distinguished, a coarser or more refined sacramentalism is the result. The church is then in danger of seeing itself in the sacraments. Baptism will be declared to be a rite of initiation into the church. The Lord's Supper will be seen as a fellowship meal in which the church celebrates its own fellowship instead of its participation in what Jesus Christ did on its behalf. Binding and loosing in the name of Christ can also be misused as the guilty are excommunicated from the church. At the same time, if we rigorously separate what the church does from what God does, we burden and overload it with the claim that it must either make a suitable and convincing response to the work of God or fittingly present its own work to others.

We thus have the life of the church in view in the sense that there is an indirect and often unexpressed connection between what must be done unconditionally and what must be said in all circumstances. We have to know what to do and why we do it.

21. Dogmatics is directed primarily toward uncertainties and conflicts in the church. It concerns that which is or ought to be debated among Christians when what is at issue is belief or disbelief, talk of God or concealment, discipleship of Jesus Christ or a refusal of discipleship, and in all these things whether the church really becomes the church and continues to be the church.

Uncertainties have to be debated even when they do not appear to be such but are unquestioned realities of what "the church is doing" either because the church has (ostensibly) always done this or because it is (apparently) necessary. Dogmatics must explain what is not clear. It will do so by speaking about the notes of the church. Thus many sermons and church pronouncements today urgently should open up the question of what proclamation really is. We must also ask whether the true character of baptism is infant baptism or not. We must ask what is in fact celebrated at the Lord's Supper. Is it a feeling of togetherness among those who assemble for it?

Dogmatics does not deal only with the proclamation of the Word and the sacraments. The Augsburg Confession did, of course, state and declare that the preaching of the gospel and the administration of the sacraments were constitutive for the church and were sufficient to give it its true unity (Articles V and VII). Protestant dogmatics followed the reduction of the notes of the church to "Word and sacrament," and it followed the reduction of the sacraments to Baptism and Eucharist, while marginally admitting the forgiveness of sins as a sacrament as well. One motivation for this was the critique of the rampant sacramentalism of those times, which was supported by the argument that the central actions of the church are limited to that which is specifically instituted by Jesus Christ. But it must still be asked whether the argument holds good that at its core the church is limited to what was specifically instituted by Jesus Christ. Were all other things humanly instituted and can thus be treated as adiaphora?

The question of actions that have been entrusted to the church is as a rule much broader than the question of what constitutes the true unity of the church. In times of crisis like that of the Reformation, a more limited questioning is unavoidable so that the church may be able to act once more. At other times, however, other spheres of action call for consideration when the church treads and has to tread slippery surfaces in its involvement. All the more decisive it is, then, that a sharper line should be drawn between divine and human action. Diaconate is one such note, and sadly it calls for little discussion today. There exists an agreement about it, which, though nourished by the best intentions for humanitarian aid and "Christian ministry of love," is so little considered that it must urgently be debated (IV.3.2), and not just when it is given prominence by a decline in church funds and there has to be debate about the most urgent needs.

It has become customary to refer to dogmatics as a function of the church. This was understandable and gave orientation at a time when dogmatics and theology as a whole, and theological training, were regarded as subject to other purposes, and a scholarship of religion and culture had to be organized afresh. Theologians referred to dogmatics as a function of the church that in other matters took very different paths in its development; for example, Karl Barth,[5] Emil Brunner,[6] Paul Tillich,[7]

---

5. K. Barth, *Die christliche Dogmatik im Entwurf,* vol. 1: *Die Lehre vom Worte Gottes. Prolegomena zur christlichen Dogmatik,* 1927, ed. G. Sauter (Zurich, 1982), p. 585; *Die Kirchliche Dogmatik* I/1 (Munich, 1932), p. 1; ET, *Church Dogmatics* I/1, trans. Geoffrey W. Bromiley (Edinburgh, 1975), p. 3.

6. E. Brunner, *Dogmatik,* vol. 1, 3rd ed. (Zurich and Stuttgart, 1960), p. 3; ET, *Dogmatics* I, trans. Olive Wyon (Philadelphia, 1950), p. 3.

7. P. Tillich, *Systematic Theology,* vol. 1 (Chicago, 1951), p. 3.

and Dietrich Bonhoeffer, who called theology "a function of the church. For there is no church without preaching, nor any preaching without remembrance. But theology is the memory of the church."[8]

We can call dogmatics a function of the church because the church is a creature of the Word and Spirit. Dogmatics has to say this and not something else. In a way that cannot be mistaken, it must remind the church of its origin. As such it is a sign of hope. It promotes acceptance of what God is doing *(consensus)*. It helps to create agreement among those who want to believe. It helps them remain in the fellowship of faith.

Without dogmatics, and the acceptance of God's work that it promotes, every church courts the danger of falling victim to debates about convictions, conflicts about worldviews, and the multiplicity of religious opinions. Dogmatics can give the church the freedom to say and do what is appropriate to it. By no means does this mean that it can declare itself to be an opponent of the church, as a place, perhaps, of licence that accepts no responsibility. Yet "church dogmatics" should not advocate a theological position that clings so closely to the "church" that it always pays heed to church leaders and their claims. It should never be a tool that these leaders can wield. That has been the painful experience of theologians who were led by the nose by church leaders and their policies in Eastern Europe, for example, under Communist regimes in which the church functioned authoritatively within a totalitarian state.[9]

An institutional autonomy of theological teaching and research can offer some protection here. But the opposite danger can then arise when, for apologetic reasons, dogmatics goes along with another forum of opinion, that is, for example, that of imagined critical contemporaries, or the spirit of the age, or public academic discussion of open topics. At the same time, it is helpful not to be defensive against other models of exposition, for example, psychological or sociological ones. The striving to maintain theological "purity" might inadvertently functionalize theology, namely, on behalf of a permanent strategy of defense.

Theological arguments suffice; they need no other support. This is part of the "churchliness" of dogmatics. The church is the natural forum of theological conversation. It is the place for consensus on what has to be said unconditionally and in all circumstances in faith and in hope and in love.

8. D. Bonhoeffer, *Akt und Sein,* ed. H.-R. Reuter, *DBW* 2 (Munich, 1988), p. 128; ET, *Act and Being,* trans. H. Martin Rumscheidt (Minneapolis, 1996), p. 130.

9. An example of such a problematic "church dogmatics" is Elemér Kocsis, *Dogmatika. A református keresztyén tanítás rendszere* (Systematics of Reformed Christian doctrine), 2nd ed. (Debrecen, 1987).

When the church is claimed by theological statements, it is the factual sphere of their validity. This sphere of validity is not identical with the (theo-logical) range and *scope* of theological statements, that is, with their talking to God. God's action reaches further than the limits of the church. The church does not say all that can be said, nor does it seek to speak for all. That would be no more than a disguised imperialism. We must always distinguish between the scope and the sphere of validity of theological statements. This distinction is of especial concern in presenting the theological grounding of mission (II.9.2). The truth of theological statements does not depend on the number of those who accept them (cf. IV.1).

For this reason the church is much more than a haven for dogmatics or a safeguard for speculation and intellectual self-satisfaction. Existence in the church means dependence on the externality of the promise.

22. Dogmatics states the inner grounding for what the church does. It is a practice in thinking. It is meaningful in itself. It does not depend on its appropriateness to other things. Therefore it is not a "function" within some superior definition of the church. It thus has what one might call an unrestricted feature, which is a further way of expressing dogmatics as an academic discipline, theology as unconditioned and free from all other presuppositions. It must show the validity of its own grounding. It must not find the grounding elsewhere. It must not let itself be determined by what is thought to be useful or valuable.[10]

The actions we shall look at more closely as examples are marks of the perception of faith and references to the work of God that is so full of promise.

II.2. Recognition of Guilt in Prayers for Forgiveness

II.2.1. Confessed Sin

How can we call upon God? Liturgically this finds expression in the confession of guilt. We see here how we stand in the presence of God, not just at lofty festivals, but always and everywhere. But why precisely is this confession of guilt necessary?

10. Cf. Martin Seils, "Die Rolle der Dogmatik in der Praxis der Kirchenleitung," *EvTh* 44 (1984): 2-11, esp. 8.

"God, be merciful to me, a sinner." That was the cry of the tax collector in the parable of Jesus (Luke 18:10-14). And according to Jesus, he was justified. For he knew that his own righteousness would not avail when he stood before God. Thus he subjects himself to the righteousness of God, without being able to confess it yet, that is, to make it apply to himself. If the tax collector had simply felt himself to be guilty because he had done so many bad things, as he probably had, then his remorse, his "readiness to repent" (a frightfully treacherous term!), would have been preconditions of his justification. He would have unwittingly taken up the same position as the Pharisee, who thought he knew what he needed if he was to find justification.

The tax collector invokes the mercy of God *as a sinner.* What he thinks about his past misdeeds is now unimportant. The decisive point is simply that he has nothing to say for himself, that he cannot compare himself with others as a basis of his own self-awareness, as the Pharisee does. He does not think of himself as a sinner in comparison with others who might claim their integrity. He stands in isolation, at a distance *(makrothen hestōs).* He does not even seem able to grasp his situation. Calling upon God, he humbles himself. He subjects himself to the grace of God. In his prayer for forgiveness he states what he thinks of himself. He *is* a sinner. He is not just "guilty" of this or that. (That is, not in the sense that he would be able to say: "Thank God, I am not guilty of other things" — these would be the words of the self-righteous Pharisee!)

23. In confession of sin to God, and in calling upon him for mercy, we can put our trust in the verdict of God. We recognize that we ourselves, and the "things" we have done that now accuse us, stand in need of God's forgiveness. They have become a matter for him alone and are subject to his action.

The confession of sin is therefore not an entry into a holy place which has previously been opened up by atonement or even self-purification. When we recognize that we are guilty before God, we make it known that there is nothing more that we can say about ourselves except only that we are now trusting wholly in God. What lies behind us, and reaches out into the future, is in a certain sense at an end. What has taken place has done so irretrievably because it is in the hands of God. It can no longer provide material for incalculable conflicts with oneself and others. Illusions would result if we sought to revise the event that took place, or to the pain it caused, by a critical "reconstruction," by working on it, both in thought and feeling, so as to be able to "do something about it."

That this is impossible is shown, for instance, by the fact that when death comes, it intervenes between ourselves and others to whom we owe a decisive debt. The guilty ones are left alone with their feelings of guilt. This will be true even though they may think they stand related to the dead, and that they can cleanse this relation. A sense of guilt can give us the false impression that possibilities still exist. Such impressions can often enough lead us into forced actions in an attempt to master what has been done. Or an inability to forget might promote imperceptibly the standpoint that the power of recollection controls the present and claims the future.

Expressing experiences from which we have not yet been cleansed can clear the air. If a far-reaching omission or disturbed relation is brought to light, a catharsis might result. But an admission of this kind cannot really free us, since it ties us to our own possibilities. In social life it refers us to those who can, and will, forgive. Such people can give the guilty ones a fresh start and freely release them from the burden of their wrongdoing, and at the same time release themselves, by "forgiving, [remitting,] in order to make it possible for life to go on" (Hannah Arendt, *The Human Condition*, 2nd ed. [Chicago, 1998], p. 240). If it were not so often misconstrued, things would be much better in everyday life and in international relations. But this freedom does not stretch to the confession of guilt.

In the liturgy the confession of guilt has to take basically the same form as that of the tax collector: "God, be merciful to me, a sinner." The tax collector calls upon God for mercy. He says in fact much more than we might suspect from the petition. Why can he speak of grace and sin at all? Above all, what allows him to relate himself to God, to use the personal pronoun "to me" *(dativus sociativus)*? What underlies his request for mercy is the fact that God has addressed him. Otherwise it would not be possible for him to address God. Do we not have here a concealed reference to his creatureliness in the presence of God? He can therefore pray in silence for a new beginning based on the grace of God.

24. The inner grounding of confession of sin is recollection of the act of God. It is a sign of the beginning of knowledge of God and recognition of the self.

II.2.2. In the Presence of God

When we see that we are sinners, we think of ourselves as those who are being affected by the work of God, and we stretch forth our hands for this work to be done in us.

Luther had this in mind when he stated that sin had to be "believed" (*WA*, 56:231.9-11). This does not mean that we must believe in it because a higher value attaches to it than to an insight into mistakes and failures, or because human life with all its depths and entanglements is always a puzzle and an added factor must be found if a balance is to be found. No, to believe in sin is to concede to God and to see ourselves as we really are. In the confession of sin we find the true subject of theology. Luther could thus write that the characteristic subject of theology is, on the one hand, the lost and guilty self, and on the other, God who justifies and saves sinners (III.2.1). This confession is the heartbeat of theology. It gives it its rhythm.

Luther reached this conclusion when expounding David's confession of sin in Psalm 51:4:

> *Against you, you alone,* have I sinned,
>   and done what is evil in your sight.
> so that you are justified in your sentence
>   and blameless when you pass judgment.

A king spoke thus, one who had sent a subject to his death in order that he might have his wife as his own. Had he done anything different from what was regarded as right and reasonable for Near Eastern rulers? The prophet Nathan told him the story of a poor man whose last possession had been stolen by a rich neighbor. The king's sense of justice was offended, and he condemned that inhumane person. But Nathan then cried: "Thou art the man." David had pronounced the death sentence upon himself. He was compelled to see that he, like all others, was subject to the law, for it is God's law. David was no despot standing above the law.

The narrative thus far tells us that under the divine law we are all equal. Perhaps we might think of the "Golden Rule" of Matthew 7:12. This saying puts it more pointedly that we are all dependent on each other and must act accordingly. David, however, does not admit only that he has been lacking in co-humanity and is therefore in debt. He confesses that he has sinned against God. He not only follows God's law, the law that makes us equal and links us to each other. He places himself under the judgment of God. And the forgiveness of his sin pronounced by the prophet means no less than deliverance from death, though at the cost of an innocent life (2 Sam. 12:1-15).

The death of Jesus Christ gives new and different contours to the recognition that sin means guilt before God. Christians can see their guilt only by clinging to Jesus Christ, the embodiment of God's act of judgment and salvation on behalf of all. Jesus took to himself the sin of the world, the immeasurable guilt that no one can blot out. The guilt is immeasurable, but not because it is odious beyond human measure or because a scrupulous sense of guilt prevents us from thinking that "renovation" of our deeds is possible. The guilt is unbearable because it has its origin in the sin with which we try to escape from God. We owe our very being to God, yet we are unfaithful to him if we do not praise and reverence him even in our relation to other creatures. We cannot escape this guilt, for we always seek ourselves, not God. We cannot therefore make it good by any deed of our own.

We must state this radically. We must not excuse any offenses, great or small. For we cannot measure guilt before God on any scale of human ability or lack of ability. It belongs to a different "order" from the moral order. The usual sequence — recognition, confession, and clearing away of sins — does not apply here. We are aware of our relationship to God only by looking at Christ. In him God has taken away the sin of the world. The old is past and the new comes, the righteousness of God with which he justifies the godless (cf. 2 Cor. 5:17, 21). Part of this new beginning is the confession of sin, not as a precondition, but as an element in the actual new beginning.

II.2.3. A New Experience of Time

When our action relates to God's, new beginnings are possible. This possibility has its origin in the forgiveness of God. It may be seen already in the confession of guilt, even though this is not demanded or sought. What we do is thus related to God's action. In all that we are able to do, that which has been granted to us in grace is plain to see: first and foremost our freedom to confess.

It might be asked: What do we usually try to explain or to charge ourselves with? Are there inner or outer reasons for our confession? The desire to accept responsibility for what we have done and for its consequences, and thereby to mature, frees us, we think, from the burden of what apparently cannot be changed. A right use of this freedom will finally help us toward a better future. All this, however, presupposes that we can know ourselves — yes, even to our very core — as we look at our actions, their causes, and their consequences. And this kind of knowledge is the very fate of a will that is not free, that seeks the good but involuntarily does the bad, for it thinks that it can discern the two. Those who confess their guilt to God are snatched away from this spell. Self-recognition means confessing that we are guilty in God's sight.

The freedom to confess rests on self-knowledge in the presence of God — *libertas confitendi implicat cognitionem Dei et hominis.*

25. Christians can confess their guilt only because they know that all their guilt is borne by Jesus Christ; otherwise they would find it to be intolerable.

Seeing this fact frees them from what would necessarily be attempts to extenuate and excuse themselves. It also releases them from accusation, from attempts to purify themselves, and from the illusion that making a declaration of guilt will clear the slate and thus be able in and of itself to make a new beginning possible. They are similarly freed from the self-deception that through a change of course marked by "penance" they can in the future start upon a guiltless or less guilty style of life. The probability of a fresh lapse is, of course, too great for anyone to count on achieving a state of complete freedom from guilt. On this view, however, "confessing one's guilt" presents a person with the ability to choose an alternative, to "convert," and thus to renew oneself. This opinion rests on the conviction that guilt is quantifiable. It is thought that it can be made good by other things, and that some part of it may be attributed to others. From first to last, however, a Christian confession of guilt can only be a confession of Christ.

The pledge of grace savingly intersects this endeavor to become free of guilt once again with a new frame of mind and corresponding conduct. Liturgically this pronouncement comes right after the confession of guilt, like the proverbial amen of the church. The change of address stresses the fact that the monologue is interrupted here where we are wrestling with our own doings, circling in hopelessly upon ourselves. No one is able to grant oneself forgiveness or to provide relief. We can basically do this to ourselves only when we *together* call upon God: "Forgive us our debts . . . for thine is the power, and the glory." When we thus call upon God together, forgiveness of each other's sins can also be pronounced. In a very special way the church becomes visible in both.

The prayer for God's forgiveness, which never becomes out of date, extends to all that we do, to all that we fail to do, to all that we endure, and to all that we end and begin. When God makes our deeds and misdeeds his own affair, he does not erase their consequences, but they are now seen and experienced only as in the petition: "Forgive our debts, as we forgive our debtors." In this petition they are set aside along with our abilities to forgive. Perhaps many things will now be different and be differently ordered. But this is not the point of the confession. When we confess our sins, we place ourselves in God's hands. We acknowledge the limit of our power to judge.

Confession of sin is always an erratic block in life's reality, which is determined by the mutual accusations and excuses of individuals, groups, and peoples. Our Western social world has since the eighteenth century established itself as a supradimensional tribunal at which people serve as defenders, prosecutors, and judges amongst themselves, often being their own prosecutors, their own advocates, and even the final court of appeal.

Theologically, the confession of guilt is grounded in the recognition of self which is continued in recognition of God. This self-recognition is already a sign of grace and of the freedom that it brings. In it, the will that is not free is liberated: freedom comes to the deeply embedded religious desire to do good, to obtain life, and even to stand at God's side in fighting evil in the world. Why, actually, should we not be able to want these things? So we might instinctively ask. That this means a practical denial of God and a deluding of the self can only be recognized and confessed but not demonstrated. For this reason confession of guilt, even in public, is an event between God and the self. Dogmatic reflection is needed, however, if we are to know the outlines of this event and not in fact to link other things to it. We must take dogmatics the more seriously because confession of guilt does not allow us to make excuses or dispense us in the least from speaking the truth in front of others.

Confession of guilt within the prayer for forgiveness is grounded in the freedom of self-knowledge. We cannot get behind this freedom. It is liberation for a new beginning. We are free to call upon God and there are no presuppositions. When we begin in this way, we do not need to justify ourselves, not even by an exhaustive investigation of our own acts, omissions, and encounters that would show us what might have a future.

To recognize that we are guilty while referring to Jesus Christ upon whom the sin of the world has been laid (John 1:29), is to recognize that he has borne our otherwise unbearable guilt. There is no method that leads on from a bad conscience to insight into our failings, then weighs up what may be done through repentance, through efforts at amendment, and through entrusting to God that which is beyond us. But the sequence of recognition of guilt and recognition of Christ is a theological sequence that stands on its head all our causal thinking about morality, the relation between freedom and bondage. It also overturns our experience of time relative to our guilty past. That past can never simply "have been," for it constantly forces itself upon us as the horizon of our future. We are mistaken, too, if we think of the action of God only as a *reaction* to our own deeds and misdeeds.

The confession of guilt combines our basic theological insights, which demand dogmatic formulation: God's action, which is full of promise, is the externality of all that we have to say about God and also about ourselves, who we are and what we can be.

II.3. Forms of Prayer

II.3.1. *"Lex Orandi–Lex Credendi"*

A particularly ancient and very typically contemporary example of the interchange of liturgy and dogmatics is to be found in interceding for other people in prayer before God. In intercession the needs of individuals known to the community are brought before God, and also the needs of groups, of nations, indeed, of humanity and of the threatened creation. Such common emergencies — sickness, poverty, perils of all kinds, death, and threatened self-destruction — are all entrusted to God with gratitude for the indispensable help that is given by social and political institutions, which themselves, of course, stand in need of right direction.

In intercession we do not directly or indirectly speak only about the actual needs of the congregation assembled for Sunday service. We speak about that which the congregation shares with others, with neighbors near and distant, with the social groupings in which they live, with their own nation and with larger political societies. Why should we not also mention the dead here? The Roman Catholic liturgy intercedes for them, but not in order to do something about their future destiny. This indeed would contradict our Protestant eschatology and is why Protestant forms of worship have been very cautious (perhaps too cautious) here. Roman Catholics pray for the dead because they belong to the church. It might be asked why we should not remember them as we pray for the mercy of God, too. Is it because their fate has already been decided and we can thus no longer include them in the human race?

Intercession raises the question of the nature and range of Christian hope. But behind this question lies the deeper and more far-reaching one: Why are we allowed to intercede, and why in this way and not in another way? An answer to this question will tell us whom to pray for and what to ask God for.

111

We find the inner grounding of intercession in 1 Timothy 2:1-4, where the apostle urges that "supplications, prayers, intercessions, and thanksgivings should be made for everyone," for it is God's will that *all* should be saved and come to a knowledge of the "truth." As we pray for others, we should let our conduct toward them be defined by our prayers. Otherwise we contradict ourselves.

The unity and uniqueness of God open up those who pray toward all people. In intercession they experience the fact that along with all others they stand in need of redemption. Intercession points us to the inner grounding of all prayer. The disciple of Augustine, Prosper of Aquitaine, in a work written between 435 and 442, wrote about this interconnection when relating liturgy to formulated belief. He found a formula for it: *ut legem credendi statuat lex supplicandi* ("that the law of intercession establishes the law of believing," *Indiculus de gratia Dei* [435/442]: PL, 51:205-12, 209). We can put this more succinctly and in a more general form as *lex orandi–lex credendi*.

26. The rule of faith rests on the rule that prayer follows. Intercession, our prayer for other people, points us to the grounding of prayer which must be the subject of dogmatic reflection.

If we know the basis and grounding of belief from the rule of prayer, this means that without clarity of belief we cannot pray aright.

Behind Prosper's formula stands Augustine's doctrine of God's prevenient work, later known as *prevenient* grace. The grace of God embraces us. God's work is there before us. Of ourselves we cannot enter into it. For this reason our praying is a way — perhaps a fairly complex way — of assenting to this action that we enjoin upon those for whom we pray. All our beliefs and prayers for others must be related to the redemption which they all need. Intercession is in fact based on the fact that we have to speak about the grace of God. We do not pray that the eyes of others or ourselves may be opened to it.

By showing us the inner grounding of prayer, the liturgy becomes a gushing spring, an elixir, of dogmatics, and especially of the doctrine of grace. We see now that the doctrine of grace is not just an optional part of dogmatics. Rather, it stands in some respects at the very beginning, namely, when we have to ask: "Why do we pray? For what and for whom?" The doctrine of grace provides the answer that gives prayer its intention. We entrust ourselves and others to the grace of God. This intention underlies intercession. By it we are to measure the practice of prayer. Dogmatics for its part speaks about this intention and develops its theological context. For this reason dogmatics serves the criterion of prayer. At the same time, it is dependent on prayer lest it become intellectual and rhetorical artistry. But dogmatics is not a musical accompaniment of liturgy. It follows the same rule, but it does so in its own way, as prayer does in its way.

We do not find any actual prayer in 1 Timothy 2:1-4. But the passage shows clearly what intercession must not omit. It also tells us clearly that we may intercede for others only if we believe in the grace of God. And that means that we so reach out for it that we expect it not only for ourselves but for all people, for the grace of God knows no limits. Those who trust in it are forced to pray, and to pray with hope, even and precisely for others. They will then meet the others on the horizon of this prayer, with the focus on "God our Savior," who wills that all should be saved and come to a knowledge of the truth.

This has an unmistakably different sound from the hymn to humanity of Friedrich Schiller, which states in his "Ode to Joy":

All humans become brothers,
where your soft wing lingers . . .
Brother! Over the starry sky
there has to live a lovely father.

Schiller's statement poetically interprets Immanuel Kant's categorical imperative that imposes the same duty upon all of us and finds all of humanity bound together in absolute mutual responsibility. Here, however, we are directed to prayer simply because God wills to save all. The "we" who thus call upon God as their Father are related in this way to all. We give thanks to God, to his proffered will to save, and to the mediatorship of Jesus Christ, whose sacrifice avails for all (vv. 5-6). This thanksgiving is not directed to a finished event that must now merely be recorded and made known publicly. It becomes a common intercession for those whose lives are in view as thanks are given to God for his action that is so full of promise.

Such intercession is politically most explosive, because it does not specify individual groups for which the Christian community should intercede. Of course, there are certain people who need solidarity in particular ways. It might mention them, and its prayers will then have special distinctness. But their theological clarity will undoubtedly be lost if they become a type of mobilization of some against others. Intercession leaves no place for enmity, often the converse of solidarity. Interceding for all people before God is not easy without resorting to global rhetoric. It is much easier to denounce grievances, to bewail the innocent, and to brand the guilty and at the same time to seek to liberate them from erroneous convictions and to change their course in a way that will be truly helpful to all. Taking that path might seem to be "concrete," but it is often only a hidden form of agitation. It also includes a political judgment, which — regardless of how farsighted this judgment might be — subjects the petition in the prayer to a human restriction, although the prayer is directed to God.

In 1 Timothy 2:2 "kings and all those in authority" are included in our thanksgivings and prayers (I.3.3). That hardly means a mere revering of those who exercise political power. Even much less is it restricted, as some think, to confessing loyalty to democracy. Intercession sets the political order in the context of the sovereign uniqueness of God and his will. It does not religiously embellish that order or give it autonomy. The state is also mentioned in the church's intercession because it is inevitably made guilty by the limits of its knowledge and its organizations for the common good. Therefore intercession is a sign that we exist politically.

At the same time intercession raises the sight of the community above the immediate horizon of its experiences, for "God wills that all should be saved and come to a knowledge of the truth." One does not go without the other! The basis of intercession is that God will work, and that we and our acts and omissions should not stand in his way. This is not a call for passivity according to the slogan "Best leave everything to God!" It is a call for vigilance and for the recognition of true reality, namely, the grace of God, God's will that all should be saved. Letting God work means relating to others only by giving thanks for their existence and by interceding on their behalf. Prayer demands a right answer to the way in which the acts of those who pray are brought into this relation, and prayer itself is to be counted among these acts.

When we intercede with God for others — indeed, for all — we follow this right answer. By praying, we are not evading what we ought to do and can do. But we grasp what we ought to do and can do in the course of our thanksgivings and our prayers. In that way we pray that they will be brought into line with the will of God and give thanks that this happens. The doctrine of grace and theological anthropology offer clarification with their theoretical distinctions, for example, between cause and effect, or between divine and human actions. At this point dogmatics has to pose unavoidably complicated questions like that of the divine omnipotence and human free-

114

dom. But discussion of such issues would be left hanging in the air without prayer. Such discussion is constantly referred to the practice of prayer, not merely because it will thus be embedded in life, but above all because in the act of intercession it may expect that unity which we so urgently need in relation to both God and all others. When we look for this unity, the spirit and even the words of our prayers will be different. We will not be merely focused on the emergencies that confront us or are brought to our notice, so that we are motivated to put forth even stronger efforts.

If there were no trust in the grace of God, intercession would be a kind of substitute for action, a place where we can dump problems that are beyond our control. Alternatively, intercession might become a heartfelt sigh of neediness that can be quieted only by a higher being. Perhaps in secret it has long since become a cry into the void, and the community itself is filling that void. It has inadvertently become the one addressed in prayer: "Leave everything to us, we will tackle it!" Our prayers might in this case sound like prayers, but they are no longer real prayers. Sooner or later they acquire a different content. They perhaps become recitals of what we have found to be especially distressing in reading the newspaper or in watching television. They might be complaints about our own experiences as pastors which we press more inwardly on the congregation in prayer than we could in sermons, which have to keep a certain distance. This would be a macabre distortion of prayer, when it becomes instruction by other means or even "preaching at" people.

Apparent externalities such as the form of address, the use of "we," the choice of words, the mentioning of individuals or topics, the sequence of "presentation" and "invocation," and inner gestures of language, all raise important dogmatic questions. For they all relate to issues in the practice of prayer: At what point does intercession threaten to become a means whereby we reach a self-evident view of the world and of the actions that it needs? How far is the theology changed that sees in prayer only an especially refined form of indoctrination? Do we not become so "conscious" of this or that emergency that we must all of us unite in a "consciousness of problems" and be incited to common actions that will weld the community together?

II.3.2. Talking of God in Lament, Petition, and Praise

27. Prayer is the path of consent to the work of God and its dimensions. The forms of prayer denote stages along this path and as well as contours in talking of God.

In lament we call upon God to counter our experiences in the world. In the presence of God we invoke the God whom we have learned to know in whatever way. We have experienced, we think, his power and his goodness. But the acute problem is that these two attributes no longer coincide. Job, for example, had been taught that God will bless the upright and punish evildoers, but he can find no explanation for his own troubles. He calls upon God, asking him to demonstrate his justice in the things that have happened to him. We see here two opposing contexts. First there is the experience of troubles. Then there is that the one thus afflicted knows to speak about God.

In lament the one context does not explain the other so that the two are reconciled. God is invoked as the one who has promised his faithfulness and righteousness, and therefore life and blessing. Those who pray urge God to come out of his concealment. They want knowledge of the truth of God and not merely a religious sublimation of their ideas of their own unbearable fate in order that they may deal with it. Those who complain are not merely bewailing their lot or making a protest in order to make their dissatisfaction with their sufferings more productive. They are turning away from their experiences in the world that do not seem to be compatible with the promise of God and that all interpretative skills seem unable to cover. They are turning to God, whom they have learned to call the true and righteous and living God, and they are asking: "Where shall I find thee?" In the lament of those who pray is the contradiction between what they may expect from God and what has really happened. They face the hiddenness of God.

Jesus cried out on the cross: "My God, my God, why have you forsaken me?" (Mark 15:34). Distant from God, he uses the traditional words in his search for the will of God, for the presence of his action in these human acts that are trying to separate him from God. Jesus was facing death, which would not merely snatch him out of the fellowship of the living, but would also separate him from the people of God and the inheritance of the promises. In this complete alienation, he casts himself upon the infinite silence of God's concealment. He does not appeal to his communion with God. He prays toward the fellowship with the living God even when all we can hear is this cry of dereliction: "My God, how far you are from me!"

In our prayers we ask that God will emerge from his hiddenness and factually declare himself. We want to be able to tell at the same time what God wills and does, and what we ought to will and do ourselves. In some sense, at the right time and the right place, our consent with the acts of

God should be decided and stated. The Lord's Prayer is a general outline of this prayer. It is not a list of the things we want. It tells us what we need and expresses our needs.

Prayer as petition, looking at our experiences and prospects, expresses hope in God and asks what we might expect and hope from him. It speaks of God's coming, which does not have a different timing from our own acts, but is still not subject to the march of time in which we live and act. So in hope we go to God, who in his work always precedes us, yet not in such a way that we might look back and use that work as an advanced starting point.

Petition specifically characterizes prayer. It is an expression of hope. By it those who pray are linked to all other creatures. Petition therefore expands into intercession, into representative prayer, into the prayer that others too will go out in the sign of grace. In this prayer we ask that whatever happens to others, including the outworking and indirect ramifications of our own acts, will always prove to be God's good and gracious will.

Thanksgiving, invocation, and praise articulate the unity we seek and expect. God is present. He has shown himself. We can consent to what he has done. Those who give thanks make it clear that they are in the presence of the giver of all good gifts. Those who offer praise do not extol God in general, but recognize God in the fullness of his deity. Thanksgiving represents a step forward in knowledge. We see that we are to give thanks only to God even when assaulted by his hiddenness and in spite of all the troubles that may come. We are finally to give thanks that with the laments, petitions, and praises of others we can all call upon God together. In the glorifying of God, in doxology, the fellowship of faith may be recognized. For this reason there is a genuine place for doxology in worship.

Thanksgiving does not symbolize our elevation above the world of facts that leaves behind our subjection to the normative power of the factual. The praise of faith is, instead, a confession of the one to whom we owe our freedom and the open future to which it leads. What is to come and what is present are united in thanksgiving. The present no longer simply continues the past, and the future is no longer that which has still to come. Thanksgiving associates what our experience of time divides, the consummation of the life that has been made by God. In this sense, not withdrawn from a world that is under many threats, caught in the perpetual struggle of humankind to master its own existence, the church is a sign, not only of the unity of all humanity, but also of the unity of its origin, work, experience, and expectation: the unity of the love of God with which he first loved us (1 John 4:19), and of our own resources which God has liberated so that they might serve his creation.

At this point prayer takes a final and decisive step that takes it beyond both self-reflection and the corporate reflection of the community. For here the Spirit of God begins to speak. He "intercedes for us," as Paul says in Romans 8:26, because we do not know what to pray for "as we ought," that is, in accordance with how it has to be done in the sight of God. Our prayer, then, ceases to be an expression of our longings, even though it asks for what humanity and the world truly need.

Does this mean that we cannot express ourselves in true prayer? Are we at best only a means through which God relates to himself all the negativities of the world that is alienated from him? Does prayer cease to be a human monologue and become instead a dialogue either of God with himself or of the divine in us with God? No, we reply. The Spirit's intercession for us in prayer for redemption does not mean our exclusion. On the contrary, he takes our place and speaks for us, and speaks in and through us because we are confronted with the limits of human speech. For this reason Paul refers to the "ineffable sighings" of the Spirit, to expressions that transcend the world of speech and that turn both himself and us to God.

How do we relate to God in prayer? We come up here against a rule of dialogue (I.3.2) that differentiates but does not separate God and ourselves. This applies to prayer. It applies precisely at the point where the language of prayer reaches its limit.

The reverse side of our inability to cross this boundary when we pray to God is the dividing up of lament, petition, and praise in time. They can never be simultaneous without becoming schematizing. They cannot flow into one another. Each is possible only at its own time. They remain finite forms of speech which the children of God, who have received the beginning of reconciliation, use when they bring the promised redemption of the world and humanity to their Father (Rom. 8:15ff.). This is precisely the way that the coming of God takes place.

Thanksgiving expresses the fact that we are placed in that which comes from God. That is why ecstatic joy often accompanies thanksgiving and invocation. Assurance is proclaimed that we truly live in fellowship with God.

Doxology extends just as far as the point where God reveals his Godhead and we ourselves enter into the fullness of his work as Father, Son, and Spirit.

II.4. Proclamation

II.4.1. Listening as a Self-Test

Christian preaching displays many different and confusing faces. With eyes open and wide-awake, it might approach and say unobtrusively: you are observed to the very depths of your being. It might also acquire a significant look because it has something arousing and stimulating to impart. It might seem to be full of understanding because nothing is strange to it; it gives a sympathetic nod to every happening. Or it can adopt a different posture when what it has to say does not accord with what it sees and hears. It might want to draw attention to itself, even pulling faces in so doing. It might be painted crudely because it does not want to be ignored, though this might conceal a doll-like emptiness that avoids all experiences that would etch themselves on the face. Raised eyebrows are a sign of pitiless skepticism that might if possible become a mask. The corners of the mouth might droop morosely if what has to be told is a story of misery, loss, and confusion, and the conciliatory smile that might follow is most unnatural. Or the face might become all ears if unheard-of things have to be recounted or announced.

The physiognomy of preaching can easily become a caricature of preachers. We must ask, therefore, what real proclamation is.

Many sermons let us see a structure that imprints itself on the message. This structure reveals the preacher's version of theology, theology in the sense of a line of thought, or more usually a schema of perception, or a total worldview. We can read it from the form rather than the content of the sermon. It will come to light at some decisive rhetorical point, or perhaps in the freezing of what is said into stereotyped gestures. In this case the proclamation is the pointer to an obligation in the pulpit: it is that which the sermon should achieve.

For example, the preacher might point to a structure of contrasts: "This is how we see the world. This is our picture of it. But God tells us something very different, for he is very different. He is the wholly other, and therefore the one who changes things." The "but" introduces the theological section, but other variations of this "but" are also possible. The use of the "but" marks a rhetorical turning point, particularly when the sermon aims at repentance or conversion or a change of outlook. It seeks to inform and to transform. What those addressed are now told is destructive. They have been thinking wrongly, acting wrongly, believing wrongly, living wrongly — it is only after such a repentance that they can truly be given fresh heart. Behind this schema of contrasts, though silently and often unwittingly, there lies the idea that the preacher must bring God into a world that is ungodly, or at least remote from God. The weight of a corrupt world lies on the preacher's shoulders.

Another kind of sermon is from first to last affirmative. It seeks to give awareness to what we have long since known but have never had the confidence to say in that way. A light of understanding is shed on everyday things. A lofty and edifying tone sets them on another level. We see this when "nature" and "grace" are brought together as in some Anglican theology or in the Roman Catholic tradition: "Nature" is never without "grace." Otherwise it would not be nature; indeed, it would be contrary to nature. Our world is never without God. This is a momentous statement, and it constantly leads us to go in search of vestiges of the presence of God.

We are subtly reminded here of fundamental and far-reaching theological questions. These might well be embedded in confessional distinctions, in statements or pronouncements of church doctrine or its substitute forms that affect the structure of the church and also the inner orientation of preaching. Preaching is embedded in the liturgy and thus is influenced by liturgical variation. The Eastern Orthodox churches think their very rich liturgy imparts so much that preaching is hardly necessary. Only when parts of the liturgy have to be expounded, for example, on a saint's day, is there room for catechesis. The Church of Scotland and North American Presbyterians view preaching as the basis of a comprehensive program of instruction supported by exegesis of the Bible. Preaching tells us how to live, and one of the risks that this incurs is that preaching will be too closely identified with the Word of God. On the other hand, if the appeal to the Word of God is less convincing or totally lacking, then the sermon can degenerate into little more than a means of enlightenment. Preaching borders on indoctrination when there is no doctrine either behind or before it that reminds it of what stands outside it.

Faced by such phenomena, we are forced to ask how far preaching can be proclamation that demands a hearing. It is a proclamation that calls to faith and kindles hope, for faith derives from hearing, and hearing from the Word of Christ (Rom. 10:17)!

Christ-talk not only seeks to be heard and accepted by those to whom it is addressed; it derives itself from hearing. So, too, does the work of the "Spirit." We learn from John's Gospel that the Paraclete is the "Spirit of truth" and that he fulfills the work of Christ by reminding us of him. "He does not speak of himself. He speaks of what he has heard, and will also tell of things to come" (John 16:13). Faith derives from the message that is heard, for this message itself is received. It is then entrusted to believers for them to proclaim it. They are not just to hand it over or transmit it. They must help people receive it as a message they have never heard before.

28. The hearing of proclamation is a beginning behind which we cannot go. Therefore all proclamation gives constant life to the question of the commencement of talk about God, no matter what form it takes. The inner grounding of all proclamation is surprise, surprise at the interjection of God that is so full of promise.

This specific hearing, the hearing of proclamation, implies a beginning with no preconditions. It lays its impress upon faith from first to last. It also lays its impress upon the dialogue of faith.

Ricoeur has noted that

> when we confess that we are hearers, we commence the game that breaks with the plan that many if not all philosophers follow, to open up the dialogue without presuppositions. We break with common practice in just commencing this game. Thinking without presuppositions is the same as starting to think itself. Only on a particular presupposition can we occupy a position as hearers of the Christian proclamation.
>
> I assume that what is said makes sense, that it is worth looking into. I assume that its investigation can accompany and lead the transference of the text into life, in which it will comprehensively prove its worth. (Paul Ricoeur, "Gott nennen," in *Gott nennen. Phänomenologische Zugänge*, ed. Bernhard Casper [Freiburg and Munich, 1981], p. 45)

The presupposition of Christian proclamation is not a position that we ourselves adopt. That is a basic and decisive point. Proclamation stands in the way of our own positions and conclusions, of what we can say for ourselves even in the form of collective monologue. God precedes what we say. He transforms us into hearers when, rather by habit than by nature, we would much rather hear ourselves speak, or interrupt others, or just be spectators who make comments.

This switch cannot be described rhetorically. If it could, we could count on it, and where would be the surprise if it could be traced back to approaches or gestures that know in advance what will surprise us! Many sermons use things that should "concern and touch and disturb and shat-

121

ter us," and the surprises they bring are really no surprises because they are well-known gestures in so many sermons. The inner basis of proclamation resists being expressed that way. Attempts in that direction do not leave room for what proclamation itself will do. A notable point here is that faith refrains from presenting itself. This self-forgetfulness cannot be programmed in advance.

Proclamation confronts its recipients with the message that it gives. But this confrontation certainly cannot be staged by preachers confronting their congregations in the pulpits. Adoption of this position is one of the accompanying circumstances of preaching that needs to be thought out theologically. What does it mean to be a minister, a servant of the Word of God, at a time when nearly every form of confrontation has become a problem? We cannot solve the problem by ending the confrontation. Preaching may have different forms, but the strangeness of the message that is the boundary of proclamation is decisive. On this side of the boundary is all that we can say to ourselves, all that constitutes our everyday speech to ourselves and others, and much of this may flow into our sermons unless we remove it artificially. But then something that we really need to hear startles us. The preachers have perhaps been startled even before their congregations. They can have this lead, perhaps, because of the time given to meditate on the text. In this way the proclaimers become the first hearers of the message they have to pass on as messengers. Implicitly, then, it becomes clear that those to whom proclamation is committed cannot be the people who tell others what they cannot tell themselves. They cannot grow beyond what they are entrusted to say to others. That would be an arrogance to which hardness of hearing would be the answer. At the same time a gesture of modesty is not much better. The preachers perhaps speak of things they can vouch for, but something will come out of it only if God pleases. Why should we give time to others, and listen to what they say, when they can tell us only what has happened in their own lives? If preachers are so modest that they range themselves with their congregations, is not this a sign that they have nothing really to say except for adding something more to the common picture of reality?

29. The promise of proclamation is that God precedes our speaking.

This promise can take different forms. It can be a clear contradiction of what we might say to ourselves. It can mediate the hope of that which comes only from God's pronouncement. It can be a liberating insight that shows that at root we already live in the presence of God. *Proclamation tells us what is,* not what must be or ought to be. The different forms of the promise can work in favor of preaching, though preaching is not the only form of proclamation. Proclamation sheds light on liturgy and on pastoral care, demands notice in church leadership, finds expression in instruction, and motivates mission. In what the church does in these fields proclamation is not much in evidence today. This is perhaps because those who are called to work in these fields are afraid lest they should have to embody in person that which has encountered them from outside themselves, which would be an intolerable expectation!

Because so many angles are present, proclamation is an especially sensitive point at which church action and dogmatics intersect. No wonder, then, that in many theologies proclamation in the form of the sermon holds a key position and dogmatics is cut according to this cloth! We might mention four examples.

Irenaeus depicts preaching as an outstanding part of the work of God in salvation history. By means of it the drama of salvation is enacted with which God has overthrown the hostile powers of death, sin, and misery (Gustaf Wingren, *Die Predigt* [Göttingen, 1955]; ET, *The Living Word: A Theological Study of Preaching and the Church,* trans. Victor C. Pogue [Philadelphia, 1960], pp. 58, 149).

Augustine, in his *De doctrina christiana,* follows ancient rhetoric but adjusts preaching to it in a way that transcends it. Christian orators are meant to convince and thereby to confess, not just to persuade. Preaching changes human self-love into love for God. It gives the hearers a new vision which will help them restructure the world of things and overcome their emotional attachment to the transitory. In turning to God we will seek and find our true selves. What preaching does along these lines is in keeping with the orientation of theology. Directing itself toward God, theology serves also to move us toward God. Proclamation sets this movement in motion and directs it toward its goal, helping it to avoid deviations and perversions. Its task is educational, but the goal of education here is of such a sort that it far surpasses the goal of any other form of learning.

For Martin Luther, and the Reformers who followed him (especially John Calvin, though only in part Philipp Melanchthon), proclamation again became the center of all that the church does and the central point in theology, for it is the promising address of the gospel and the communication of the divine promise. In this way God himself gives faith, which opens the door for all the further workings of the triune God.

In proclamation God makes himself present in human words. He

123

meets us here. His deity unmasks all idolatry, all false deification, all self-deification. It also reveals to us how God is for us and we are for God. To that extent preaching is a pronouncement of the presence of the triune God.

The predella of the altar of the city church of Wittenberg, where Luther preached, depicts the reformer in the pulpit. He is pointing to the crucified Christ, who is exalted between the congregation and the preacher, so that the eyes of all will fall on him alone and not on the eloquent preacher. This is perhaps the most concise reference possible to the externality of Protestant preaching. The preaching of the gospel is the message of the cross, the acceptance of what Christ has done by letting God act in him. "A theologian of the cross calls the thing what it actually is" (Thesis 21 of the 1518 Heidelberg Disputation; ET, trans. Harold Grimm, *LW,* 31:40; *WA,* 1:354.21-22). It directs us to look at what God has done and thus follows God's action (Thesis 20).

Karl Barth said that a task of his whole *Church Dogmatics* is to test the relevance of Christian speech. "Talk about God in the church seeks to be proclamation to the extent that in the form of preaching and sacrament it is directed to man with the claim and expectation that in accordance with the commission it has to speak to him the Word of God to be heard in faith. Inasmuch as it is a human word in spite of this claim and expectation, it is the material of dogmatics, i.e., of the investigation of its responsibility as measured by the Word of God which it seeks to proclaim" (thesis of §3, I/1, 2nd ed., trans. Geoffrey W. Bromiley [Edinburgh, 1975]).

Dogmatics inquires into the foundations of the proclamation that is entrusted to the church. These foundations do not consist of a distant goal or norm or ideal. Rather, they can be heard in proclamation as God's speech. To this extent, preaching is a form of the Word of God (§ 4) — not even mere revelation! — and for this reason dogmatics is rooted in preaching as a phenomenon, even though this phenomenon is the word of humans. But dogmatics has to deal with the possibility that God's speech can be heard through preaching; that this actually happens is down to God alone. For the sake of such hope, the talk of the church about God is the theme of dogmatics. The theme is not God himself in a direct form. God has willed to express himself in preaching. Faith, too, is not the theme. Faith arises only through preaching, and preaching constantly confirms it. Only God himself can verify what is said with reference to him.

These are four different definitions of proclamation, and behind the differences lie dogmatic statements which find expression in the doctrine of God and the Trinity. These definitions all impressively stress the interconnection between dogmatic theory and church practice. Nevertheless, they are inclined to reduce dogmatics to a norm of church practice. Even if they attempt to find the totality of theology and the church in the conjunction of divine and human action, they surely cannot find it in a cardinal theme, no matter how central and normative it might seem to be. If this cardinal theme is treated as a pattern for preaching — an example would be the Word of God as a contrast to present reality — then it can become the source of a monotony that causes long-term damage to our ability to hear proclamation.

II.4.2. An Unrequested Message

Why should we listen to the Word about Christ? How should we do so? This Word that draws near to us is a strange Word, an alien Word. It does not have its origin in us. It does not always answer our expectations. It announces the promise of God with which he draws near to us. It can never lose this unexpected strangeness no matter how often we hear it. It continually makes this strangeness apparent to us whenever we listen. An element of this is that preaching is related to biblical speaking of God, without always having to be preaching on a certain text. It thus puts us on an unfamiliar track: we are compelled to bring out something that runs counter to the proportions of dogmatics or simply goes against the grain of our theological convictions. We can never say to ourselves the message of the unknown proximity of God.

As the preaching of Christ, preaching derives from hearing. It is the message that Jesus Christ is risen. The sermon at Pentecost also refers to the Easter message (Acts 2:22-36). That does not mean that every sermon must be a variation of the Easter message. What it does mean is that it must have the "unrequested" nature of the Easter message.

Originally the Easter feast was related both chronologically and materially to the Passover (I.5.3).

The oldest Easter sermon known to us is the Passover homily of Melito of Sardis (d. ca. 180). Melito clearly associated redemption through the death of Christ with the liberation of the Jewish people from oppression in Egypt. Christ has brought his own people "from slavery to liberty, from darkness to light, from death to life, from tyranny to eternal royalty," i.e., to the everlasting kingdom ("On Pascha" 68, in *On Pascha and*

Fragments, trans. Stuart George Hall [Oxford, 1979], p. 37). For Melito the exodus story is thus a prefiguration of the passion of Jesus. But we should not overlook an essential difference even though there is only an inkling of this in Melito. Jesus Christ did not break into the kingdom of freedom with power, as a liberated liberator. He overcame death by his own death. The only Son of God was not spared like the firstborn sons of Jewish families. He was given up for us all (cf. Rom. 8:32). He did not seek eternity passing through the portals of death. The living God revealed himself by raising him from the dead. Along these lines the Easter message is the antitype of the exodus narrative.

Another feature is even more striking. It does not appear at all in what the Easter message says, but it marks this message as a whole and is quite unmistakable, distinguishing the Easter message from the Passover Haggadah, the story of the exodus that is the heart of the Passover feast. According to this account, a question has to be put by the youngest in the family. He asks what is the meaning of the elements of the feast that he sees before him, the bitter herbs, the unleavened bread, the cup of blessing. The answer is indicated by the recitation and the symbols of the story of liberating salvation. By this answer those who are questioning, as the youngest members of their people, are now integrated into the people whose history began with this exodus by night that redeemed it from slavery. And the eating of these symbolic elements by the family incorporates that family into the history of their forebears.

A similar practice, however, would be unthinkable in the Easter celebration. In relation to the history, where would be the symbolic signs about which to inquire? A crib would fit Christmas, but an empty grave or a stone would hardly be suitable for Easter. Such things would in fact mislead us (as indicated in Mark 16:8). We cannot raise any further queries about the answer that is given by the Easter event. The Easter cry: "Christ is risen, he is risen indeed," is an unrequested answer, the Easter message in the absolute.

To establish this message, metaphorical exaggerations or extensions taken from the story of the exodus are not enough. Theology is concerned with another question, a decisive and normative question for the Christian church. That is the question: "Who is Jesus Christ?" The question has to be dealt with in a way that is clear and allows for no mistakes if the underivable answer given by the Easter message is not to be obstructed by false lines of inquiry. The answer that is given must always retain its character as a message.

The Passover feast took a narrative form. In it the story of the liberation of Israel from subjection to Pharaoh was recounted. God had saved his people from the hands of the enemy. The people of God were to tell this story from one generation to another. Jews must hold fast to this story. They will then not be helpless when new threats face them.

If we hand down the story of Easter as though it were a Passover Haggadah, we would have to treat the Easter event as an exodus of higher rank. Not only would the foes of God and his people have been conquered. The hostile and dark world as a whole would have to be broken up. Easter would symbolize an exodus from an existence that has fallen under the sway of death. In this case the resurrection of Christ and the fellowship of Christ would be a typologically enhanced exodus. What is prefigured is redemption from danger. The figure can take different forms, but the persons depicted are the same: the oppressed who are liberated and the oppressors who must fail.

This configuration lies behind the narrative theology of Judaism (Schalom Ben Chorin, *Narrative Theologie des Judentums anhand der Pessach-Haggada: Jerusalemer Vorlesungen* [Tübingen, 1985]). The Haggadah tells of the enemies of enslaved Israel and points all later generations to its liberation. The exodus narrative achieves this: in this narrative the people's history carries on and continually establishes its identity. Jews can identify themselves by mentioning their threateners, the threats, and the help that is given them. In the constellation of threats which has returned again and again, the prospect of the exodus has upheld the Jewish identity.

At the Easter feast, however, members of the community are given assurance of their participation in the history of Jesus Christ, and only then does the community of Jesus Christ come into being. It is called forth from the whole world, whose frontiers have been burst open by the death of Jesus.

At the Easter feast God is worshiped by the Christian fellowship. The members of the church have experienced that Christ is risen, and they look forward to his coming. We are not Christians by right of birth as Jews are. Being a Christian can be understood only as belonging to the church. But in that case, what is the church? How does it arise? How is it constituted?

The celebration of faith cannot be produced by "actors" and watched by "spectators." Even the ministers are addressed by the message that they are directed to proclaim. They do not address families as parts of a people. They invite the family of God (*familia dei*) to the festal celebration. A greater compulsion is laid upon individuals than it is for Jews, who belong to a given community that binds their offspring to them. The Passover is typically celebrated in the family, the household fellowship, which is charged to pass on the tradition of faith.

In the Christian church, family and people are not so constitutive that we are born into them and can thus speak of the "God of our forebears" who brought us "out of Egypt, out of the land of bondage." With what right can Christians, too, speak of this God? Considered more closely, this question stands behind the trinitarian and christological dogmas. But a further element enters in. From the days of Constantine church and state have overlapped. The more important it is, then, to draw the boundaries of the church so clearly that different opinions of faith, liturgical variations, and other differences cannot dissolve it from within. It is only by essential agreement in faith that the church can protect its unity. To this degree we should view the conciliar decisions as theological rules. They are not a symptom of the unholy alliance of church and state. They are efforts to define the church theologically and to find guidance in the consensus of faith. This consensus finds itself referred to the question posed by Easter. What is that world from which Jesus, by dying in it, withdrew so radically as to shatter it to the very depths? And what will be our human destiny now that the power of death is broken, the death to which we had all become subject?

II.4.3. The Presence of the Spirit

We can now add various points to the inner grounding of proclamation mentioned in thesis 28.

30. Proclamation delivers an unrequested and unexpected message. God has acted and we are now addressed. The promise of his action is pronounced to us. We are thus made aware of the fullness of the presence of God, of his unrecognized nearness.

Focusing on the question of how our talk about God begins, proclamation stands close to homology inasmuch as it joins in the unrequested message (I.2.1). Dogmatics is directed to proclamation because there perceptive hearing is exercised. Proclamation is admonished by dogmatics to let the answer given by God be heard clearly and not to lose sight of its ramifications.

Proclamation is exposed to two complementary misunderstandings that dogmatics brings to light. One is that we have to bring God into the world. The other is that we can catch his presence from what is around us so long as we look intensively enough and penetrate to the depths of what we see.

The inner grounding of proclamation is the prevenient action of God. It is only thanks to this action that the presence of God already embraces all of us: speakers, hearers, the people we speak of, the people we pray for. We dare not make this point except in faith, hope, and love. Yet the expectation it gives us is a most powerful weapon against indoctrination, which is the greatest misunderstanding of proclamation. The community on no account should experience exorcism. It confesses its sins, but this does not allow preachers to root out those who must be excluded on account of their "unbelief," and in this way led to "faith."

The prevenient action of God is the presence of his Spirit. God is present with us before we are aware of it. He acts in relation to us even before we are believers, even before we can speak meaningfully about belief and unbelief, even before we know what these terms signify. He has confronted us for a long time. Were we aware of it? Could we be before his message reached us? He is at work among us, but are we where he is? His promise leads us beyond ourselves into faith, hope, and love.

The fact that proclamation is grounded in the presence of God's Spirit does not usually form part of the content of proclamation, but it does form its theological premise, which can come to view in its fine structure. Proclamation and dogmatics are thus interlocked. Dogmatics unfolds the theological grounding of proclamation. We also find in dogmatics the practice of proclamation to which it relates. What does it expect from proclamation? Does it know the line of approach? Does it really begin at the beginning? Or does it put the cart before the horse?

Pronouncing the message of God's prevenient grace, proclamation is at its heart *kerygma.* In the narrower sense, that is, that of form criticism, kerygma is missionary preaching signifying that people of all kinds are called into the Christian fellowship, not born into it. Along with this an outward reason is mentioned that is not restricted to mission, namely, that Christian communities have arisen, and still arise, as individuals are called *out* of their particular circumstances and *into* the history that God has founded with humanity *(ecclesia).* For the sake of this message, ambassadors are needed who will proclaim the fact that Jesus was sent into the world. Proclamation needs messengers to transmit it, to do so plainly and simply, announcing the unknown proximity of God. They will not impart either doleful messages or songs of victory, but the message that has itself been given, the Word that comes from God and will not return to him empty (Isa. 55:11).

This message is new and strange, and not merely for those who have not yet heard it, that is, on the mission field, but also for all those who hear far too many voices, not least their own. The message tells us who God really is, who we ourselves are in his presence, and what is real. It will surprise us often enough, and at times alienate us, but it will at least cause us to address the question: Who are you? How do you live and how will you die? What have you to do or not do?

The inner grounding of proclamation is the inexhaustible fullness of the presence of God's Spirit. The paraphrase "God's address" describes this fullness. The fact that the situation of the hearers varies so widely is a sign that this fullness can never reach an end. If this were so, then proclamation would rest on a general program that we must execute point by point.

The inexhaustibility of the presence of the Spirit relates to the fact that the Spirit is linked to the Word and thus to the many ways in which the Bible speaks about God (for the literal sense of Scripture, cf. III.3). As proclamation is dependent on dogmatics (so that we do not lose sight of the infinite range of God's action), it is also dependent on the canon. A multitude of voices are heard in the biblical Word, all in tension, yet all in secret agreement as regards God's action. As we listen to these voices, proclamation will show us how manifold is the work of God. Dogmatics is again an aid to memory at this point, and the church year gives additional support (I.5.3).

The inexhaustible presence of the Spirit of God intensifies to proclamation, actually demanding that preaching and pastoral counseling be one-sided in their aim at specificity. This is not just because no one can say everything at once. Proclamation is pointed just because it encourages us to go beyond this point. It leads us into unknown territory that may seem to us to be no-man's land at first glance. But we can take this step, for proclamation does not stand alone. It is accompanied by all the other activities of the church. We may take the step indicated by proclamation because it is supported by lament, petition, and intercession, by praise and thanksgiving.

Why is it never enough to hear only one sermon, no matter how incisive for our lives this might be? Proclamation as kerygma extends to us a message from outside that we cannot grasp, that might easily be buried under other things, so that we have to hear it time and time again in various situations and with many nuances. It will always come to us as something new and different, yet it is always the same, for God himself speaks to us. He speaks to us in unexpected ways, and even though we go to meet him, his Word *strikes* us. He finds us in ways that we do not recognize ourselves, or do not want to, and addresses us in ways that we can never speak about ourselves. God does not give us one angle on which to answer our questions concerning our Whence and Whither. He does not simply give us a basic confidence in our existence. At any rate, this is not where theology begins. God begins to speak to us. Dogmatics prepares to deal with the dimension of this self-impartation of God, for it begins with the acts of God and the promises of God.

God's unknown proximity is not uncovered by stages in proclamation. Fresh hearing, then, is always demanded even though it leads us forward. We will never reach an end, however, for the unknown proximity of God is inexhaustible, because he remains concealed in his revelation, but in his concealment he is near to us.

In proclamation God draws near to us when we note what God has done in the lives of people who by their very existence point to his work. We thus perceive that God is near. God's known proximity makes us sensitive to his unknown proximity, though it does not open our eyes at once and enable us to see clearly all that had previously escaped our knowledge. To proclaim in the light of God's known presence is to speak about this presence as it relates even to what cannot be shown to be in harmony with what we know. Even that which still escapes our knowledge does not escape God's knowledge.

Proclamation steers between the Scylla of religious common sense and the Charybdis of indoctrination. Can people be addressed with things that are common knowledge? Or must we "orientate" them, thinking for them and praying for them? Does proclamation mediate something wholly different? Or is it simply there to bring God into the world? That would require first of all that the world is godless. (How many sermons, in both structure and content, seem to be guided by ideas of this kind!) What proclamation tries to communicate will be partly determined by whether it holds to a steady course, avoiding these two perils, by whether it learns to see that God encounters us in his fullness and that he does indeed anticipate all that we may think and say and do.

II.5. Worship as the Blessing and Upbuilding of the Congregation

Blessing is the cardinal point or axis of worship in all its forms.

What is worship? When we ask this, we are asking whether and how we can expect the presence of God at specific places, at specific times, and

·

131

in specific ways. The Eastern Orthodox and Reformation churches agree when they reply that:

31. Worship is the form of God's action that directly demands that we should serve God by letting God do his own work with us.

At various points we have referred to the activity of God without any closer elucidation. What we have been saying is that God "encounters" us, that we come up against his "work," that through his "acts" we are linked with him, that he addresses us and "wants to have dealings with us." In his acts he speaks to us, and in his speech he acts upon us. His work is not a dumb work. His Word does not merely explain what happens at all times or what happens in such inconceivable ways that a supernatural explanation has to be given. His speech and his acts are one and the same thing. In them he confronts us, so that we are no longer left alone with ourselves or with others like us. He himself is with us. The will of God can be known through the events in which he speaks to us. This is true even though we are only beginning to ask about him.

In Christian theology the thought of God's action is defined as follows: God, the one and only God, encounters us "in person." He mediates himself to us through his acts (I.2.2) He does not hide his face from us but is devoted to us and is open to us. He is known to us by what he has created, redeemed, judged, preserved, confirmed, rejected, promised, and fulfilled. In these acts he posits the relations in which we gain perception of God himself, of ourselves, and of our being in the world.

Worship discloses these relations to us. In worship, in other words, we move within them. It incorporates us into them. It anticipates both what we can expect of it and what we ourselves can do there. God comes to our aid by showing us where we can hear him, receive his promises, and be prepared and sent to live at his side. His will is that we should know him and value him as the one he is, also as the one who is for us. The term "worship" is based on the Anglo-Saxon "weorthscipe," which means "to ascribe worth," "to value people as they really are."

God's action does not only have to be followed by human action. It need not and cannot be simply represented by specific acts or imitated by them. Worship does not represent God; it is neither a depicting nor a supplementing nor even a substituting action. What we rightly say and do in worship, or what we omit to say and do, accords in different ways with God's own distinctive work. To this extent it is "service," serving what God wills to do toward us and through us.

In a special sense this occurs as the blessing. Blessing "inaugurates" God's action, the activity that he himself denotes in the words of blessing. God wills to tell us what he is doing as blessing is pronounced. The form of blessing opens the door to God's work by opening those who receive the blessing. It opens them for the future of the promise. Blessing gives hope, and thus inaugurates the future.

We see this in the introduction to the Aaronic blessing in Numbers 6:22-27. Aaron and his brothers are charged to put the name of God on Israel, to put upon it the weight of this name.

God's name shall be laid on Israel in a threefold form. "The Lord bless you and keep you": *God accepts responsibility for the lives of those to whom he turns.* He is to care for them, to set them under his providential eye, not to let them perish. They are no longer left to look after their own lives. "The Lord make his face to shine upon you, and be gracious to you": *God's face is radiant.* It shines, so to speak. God is to look at them, so that they are enabled to look at him. All eyes should bow before the majesty of God — who can behold him? But God, as it were, lifts our heads with his hands and draws them to himself. They are lifted up so that they can stand and move before God. "The Lord lift up his countenance upon you, and give you peace." *God is to look upon those who need his salvation.* He is to keep them in view. He is to watch over them and to prepare salvation for them.

What a shocking demand — to God! The grammatical form of the jussive is not confined to a request; a claim is made on God, in another way than in proclamation or prayer. It is a command, entrusted to those who do the blessing. But they are thus oriented on the action of God and are kept from trying to conjure up this action by their words of blessing.

32. The inner grounding of blessing is the pronouncing of God's saving presence.

The name of God is placed upon his people. They carry this name. Yet it is not a burden. It is a cover for them as they are sent out into a world in which the blessing of God always stands before them, expects them, and accompanies them.

The inexhaustibility of the divine blessing is a prefiguration of what dogmatics has to say about the doctrine of the Trinity, namely, that God discloses himself in the fullness of his deity. God is not there merely for himself. He does not simply enter into relationship with us. In his acts toward us he discloses himself. But in mediating himself, he does not exhaust himself. His action is indivisible, but it wants us to know its different features.

The doctrine of the Trinity has made a rule of this (cf. the scholastic

133

Wilhelm de Rubione in a commentary on Peter Lombard's *Sentences,* 1518, 134 verso): "The works of the triune God are outwardly [in relation to us] indivisible."[11] They constitute the unity of God's communal work. Father, Son, and Spirit make no individual contributions that might be traced back to one of the three. All are present in everything that God does. This rule solves a problem of biblical theology which was raised by speaking about God the Father, Son, and Spirit. Was the Father active only in the creation, and the Son only in the reconciliation and redemption; is the Spirit active only later and possibly not until a completion that is yet to come? The response is: the kinds of God's effectiveness are only coordinated to Father, Son, and Spirit. God is always present himself. We cannot divide the Godhead into different functions, into a God of providence, a God of omnipotence, a God who helps. These "functional" gods, then, could be called upon and needed to be called upon as required. When we hear that "God cares for us," we also know that he is the Lord who confronts us, and that as such he is the one who stands by to help us. He will resist us if we try to resist him, but even this resistance can have the form of help.

We have often referred to "we," but now at last, in relation to those who are promised God's blessing, we must inquire into the inner grounding of this "we."

In the Lutheran liturgies the assembly that gathers for worship is often expressly addressed in the invitation to confession and prayer, or in the salutation "The Lord will be with you" before the Eucharist and in the pulpit prior to the sermon. I will select 2 Corinthians 13:13 as an example of this special form of address: "The grace of the Lord Jesus Christ, the love of God, and the communion of the Holy Spirit be with you all."

To what extent do we find dogmatics here? In two ways: this formula of greeting contains already at root elements of the later doctrine of the Trinity; and it also answers the question why individuals of different backgrounds and situations can be addressed in common, why and in what ways they are related to one another.

33. The address that contains the divine greeting constitutes the "we" of the Christian community. Related to this fact is the inclusive language of dogmatics.

In 2 Corinthians 13 the greeting and the "holy kiss" (v. 12) form a transition to the celebration of the Lord's Supper. This was the place where Paul's epistle would be read. For many years this richly freighted greeting

11. Opera trinitatis ad extra sunt indivisa.

would precede the Eucharist. From the Middle Ages onward it has also come before the sermon, retaining its character even though the sermon is now separated from Holy Communion. For it still tells the congregation in whose name they are being addressed, and to what end.

Paul relates what he has to say to a liturgical context, and by the greeting he also draws attention to the inner grounding of the celebration. His instruction is called forth by the challenge of many in the Corinthian church to the legitimacy of his apostolic office. The greeting does not simply bring this controversy to a close. Instead, it points to the consensus which discloses the meaning of all foregoing arguments. It also makes it clear that apostolic authority has its basis in a fellowship which includes both Paul himself and the congregation.

Whence does Paul derive his authority? How can he make the claim that others should listen to him? With what right does he speak as strongly as he does in this letter? And why should he even break into tears? This could hardly be because he wept so easily. The strife concerning his legitimacy has cut him to the quick. His concern is not for himself alone. He is stunned, and the fact that he weeps is an expression of his inability to control the situation. But he need not control it. What he has to say rests, like the invitation to the table of the Lord and to participation in Christ's presence, upon the grace of our Lord Jesus Christ, the love of God, and the fellowship of the Holy Spirit.

Let us consider the dogmatic implications of this greeting. Its three elements point to one theme in the doctrine of the Trinity, namely, to the "economic Trinity," to the presence of the triune God in the unity of his "work of salvation" *(oikonomia)* toward us on the world's behalf. The three names, Jesus Christ, God, and Spirit, are not alone in announcing this theme. Paul tells us what goes with these names, what derives from them, and what ties them together. Dogmatics knows this as the doctrine of the relations (I.2.2) and appropriations of the triune God. The fullness and unity of God's work of salvation leads to the mystery of the so-called immanent Trinity, the essential relations of the Father, Son, and Spirit with one another.

The relations between the three persons of the Trinity bring their actions into association. God himself encounters us here. From his fullness flow grace and love and fellowship. They cannot be thought of as separate. When we say fellowship we point to the love of God, and we find this love in the grace that is revealed in Jesus Christ. Love and grace and fellowship are inseparably bound up with the essence of the triune God. They lead us into the very depths of God himself.

135

All this was later developed in the trinitarian teaching of the early church, though not specifically in relation to 2 Corinthians 13:13. One concern of this teaching was to achieve a clarification of terms as it wrestled with contemporary thought. But it was primarily unfolding what lay behind that address to a Christian community. Conversely, the doctrine of the Trinity was needed if the address was to be rightly used and its real meaning understood. This doctrine has, among other things, the task of showing that love and grace and fellowship are "acts of God in person." We can say that grace is not a relation of a transcendent divine reality to a needy world only because Jesus Christ was sacrificed in order to do the work of reconciliation, letting himself be declared guilty "so that we might be made the righteousness of God in him" (2 Cor. 5:21). Jesus in this way freely submitted to the will of him who sent him. He underwent the most profound alienation from God, but thus brought to light the love of God that would achieve fulfillment as fellowship with him was established and peace among us was effected. If we ignore, forget, or misunderstand these relations, confusion follows in what we say about God, with unforeseeable consequences for both the "church" and the "world."

We need dogmatics if we are to keep these relations in mind and not misunderstand the intention behind that address. Dogmatics for its part is rooted in the fact that we are now entrusted to the presence of God and are addressed in his name. Preaching and the sacraments have been established as the "ministry of reconciliation." The authorized greeting and invitation define the content and administration of preaching and the sacraments (lex salutandi constituit regulam praedicandi et administrandi sacramentorum). The address shows us what form the church takes. It is greeted and constituted as a community that is gathered for worship.

Who addresses whom, and how? This is not an indifferent or formal question. It is connected with what is said, and also with how it is received. The ministers and preachers say "Beloved congregation," not "Ladies and Gentlemen" or "Comrades." They thus make it clear that they are speaking to people who belong together, even if they are not yet at all aware of it and even if all things that might create a sense of community may be missing. They perhaps have little in common and are completely different in nature, custom, and outlook. The edifying term "Brothers and Sisters" might perhaps conceal the strangeness. It gives a sense of community that is obviously well-meant. Why should not the worshipers feel at home? But the divine greeting says much more and puts it very differently when it tells people of the reconciliation that they need even if they have been for long enough familiar with the Christian tradition. As those to whom the grace of Jesus Christ deriving from the love of God applies (and who are in the community of the Spirit), they are now a "we," a corporate person, not a sum of individuals or a group of like-minded people. They confront the ministers and preachers in a certain sense if they speak, for they speak in the name of God. They have to give them a message and speak on Christ's behalf. Yet the ministers and preachers, too, belong to the community before God, and they are thus caught up in that "we."

The address to the congregation is not a rhetorical device that preachers use to capture an audience. Behind the possibility of saying "we," and thus addressing others, there is concealed a truly far-reaching social question. With what right and in what sense can preachers say "we," and do so in a way that does not simply sound edifying? Would it not be more honest if a preacher distinguished himself or herself from the listeners by using "I" and "you"?

The congregation is a gathering of those who for various reasons have come to worship. It is not an assembly of listeners. Nor is it united by common interests and tasks. It is not a society of academics, a scientific community. It is not a political party. Those who do not speak or write specifically for these kinds of groups realize that the use of "we" is meaningless. It can be used seriously only with reference to points in common that have still to be substantiated. In relation to ethical problems, which of us today can simply refer back to a "we"? And what really occurs when those who encounter a similar analysis of a situation believe that this fact brings them together? Worship is not immune to such doubts and objections. But in the various parts of liturgy God imparts elements of his work. Along these lines he constitutes the "we" that allows dogmatics, too, to speak inclusively (I.1.2).

II.6. Pastoral Care

II.6.1. Pastoral Care as a Stimulus for Dogmatics

Tillich described pastoral care as "a continuous source" of "systematic work" (Paul Tillich, "The Theology of Pastoral Care: The Spiritual and Theological Foundations of Pastoral Care" [1958], in *The Meaning of Health: Essays in Existentialism, Psychoanalysis, and Religion,* ed. Perry LeFevre [Chicago, 1984], pp. 125-30, esp. 128. See also Paul Tillich, "The Impact of Pastoral Psychology on Theological Thought" [1960], in the same volume, pp. 144-50). It commends itself as a far-reaching support for various forms of life.

Normative in this regard is the question of meaning. People naturally ask what is of ultimate concern for them. They are looking for a point of reference that will give them orientation, and Tillich emphasizes time and time again that this can help them forward only if they are prevented from entrenching themselves in any one aspect of life's experience. The meaning of life and of the world is manifested in the revelation of God in Jesus Christ, in what Tillich calls the "new being." We cannot pass on this answer to the question of meaning merely as information, for it leads us into historically shifting questions that concern all of us. When we experience the meaning that is given by the name of "Jesus the Christ" as the answer to our primal questions, then we also experience the salvation that he brings, and we transcend ourselves. We experience a foretaste of the totality of an essential life that is unbroken. We thus regain our health for living in an ambiguous world (cf. *Systematic Theology*, vol. 3 [Chicago, 1963], IV 1.C: "The Quest for Unambiguous Life and the Symbols of Its Anticipation").

Pastoral care has to do with those who are seeking meaning. In this sense it is a continuous and constant source for theologians who are concerned about order and systems, like Tillich. This kind of pastoral care is an ongoing stimulus for a systematic theology that dedicates itself to the question of meaning in its full compass: the general riddle of the world; the basic question of the being of things and the goal of history that unites all humanity and gives validity to all cultural achievements in spite of the fact that they are so relative and provisional. Systematic theology depends on pastoral work because it needs its help in tracking the intellectual and spiritual situation of the age (and, conversely, pastoral care can only hit on its goals if it is introduced to the spiritual situation of the age). In probing this situation, theology will meet with that which drives our contemporaries, that which threatens them, and that which they need. But we can recognize the modern situation only if we do not abandon ourselves to these drives but know their limits, namely, the context that enables us to see the inalienable and permanent human questions in the flood of information, and helpfully, therefore, to shed light on the nature of humanity.

When we look at them in this way, systematic theology and pastoral care are very closely related. We might think of systematic theology as the theory of pastoral care, of a pastoral care that aids in promoting a vital and goal-directed life. Systematic theology thus provides a comprehensive basis for a religious diagnosis of the time. Preaching, instruction, and prayer are specific forms in which this therapy finds application.

II.6.2. The Relation of "Nature" and "Grace" as Configurations of Self-Recognition

Paul Tillich's systematic concept provides a (quasi-metaphysical) framework for what is theological and philosophical. If instead we inquire into the inner grounding of pastoral conversations, we quickly see that these cannot have their basis in themselves. The rules that direct them have a wider reference. They cannot just be answers to existential questions, no matter how extensive systematically. Therefore, pastoral discourse does not stand alone. It is embedded in prayer, even though this does not always come to expression in pastoral work itself. At such points we can see a structure of dogmatics that characteristically differs from the view of Tillich.

Instructive in this regard is the contribution of Augustine. Debating with Pelagius, Augustine tried to clarify the relation between divine grace and human freedom.

The theological program of Pelagius rested on a view of pastoral care that he had taken over from the tradition of antiquity. This view had a philosophical basis. It aimed at a lifestyle that presupposed an adequate knowledge of humanity, a thoroughgoing anthropology (*De natura* [410], preserved in fragmentary form in Augustine's counterblast, *De natura et gratia* [415]. Cf. for what follows II.2; CSEL, 60:234.10-27; ET, *On Nature and Grace* [NPNF, 5:122]). If we want to help people, we need to know what they are and what they can be: able to live aright, to strive after the good, to do it, and not to turn aside from what distinguishes true humanity. As a Christian theologian, Pelagius is not fully content with this view. The help of the grace of God, he thought, must be added. None of us on our own can accomplish what we ought to be. God, however, will strengthen our freedom to do what is good, that to which every instruction to live a righteous life appeals.

A specific schema lies behind this theological classification of education as anthropological knowledge. The grace of God transcends our human ability, but it presupposes a human readiness, in intention at least. For only if our "nature" is so constituted that we want to live aright can we be urged to a good life and our ability not to sin be strengthened. If we were made differently, the will of God would be thwarted. But that is no less unthinkable than an address that expects the recipients to have no means of understanding it.

On this view, nature and grace work together in our relationship with God. This type of calculation fits in well with a rhetorical and didac-

139

tic scheme. But the impression is left that the grace of God is something added to human ability, that it crowns that which we can achieve for ourselves, that it is the seal upon our destiny. Our basic anthropological structure remains untouched. Our disposition is to do good. So divine grace is made into an offer that we might accept or reject. We can decide in favor of it or against it.

Augustine's criticism of Pelagius focuses first on this understanding of grace as something that can be calculated anthropologically. He agreed with Pelagius that we need the help of God. Pelagius also could have agreed with him that God alone makes righteous action possible. "He gives what He commands when He helps him [the person] to obey whom He commands" (". . . adiuvat ut faciat quod iubet," *De gratia et libero arbitrio* 15.31 [425], PL, 44:899; ET, *On Grace and Free Will* [NPNF, 5:456]). But how are we to read a sentence of this kind? Pelagius simply read it along the lines of his moral and pastoral teaching. The help of God's grace is the presupposition of righteous action that is pleasing to God. But this presupposition, as it were, only indicates the condition before an anthropological reasoning. The grace of God is the primal grace of creation to which we must always refer back because it defines us constitutionally.

Augustine, on the other hand, speaks of the presupposition of grace in prayer, and in so doing he indicates the theologically decisive point of controversy, for in prayer we beseech God: "Give what Thou commandest, and command what Thou wilt" ("Da quod iubes et iube quod vis," *Confessiones* [396/98] 10:29.40; CSEL, 33:256.24; ET, *Confessions* [NPNF, 1:153]).

The command of God and the living will of God are both imparted to those who pray, and they are unable to separate what they receive and what they are asked to do. "What do you have that you did not receive?" Augustine sees in this saying of Paul (1 Cor. 4:7) a reference to God's *creatio continua,* his continuous creation ("profecto et ipsum velle credere Deus operatur in homine et in omnibus misericordia eius praevenit nos," *De spiritu et littera* 34.60 [412]; CSEL, 60:220.17-19; ET, *On the Spirit and the Letter* [NPNF, 5:110]: "that it is God who both works in the man the willing to believe, and in all things prevents us with His mercy").

Human free will in human responsibility, Augustine emphasizes, is not excluded. God's prevenient action also includes the new creation that we owe to the death of Jesus. We cannot simply look back at this work of God. Rather, we can keep it constantly in view, as it is there before us. Again, we cannot integrate God's action into a basic human structure. It has an autonomous dogmatic grounding.

140

Augustine therefore agreed with Pelagius that we have unconditional need of the grace of God and that this grace is a gift. Pelagius, however, found in the gift of grace the basis of a task. The grace of God sets a
task before us, not just any task that we can carry out in various ways, but
the total task of a life that has to be lived. A true theological understanding of our humanity must result in action. But Augustine took an opposite view, perceiving that "being given" is the essence of grace. "Give what
you command and demand what you will." For Augustine we do not have
here a presupposition linked to consequences. We have instead the union
of gift and command. No one can put the gift of God under human management — "What do you have that you did not receive?" — unless it be
through misuse of our own created will.

Out of his pastoral concern to give a correct direction to life, Augustine takes up the question of the relation between the work of God
and human freedom. He finds the *dogmatic* answer in his dissatisfaction
with the idea that the work of God is simply not put at our disposal.
When grace comes to us, as it does in prayer, we *receive* freedom, and our
wills are wholly and utterly oriented to God. Grace does not supply what
we lack. Instead, it puts us in a position where we can know and will the
good.

*34. The inner grounding of pastoral care is the grace of God that orients our human
wills to God.*

Prayer is a very different speech act from a command, as an imperative
that communicates God's commands to us ("Thou shalt . . ."). Prayer sets
what we do within the context of what God does, which can be formulated
only dogmatically. Prayer, then, finds its life in God's continuous creation.
It is a constitutive feature of the doctrine of grace and of a true understanding of human freedom (*De natura et gratia* 12.13-14 [415]; CSEL,
60:241.2–5.12; ET, *On Nature and Grace* [NPNF, 5:125]). Concerning Pelagius, Augustine writes that as "we know the will of God from his commands, he may know God's grace by prayer" (*Epistula* 177.5, to Pope Innocent [416]: "Sicut ergo agnoscimus voluntatem, cum haec praecipiuntur,
sic et ipse agnoscat gratiam, cum petuntur"; CSEL, 44:674.18ff.).

Theologically the consequences can be quite different. Pelagius
views the help of God as a means of perfecting what we can do. Augustine,
however, puts the question: What does it mean to *will* to do the good? And
he comes up against the riddle of human will that is perverted and yet not
aware of its perversion. Only when by the grace of God we receive forgive-

ness for our sins does our will no longer stumble over itself. Only then does it learn to know what it really wills. It is restored and given a completely new orientation rather than being perfected in the sense of quantitative enrichment, following Pelagius.

Augustine is confronted by the fact that our will resists the good that God has given and posited for us. This resistance must be overcome, and the first and decisive step in this direction is the knowledge of the good that God has granted to us with his grace. The question how we can *become* good is left open. At this point Luther would add that we can perceive God's will only by receiving God's righteousness and being pronounced righteous.

II.6.3. Broken Self-Knowledge: Perceiving the Self as God Judges

Luther asked the question: "Can we know what God wills?" The answer that he found in the practice of penance (clarified by the Council of Trent) rested on a complex interrelating of God's action and human will. We must grasp the grace of God without acquiring it by our own work. Sin has permanently interrupted this relation; it can and must be restored by penance and contrition.

But what really takes place when we look into the mirror that our father confessors hold up before us in the name of God and take note of all our deeds and misdeeds? The penitential mirror shows us what we could be by doing or not doing specific things. This self-examination might be a first step on the road to betterment according to our own judgment and knowledge and conscience. But is this really self-knowledge? That is the counterquestion of Luther. If in a mirror we were to see ourselves as we really are, we would be frightened![12] If we really wanted to see ourselves thus, it would slay us. If we measured ourselves, and not just our deeds or misdeeds, against God's manifested will, it would destroy us. We would be

---

12. Cf. M. Luther, *Treatise on Good Works* (1520), trans. W. A. Lambert in *Works of Martin Luther* (Philadelphia, 1943), 1:231: "There is no better mirror in which to see your need than simply the Ten Commandments, in which you will find what you lack and what you should seek." This is toned down again in the *Formula of Concord*, Solid Declaration VI: "Third Use of the Law": "For the law is a mirror in which the will of God and what is pleasing to him is correctly portrayed. It is necessary to hold this constantly before believers and continually to urge it upon them with diligence" (*The Book of Concord*, ed. Tappert, p. 564).

taking a "hellish journey of self-knowledge," as Hamann puts it, that would paradoxically annihilate the "self."[13]

The image of the mirror as a metaphor of self-knowledge switches direction when we discover in Christ "a mirror of the fatherly heart" of God (*Great Catechism*, third article, in *The Book of Concord*, ed. Tappert, p. 619). For we now see ourselves as the eyes of God see us. Knowing ourselves in Christ, we see ourselves as we are in the presence of God. The Christ who suffered under the divine action is an "earnest mirror" ("Sermon on the Holy Sufferings of Christ" [1519], *WA*, 2:137.35; ET, *Sermons of Martin Luther*, ed. and trans. John Nicholas Lenker [Grand Rapids, 1988], 2:186). "In this mirror we can see the truth of our human existence, a truth that we do not find in us but over against us, a truth which is our truth and our self-knowledge only by faith in Jesus Christ" (Hans Joachim Iwand, "Die Predigt des Gesetzes" [1934], reprinted in *Glaubensgerechtigkeit. Lutherstudien*, ed. G. Sauter, 2nd ed., TB 64 [Munich, 1991], p. 154). For in Jesus Christ alone can we know God as both our Judge and our Savior.

The truth of God that confronts us distances us from ourselves. Knowing ourselves in God, we are detached from self and its life achievements. This view confronts us with the old life. We no longer live from this life. We live the life of forgiveness received from God. God now sees to our past. It is as though it had never been for us. We realize that we can know ourselves only in terms of the work of God upon us.

Insistence upon the freedom of the will as a center from which to view God and the world is now shown to be a trivial thing. Luther pointed this out in his *On the Bondage of the Will* (1525). It is pure fiction to think that we can do as we please. Naturally we can choose between different possibilities. But if we want to choose what we ourselves *are*, we quickly find out that no choice is possible. Our will is at this point profoundly questionable. The ego has no control over its will at this deep dimension where it is a matter of the totality of our lives. For this reason, the will to do what God wills, to live as God desires, as Paul points out in Romans 7:9-24, is *the* paradigm showing the fallacy that our will is free.

Luther thus describes the crisis of an anthropology that rests on human knowledge of the self. This crisis comes to the fore in pastoral care.

---

13. Johann Georg Hamann, *Kreuzzüge des Philologen* (1762). *Chimärische Einfälle . . .* in *Hamann's Schriften*, vol. 2, ed. Friedrich Roth (Berlin, 1821), p. 198. Hamann goes on to say that "nothing but the hellish journey of self-knowledge prepares the way for deification."

35. Pastoral care can help us expose ourselves to the judgment of God and to accept this judgment.

Humanity is not defined by its constitution or its possibilities. It is defined by an event, the event of justification by faith (*hominem iustificari fide,* Thesis 32 of the *Disputatio de homine* [1536], *WA,* 39/I:176.34-35). Theology can thus deal with human beings as subjects only as they are defined by the act of God (III.3.1).

II.6.4. Surprises in Pastoral Care

Humanity, determined by God's action: such an idea brings about revolutionary upheavals, for a whole world passes away and is replaced by a new one. This was one of the pastoral insights of Johann Christoph Blumhardt (1805-1880).

This insight forced itself upon Blumhardt. By his theological education and his church background — Swabian Pietism of a Lutheran provenance — Blumhardt was well acquainted with the methods of "instructing, punishing, and consoling" that he described as spiritual persuasion or entreaty (*Verteidigungsschrift gegen Herrn Dr. de Valenti,* 1850, *Gesammelte Werke,* vol. I,1: *Der Kampf in Möttlingen. Texte,* ed. Gerhard Schäfer [Göttingen, 1979], pp. 124-299, esp. 178). The sick and those who sought help had to see what they had done wrong. They were then told how to improve their lives, and they were promised the help of God. Blumhardt, however, came to see that these "measures" only made their sufferings worse. They did not get down to the core of what was wrong and kindled resistance that did not prepare the way for healing crises.

In the first dramatic story of sickness and healing that Blumhardt would later expressly record, a first turning took place when Blumhardt told the sick person to call upon Jesus for help (*Krankheitsgeschichte der G[ottliebin] D[ittus] in Möttlingen, mitgeteilt von Pfarrer Blumhardt,* 1850, *Gesammelte Werke,* vol. I,1, pp. 32-78, esp. 40). Later, as the upshot of this account, Blumhardt recognized that this cry for help was at root a proclamation of the kingdom of God: "Jesus is Victor." The cry for help made by impotent individuals is a prayer for the coming of God's kingdom. We do not request this help even in our more pious moods. We will do all that we can to escape the will of God (*Verteidigungsschrift,* pp. 218-19). This process breaks forth like a cancerous sore of spiritual and physical sicknesses and intellectual confusions. The heart of suffering is a desperate search to outwit the course of things, to master at all costs the circumstances of life. But to do so is to cast off more and more of one's own will, for this will wants to live its own life, to be an autonomous will.

Blumhardt came to know sufferers who were no longer in control of their faculties. They were not just suffering from a weakness of will. They were impotent in both mind and soul even to the point of insensibility. In extreme cases they could no longer even respond. They were so entangled and oppressed that they no longer viewed their own situations of need as something alien to them. They could no longer say what they wanted. They could only cry out with a voice that was not their own. They had become the voice for utterances of a completely alien nature, contrary to humanity, contrary to creation. There was no longer any trace of a subjectivity that with strengthening could be restored and reestablished. These sick people were hopelessly alienated. They had become objects. They were capable only of compulsive actions. To the best of his ability Blumhardt sought to diagnose these symptoms and cope with them to some extent. He also suspected deep-seated moral failings, idolatry and superstition. But it gradually dawned on him that the suffering would display its contours only when it was overcome. We would then see that God was at work in it. He was thus compelled to adopt a totally different diagnosis by relating the suffering to the coming of the kingdom of God.

Praying for the help of God — and not just for help in general, for support in mastering life, for a strengthening of personal powers — means learning to pray: "Hallowed be thy name, thy kingdom come, thy will be done on earth as it is in heaven." The prayer for help has to do with the hallowing of God's name, the coming of his kingdom, and the doing of his will. The first three petitions of the Lord's Prayer go together. If we do not do God's will, we break the first commandment and cannot differentiate God from idols. We let that reign over us that we ourselves have produced or allowed. We do not do God's will if it is not pleasing to us. We do not see that the rule of God liberates us as long as we see it only as a limitation of our own powers.

The question of self-knowledge is very acute here. What do those who suffer recognize in their impotence, not those who passively suffer, but those who are bound and tormented? What do they perceive if an assault is made upon the relation of soul and body and their physical nature is grasped and shaken? They do not only need help; they need salvation. What they can and cannot do takes us far beyond the relation between grace and the human will that was debated by Pelagius and Augustine. The grace of God is a redeeming act. It plucks those who risk getting completely lost away from the destructive powers. The self moves on to the new creation. It can no longer be won out of self-knowledge. This self may be discerned in the cry for help which, even though those who pray may not be aware of it, is a cry for salvation, a first sign of the struggle for God's kingdom. It is obvious that in a paradoxical way we are "active" and "at work" here by letting God work. But those who call and pray are now at work, too. They are no longer helpless. For Blumhardt the cry "Jesus is Victor" was the desperate cry of a foe who had already been defeated. This foe was an alien power that had possessed someone who was sick. But the cry signaled its capitulation and was thus a confession of Christ.

36. Pastoral care participates in God's setting up of his kingdom and in Christ's victory over the powers of destruction.

Pastoral counselors can entrust themselves only to the help of God. But do they really know where their trust should lie? In what do they involve themselves when they really stand by those who suffer? At least they cannot fight as God's representatives by taking up the cause of God in their relations with them.

Blumhardt listens to what the sufferers say. It might sound surprising, strange, and even demonic. Because many of the things he heard show the personality of the sufferers to be destroyed and threatened, he addresses a self which can cling only to its Creator and Redeemer. It cannot stand up for itself and can say nothing on its own behalf. In the grip of evil, humans are so obstinately turned in upon themselves that they cannot be made straight. Those who have lost their elasticity can only be broken!

Conversation could no longer avail even on the odd chance that they might gradually come back to themselves. What would be unearthed thereby? Blumhardt never entered upon conversations that would trigger self-release. Nor did he think that the discovery of a "word of absolution" would give speech a healing power. In this sense his pastoral care was far distant from speech therapy. The needs he was confronted with were so immense that he had little time for such conversation. In the first story of healing, he did resolve, after some hesitation, upon a very sober dialogue (Friedrich Zündel, *Johann Christoph Blumhardt. Ein Lebensbild* [Zurich and Heilbronn, 1880], p. 118). Yet the only voice in reply was that of demons! As he saw it, the aim of pastoral care is not simply to heal and purify a subjectivity that has regained control. Pastoral counseling takes place with the hope that the no longer disintegrated and divided individuals belong in their wholeness to God's kingdom. This hope enabled Blumhardt to cast upon God all the needs that confronted him and also his own conflicts concerning them and his fatigue. A dramatic turn was thus given to his counseling. Yet this did not mean that what he did led to a catharsis, a high point, or a turning point that released the unbearable tension. We are not to see in Blumhardt a master of the psychotherapeutic art that cleanses the conflicts of the soul through an explosion of pent-up and oppressed emotions. Instead, Blumhardt called upon God, often crying out to him in the extreme need of involvement in sufferings that he saw to be of cosmic proportions. He gave up praying with sufferers or enforcing prayer upon them. He simply interceded for them.

Redemption frees us from the power of evil. Liberation means deliverance from corruption. By pardoning guilt, God takes us out of the entanglement in which we are caught, and it now becomes clear that an evil will has held sway in those who are tormented, though this was no excuse. A parting of the ways comes with absolution. Luther, in the *Small Catechism,* said that "where there is forgiveness of sins, there are also life and salvation" (CC, 124). But Blumhardt took this to mean something very different from what his church tradition had taught him. Life and salvation are not just imparted when inner burdens are lifted and outward afflictions are relieved. In absolution, after a hard "struggle," the kingdom of God is set up.

This kingdom is set up, and with it there dawns for sufferers the hope and expectation of God's coming kingdom. In this case the eschatology is neither present nor future. It is a consistent eschatology, consistent insofar as the hope that is based on the coming of Jesus Christ depends on God's faithfulness to his promises. Blumhardt links the confession "Jesus is Victor" to the cry "Maranatha — our Lord, come" (1 Cor. 16:22; Rev. 22:20). By so doing, he also links the certainty of the presence of Christ, and the imminent expectation of his coming, to the redemption of creation when the kingdom of God is complete. The victory of Jesus does not end the conflict but creatively continues it. Our gaze is directed to the "totality" when God will be all in all (1 Cor. 15:28).

Asked about the hope of the Holy Spirit, Blumhardt replied that he had never dared to imagine or to fix in himself the manner in which God could give to us what the apostolic period had already had, for he had not arrived at his thoughts of hope seated reflectively behind the lectern. (*Gesammelte Werke von J. Christoph Blumhardt,* vol. 3, ed. Christoph Blumhardt, *Gesammelte Aufsätze,* Teil 1: *Besprechung wichtiger Glaubensfragen* [Karlsruhe, 1888], p. 52). This was not a dig at systematic thinking and no admission of a lack of intellectual consistency but a renouncing of the im-

147

possible venture of thinking up hope even with a systematic combining of biblical quotations. Blumhardt did have his thoughts about hope, because all his experiences in pastoral counseling could only be understood as inescapable expectation of God. He did not develop his theology out of "experience" or assume that dogmatics provided thoughts which then needed to be realized. His thinking was based on what had to be done.

Dogmatics was not for him a construct of thought and language that had then to be translated when it was applied to different situations and contexts of understanding. It was the grammar of faith and hope and love.

Because pastoral care is unthinkable without the prayer "Thy kingdom come," it needs not only the doctrine of grace and justification but also an account for hope if it is to overcome the aporia of self-knowledge.

This account for hope exposes itself to the promises of God which reveal the full helplessness of human suffering. The promises take a different view of this need from that expressed by the sufferers. This is especially true when sufferings arise from the sufferer's inability to control his or her physical or psychological constitution when it seems to be controlled by alien influences. At this point it is not enough to discuss them or to talk about them. When we hear the promises of God, however, then our human answers can go far beyond what we might say to ourselves or to one another. The answers can proclaim the divine victory. They can give us a sense of the extent of this victory if the proclamation tells us who or what is subject to God. In the invocation of God in hopeless need, battles of immeasurable dimensions are to be seen. These make us aware that speaking in faith and love and hope is not closed in upon itself. It is always oriented to the outreach of God's action. Dogmatics guarantees this orientation. It is thus indispensable to pastoral care. For it speaks to those who have come to the end of what they themselves can say, since the unity of their world has been shattered.

II.7. Christian Education

II.7.1. Learning to Believe?

When reading records of my late father from the year 1939, I came up against the question whether the vocation of the pastor would be needed in the future. Or was it even indispensable? Many pastors in the Confessing Church were dealing with this question both then and during the war years. It then became an even more urgent one than during the years of the *Kirchenkampf,* for as the war came to its end, they saw that the church now had to face both unforeseen new tasks and new difficulties. In talking with men of his congregation during the period of mobilization at the beginning of the war, my father had to ask himself whether the time had come when he should prepare both himself and others for the tasks of the pastor to be carried out by especially able and responsible members of the congregation. Was a theological profession really needed to give sermons, to visit the sick, to do pastoral counseling, and even to baptize, to wed, and to bury? Had not many incidents shown that the "office" of the pastor could be replaced?

My father came to the conclusion, however, that "instruction for the children was necessary," and for this purpose alone, maybe, people were needed who could give their full time and energy to this task. If proper instruction was to be given in the Christian faith, a comprehensive education in theology would be demanded, along with a sharpened power of judgment, the greatest care in listening, pedagogical ability, and a full deployment of all one's energies. A vocation of theology was needed for the sake of instruction in the faith.

But why? *Why* is this kind of instruction necessary? One view is that Christian faith is a tradition, and its vitality depends on its successful transmission from person to person. No religion can survive unless it is passed on to succeeding generations, who have to learn it, to understand it, and to live it out. Thorough instruction is needed for the transmission of a religious tradition and for its further development, even though this will often involve growing pains for all concerned, teacher as well as students. Does this approach have a theological basis?

No, for it states in much too general terms that instruction is just the passing on of traditions, and it would be particularly inadequate to restrict the basis of instruction to this, even if it does allow that the transmission is always a critical process. Attention focuses too much on the relation between what developed in the past and its present-day vitality. The passing on of tradition means more than transmitting what has been established and giving insight into how it has been established. It means passing on what is true, standing in the true tradition, not picking out what seems to be the most digestible in the proffered tradition, not adopting specific views of things or simply adhering to a particular lifestyle. But what is true can only be passed on in words if it is known as the truth. Otherwise instruction would be indoctrination.

Phenomenologically, "religious education" can take different forms even if we do not take into account the various theories of education or of the psychology of development. But what form it takes, or what is its inner structure, or its goal or orientation, is revealing in theological terms and has to be unfolded if a true answer is to be given to the question: "Why is instruction necessary?" and we are not to be content with a pragmatic reference to the process of passing on a tradition.

To be noted at this point is a typical distinction between Jewish instruction and Christian instruction. We have to note various similarities and points they have in common, but the point of difference is that the child of a Jewish mother is *born into* the Jewish people (II.4.2). The rite of circumcision stresses this fact. Circumcision is a sign of the covenant of God with his people; the circumcised child is now a mark of God's history with this people, in which he, too, now has a share.

But no one is born into the church, not even into a national church *(Volkskirche)*. Even if persons belong by tradition to the church, they still have to be initiated by baptism. Baptism is a sign of the grace of God. It is a sign that Christians are what they are only by divine grace. They belong to God because he has called them. The grace of God precedes every human possibility of "relating to God." It is not linked to a human readiness to believe any more than to human incapacity or a resistance to belief. Faith is a pure gift. We can only receive it. Grace is imparted in baptism, whether to infants who cannot protest against it — their cries are no true protest — or to adolescents or adults who consciously desire it.

Fundamentally, and from a historical standpoint, *Christian instruction is baptismal instruction*. At first it was preparation for baptism. It "informed" those who were to be baptized — which means much more than merely giving information. It informed theologically because at root it unfolded what takes place in baptism along with its presuppositions and consequences.

Baptismal instruction seeks to make the full compass of the acts of God familiar to us. How, then, can it ever be concluded? Will it come to an end when one stage of knowledge is reached? If the Christian life constantly goes back to its origins *(reditus ad baptismum)*, that means to the confession of guilt in the hope of forgiveness, instruction can only follow the same path to the source of faith, the path which involves no backward step.

The churches differ (though not substantially) with regard to what is to be taught. For instruction is related to how the church manifests itself and what preparation must be made to meet it, to enter it (not just a formal admission), and to belong to it (not just to be a nominal member).

In the Eastern Orthodox churches instruction focuses on making candidates familiar with the liturgy. Training in the liturgy is a constant treading of the path of the church's faith set forth liturgically. And since the whole world is included in the liturgical extolling of God, divine worship shines into everyday life. Everyday life is shown in the liturgy to be transparent to the presence of God.

For Roman Catholics instruction means participation in the faith of the church and sharing in the church's tradition. In Catholic doctrine, tradition is the deposit of the workings of the Holy Spirit, who has guided the church and kept it constantly in the faith. In this sense Blaise Pascal said aphoristically:

> There are three ways to belief: reason, habit [*coutume*], and inspiration. Christianity, which alone has reason, does not admit as its true children those who believe without inspiration. Not that it excludes reason and habit; far from it. But we must open our minds to proofs, confirm ourselves by habit, and offer ourselves humbly to inspiration, which alone can produce a true and salutary result: *Lest the Cross of Christ should be made of none effect* [1 Cor. 1:17]. (*Pensées* [1658-62], fragment 482, ed. Jacques Chevalier [1954]; ET, *The Pensées*, trans. J. M. Cohen [Harmondsworth: Penguin Books, 1961], pp. 165-66)

This might sound traditionalistic, but it reflects exactly that which "coming to faith" means, namely, sharing the faith of the church. It means learning to pray, finding oneself in the biblical stories, and, having been taught by them, asking questions and receiving answers. Pascal's *Mémorial,* his personal confession of faith, which he always wore in his coat next to his heart, bears eloquent testimony to this fact. It speaks of an experience of God which grew out of deadly separation from God and was sustained in the hope of life in God, using among others the words of Ruth when she accepted incorporation into the people of God: "Thy God shall be my God" (Ruth 1:16). And these very personal and biblical statements lead on to the insight: "It is only on the ways taught by the gospel that we can retain God." This confession makes us conscious of the dialectical relation between this kind of confession and what a dominant theology prescribes for the "faithful," namely, in Pascal's day a watered-down doctrine of grace that knows nothing of the profound alienation that Pascal himself experienced. The tradition of the church, when saying why instruction is necessary, does not in any sense equate this instruction with a simple form of instruc-

151

tion, least of all when it pays attention to the inner theological tension of the transmission of faith. Here is the inner grounding of the necessity of instruction in the faith — not just for the teaching institutions as such, but wherever others are to be inducted into this faith, and even though the instruction be "only" informative.

For the Reformers this tension was reason enough why they should view catechesis as a theological task in a new way and with new methods. Along these lines they transcended the usual answer to the question why instruction is necessary, or rather they sharpened and deepened the answer. Behind what they did lay a different understanding of God's action and the work of the Holy Spirit, and therefore of the church, which was for them a creature of the Word, created by the gospel of God's free grace, to which faith owed itself.

Instruction in faith, then, has the task and goal of teaching that "faith" cannot be learned. This paradoxical aim of teaching arose out of the nature of believing, which we can learn to know only as "faith" is articulated, though never completely and once-for-all, but only as we state what "believing" establishes and how "faith" itself is established. All this must be said in a way that is as elementary as possible and as comprehensive as necessary. In this regard instruction in faith resembles the teaching of evangelical theology. It does not have to try to say all that "the church believes," that is, all its binding statements to this day. That is the view of Roman Catholic teaching, and therefore Roman Catholic catechisms are as comprehensive as they can be. The binding doctrine taught by evangelical theology (I.5.1) is not poorer in content than what the magisterium of the Roman Catholic Church has defined over the years, but it always makes it clear what has to be said unconditionally and in all circumstances in faith, hope, and love. Hence what it offers is more a profile of faith and hope than an unbroken exposition of doctrinal decisions. From the very first, evangelical catechisms should not be seen as an educational program, but as true "teaching" in the evangelical sense of the term, namely, as a description of what the Protestant church has committed itself to say, and sees itself as committed to say, when its essence as a church is questioned and it replies by pointing to that which guides it in faith, hope, and love (I.4.1). The compass of such statements might be large or small. Luther's *Small Catechism* puts things briefly and concisely; his *Great Catechism* was arranged in a more extensive manner but was materially no richer. Calvin systematically developed his teaching in the different versions of the *Institutes of the Christian Religion,* which had his catechisms as a basis. In his *Examen Ordinandorum* (1552) Melanchthon linked his catechism very closely to doctrine in an educational way (Hans-Jürgen Fraas, *Katechismustradition. Luthers kleiner Katechismus in Kirche und Schule*, APTh 7 [Göttingen, 1971], p. 76).

37. To be instructed in the faith means to learn that faith cannot be learned. Yet it must be practiced as we learn to formulate all the questions that arise under all circumstances with a reference to the promises of God, and thus to answer them, although not in the sense of giving an answer once and for all.

We thus learn what it means to have fellowship with Christ, who says: "Come to me . . . and learn from me" (Matt. 11:28-29).

Agreement about what God does for the world and humanity leads to the fuller agreement that we call consensus (I.4.3), in which the fellowship of faith finds expression. If each time afresh we are to see the nexus of God's work in the expectations and experiences of faith, then it is pivotal for us to communicate and to share our perceptions.

Learning from faith and in the direction of faith arises out of such joining in, and consensus is the goal. We have here a critical process. It is not at all an instruction seeking harmony. The core of the process consists of the building of theological judgments (I.3). As education, it may to some degree be learned. Dogmatics makes specific experiences possible as faith experiences as it helps to teach how to become experienced in faith. Learning of this kind must pay attention to the faith tradition. It must do this more than adequately. Yet tradition itself always demands investigation when dissent arises. It will prove itself, and show that it is binding, when it helps to achieve a consensus that will allow us to express the truth of faith in new and often unexpected if tentative ways.

In church instruction and religious education the building of theological judgment is the core of the matter, at least when it takes the form of an objective and committed presentation of judgment or an invitation thereto. It takes place with the pausing and continuation of the instruction that has faith as its boundary and that measures, by this boundary, where it is going and into what it can enter, namely, the new creation of God. If judgment is truly formed, it will not block off everyday instruction from faith, nor lessen joy in learning discoveries when we try to speak about faith in the light of the everyday. A "concrete" judgment is one that seeks to be upheld in different situations. It is not a reproduction of theological concepts on the level of illustrative material that passes as real in the immediate situation, even if it is often a reality put together and evoked by association. We can perceive what is to be said in faith, though

153

when what must be said in faith is meant to be illustrative and not just elementary, it must accompany and not replace what we say specifically in faith.

Nevertheless, the building of theological judgment must help to avoid the fallacy of trying to "learn to believe" as though it were a program of conduct or a way of mastering life. "Learning to believe" in this way sounds attractive at a time like our own when many people are seeking firm convictions, unmistakable guidelines, and final certainties about life's decisions. With no religious arrogance, the building of theological judgment must drive out such wishes in order to give people a sharper view of the distinctive assurance of the Christian faith that anchors Christians in the promises of God and not in their devoutness.

As we read in 2 Thessalonians 3:2, such faith is not for everyone. Can learning help everyone, or is it only for those who already believe, or at least think they believe? We cannot answer this question at once. Its limits will be seen only in the process of forming judgments.

II.7.2. Learning to Respond

Though faith cannot be learned, naturally this does not mean to say that we cannot learn anything about "faith," possibly by giving the reason that it is not a structure of thought that we can develop by our own efforts. Friedrich Schleiermacher's definition of "religion" pointed in this direction (*Über die Religion. Reden an die Gebildeten unter ihren Verächtern* [Berlin, 1799]; ET, *On Religion: Speeches to Its Cultured Despisers,* trans. Richard Crouter [Cambridge, U.K. and New York, 1996]). We have to maintain, however, that we can and must learn to move in the language of faith. On this ground cognitive elements are indispensable. A Protestant understanding equates "faith" with acquiring and cultivating knowledge. This learning process needs to be facilitated. Otherwise the admission that we "simply cannot believe" might become an evasion and even lead us to the fancy idea that faith depends on some genetic disposition.

We can speak about faith only as we speak about the acts of God which precede all our unbelief or delusions that faith belongs to us. We can learn as we ask each time afresh concerning the outreach of the divine action in various situations, those of ourselves and those of others. We can learn, for example, to read the biblical stories with the goal of being able to narrate them correctly, taking account of the breaks and the sequences, and making a note of what they do not say where we might have expected information from them. At this point dogmatics can give us help by pointing out how far-reaching is the work of God.

Instruction can help people "come to faith." But it can never rest content by treating faith as a pure gift that is granted to some but not to others, as a gift that falls to our lot. There is, of course, *some* truth in this, yet we must then also say *why* it is the case. And this brings us into the movement of coming to faith and to the steps that we either take or do not take so far as it depends on us. There are indeed some learning steps of faith, though these do not lead step by step to faith, as if to make faith the goal of learning that we can reach at some point and that will then be surpassed by new goals.

In his *Training in Christianity* (1850; ET, trans. Walter Lowie [Princeton, N.J., 1972]), Søren Kierkegaard tracked down the paradox of learning faith to a leap of faith that leaves all securities behind, even the securities of our own acquired knowledge and of the awareness of what we can or cannot do. Faith can only be "indirectly imparted" as we are told what calls us to faith and places us in the history of Jesus Christ. Can we practice this as a basic religious attitude? Does not our training mean to learn to move in the language of faith without ever having it fully at our disposal?

A theology that follows this insight can never adopt a theory of education that counts in any way on our ability to achieve the grace of God, and faith as the divine action upon us, whether by cooperation with God's working, by acceptance of the divine impulsion, or by the development of a disposition. This fundamental problem lay behind the debate between Augustine and Pelagius (II.6.2), and also behind the criticism of the Reformation doctrine of justification by the Council of Trent, which revived penitential discipline as a form of training in the faith, and along with it also revived instruction in the role of the sacraments in the Christian life. In this way Christian perfection was relativized "realistically" and thus became attainable. This problem always recurs when "education" is seen as a "matter of faith" and when we have to believe in lifelong education if we are not to lose our trust in humanity.

"Faith," however, is not a goal of education. Rather, the related goal of learning consists of a distinctive structure of questions. Faith is linked to specific questions and their answers, namely, to those that unfold what "faith says" and that show how wide and far-reaching the statements of faith are. The catechisms of the Reformation age are structured along these lines.

The Heidelberg Catechism (1563) covers the questions that all

Christians must be able to pose when facing questions of life and death. The catechism prepares us to meet these questions, for we can none of us know when and where they will encounter us, or whether we will have time and opportunity then to search out answers for ourselves. It limits itself to questions that have to be answered, as it were, off the cuff. But these are questions that always confront Christians, that they must deal with throughout their lives, and that have answers that will always be with them, in this life and beyond. The questions are formulated in such a way as to lead on to continuous reading of the Bible and to give us training in it. We can thus see how far-reaching is the work of God and in this way become aware of its inner theological context. There is thus a constant interplay of questions dealing with the comfort that we need and the way God's action has met this need, with biblical references to the promises of God.

Luther takes up expressions of faith in his works: prayer, confession, baptism and the Eucharist as participation in Christ's life and death, and joy in the will of God stated in his commandments. Luther's expositions assist in the formation of judgment. If we ignore the question-and-answer schema, which seems outdated today, training is given in the perception of elementary matters. Individuals ought to be able to say in the middle of their everyday affairs: "This is how it is, and nothing different." This way of forming judgment differs essentially from setting up a framework which one can acquire, a model of interpretation and conduct with the help of which we can always anticipate in advance the reality that encounters us. To this extent instruction in the faith prepares us for maturity by teaching us to say specific things in specific ways.

For a check-test we might look at the attempt to transform theology into a cultural institution by religious education. In 1875 Albrecht Ritschl published his *Instruction in the Christian Religion,* which was destined "for use in the graduating class of Protestant high schools and colleges" (*Theology of Albrecht Ritschl,* together with *Instruction in the Christian Religion* by Albrecht Ritschl, trans. Alice Mead Swing [New York, 1901]). As the author emphasized in the preface, it was meant to be instruction in religion and not in theology (not in the American translation).

For Ritschl the transition from systematic theology to instruction in religion was still relatively simple. As he saw it, the didactic problem was the challenge that technical rationality posed to the Christian tradition, as it began to determine the character of school education, especially through the teaching of science. To thought and action controlled by the question of causes and effects, and seeking to control in this way the conditions of life, Ritschl opposed his system of values and goal-directed action. The religious quintessence of this was the kingdom of God as the basis and goal of communal and value-related activity. What we see here is the perspective of an experience of historical meaning that gives coherence to the world. Its aim is to reconcile the Christian tradition with the conditions of modern life by giving prominence to a religious evolution that would counteract technocratic destruction.

"Faith," then, is surreptitiously changed into a goal of education which demands an attitude of mere receptivity. Ritschl wanted to apply the Reformation doctrine of justification by liberating faith from all the activity of works. Faith cannot be "learned," for it is opposed to every effort of our own. But we need to train this distinction, and for this reason instruction in the Christian religion is indispensable. For the Christian life means adopting a different standpoint from that of our contemporaries, who are trying to master its reality. God and his kingdom have no place in their world. The place of God is the kingdom of values that are worth living for and dying for. Theological terms express this new outlook, and thus they can and should be learned, for they semantically confirm faith as a basic approach.

Ritschl, then, reinterpreted theology from a theory of action. In so doing, he demonstrated the social character of Christianity and helped to solve the problem posed by the existence of the church in the world. The result, however, was to foreshorten and flatten theology with unforeseeable ramifications for religious instruction. For if theology is changed into a kind of adult education, as it has nowadays become under the influence of Paul Tillich, then it might perhaps for some time share in the general interest in education that deals with the world of values and the question of meaning, but it will have lost in the process that which makes it "instruction in faith."

Why should we be taught? To what end? Because teaching (or doctrine) is a necessary part of the Christian faith, the kind of teaching that is irrevocably dependent on free consent and for this reason opens up the learning process, a learning that leads to various forms of knowledge. This is the heart of the instruction in faith offered by Protestant theology, the *doctrina evangelii* of CA VII (I.4.3). Teaching is meant to protect the call to faith against misunderstanding and misuse. It thus serves to protect the freedom of this call insofar as this is a matter of human responsibility. Teaching should not seek to give rise to conviction. By what it says, and how it says it, it tells people that they are able to come to faith only because God calls them and brings them together, so that they will receive

157

their future in fellowship with him. The teaching of faith sketches out the area in which we can know the details of this promise and demand. To be able to move in this area, we must know its limits and also what is specific. We can say this objectively and with no converting zeal, which is a real hindrance to instruction and might make it impossible.

II.8. Church Leadership

"Leadership" is a noun of action denoting guidance of or giving direction to the church. We misunderstand it when we relate it to a group of leaders. "Theology" and "church leadership" are not two opposing institutions. We must ask instead — we differ at this point from Roman Catholics and the Eastern Orthodox — where, and in what form, we encounter church leadership. The Barmen Declaration has taught the German Protestant Church that even in matters of administration, leadership is possible only when a genuine theological responsibility is present, which is rooted in the realization which leads to confession and is thus no less than a binding church doctrine carried out. Thus the Barmen Declaration is church leadership and simultaneously expounds a Protestant understanding of church leadership.

Thesis IV of the Barmen Declaration tells us that "the various offices in the church establish no rule of one over the other but the exercise of the service entrusted and commanded to the whole congregation (CC, 521)."

What does this mean?

II.8.1. Church Leadership as Theology

We will glance first at the biblical text which forms the grounding of the thesis:

> You know that the rulers of the Gentiles lord it over them, and their great ones are tyrants over them. It will not be so among you; but whoever wishes to be great among you must be your servant. (Matt. 20:25-26)

If we view these two verses in isolation, they might seem to be contrasting "force" and "service." But then the issue of influence and domination would still be decisive. A different and even opposing practice could be compared to that of secular governments. The wish, however, would still be the same, the well-intentioned wish of subtly achieving power.

But let us consider the context of these verses. Then the ground will be quickly cut from under such an interpretation. Immediately before them Jesus had been announcing his passion, his being delivered up to the Gentiles, and his resurrection. The mother of two of his disciples then asks that her sons might have a special function when the messianic kingdom is established. To this request Jesus replies that she does not know what she is asking for, and in this way he brings to light her misunderstanding. When the two sons are ready to participate in Jesus' cup of suffering, which will, they think, enable them to enjoy to the full his triumph, Jesus rejects this perspective, because sharing judicial power in God's kingdom does not lie in his hands. He indicates in this way that the rule of God differs quite radically from what his disciples expect of him. It is not by any means a secular rule which uses power to enforce order upon people to their own good. "It will not be so among you," says Jesus. He sets his own ministry in opposition to this type of rule. In so doing he shows that he himself incorporates what service in the kingdom of God involves: "The Son of Man came not to be served but to serve, and to give his life a ransom for many," that is, for all (v. 28).

At root it is not really a matter of "serving" *or* "ruling." Humanity has to be saved by the redeeming act of Jesus. This redemptive ministry is not a final and desperate effort to bring peace to the world by an unusual means, that is, by powerlessness. No, it is the giving up of the life of Jesus in subjection to the will of God. This is what brings fully to light the misunderstanding of the mother and her two sons. It is made clear that force cannot restore order to our human world. We have to be redeemed. And this redemption will not be achieved either by militant suffering or active resistance. It will be victoriously accomplished only when God's will is done on our behalf.

Only in this light can we understand what can be meant by "ministry" in the church. The password "ministry" is by itself so ambiguous that the community of Jesus Christ cannot be adequately distinguished from orders of government and structures of subjection that prevent the church from truly being and becoming the church. The Prussian king Frederick the Great, as is well known, called himself the first minister *(Diener)* of his state. What he meant was that he was committed to the state and to the laws which he had given it. He was so committed that appeals for justice should not finally be made to him as governor. The laws themselves were the final court of appeal. The rulers and sovereigns of today's world have long since become accustomed to calling themselves "ministers" — at least as ministers of a higher aim — so that the term "ministry" is no challenge to secular government, whether in great things or small, whether in an ideological sense or a constitutional sense. On the other hand, "ministry" knows superior and inferior orders. The former can relatively rule over the latter. It involves a sharing of authority and a regulation of responsibilities. When we speak of "ministry" — and this takes place emphatically and almost too readily in the church itself — it is not at all clear whether this gives an essential expression of the form the church should take.

The ministry of Jesus Christ to which Thesis IV of Barmen refers is, of course, incomparable. None of us can repeat or imitate the self-sacrifice of Jesus in any way. Our task is *to bear witness* to the unique ministry of Jesus Christ, to proclaim the free grace of God not only by word but by action growing out of the sacrifice of Jesus. The ministry of redemption is not entrusted to us, for we ourselves need the redeeming work of God that has found a place in our world through Jesus Christ. But insofar as we are the "body of Christ" (cf. Barmen III, quoting Eph. 4:15-16), our existence in the church and as the church is a constituent part of the ministry that finds embodiment in Jesus Christ. In the light of Thesis IV of Barmen, the metaphor "body of Christ" is much more than a similitude. What it depicts is the *embodied* presence of Jesus Christ, his *being there for others* in his death, in his acceptance of the will of God, and in his entrance into fellowship with God.

Being there for others! Is not this the key to what we can rightly call "order in the church"? "Order" here does not mean primarily that some are superior and some inferior. It points to *coordination*. We are dependent on one another. We need one another. This reciprocity must find expression in order. It calls for regulation. Yet the decisive thing is that coordination must be recognized even in obscure and difficult cases. It must never be ignored. At first we do not need spheres of competence and the orders based on them. Our first and primary need is for regular interplay and interaction in meeting different needs. Christians can be there for others only if they are there for themselves. In 1 Corinthians 12 and 14 Paul explains that the charisms, the different gifts of grace, are there to minister to the Christian community. He takes it for granted that all Christians will serve, for all have received specific gifts. The individual gift is always dependent on the gifts of others. It complements all the other gifts. Hence all the ministries work together to serve the "common good," the upbuilding of the church of Jesus Christ. Within this "structured ministry" there are, of course, different levels, superior and inferior functions.

But the normal evaluation of gifts does not apply. Ecstatic utterances, for example, need interpretation in order to become intelligible for others. For the utterers rise to the highest peak imaginable for human language, nearly entering God's new world with no regard for the understanding of others. Only then can they say what they are supposed to say. For this reason the prophet, who intelligently articulates the presence of God for others, is rated more highly than the ecstatic. Nevertheless, there is no real ranking. Nor does the multiplicity of gifts of grace imply a division of tasks. According to 1 Corinthians 14:33, the decisive point for Paul is that there be no disorder. God is not a God of disorder. But he is also not a God of order, for what we read in Paul is that he is a God of peace. Peace among us is a testimony to the saving unity that God has created, the subjecting of all that we do to the lordship of Christ. "Order in the church" can only bear witness to this peace. It points to it. It expresses it in such a way that nothing that we say or do will resist or contradict it.

In this derived and relative sense we can speak of "church order."

38. Order in the church rests on the fact that Christians must always be ready to let the decisive thing be said to them, and to hear it also from others, who thereby become their brothers and sisters.

Order in the church contradicts the supposedly pious view that when brotherhood and sisterhood are fully achieved no one needs to say anything to others because they all know what to do already and at best can only give expression to an existing agreement. This is sometimes how the much discussed "priesthood of all believers" is understood, namely, as an egalitarian association of all congenial and like-minded people who only share with one another what is on the hearts of all of them.

First Peter 2:9, however, tells us unmistakably that the priesthood of all believers refers to the people of God that is set apart for the service of God, that is God's own possession, and that is subject to his lordship alone. God deals directly with each individual so that, like the priests of the old covenant, they all stand before him and need no intermediaries. This is exactly what the "priesthood of all believers" means, namely, a common standing before God in rendering him service. So "immediacy to God" does not mean self-sufficiency. We are brothers and sisters because Jesus Christ *became* our Brother. When he is present, we *become* brothers and sisters to one another. Brotherhood and sisterhood, therefore, are grounded in the imparting of the free grace of God and are a sign of reconciliation.

The church is a fellowship that ministers the reconciliation of the world with God. As we try to make its profile plain, we must also think of political ideas of government. The Barmen Declaration rejected the principle of the leader *(Führerprinzip)* of National Socialism. It did not reject leadership as such. It rejected a specific style of leadership, namely, leaders who were equipped with all the powers of government but did not engage in a ministry of reconciliation. What they had in view was an authoritarian exercise of moral and spiritual power, an autonomous imposition of law. In no circumstances can this ever come into question in the church. Nor should church movements from below decide on what is binding for faith; questions of truth cannot be settled by plebiscite. In contrast to both these errors, the church of Jesus Christ views itself as a fellowship which is not self-constituted, which cannot tell itself what it must communicate, and which cannot be told this by anyone either inside or outside the church. The church is called upon to engage in the ministry of reconciliation under the lordship of Jesus Christ. It must plead with people: "Be reconciled to God!" (2 Cor. 5:20). (Cf. Heinrich Vogel, "Wer regiert die Kirche? Über Amt, Ordnung, Regiment der Kirche," TEH 15 [Munich, 1934], reprinted 1980; Hans Asmussen, "Theologie und Kirchenleitung," TEH 31 [Munich, 1935], reprinted 1980.)

The third thesis of the Barmen Declaration explains this truth after first recalling Ephesians 4:15-16: "But speaking the truth in love, we must grow up in every way into him who is the head, into Christ, from whom the whole body [is] joined and knitted together."

The church is the community of those who have experienced the justification of the godless, and therefore it cannot shape its "order" according to its own desires nor adjust itself to prevailing political concepts of order (cf. the statement in the anathema). For:

> The Christian church is the community of the brethren, in which Jesus Christ presently works in the word and sacraments through the Holy Spirit. With her faith as well as her obedience, with her message as well as her ordinances, she has to witness in the midst of the world of sin as the church of forgiven sinners that she is his alone, that she lives and wishes to live only by his comfort and his counsel in expectation of his appearance. (CC, 520-21)

Does the constitution of the church resemble the structure of a democratic state? This point was considered not only after the Third Reich ended but already during the *Kirchenkampf*, especially since church and theology seemed to be so dangerously apathetic to the attempt to establish democracy under the Weimar Republic. The principle of a division of powers (legislative, executive, and independent judicial) relates the different forms of politically necessary action in a way that forces them to cooperate with one another, and thus excludes both authoritarianism and rule by plebiscite. Can we apply this kind of model to the church?

Hermann Diem, in a work planned while he was still a prisoner of war, did not think so. He stated ironically that "in our democratic church constitutions the synod would play the role of parliament as the legislative branch, church leadership would exercise government as the executive branch, and an independent disciplinary court would see to the formal upholding of the law as the judicial branch" (*Restauration oder Neuanfang in der Evangelischen Kirche?* [Stuttgart, 1946], pp. 96-97). But a church disciplinary procedure cannot be contented with a mere calling up of theological formulae. It must inquire into the articulated truth of the faith. The question of truth is the cardinal question for church law and church order, for it links the existence of the church to the promise and direction of God. Instead of the political division of powers, we find in the church the working together of the Bible, the community, and theological consensus.

II.8.2. Building Consensus

Without community, consensus would be a mere phantom. Without the Bible the community would be a spontaneous association of congenial and like-minded people. Without confirmed and developing consensus, the Bible would be a museum piece. If consensus is lacking, we could all read the Bible as we saw fit. We need the witness of our brothers and sisters if we are not to identify our own perspective with real knowledge. It is for this reason that consensus arises in the church.

39. Consensus, as agreement in the faith, is an expression of church leadership.

It realizes church leadership on various levels and in different fields of the work of the church and in specific situations and questions which the church faces.

Building consensus is needed when dissent arises, not always and in all circumstances but when conflict comes, or has to come, for the sake of faith, hope, and love. Conflict is a first and essential step in church leadership. Where there is indifference, resting on false agreement, consciences must be aroused, vital differences have to be recognized, various possible paths have to be noted, even though there is apparently no way forward. There is a road to consensus. Steps are needed in this direction. We must move on to the various stations indicated by the promises of God. Consensus always leads the church past the status quo. It is a step into the unknown. It brings us into line with the work of God which is the basis of all human agreement in faith and hope. This agreement lifts us out of ourselves and brings us together as we meet in something far greater than our own presuppositions, motivations, and resources. For this reason church consensus always poses a demand upon all participants, a demand in a positive sense, for it summons us out of what is customary for us and into the truth, which releases us from imprisonment in the personal and unites us in a reality in which we gain a fresh view of ourselves. The demand of truth, and its vigor, does not merely help us to endure the bright and often painful light of the truth. It also helps us to live in the truth and to do what is in accordance with the truth. In acts of this kind consensus reaches its goal. No common action can succeed unless it is referred to God and confesses God.

Church consensus is always a forward step even though it might not be regarded as progress in the usual sense. Dissent arises over the very question of what "progress" means for church and theology, and this presents a task of church leadership. If I see the existing situation of the church correctly, it is marked by increasing polarization. Ecclesiastically as well as politically our attention focuses on the right wing and the left wing and the battles between them. These are the alternatives which we then soon regard as decisions of faith. In the church, as in society, there is no place for a firm and reconciling center. By this center I do not have in view the silent majority of which we hear so much. No, I am thinking of Christians and citizens who do not see themselves as facing the alternatives of conservation or change, but even though tensions arise, try to do what is needed to keep things going. This is a vital problem, and as I see it, a problem of survival for our political culture.

Much more seriously the church faces an increasing radicalization, at least in its preliminary stages, as decisive questions are terribly simplified into choices. We have been brought up in such a way that our orientation is to antitheses like belief and unbelief, hope and despair, salvation and perdition, and an underlying God and false god. In Germany the either-or took a sharper turn that resulted from the *Kirchenkampf*, which taught us not to trust in any both-and, and any hyphenated Christianity. No text of the Bible is more frequently adduced in support of this view than the criticism of the church at Laodicea that was neither hot nor cold but only lukewarm, and that would thus be spewed out of the mouth of God (Rev. 3:16). Often believers miss the real point here. They construe heat as the passionate commitment that God is seeking and that will reach a boiling point that will change humanity and the world. A cold tenacity would thus fall victim to the divine No, no less than a lukewarm indecisiveness.

The Christian community, like the civil, is well (or badly) hooked on alternatives. Public opinion shapes us this way. The press, the radio, and television teach us to think only in alternatives. It is easy enough to discern both light and darkness. But what does the habit of seeing black and white do to our sensitivity to ordinary facts, to everyday life and its decisions, and to truth and falsehood, which we can often discern only in intermediate shades?

What has all this got to do with theology and church leadership, or with church leadership as theology? A primary point is that too long an exposure to this exaggeration threatens to ruin our sensitivity when theological decisions have to be made. We no longer see sensitive questions because they are covered over by antithetical forms of action or by political commitments. A first and decisive act of church leadership is to give us a better insight, to enable us to see what we must contend for when it is a matter of faith and hope and love.

Church leadership must undertake the painful and most unrewarding task of bringing to light true theological reasonings and counterreasonings, and distinguishing them from the many other motives that guide our actions, even from the vocational sicknesses of theologians who try to present and profile themselves as those who offer comments from a lofty moral watchtower when they will not accept the burden of real responsibility. To be able to make such distinctions, a developed theological judgment is needed that can only rarely be replaced by intuitive insight. Theology and church leadership directly intertwine at this point. Certainly faith is not dependent upon theology. Nevertheless, the formulation of questions of faith demands an exploration of theological grounding and a knowledge of past and present history if abysses are to be avoided. For this reason taking responsibility for examinations in theology is one of the tasks that is indispensable to church leadership.

We can recognize a sufficient theological grounding by the fact that it is shared by all concerned, though this does not mean that they are a common good! In other words, if theological arguments really direct our attention to God, then they support the promise that with their help we can reach the free and unforced agreement that will give us the courage to move ahead into God's future. The mist of mere hypotheses will then be dispelled, and we will be able to glance freely at the coming of God. Here is the unifying power of church consensus. We do not invent or establish but *discover* together what we can now do as a body together. When consensus is discovered, the moment is always one of surprise and astonishment. This is always the case when we see that we cannot just repeat what is familiar but can simply say: That is the way it is and not otherwise.

Theological consensus is hardly attained when some people press on ahead and try to get as many of the others as possible to stand behind them and shape up to their ideas. Nor can it be reached when believers simply repeat at length traditional statements until no one can come up with anything new. Nor can we reach consensus by sharing every conceivable standpoint. Rather, in Romans 15:1-6 Paul tells us that consensus comes by the reconciling of the strong and the weak. Believers have to be *for* one another in what is a ministry of reconciliation. Some members of the congregation feel that they are so independent and so immediately in touch with God that they show little concern for the anxieties of others even though these anxieties trigger a need for protection by causing them to cling timidly to whatever spares them from the dangers of unusual experiences. The weakness depicted here is not psychological weakness that can gradually be overcome by exerting spiritual strength — for example, by training in ways of thinking and acting more freely. It is weakness in the threatened and threatening state of the world in which all of us live, both weak and strong. Compromises between the strong and the weak cannot cope with it. It is not enough to bring the two into line. This can only produce the half-strong who are also half-weak. Yet the strong are always in danger of simply displaying their own freedom, their independence of extraneous considerations and precautions. They do not share their freedom with the weak. They are in danger of leaping too far ahead when only small steps are possible. For this reason they need the weak who, voluntarily or involuntarily, are still chained too much to this world. By means of perceiving and respecting one another, both the weak and the strong might then become sober in their hope and audacious in their expectations.

This is a touchstone of true church leadership. But a distinction must be made. When different positions are integrated and room can be left for divergences without undermining the whole, this is without doubt a social achievement of great value. But it does not represent real church leadership. I will speak briefly about the distinction.

The best thing that can happen in this situation was formulated more than 190 years ago by Friedrich Schleiermacher when he advanced the thesis that the goal of theology is church leadership (*Kurze Darstellung des theologischen Studiums*... [1811], ed. Heinrich Scholz [Leipzig, 1910; 5th ed., Darmstadt, 1982], §§3-5, ET, *Brief Outline of the Theological Study*, trans. Terrence N. Tice [Richmond, 1966], §§3-5). What Schleiermacher meant by church leadership was a conjunction of different forms of piety within the Christian community, so that all the notes would be sounded forth. Schleiermacher was an enthusiastic chorister who probably had polyphonic harmony in mind. He said that in the church there is always tension. Two forces pull in different directions. There are the defenders of tradition who want continuity. There are those who look ahead, who move out to the limits of what faith can do, and even cross these limits, venturing out into new fields of religious experience. For Schleiermacher church leadership was embodied in the "princes of the church" (§9). These should not simply bring those forces into line or even restrict themselves to watching over their coexistence. This seems to be the desire of church administrations today, as may be seen at synods and conferences. No, what Schleiermacher wants is to keep the church alive, and this will be possible only if an equilibrium is reached between those who lag behind and those who forge on ahead. Those who forge on ahead must accept responsibility for the identity of the church and therefore have regard for historical continuity, while those who cling to tradition must still look ahead to the church's consummation.

Schleiermacher is the best theoretician of pragmatic church leadership. He is unexcelled in describing what goes on in the church's history when Christian groups answer the challenge of their day but do not lose themselves to it in consequence. But this is predominantly a sociological view. The church directs itself by adopting everything that will enhance its own vitality and sooner or later discards what will threaten its ability to survive (I.1.1).

II.8.3. Freedom for the Free Grace of God

A theological definition of church leadership must take another essential step, and this step will lead it into sociologically uncharted territory. What church leadership means is that it should cause all the church's actions, all the expressions of its life, to become ministry to the "message of the free grace of God." Thesis VI of the Barmen Declaration puts this well: "The Church's commission, upon which its freedom is founded, consists in delivering the message of the free grace of God to all people in Christ's stead, and therefore in the ministry of his own Word and work through sermon and sacrament." The primary task of church leadership is to make this proclamation as far as is humanly possible.

Schleiermacher was motivated by the question of how the church is to keep in step with the history in which it lives. Significant answers had to be given. But is this really one of our most important concerns? Is it not one of the things that, according to the words of the Gospel, will be added to us if we seek first the kingdom of God and the righteousness of God (Matt. 6:33)? To seek God's kingdom means giving God space to will and do what he wishes, that is, not to get in his way. If we give space to the will of God, we will have no reason to stage for ourselves what we think that will ought to be. Instead, we shall ask ourselves what does not resist God instead of seeking what "corresponds" to his action. Just as important as the question of what church leadership should be doing is the question of what it should not be doing for the sake of God, of what it should leave undone so as not to get in the way of faith, and let false expectations extinguish hope, and kill love by frenzied overactivity.

Church leadership gives us liberty for worship, for common calling upon God and expecting him. Church leadership faces a decisive situation, however, as regards proclamation. Do we not have a real crisis when people come from Sunday worship depressed because they feel hopelessly overburdened by moral demands and pious ideals? It is not the drowsy and indifferent who are finally scared away when the fate of the whole world is laid upon their hearts, not just commended to their hearts! Those who are oppressed today by sermons and church pronouncements and church actions and even prayers are often the wide-awake, the too wide-awake, who perhaps take what is said much too seriously because it is pitched in exaggerated terms. What is demanded by the consensus of faith and hope and love is quite different: Consciences that are under assault are comforted and encouraged.

Church leadership is displayed in a common confession, a common hearing, and a common obeying. Authority and freedom meet at this point, and a ministry of reconciliation is executed. Here is church order in every field. Achieving this order is the task of "church leadership."

II.9. Mission

II.9.1. Mission or the Expansion of Christendom?

The Christian churches did not always and everywhere engage in "mission" by sending out missionaries to foreign lands. Martin Luther equated mission with the reformation of the church. The church, he thought, must be open and ready to *send out the Word of God into the world*. Only thus will its origin and constitution be manifested. The world was for Luther, however, the place in which the church was put. It was a sphere full of change. It was overrun by the slogans of contemporaries. Many of these claimed to be sent by God and wished either to reconstruct this world or to introduce a new and true world. For Luther the world was not the "great wide world," or the "new world" that had then been discovered and for which people had different expectations from those that the church derived from its origin by the Word and Spirit of God. The Reformers were not concerned about the expansion of the church. Its inner health was their concern.

The sixteenth-century Roman Catholics seemed to have introduced the equation of "mission" and "sending." This usage went hand in hand with the policies of Spanish and Portuguese expansion — a fatal legacy. For the most part it was only gradually that mission came to be seen as Christian expansion. The "Christianization of the world" is a program of modern Christianity in the West. The accompanying cultural imperialism and colonial ramifications are so much in the forefront today that little heed is paid to the understanding of mission as preaching the kingdom of God up to the end of the world and building a new church by evangelism. How theologically questionable this is is also only rarely considered today. Usually the "end of the world" was taken in a spatial and temporal sense, and it was thought that world mission would bring with it the end of history as we know it. But this is only one chapter in the history of Christian mission, even if it is a highly significant one.

The churches in Asia tell the story differently. There the problematic factors that typify the being of the church have come to light more clearly across the centuries. These include the importance attached to doctrine, church divisions through doctrinal controversies, the way church unity is constituted, the relation with changing state forms, the inner threats through close contacts with peoples and social groups, and the dissolution of congregations by cutting off these relative relationships. In general, tension arises between a strange and incredible message and the people to whom it promises a life that will open them up in unheard-of fashion, calling them out of their present existence and into a new one (Samuel Hugh Moffett, *A History of Christianity in Asia*, vol. 1: *Beginnings to 1500* [San Francisco, 1992]).

Thus far Protestants do not have a theology of mission worth mentioning. We do have evangelical and fundamentalist theologies. These focus upon winning the "world" for Christ, upon the saving will of God, and upon redemption from alienation and sin. They have little to say about the church as a fellowship of justified sinners exposed to divine judgment. Do theology and church still inquire into the inner bases of mission as something the church should do? This silence conceals serious uncertainties regarding Christology. What, after all, is the answer to the question: "Who is Christ and what is the relation between humanity and his history?" How does the church understand itself in its relation to "others," to other religions, to other ways of believing and thinking?

The "missionary command" of Jesus Christ first points to the presence of Jesus Christ with those he sends forth, his government of them and of all they meet, as we certainly read in Matthew 28:18-20:

> All authority in heaven and on earth has been given to me. Go therefore and make disciples of all nations, baptizing them in the name of the Father and the Son and the Holy Spirit, and teaching them to obey everything that I have commanded you. And remember, I am with you always, to the end of the age.

Only secondly does this command direct our attention to the relation of the disciples to all others, but this attention could give rise to erroneous conceptions, to a rapid expansion of the body of disciples, to a concept of a gradual expansion of Christianity, to a fusion of many peoples into the church. On such views the church is betrayed into doubts about itself if expansion declines.

Although not at all times and in all places, nevertheless time and again Christianity has found the missionary command to be an adequate reason to do missionary work. But has there always been a clear understanding of the inner basis of this work? Matthew 28:18-20, we recall, speaks of the enthronement of Christ and its ramifications. People are to be baptized, called to be his disciples, and given a share in his history. Why is this? Because Jesus Christ has been elevated to be the ruler of the whole world. His dominion takes shape in baptism. Baptism signifies the prevenient action of God. Individuals receive this in full freedom; their act of receiving is the first act of the freedom they are given. There is an obvious contrast between this form of lordship and all other views of lordship and of the ways of executing it! The unique and incomparable power of Christ does not force subjugation. Baptism neither can nor may be an instrument of subjugation. Jesus Christ holds true to his promise that always and everywhere he will be present with those who bring his dominion to others, who bear witness to it by first subjecting themselves to it and showing that they participate in it.

Christ will be with his people to the "end of this age," that is, always and everwhere. But what is the relation between this temporal promise and the spatial world? Does Christ's rule need spatial expansion? Will it be achieved only when his messengers reach the far corners of the earth and deliver their message, so that no one can claim anymore that he or she has never heard?

Other motivations can be linked to the missionary command, not only the lesser motivations that have insinuated themselves into it. They are motivations which are suggested by the words "all" and "end of the world" on the lips of Jesus. How are we to construe these words?

A first motivation may derive from a sense of mission. Mission in this sense inevitably suggests expansion. A common phrase is that what does not expand withers. People of conviction are convinced that things they regard as essential must not be kept to themselves. What they have found to be true will be true for others as well; otherwise it would not be really convincing. But we cannot reduce faith to mere conviction. If we do, the communication of faith will wither away and those to whom it should be communicated will be misused as an audience which is to be won over to the speaker's conviction.

A second motivation rests on the *universal claim of the message to be proclaimed.* "All power is given to me," said Jesus, "and therefore go to all peoples." Does not this obviously suggest that Jesus Christ will become Lord only when all are subjected to him, or when they have at least heard of his lordship? This conclusion has indeed been a motive force for much missionary endeavor, and it finds added strength in the fact that God has made Jesus Christ Lord over all people and all things in virtue of his unrivaled deity. He is the one true God. He alone is God.

But a similar thought gives relentless missionary energy to Islam as well. The worship and the embedded law set up by the prophet will overwhelm the whole earth. It should be noted, however, that no mission was derived from Judaism's confession of the uniqueness of God. The expectation of the Jews is that the peoples will make the pilgrimage to Zion (Isa. 2:2-4; Mic. 4:1-5). Tragically, the Jews were then expelled for centuries from their holy places and scattered among the nations. The hope of Christians is not directed to any holy place, nor does its fulfillment depend on a worldwide expansion, though a motivation of this kind appears in Paul and gave wings to many missionary efforts, especially in the eighteenth, nineteenth, and early twentieth centuries. We need to distinguish carefully between what is primary here and what is secondary. If the coming of God's kingdom is linked to the expansion of the church, the idea might creep in that the church must bring God into the world, or at least make it plausible to the world that God is its supreme Lord, so that he may truly be "all in all" (1 Cor. 15:28).

Today many churches have lost their readiness for mission or transformed it into a vague readiness for dialogue with new forms of Christianity or with other religions. But this is the other side of the same coin. The need to expand the church has given way to anxiety to ensure its standing. The church must concentrate all its forces here lest this standing be lost. In these churches the desire to expand Christendom seems to have been lost altogether or to flicker on uncertainly only as wishful thinking. Mission is abandoned, for every "outward" push seems to involve the danger of "inward" losses.

Both these motivations are thus ambivalent, and neither of them tells us what the grounding of mission is.

Theologically the grounding for mission is not to be found in the need to communicate religiously. Hence the complications of communicating with others do not constitute a boundary for it. "I believe and therefore will I speak" (Ps. 116:10, quoted in 2 Cor. 4:13). This does not mean that a "believer" wants to express himself. The statement is much rather a counter to the anguish in the face of which one is left speechless. This anguish is indeed a plight, insofar as it enters a relationship to the acts of God and his promise. It shows that our situation is one of need as we come to stand in relationship to the acts and promises of God. "Those who believe can speak about it, making it plain both before God and before others." Pain, temptation, hostility — to all these we may refer when confessing the risen Christ. We can do so without inhibition. This does not mean, of course, that we transform what is inward for us into something outward. We must not do this. That would be a psychological phenomenon and one of communication.

The inner grounding of mission finds clearest expression in 2 Corinthians 5:18-21:

All this is from God, who reconciled *us* to himself *through Christ*, and has given us the ministry of reconciliation; that is, *in Christ* God was reconciling the world to himself, not counting *their* trespasses *against them*, and entrusting the message of reconciliation to *us*. So *we* are ambassadors for Christ, since God is making his appeal *through us*; we entreat *you* on behalf of Christ, be reconciled to God. *For our sake* he made *him* to be sin who knew no sin, so that *in him we* might become the righteousness of God.

40. Christian mission takes place when, without restriction or limitation, we beseech people to be reconciled with God (2 Cor. 5:20), to let the reconciliation with the world that God has made in Jesus Christ occur for them, to expose themselves to this reconciliation.

How is mission given reasons for? God reconciled the world to himself in Christ. For this reason we are ambassadors for Christ. We beseech and implore people to be reconciled with God. Only because the human world is reconciled with God *"in Christ"* can "Christians" then turn to all others. They can and must tell them that Christ is there for them. Mission can only take the form of this beseeching. Drawing attention to what has happened, it is an imploring that does not force it upon people but bears witness to it. This means for Christians that Christ encounters them in others. Christians do not bring Christ into the world. But they are in the world not to get in the way of Christ. In what they say and do they must leave room for Christ. Jesus Christ died for all. He is therefore the hope of all. We must cling to this fact, the fact that defines our relation to all "others."

Becoming reconciled and being reconciled form the sphere, the force field, into which both those that beseech and those that are besought are called. They are directed to one another by the word of reconciliation, by God's act in the Word. They are set in motion together; that is why we emphasized the pronouns when quoting 2 Cor. 5:18-21.

Here, then, the inner grounding of mission is broadened. Therefore the message of reconciliation is the counterpoise to the sending out of the disciples in Matt. 28:18-20. It characterizes its task in which the disciples are involved. It prevents us from restricting our gaze to the relation between the church and the world. The messengers are subjected to the fact that their mission is one of beseeching. Only in this light can we properly understand the power and the lordship of Christ.

We should not speak of "winning individuals *for Christ,*" since their lives have already been won *by* Christ. All people are present before God "in Christ" (cf. Rom. 5:6-19). Those who beseech others can and must do so on the basis of the fact that Christ is there for them. They must not only recognize this but state it.

The "motif of sending" is a broken one. Jesus Christ was sent by the Father, but he fulfilled this mission by the death he died for all. By this death they all have become different before God from what they once

173

were. What can those who are sent add to this? They do not help God by pushing him into the world or extending his dominion over the world.

Mission derives from the sending of the Word (Isa. 55:11), the sending of the Son (John 3:17; etc.), and the sending of the Spirit who glorifies Christ. The Spirit does not speak of himself but proclaims things heard and things to come (John 16:7b-11, 13-14). Here is the trinitarian drive of mission. The Spirit who is sent does not speak of himself. He proclaims what has been heard (John 16). He causes it to be heard again and seen again (John 15:26). It is only in this way that Jesus sends out his disciples (John 17:18; 20:21). Barth sees in this sending a possible basis of a theology of mission in the doctrine of reconciliation (*Church Dogmatics* IV/3, §72, pp. 681-901).

Christ, in whom God has acted for us, beseeches us to be reconciled with God *(passivum divinum)* and brought into God's action. This action restores a completely broken relationship (a "new creation"). It does not simply repair one that has been disrupted. In consequence broken and even destroyed human relationships are not just glued together again but are newly established.

Those who beseech others expose themselves. They have to communicate unheard-of things, things they could never enforce upon others nor impart by mere persuasion. God's work of reconciliation does not impose demands. The beseeching makes us helpless against those who are besought and their reaction. We become vulnerable. The beseeching cannot force reconciliation. It simply points those who hear it to God. Why should they not let this happen to them?

We have to take seriously the answer to this request even though it be a strong and even violent rejection. If we do not do this, we violate the integrity of those to whom we put the request. They are then told that they are part of the world that has been reconciled with God even though they are not yet aware of the fact. But if, in so doing, we draw conclusions as to God's action from the reaction of humans to the message of reconciliation, then a fatal theory is deduced, the doctrine of twofold election (predestination), which seeks to overcome the fact that not all people believe by pointing to the decree of God to condemn such people instead of saving them. Believers, on the other hand, confirm their election to salvation by their faith and possibly by their conduct too. The opposing and complementary theory, of course, is that of universal atonement. Since God has reconciled the world to himself, no one and nothing is excluded. In some way and at some time all people and all things will find themselves in God. This would mean that all people, in theory, are brought within the pale of the church no matter what, and Christians could thus sleep peacefully. This strategy of embracing is the alternative to reflection on the inner life of the church, and the one is just as fatal as the other.

The command of Jesus is to go. He does not ask us to "wait until they come" (Martin Kähler). Yet with the command to go we should also remember the invitation: "Come unto me, all you that are weary and are carrying heavy burdens, and I will give you rest" (Matt. 11:28). What is the relation between *going* and *coming to Christ?* We go in order to pass on the request of Christ, no more and no less. We see that others are in need. Their needs are different, but just as acute as ours are. We can only ask others because we have ourselves been asked. Christian mission is not a sense of missionary sending that rests on feelings of superiority.

Beseeching paradoxically expresses the force and power of Christ. Those who beseech are helpless and vulnerable. They want people to accept their request. But beseeching can become importunate. It can get on the nerves of those who are besought. The specific request to be reconciled takes the form of a reference to what God has done. God was in Christ reconciling the world to himself. Christ, then, comes to us from outside. In those who need reconciliation our concern is with God's action. Such people do not belong to a "latent church" (Paul Tillich, *Systematic Theology,* vol. 3 [Chicago, 1963], p. 152), nor are they "anonymous Christians" (Karl Rahner, "Observations on the Problem of the 'Anonymous Christians,'" in *Theological Investigations,* vol. 14, trans. David Burke [New York, 1976], pp. 280-94). Such vague descriptions do not make plausible the fact that God's presence and God's grace reach far beyond the explicit acceptance of faith. God is greater than our hearts (II.4.3); we ourselves and our inner lives do not bring God into the world (II.5). The work of God reaches far beyond the confines of the church.

In missionary practice, experience shows that only a second stage gives prominence to the grounding of mission. The first stage is for the most part a commitment to a different lifestyle. Communicating the theological reasons is a test case as regards instruction in the Christian faith (II.7), in which we have to speak about the inner grounding for what the church is doing.

II.9.2. The Scope and the Sphere of Validity of Theological Statements

"In Christ God was reconciling the world to himself" (2 Cor. 5:19). That is a universal principle. It is indeed the basic principle of theological universality.

The character of this universality means that none of us have a superior claim, or a claim to better knowledge, than others. It also means, however, that we can come to others without fears or excuses. The gesture of beseeching sets all these things aside. Those who beseech are very much secondary to that which stands behind them. The impotent God is powerful in this way, hidden in the cross. Does this violate others? The request to be reconciled with God is addressed inwardly first of all, to the community. It is made incessantly. I can beseech others only if others have besought me.

The universal "significance" of Jesus is his being for all. From this, however, we cannot deduce any theoretical angle from which to view our relationship with each other. Theologically Jesus opposed no one. He died for all. We must not halve this statement!

We pervert the universal significance of Jesus the moment we use it as something by which to define the relation between his "followers" and "others," between those who are his and those outside. For in this case the others are then part of a comprehensive picture of the world of religion of which Christianity is another part. On the one hand, those who see it this way want to fit themselves into a whole. On the other hand, they take a comparative point of view and therefore stand over all as a self-contained part of this world of religion too. With a highly problematical shift of perspective, this twofold position is the root of two evils that are rivals within Christianity. The self-appointed champions of Christianity either see themselves as much superior to all the rest and base their missionary work upon this fact. Or they see themselves as equal (or inferior) and abstain from mission.

The word of reconciliation alone can help us to say what the relation of the "we" of the church to "others" really is. If we speak in faith and hope and love (and how else are we to speak!), our attitude to others will be that of those who need reconciliation just as much as they do.

41. The range and scope of theological statements is just as unlimited as is God's work of reconciliation. The sphere of validity of theological statements is the church, though this fact does not reduce their scope.

A confusing of *scope* and *sphere of validity* leads to a typical error of thought that we can fall into unawares. This error damages the church's understanding of itself and makes mission impossible. That "God is all in all" is made into a program for the extension of what we say about this God. The "universality" of God will be demonstrated only when the universe acknowledges God. "Can God really be God before (or unless) all people come to believe?" This question is falsely put, and therefore the answer to it will also be false. The statement that "God is all in all" (1 Cor. 15:28) has to be made in faith and hope. The perspective is eschatological. It has in view what the coming Jesus Christ will do, namely, subject himself to God, though without merging into him. This is not the kind of universality that can be transformed into mission.

The typical reverse of this error is the widespread modern anxiety that confessing Christ might violate others and must not be demanded of them. Instead there must be an exchange of dialogue in which a common denominator of religious convictions and values and goals is reached. This error perverts the way Acts 4:12, for example, is understood: "There is salvation in no one else, for there is no other name under heaven given among mortals by which we must be saved." The "we" here is constituted by the action of the triune God. It is not a numerical "we" which can be increased by the addition of others or decreased by their subtraction. This saying does not give to Christendom a right of possession which can then be renounced in order to make coexistence with other religions, especially Judaism, more easily possible.

The distinction between theological scope and sphere of validity with respect to the church should help us in our efforts *not* to try to verify what we say about God at all empirically, as though the illimitable scope of the work of God could be equated with the universal validity of what we regard as credible. All attempts in this direction will either favor an ecclesiastical imperialism or will sanction a sense of inferiority face-to-face with a disinterested public or one that is hostile to the Christian faith because God is spoken of as one who avails only "for us" or even perhaps "for me."

The church is the space for theological dialogue. It is the sphere in which "we" (II.5) rely on that which can be said in faith and hope, the sphere in which we can agree on the validity of theological statements and also have to subject them to debate, the sphere in which we can talk and dispute, but in so doing *know how to begin*. The more freely we move in this sphere, the more uninhibited we shall be in conversations outside the area of consensus. We can discover theological contents for the very reasons that we are not concerned about where theology can have a place in our everyday dealings. We need not be afraid when handling religious questions or talking about God because we know that those who speak with us, like ourselves, are already embraced by the work of God. Whether or when this can find expression is by no means essential. The presence of God is not dependent upon it. If we do not really know where to start, the anxiety of others about where they should start would not really concern us. We cannot understand this anxiety if we have not constantly had the experience in the church of starting ourselves.

The church is the linguistic sphere in which I know *where to begin* if I am to speak in faith and hope (I.2). It is the pragmatic, linguistic sphere in which there can be agreement on the reach of theological statements. This changes the relation between the inner aspect of the church and its outer aspect. The inner aspect is agreement in the faith. We must not confine it to an internal dialogue between those who already understand one another, who have developed a sense of fellowship which marks them off from those outside, perhaps through the use of pious language, a collective form of private speech which others cannot understand. In the church, talking in faith is natural. The outer aspect of the church means encounter with those who explicitly or inexplicitly are motivated by the question of where they are to start to have faith, to hope, and to love.

II.9.3. Encountering Others

42. Mission takes place when the statements of faith venture out into a sphere of communication in which they are not yet valid but are seeking validity.

Mission involves the sending of people to other people, but also the sending of their words and deeds to other spheres of validity. The question always arises, "How can what has happened for all really be of benefit to them? And how far does responsibility fall on us?"

A distorted question also arises at this point: What is the relation between "Christians" and "non-Christians"? It seems that Christians are those who know that they need reconciliation, God's reconciliation of the world to himself in Christ. They can thus *address* others as those to whom this reconciliation also applies.

Unmistakable clarity is given to this answer if we add at once that although God has reconciled the world in Christ, not all are included in this reconciliation. Reconciliation is not a consummated action in which "all" can be counted and by which all are "embraced." An all-inclusiveness of this kind would be a fundamental mistake. Why?

It would make "others" an element in defining my own position. It would put both of us in the same sphere. I compare myself with them, and I compare my own position with the otherness of others. To some extent, of course, this is unavoidable if I really want to communicate with them and not isolate myself. Nevertheless, communication means primarily perceiving others as truly others. It means seeing them as they are and as they wish to impart themselves. And that means that I, too, must show them who I am. Theologically that means sharing with them all that constitutes "my faith," which is not only "my" faith but faith with a distinctive outreach.

The relation to others changes at once and fundamentally when "my faith" confronts the faith of others. Sooner or later comparison again arises. I see myself in relation to them. This is a step toward theorizing. Others are part of my view of the world. A comparative standpoint is adopted. The science of religions describes it. Dogmatics, however, has nothing to say about this description. Comparisons abandon the place at which we speak in faith, hope, and love. They do not say what we have to say more relevantly or make it more faithful to its object (III.2). They assiduously put in place of this speaking expressions of inner convictions which stand at our disposal. All this has direct ramifications for any future understanding. From a comparative standpoint I do not meet with "others" dialogically. Even in communication with them they have surreptitiously become part of the way I define my own position.

Constant reflection on the relation between those that are in the church and those outside is a serious threat to mission and can be a cause of failure. When we think along these lines, we could give up hope about the inner grounding of what the church is doing because it does not make itself plausible "outside." We may note that others do not believe, or believe differently, but this can never be a meaningful approach to the question of what "we" believe, that is, what we can and should say theologically. We must remember this when we ourselves study this approach (IV.1).

This chapter has investigated the bases, the inner grounding and justification of various church activities. The question might take different forms. Perhaps we have to inquire into the theological reasons for customary and all-too-familiar ways of life and work, so that their dynamism can be restored to them. Or the aims of action may have become diffuse and stand in need of theological clarification. Questionable motives may have insinuated themselves. Only by learning to see what action, or inaction, is promised and commanded for the Christian community can we understand how dubious these motivations are. Or external pressure has influenced and perhaps already deformed the church's life and work, so that it has lost its sense of direction. Its way of doing things, which has come to be regarded as self-explanatory, may need to be compared and contrasted with very different forms.

From different angles we have put these various questions (with no claim to completeness) in order that we might see what dogmatic thinking means in practice. In this practice we have come across the detailed structure of linguistic forms and movements that encountered us in the first chapter. It has been seen to cover a very wide field. But now our task must be to become more intensively acquainted with the systematic structure of dogmatics so that we do not think that a kind of labyrinth confronts us. We must learn how the thematic interconnections of dogmatics arise to form a direction-pointing nexus or *systema* (III.1). With what "basic statements" can we start that will influence the movement of theological argumentation (III.2)? We then consider (in III.3) why and how dogmatics refers to biblical texts as "Scripture," so as to make it plain why and to what end biblical passages are quoted so frequently in this book. This will also help us deal with questionable approaches and points of departure that might put us on a false track (IV).

III. Dogmatics Put in Motion

III.1. The Range and Scope of Theological Knowledge

III.1.1. Growing into the Theological Context of Justification

In the second chapter we drew attention to various ways of looking at the inner grounding of what the church does now that God has entrusted his promises to its members and counts on them to do his stated will by imparting these promises. The grounding points us to the work of God both by telling us on what we can rely and by directing us to the goal toward which we are to strive. By way of example, and with no claim to fullness, these dogmatic formulations taught us the practice of thought whose structure we encountered in the first chapter when studying linguistic forms and movements.

At the same time we also took some steps toward a theological knowledge by seeing how the various reasons underlying the church's work are all interrelated and how they all point us to the extensive range of the work of God, to its inconceivable depth that gives faith its transverse strength, to its immeasurable width that gives hope its elasticity, and to its intensive density that is the source of love.

The dogmatic reasons are no more than formulas if they do not lead us to this kind of knowledge. It deals first with elementary questions. Why do we pray? Why do we constantly and unceasingly read the Bible? What would it mean if we wished or were forced to stop? How do we relate to others and to ourselves? What does it mean for us to talk about God? If we can really get a hold on such questions and not dither about with them, then some things become plain at least in outline. When we follow the linguistic contours, a plastic profile gradually emerges of what is really true in faith and hope. Although outside us, this is directed completely toward us. This way of looking at things shows us what to look for. It helps keep us to the point. It also unleashes for us the ecstatic astonishment that always accompanies true knowledge. Unsuspected links open up, dimensions encouraging further thought. We can perceive and grow into these without giving ourselves airs. The mist of prejudice is dispersed. We now see a further stretch of the way clearly as questions are answered, but this does not prevent us from searching further.

Our present focus is only on the linguistic form of this knowledge, and especially on its formative principles, the formulated principles rather than the prelinguistic and nonlinguistic factors to which this knowledge is also indebted. We might express the linguistic form of this knowledge as follows:

43. *Theological grounding is linked and interrelated in such a way that it forms the theological context of justification. It unites the basic statements that have been gained from experiences in theological thinking so far.*

These experiences are experiences in common. To be sure, individuals go on ahead and have to help others, gradually and with much difficulty, to follow in their steps. Our present state of theological knowledge rests on the theological context of justification (I.1.3) which is the core of dogmatics.

This theological context of justification receives its unity and inner coherence from the fact that in both the whole and the part it points us to the work of God in all its dimensions, setting this work before us. This context expresses the externality of what God does. It enables us to move within this as we study it and expectantly recall once more all that God has said and done. Recollection makes further knowledge possible. In no sense is theological knowledge a simple repeating of what has been said before, valid though it might be. It is not exhausted by a mere repetition of earlier thought experiences. It adopts what must be said unconditionally and in all circumstances in faith and hope, and measures it as it relates to our own lives. This permits us to say something specific though without a comprehensive grasp of things.

44. The theological context of justification stands over against the church as a sign of the faithfulness of God, of the breadth of his promises, and of the range of his divine activity.

It will help to give the church stability when it might be hesitant and uncertain, for it gives orientation to what the church says and does. It can also mean, however, that on theological grounds the church is interrupted or prevented from doing certain things.

Because this context expresses the externality of faith, it is not the same as a theory of the church's work. For it addresses the church. The church does not express itself in it. By no means is it a showcase in which the church presents itself. Being responsible for the theological context of justification, dogmatics confronts the church (I.1.2). It is true that when dogmatics is divorced from the life of the church it can depict only a virtual reality, yet at the same time it would surely perish if it became a mere reflection of the church's power of achievement.

Since theological principles are interrelated, even within this context we can think of them in their own context independently, with their own claim to truth. The theological context of justification also differs from a background of motivations that we can decode psychologically or socio-psychologically. The latter is a mix of reasons deriving from different sources, for example, from desires and demands, from traditional values, and from the thrust for self-preservation. Dogmatics barricades itself off against all attempts to confuse the inner reasons behind the church's work with a balance between pious custom on the one side and an ability to adjust oneself to the age on the other.

Theological principles are interwoven. Does this web give evidence of a specific pattern? Can the full extent of the work of God about which dogmatics speaks be sketched in a way that is binding?

Textbooks, compendia, conceptions, and lecture cycles that deal with dogmatics all give a systematic impression. The fullness of the material is arranged in such a way that a total picture emerges of what theology needs to know. What is stated should correspond to the full truth of faith, to the abundance of God and his works from their origins to their completion.

Two types of presentation have become customary, though these can vary considerably. The one begins by speaking about the triune God, Father, Son, and Spirit — Creator, Reconciler, and Consummator. The other sketches, as it were, the history of the work of God, having first explained who God is and why we can speak about him.

These time-honored types are the final product of a lengthy development that we cannot describe here. I should mention three problems relating to systematic study of this kind. I constantly encounter these risks and side effects when talking with students. Students very often miss the enjoyment that a study of dogmatics ought to bring and find that their concern for a true theological knowledge is frequently overwhelmed.

First is the problem of completeness. Does not dogmatics seek to garner a knowledge that covers every angle? If this is so, does it not also have to compress, to give only basic information, which can then be developed and expanded as need arises? Is it not a root theology that the waters of eloquence can fructify?

Next is the problem of putting the themes of theology in a sequence. How is it to achieve an inner coherence and consistency? Most often an impression of chronological arrangement is given, especially by the second of the two types mentioned. The origin comes first, and then the story is carried forward to the end. It seems to take a similar course to the Bible, though in a very different form, for it does not use narratives and many different genres. But it arranges all events in their relation to God, the world, and humanity, and to that which underlies this relation before and outside all time.

Finally there is the question of the kind of overview that dogmatics must offer. What is our own relation to dogmatics? Can God's perspectives, plans, thoughts, and impulses be ours? What have our recollections and expectations, our sense of nearness and distance, of time and space, to do with all this? Does dogmatics perhaps lead us to think of God, the world, and humanity as a single construct that might correspond to our need for direction and clarity but fails to do justice to our present situation? Is what we get a bird's-eye view, which a stricter reading shows to be and to stay a worm's-eye view?!

Problems of this kind are not merely technical. Basic theological questions lie concealed behind them. In order to deal with them, and if possible to answer them, we must turn again to the church year. We mentioned this already as a proven aid to recollection in I.5.3. Now we refer to it as a plan in dogmatics. It gives dogmatics a specific chronology. It thus enables us to handle our earlier problems, that is, those of dogmatic sequence. It thus prepares the ground for the putting of basic dogmatic questions (III.1.3) and for varied surprises at the inner logic of dogmatics and its awaited fullness.

In this section, therefore, we shall be inquiring into the structure of dogmatics as an extensive context of statements that tries to follow the full scope of the work of God, depicting its fullness, or at least giving some trace of it. But which questions and answers do we come upon first? And which questions and answers come next, and why? Where, too, must we always return to so as not to go off into byways or to fall into error?

III.1.2. The Church Year as a Plan of Dogmatics

From the arrangement of the church year (I.5.3) we derive a specific rhythm defined by the incursion of God into human history and destiny. The creed stresses that this intervention was not expected by having the coming of Jesus Christ break into creation without mediation. It then scans the elements of Christ's history in segmentary form. We see that his birth, his death, his resurrection, and his exaltation as judge — each in its own unmistakable way — are new beginnings, not stages of development. The points marking these beginnings constitute a stretch or path that is not identical with the passage of time. The full scope of faith refers to this temporal process. It allows us, then, to measure time, namely, with the length of the strides of faith denoted by the sequences of the festivals of Christ.

Thus a different reckoning of time is given from the so-called Christian reckoning which makes a break between the time "before Christ's birth" and the time "after" it. This reckoning, however, can all too easily lose the sense that recollection and expectation of Christ ought not be divided into two spans of time but are interrelated. The longer that reckoning continues, the more it will give the impression that we are irresistibly moving into a post-Christian era.

The Christian festivals celebrate the great acts of God. The message of each one discloses a specific aspect of God's surprising work in and with Jesus Christ. Unsought and unexpected, it calls to be heard. It might be that several expectations preceded what took place when Jesus of Nazareth came, but his actual coming disrupted the assumptions. The situation suddenly became unclear, and the accustomed way of measuring time ran into confusion. Time is now measured by the Christian festivals as the recollection of Jesus Christ leads on to the presence of God. In its own specific way each festival invites us to accept God's newly creative act and thus to wait upon God. Against all our expectations these festivals train us in hope.

Recollection of Jesus Christ takes place with the declaration of the unsought message that "Christ is risen" and extends into the hope of Christ as the Coming One.

45. The Christian festivals permit us constantly to begin once again and yet to move forward according to their rhythm, although even step-by-step we can never catch up with the fullness of God.

The sequence of the festivals is not a spiral in which by an incessant process we have to wind ourselves up to God. Nor does this sequence demand of us that each time we should experience or even imagine something more and thus gradually come nearer to God's fullness. We are not even able to produce this fullness by achieving new aspects each time we work through the festivals.

A believed faith lets its full extent be known, but we must keep to the length of its strides. We cannot rush ahead or miss out on anything. Christmas does not stand in the shadow of Golgotha, or Good Friday in the light of Easter. We get a foreshadowing of Good Friday at Christmas, as Johann Sebastian Bach realized when in his Christmas Oratorio he used the tune of "O Sacred Head, Sore Wounded," or as Joos van Cleve (1480-1540/41) did in his painting when he had Mary offer her child the cup of suffering (Museum of Fine Arts, Budapest). But a systematic synopsis of this would be fallacious. We must rejoice for a time at the crib, but only for a time. We must also tarry for a time at the cross. We cannot leap over the abyss of Holy Saturday. It is fatal to cling too closely to Christmas and to seek to celebrate it forever. And we shall turn into pillars of salt if we look too long at the cross.

46. The arrangement of the church year releases us from the hopeless attempt to say everything decisive at once, or always to want to say something completely new.

Adopted by dogmatics, this arrangement is an effective tool against monotony. Everything cannot be brought under a single concept or led back to a single concept, even the concept of Easter, earthshaking and momentous though this undoubtedly is.

The recurrence of the festivals is a sign that God will not let us be cut off in a stretch of time that we construct and design and survey. This is how we must traverse (and celebrate) the church year. This year is a period with its own meter. Nevertheless it is not a closed cycle. The festivals do not coincide with our ordinary yearly calendar. Their sequence has a different rhythm.

The usual yearly cycle involves a steady progression from becoming to perishing and to renewed becoming. Every year sets this regeneration before our eyes. It runs in the blood. The measure of time is consonant with the biorhythm of becoming and perishing. If we do not abstract away from nature, then in the yearly cycle we shall find a warning of our own mortality. Yet the impetus of nature lifts us up again, and shows us that the whole survives the extinguishing of the parts. Our own life span is not more than a stretch of time, but this does not really end, as long as our lives can be caught up again in the sequence which fed them for a season.

Into this experience of time comes Jesus Christ. He steps in between the becoming and perishing in which we are entangled. His person mediates to us a different time. This time is connected with his person. Thus a counterrhythm to the yearly cycle is set up, which sometimes disrupts the yearly rhythm, but the disruption is not one of disease but of liberation.

The conclusion of the church year is stamped by its beginning, the advent of Jesus Christ. The church year ends by flowing into expectation of Christ. It ends with comfort for the dead and dying. It also calls us to repentance. The Advent season is a time of preparation for Christmas ("O Lord, How Shall We Meet You?"). It is basically a time of fasting, not of joy. The end of the church's year allows us to progress but not to rush ahead.

There is thus an unceasing dialectical tension between recollection and hope. Christ has come but has yet to come. What he has achieved is balanced by what is promised us in him. In this tension we can say something definite by way of recollection and hope. The close association between the church's year and dogmatics may be seen in what theology says about a "specific time." What are we to say under all conditions specifically on this day and in this situation? What is the specific and unchangeable message of Christmas or Good Friday or Easter or Ascension Day?

Dogmatics helps keep before us the sequence marked by the Christian festivals. This sequence prevents the repetition of what we say about the great acts of God from becoming stale. We expound the story of Christ as a whole and in further theological contexts. Dogmatics does this and it thus brings out the range of all that is said about Jesus Christ. It opens up horizons that encourage us to move forward. These are the horizons of a *pilgrim theology (theologia viatorum)*. In relation to the christological sequence, the pilgrims' recollections and expectations are always open to revision. They are not, of course, outdated. We recognize, however, that they are inadequate either because they have become too shallow or because they are not fully grasped. Revision of this kind deepens, expands, and concentrates theological knowledge.

III.1.3. Thinking Further! The Outline of Dogmatics

Dogmatic decisions, which go hand in hand with the development of the church year, give support to the church's memory. What strands run through this memory? How is it constituted? How far does the anamnesis stretch back, irrespective of where it might begin, whether with shreds of recollection, with associations, or with momentary impressions?

The rule of faith, the core of dogmatic statements, came into being along with the canon (I.1.4). Both bear record that faith depends on the fact that God has manifested himself in Jesus Christ. He has manifested himself in a way that summons people of different religions, cultures, and social roles and strata to become his church and to belong to Jesus Christ. This fact has set dogmatics on its way, and sets it again and again on this way. Without Jesus Christ we could perhaps speak about God, but we would do so very differently. Indeed, we would speak about a different God from the one who has spoken definitely for us all in Jesus Christ (Heb. 1:1-2).

But this gives inner force to the question: Who is Jesus Christ? What is his relation to God, to the God upon whom he calls? Can we call upon him in the same way? Who is the God who has spoken and acted in Jesus Christ? How does he act toward us? How is he present with us? Out of such questions Christology and the doctrine of the Trinity arose, accompanied by the canon, which rests on the astounding permission to read the Scriptures of the Jewish people as a book of the church, and in speaking about God to refer back to his praise in creation.

Then the question arises of our own relation to this God, not the relation of believers alone, but that of all humanity. Who are we — before God? "What are human beings that thou art mindful of them?" (Ps. 8:4). This is the place for the doctrine of sin and grace, of creation and the fall. On the one side there develops a nuanced teaching about humanity, its origin and destiny in God's acting upon it (Irenaeus). On the other side focus is upon the church. The church is dependent on God's election and calling. In everything it does it seeks to conform to the will of God. It always sets its hope in God. Hence it is not defined by the quality of its members, by their moral achievements (Augustine).

"What is the church, and what can it do?" This question has accompanied the church and its theology throughout its history. No satisfactory answer, or definitive answer, can be found either in this history or based on it. The question becomes sharper as the church tends to look at itself and its representatives, being concerned with its possessions rather than with what it is entrusted to say and do. In consequence, people's perception of the Bible and the sacraments suffer. Worship is no longer the vital center and source of other forms of service. The dominating factor is what the church owns and can impart in order to bind others to itself and thus to compete in the fight for territory. What does the church have to represent and uphold? All this may be done with the best of intentions. The church does not do it for its own sake but for God's. Even the question "Who is Jesus Christ?" can be functionalized as the church makes itself the theme: "What is the church doing with an appeal to what Jesus Christ has done?" Anselm of Canterbury saw the same thing in his *Cur deus homo?*: the church controls the merit that was earned by Jesus Christ when he restored the honor of God that human guilt had violated.

What is the church, the true and ancient church? This question took on a sharper edge at the Reformation, to the point of division. The Reformers referred to the church's origin in the Word and Spirit of God. The Council of Trent, in defining the relation between Scripture and tradition, was concerned to establish the *authority of the church.* This line of approach led on to the doctrine of papal infallibility at Vatican I (1870-71) and then to a revised answer to the question of the church at Vatican II (1962-65). The churches of the Reformation, however, were more concerned with the question of the *authority of the Bible.* Both the Roman Catholic and the Protestant answers to this question — and these often contained very controversial distinctions — dealt with the issue of the final court of appeal for what must be said in faith and hope. Is this supreme court the teaching office of the church, which embodies the unity of the church in the person of the pope? Or is it the biblical Word, Scripture, and what does it mean to begin here and never to go behind it (III.3)?

The Reformers also took up again the thread of the doctrine of grace, which had almost disintegrated in the preceding centuries, being broken up into such questions as the relation of God's operations for us and our human cooperation with them, or human disposition of faith, or the gradual emergence of a life in accordance with the will of God, or faith and works. The Reformation question: "How can we speak about God's work?" was linked to the question of the true church, the fellowship of justified sinners who were previously without God and without hope. This led on to the following questions: "How are we to perceive sin and justification?" and "What are we to say about the Christian life?" Reformation theology asked the church about its life and its sources.

But then another string of questions very quickly arose as the full extent of God's work came to be perceived. How about the relation to God of those who do not belong to the church of Jesus Christ? When we speak in faith and hope, in other words, what is our responsibility to those who have no faith and no hope, or whose faith and hope differ from ours? How are they to understand what we say even if they do not agree with it? Is there a common forum of discussion which enables us to address all sensible people about things on which they could be convinced by arguments?

This group of questions becomes broader and stronger as theology reaches a wider public. A first step in this direction was taken when theology was not just used for the training of a theological elite in monasteries but also for discussion with those who think differently and with representatives of other faiths — Jews and Muslims, for example. The founding of the medieval universities brought theology into intellectual debate that attracted increasingly wider circles. This was the hour when theology became wedded to reason. Theology clarified its relationship to philosophical traditions. Its concern, for example, was to show that God can be proved. The so-called proofs of the existence of God resulted. Theological teachers were no longer also bishops and abbots. The universities created a stimulating forum of discussion which dealt with new questions, references, and forms of treatment (e.g., disputations), and which strongly formed theological thinking.

The change in the conditions of theological work was not just external. If "reason" was seen as a social phenomenon, as each person is claimed by it, so "faith" must be subject to reason if it is to be communicated. The relation between faith and reason became decisive if the validity of theological statements was at issue. These statements could have universal validity only if they could be shown to be rational. A wide field thus opened up. Theology had to think about the reasons for what it said, about the range of its statements, and about the sphere of their legitimacy. The more such problems controlled theology, the more strongly insistent became the question: must there not be an approach to theology that does not presuppose an explicit faith? *Religion* promises to open up such an approach. It is a universal intellectual frame of mind. We all ask where life comes from and where it is going. Some find an answer to such questions in the Christian faith, but it is not to be found there unconditionally. Theology was caught up in this question of approaches at least from the days of the Enlightenment, and dogmatics has been led from one crisis to another in this regard. New patterns of investigations have changed the face of dogmatics (IV.1-3). They have often wounded dogmatics to the quick, and it has been forced at least to find more and more room for them.

190

We can survey the types of questions that have left particularly deep marks on the history of theology and often led to very successful experiences in thinking. But we must also give some thought to some of the failures. They cast light on open theological questions and make it clear that the work of dogmatics is not yet over. Three examples might at least be sketched.

One has to do with the Holy Spirit. How are we to rate and adequately enough discuss the Holy Spirit as the creative and redeeming presence of God (pneumatology)? It is not enough simply to speak of the doctrine of the Trinity. What we say about the world and humanity and the church is also affected. But how? Christology teaches us to distinguish but not separate the deity and humanity of Christ (I.2.1). Should not pneumatology say that there is a relation between the divine life and our human life, between what God does and what we do or fail to do?

Second, is it enough to regard people only as creatures and sinners, as the early church taught us to do? It could especially appeal to the stories of creation and the fall in Genesis 1–3. It could later quote the doctrine of grace. But does all this really do justice to the wealth of tension in what the Bible has to say about humanity? What significance does the knowledge of Jesus Christ as the "true man" have for the theological interpretation of humanity? And what insights can spirituality awaken for theology (I.5.1)? Experiences in thinking can be attained even from the complication of self-perception, though this must be on guard against self-imaging. In dogmatics, of course, such experiences will find only marginal entry. In the West, following upon the Enlightenment, we have set human subjectivity alongside this self-perception and made it the central point of contact for all knowledge. "Nature" and "history" are now the framework conditioning how we see ourselves, and these have now begun to transform traditional theological views (cf. Emanuel Hirsch, *Schöpfung und Sünde in der natürlich-geschichtlichen Wirklichkeit des einzelnen Menschen*, BSTh 1 [Tübingen, 1931]). The resultant "anthropology" has given us new ways of investigating ourselves, our constitution, and our position in the world, and it has thus become a competitor with theology. It has damaged the efforts to arrive at a theological anthropology. The treasures of theological thinking about being human and remaining human have been largely buried, and they are waiting to be raised up again.

The third example pertains to 1 Peter 3:15, which tells us that we are called to account for the hope that is in us. But thus far a form has not been discovered for a convincing integration of this hope with the basic theological context of justification. We have a doctrine of the last things (eschatol-

191

ogy). Here dogmatics sheds its concluding light. And it does help us to keep in mind important themes such as the resurrection of the dead, the last judgment, the consummation of creation, and external life either with God or without him. But it is more than doubtful whether this adequately shows how a living hope is based on Jesus Christ, the Coming One.

These three themes are often pushed into the background of dogmatic interest and can thus be exploited by unchecked associations. It is particularly difficult to show what is the structure of their theological foundations. They thus constitute the open flanks of dogmatics. Erroneous lights thus flare up and entice us onto deceptive ground.

We can only give a very rough sketch of the origins of dogmatics here. We see in them a process of development which does not take it in just one direction but always leaves room for new beginnings as new questions have to be added to older ones. But pauses have to be made for an account of the path already taken to see how the additions will fit. The new approaches are not merely technical. They represent a forward step in knowledge that allows what is said in faith, hope, and love to be understood in new and broader contexts. This is the only way epochs arise in dogmatic thinking, epochs which are also turning points where different paths can be entered, but where it has also to be asked why this has happened, on what theological grounds, and whether these grounds are valid.

If the origins of dogmatics are reconstructed and told theologically and not merely historically, account has to be taken of which reasons imperatively enforce theological inquiries. With what weight do they set thinking in motion (not: *have* they set it in motion so that it is now at rest)? Are they really related to one another, and if so, how? This is irrespective of all existing or supposed historical, cultural, and social concerns that might have played some role but cannot explain why theologically this is how it is, and why no other view of it is possible!

In this way we become acquainted with the esssential features of basic dogmatic knowledge:

47. The basic dogmatic knowledge arises out of the interrelating of questions and added questions with which dogmatics starts and to which it constantly refers in seeking the right connection.

This interrelating has to be kept in mind so that we do not just record and catalogue the remembered questions and answers, but keep them alive as unavoidable questions that always fall within the field of theology.

These questions arose historically. This was inevitable. We can trace each of them back to a situation when they arose, a historical context of discovery (IV.2.3). Here is a rich field of historical theology, which directs attention to historical conditions, which focuses this attention by stressing that whatever we think and say theologically is always relative, for it is connected with all the circumstances out of which it rose and in which it developed its effect. This way of looking at things can, of course, cause us to lose sight of the inner grounds of theological thought, especially when it only records the history of ideas. It is important for dogmatics to characterize the experiences in thinking that have achieved permanence and the way in which they are intertwined. These experiences start off with elementary questions that will sooner or later find a place in what is said in faith and hope. They arrive at definitive conclusions that will always carry weight, for otherwise they would be justly forgotten. Theological discussion can always come back to them so long as they are not replaced by new and better knowledge. Dogmatics must not force these questions and their answers on anyone, but it can help people relate to them and pass on what has already been learned, often with some difficulty, many struggles, and frequent errors and confusions. In this way detours and mistakes can be avoided and much unnecessary ballast can be jettisoned.

We might learn the path of dogmatic inquiry as we do a party game. We begin with rudimentary statements perhaps taken from the NT. Thus we could turn to the saying of Jesus in John 10:30: "The Father and I are one." The participants can develop and think through this saying by gradually asking questions. This kind of game will make us aware that dogmatics is a common enterprise, or will sooner or later become such, even though it demands the intensive and extensive thinking of individuals.

In sum, we are presented with a plastic profile of questions and answers, of thinking experiences and problems, that arise in a far-reaching and richly related field of topics. We do not have a mere list of contents that we can learn and set aside. Knowledge of that kind is soon forgotten!

An outline of the origin of dogmatics is communicated by its disposition. This will show us its multidimensional scope. Topics are not just mentioned and dealt with one by one. We must pursue a path of knowledge. Dogmatic texts and a dogmatic presentation will be the more rewarding the more they compel us to take part in scanning and treading this path with all its toils, its surprises, and its joys.

Various forms of composition suggest themselves as we consider how to arrange dogmatics. Older dogmatics usually combined themes systematically. System *(systema)* originally simply meant combination, with perspicuity and purposefulness in view. It seemed that this could best be achieved through either a trinitarian or an historical outline. The greater the concern for consistency and coherence, the stronger the systematic interest. Finally, then, all dogmatics came to be developed out of one basic concept, a principle. Everything is derived from this. We must not be afraid of the term "principle." It should not make us think of a rigid construct, a speculative approach, or a monotonous execution. It normally seeks to give solid answers to questions, answers which form the basis of theological knowledge. We can start off here and constantly return here. It gives us a universal view. It enables us to achieve a fuller clarity and consistency than does a looser arrangement of themes in which all have their own importance and specific profile. Both methods have their price, however, and have their advantages and disadvantages.

It is worthwhile to study the many forms of composition. But it is much more important to gain an insight into the constitution of dogmatic thought, that is, its structure. The structure is much more than the list of thoughts and themes that we can get from perusing the table of contents of a book of dogmatics or the syllabus of a course of dogmatic lectures. We dealt with this matter in chapter I. We showed there that we must know something definite so that we can make theological judgments. The development of dogmatics communicates our knowledge of existing experiences in theological thinking. These experiences will never be one-dimensional or monotonous. They are not simply echoed in the intricate execution of individual topics. We move on from experiences in thinking to specific forms of speech — for example, to basic distinctions which include and exclude — and these form a foundation for further building. Basic dogmatic knowledge becomes accessible through exemplary learning. It no more levels everything down than does dogmatics itself. It does not reduce everything to a single massive pillar that has to carry all the rest. Basic dogmatic knowledge is not, as it were, iron rations. It cannot be put on a single page. It is not a fixed core that the shifts of historical change cannot shake, that remains a healthy tree as rings of growth are added, or that is encircled by a linguistic bark that even if it be peeled off will be replaced or will renew itself.

Generative statements, relations, and interconnections are part of the linguistic elements of dogmatics (I.3.3). They are texts of different kinds. They develop in such and such a way. They can find a place in dogmatics with or alongside others if it does not deal with theological opinions or deal too aptly with just theological topics. They might be texts of church doctrine (I.4). They might express the core of statements definitive in dialogue (I.2.2). They might convey basic distinctions (I.2.1) that can be carried through in different ways and that will prove to be fruitful in different situations. The fact that dogmatics can express itself in so many different ways helps to promote theological knowledge much better than might be expected if we could always summon up normative texts.

From this standpoint dogmatics is ongoing. It never reaches an end even though its field of subjects is limited. How could it scope the full extent of God's work of promise? It might then be "at an end" insofar as it would have died out as a thought movement and could just be retrieved as necessary. We cannot even know how great is this extent. We can still be surprised by it. The more deeply we plunge into it, the more we become aware of how delicate its movements and ramifications are. That is why dogmatics is so increasingly complex. At first glance we might find this complexity oppressive, but it will quickly display a rewarding wealth. The full scope of the work of God is something we can never measure. It extends far beyond the sphere that we can tread. Nevertheless, we embark on a path that is encircled by the divine action, so that we can at least measure it to the extent that we can know whether we are on the right path or the wrong path according to our human judgment. Dogmatics reminds us of this. What it has to say must be so oriented that the direction in which it points us does not lead to disorder. No dimension must be overlooked. Yet we must not feel that too much is demanded of us, and we must certainly avoid the false impression that we have completed the task. In this whole field dogmatics serves as a support for the memory.

For this very reason dogmatics can also relieve us, especially from our compulsion to say everything at once and to do so as quickly as possible. Dogmatics allows us to begin with a single observation and to follow it in one direction even though we do not see everything at the same time. Dogmatics, then, never gives rise to the impression of swimming around with no shore in view. Because it is limited, and within these limits does not float in the void in relation to what it has to say, but clearly relates things alongside and with one another, it is always coherent, but only insofar as its path of knowledge remains on solid ground and does not leap in the air or fall into a *salto mortale*. The path, of course, will not always be rectilineal. How could it be, in virtue of the complexity that is proper to dogmatics?

A quasi-temporal arrangement of theological themes cannot overcome time and cannot resolve the tension between recollection and expectation. At the same time an impressive "categorizing" of all the themes must not cause us to forget that each survey of dogmatic inquiries, no matter how complete, can only serve to reinforce our memory, so that we keep everything in view. Dogmatic topics have a breadth, and we can only do damage by trimming it. If anything essential is left out, one-sidedness or crookedness results. The survey will restrict itself to early impressions and to matters that call for theological judgment. But so far as is possible it pursues them with all possible width and profundity.

A true development of thought, which is not the same as drawing easy conclusions, grows out of the astonishment that lifts us above ourselves when we are gripped by insights for which our own knowledge did not originally equip us. These insights allow us to breathe more freely and to look further ahead. We see a path that we can take. It will carry us further. We are attracted by its logic. Thinking further then really involves acquiring a sense that elementary questions and observations are not the end, that interrelations are possible, that networks can be formed. How can we pick up a thread and develop a concept and measure what will result?

Dogmatics observes no law of composition. My ideal illustration is that of a Celtic chain of interlacing strands on which we can find neither beginning nor end, since they always go over and under one another, and yet they always move in the same direction and thus form a visible but not wholly comprehensible totality.

Dogmatics might begin with any topic. Some thinkers begin with God in the mystery of his presence. Some start off with God's action at the beginning of things. Some commence with the coming of Jesus Christ, whose history mediates the work of this God, so that we see how vast are the dimensions of this work. Some turn first to human beings like ourselves, with the tension between our lack of faith and our faith, with our temptations and our confidence. We must distinguish, however, between these points of departure and the fixed points of theological orientation by which the argumentation of dogmatics is directed. To these we shall now turn.

III.2. The Character of Theology

In discussing the character of theology, I will try to take up again an inquiry that has often been treated fallaciously and even erroneously. This is the inquiry into the subject matter of theology. Three answers seem to suggest themselves. The first is that God is the subject of theology, the second is that we ourselves as faithful persons are, and the third is that the real subject is the history of Christianity. These answers have shaped the story of modern theology and make many of its conceptual distinctions intelligible. We need not discuss here the complications that all of them have, whether individually or in relation to the rest. All of them tend to equate "subject" with something present, or a state of affairs that if it can be demonstrated will guarantee the unity of theological research.

Is it not far more the case that the subject matter of theology is characterized by the reality that confronts it, directs it, even in the sense of resistance, forms it, gives it character, and characterizes its procedure?

In order to characterize the "subject matter" of Christian theology, I propose, we have to name the decisive *characteristics* which make it possible to decide whether an assumption or argument fits with the constitution of Christian theology and draws attention to this constitution. That is, we discover the subject of theology in the sense of the reality, which gives form to theology and to doing theology.

In this sense the subject matter of theology does not imply the submission of theology to some philosophical or scientific definition of subjects, nor does it signify any matter of fact which could be described and established independently, and then serve as a "foundation" of theology. To avoid such a misunderstanding, I would prefer the word "character" to "subject" or "subject matter"; the character of theology is a profile or feature which cannot be mistaken for anything else and which enables us to recognize theology. You can compare it to the physiognomy of a person: A photograph may reproduce most of the details and yet it may miss the character. Conversely, a good artist is able to hit the point with a few lines, to draw the person, so that we can immediately recognize the face. In this respect, a good portrait is superior to any photograph, because the *coherence* of the lines is pointed out, the connections, which give *life* to the picture.

III.2.1. Characteristics

48. The physiognomy of theology is characterized by statements about the being of God, the self-manifestation of God, and the action of God — by the theological answers to the questions: "Who is God that we might call upon him?", "How does God address us, how do we encounter God?", and "Who are we in relation to God?"

These answers constitute the task of dogmatics. In what follows we shall be speaking of dogmatics as representative of theology as a whole.

197

Dogmatics is a vital body of language. As such it is a discipline: Like any other "normal science" (see Thomas S. Kuhn, *The Structure of Scientific Revolutions,* 3rd ed. [Chicago and London, 1996], pp. 23-34), it is characterized by a constellation, a certain recurrent structure of words and objects, that is, by a *sphere of subject.* We have to draw this structure with a few statements in order to recognize it again and again under different circumstances and in different verbal sequences.

Let us illustrate this by three paradigmatic answers to those basic questions stated above.

The first question, "Who is God that we might call upon him?" finds an answer in the doctrine of the Trinity that characterizes Christian talk of God. It refers to the triune God, to God's self-presentation, self-manifestation and self-disclosure in Jesus Christ, and to God's action toward us and in us in the Spirit. We can discern the divinity of God — God *as God* — only by his self-manifestation (and in this sense: his revelation). But he does not get absorbed in his work. He remains creator, reconciler, and consummator in relation to his work. In each of these actions he *makes himself known* as Father, Son, and Spirit, but always as God who is One.

Those who perceive and bear witness to this God as the only God are able to speak about him only as they are caught up into God's movement. We cannot fix this movement, observing it from our own standpoint. We cannot change ourselves in relation to it. We do not stand before God as a fixed point or a fixed star. Nor are we set before him in a movement that is defined by our world in its unceasing development. God himself sets us before him. When we call upon God, we are already caught up in this movement. We are not at a greater or lesser distance from God. But we perceive ourselves in a relation in which we stand before God's action. God resists our human ideas of God. He speaks his own Word even in what we say, and in so doing he transcends what we can say. The doctrine of the Trinity talks about this surprising sovereignty in such an open way that for this reason it can help us to *expect* God's unexpected presence.

The doctrine of the Trinity asserts relations: Father, Son, and Spirit; God and the world; being created and being alive. In these repetitive statements, which are extremely rich in relations, we find characterized what Christian theology has to say, that is, its subject matter.

It was along these lines that the early church profiled the doctrine of the Trinity. Through ever new approaches it critically discovered what is meant by our human knowledge of God. For example, God is not a composite essence beyond all being. If he were, he could not be the only God who is superior to the world. The doctrine of the Trinity set aside what

198

seemed at first to be compelling conclusions. It did so by pointing to the God who has made himself known. On this ground, and with no unnecessary complications, it answered the question: "Who is the God upon whom we call?" It laid down the necessary conditions upon which we can talk of God.

The second question runs: "How can we approach God?" Thomas Aquinas was much concerned about this question. He expressly took it up as the true theme of theology, and he gave it a sharper twist. At the beginning of his *Summa theologica* (I q.1 a.7 i.c) he described "sacred doctrine" as a science *(scientia)* and asked whether God can be the subject *(subiectum)* of this science. He rules out the fact that God can be defined philosophically. God is ineffable. Nevertheless, God reveals himself by his works — that is, by creation, and the ordering of all being to himself. Everything around us can be put in theological terms. It is all related to God:

> I answer that, God is the object of this science. . . . It follows that God is in very truth the object of this science. This is clear also from the principles of this science, namely, the articles of faith, for faith is about God. The object of the principles and of the whole science must be the same, since the whole science is contained virtually in its principles. (trans. by Fathers of the English Dominican Province [New York, 1947], 1:4-5)[1]

> The object of this science is that of which it principally treats. But in this science the treatment is mainly about God; for it is called theology, as treating of God. (1:4)[2]

Three parts of this definition of the subject matter of theology are worthy of thought.

First, Aquinas takes this view very freely, even though he is aware that we must not equate God with any existing thing. Second, his distinction between God and the world protects him against this misunderstanding. God posits the world as he objectifies himself in it, ordering the whole world to himself as its creator. Third, by means of this ordering God reveals himself. None of us, however, can infer that. To know the

---

1. Respondeo dicendum quod Deus est subiectum huius scientiae. . . . Quod etiam manifestum fit ex principiis huius scientiae, quae sunt articuli fidei, quae est de Deo. Idem autem est subiectum principiorum et totius scientiae, cum tota scientia virtute contineatur in principiis.

2. Illud est subiectum scientiae, de quo principaliter fit sermo in scientia. Sed in hac scientia principaliter fit sermo de Deo (dicitur enim theologia, quasi sermo de Deo).

world in its totality, we need the articles of faith *(articuli fidei)* which contain the knowledge that God himself has given. These, then, are the principles of theological science.

It might seem that Aquinas is simply introducing purely traditional authorities (Scripture and dogmas). But when we note the intricate structure of his thinking, we quickly come to see how confrontation with the sayings of the Bible opens up the way for metaphysical insights, so that God is always pervasively expressing himself. Hence theology is prevented from gaining control over these insights. At this point Aquinas's argumentation might be a standard even today.

How Aquinas attains to this knowledge, and especially whether he works back from the existing world to God, demands further investigation. In this context, however, our concern is with the complexity that Aquinas claims for theology. The basis of this complexity is the fact that theology has to speak about God without being able to comprehend God even in words. For this reason theology as a science engages in a distinctive drama from which it also gains objectivity, for it can do nothing for itself, even by a magic of words. For all his dry didacticism, Aquinas enables us to detect this.

The answer to the third question: "Who are we in relation to God?" is formulated by Martin Luther in a way that gives us direction. Luther, too, adopts the scholastic understanding of subject as subject matter, but he gives it precision by describing it as a movement that constitutes theology. He achieves this contour when he compares it with the subjects of other sciences that we now call the humanities, for example, jurisprudence, which deals with the person who has certain privileges or medicine which treats sick people. Luther uses the "scholastic" concept of "subject matter," but his characterization of theology modifies that concept: He does not set theology in competition with the humanities but points out its distinctive character. He refers to Psalm 51 *(Enarratio Psalmi LI* [1538], *WA,* 40/II:328.17-20):

> The characteristic subject of theology is humanity who is guilty of sin and condemned, and God who justifies and saves sinful humanity. Whatever is asked or discussed outside this subject in theology is a misconception and poison. (trans. Jaroslav Pelikan, *LW,* 12:311)

Luther, of course, does not propose that theology only and exclusively talks about the sinner and God the Savior who gives us his justice. The point of his determination is that true knowledge of human personality depends on a personal unity which God creates and addresses, and that true knowledge of God is constituted together with personal passion of God's action toward us as Judge and Savior. We cannot talk about God in himself or human personality *as such*, nor about the relation of God and humanity, rather of the happening we are involved in, that God justifies and saves the person, whom we can perceive only and exclusively under God's judgment and his promise of justification and salvation. John Calvin agrees with Luther in the beginning of his *Institutio* (1559), when he underscores the insolvable connection between knowledge of God and self-knowledge (I.1,1-2): "Without knowledge of God there is no knowledge of self" (*Institutes of the Christian Religion,* trans. Ford Lewis Battles [Philadelphia, 1960], 1:35.37). Blaise Pascal, in his *Pensées,* argues:

> Not only do we not know God except through Jesus Christ, but we do not know ourselves except through Him. Without Jesus Christ, we do not know what our life is, or our death, or what God is, or ourselves. (fragment 729, ed. Jacques Chevalier [1954]; ET, *The Pensées,* trans. J. M. Cohen [Harmondsworth: Penguin Books, 1961], p. 251)

III.2.2. Axioms

Where do these three sketches lead us?

49. The character of dogmatics is established by basic theological statements that stand in a specific relation to one another, and as thus connected, form a certain structure and context.

We can call these basic statements axioms because there is no getting behind them. If we want to find reasons for them, we have already misunderstood them. They are the linguistic presuppositions of all the dogmatic statements that follow. The doctrine of the Trinity and Luther's definition of the subject of theology are such axioms. In essence they are to the effect that God has both acted and promised to act at one and the same time. Christian theology can proceed only on this basis.

Axioms build the intertwining relationships of the concepts which are fundamental for a science. The axiomatic structure of theology makes it possible to assess its statements according to its own terms. At the same time, this structure may be compared to other sciences, in order to discover parallels and characteristic differences.

A first point of comparison is that axioms are always statements. They outline a linguistic field that we can traverse and within which we can move. They also mark the limits of language; they are the borderline between language and reality. Insights and intuitive perceptions may "tune in" from beyond these limits. Axioms confront language with non-linguistic reality — they force us to take into account the problem of "word and object": a fundamental problem for the philosophy of language and for the theory of scientific knowledge as well. As such it has proved to be extremely productive for the basic research in recent physics; the examination of the role of axioms in this context sheds light on the revolutions characterizing the history of sciences. T. S. Kuhn has drawn attention to this, and H. Putnam has profiled it in terms of linguistic philosophy.

Kuhn points out that axioms constitute reality for us in antithesis to the naive but widespread idea that this is done by direct sense data immediately perceived as the last resort for truth and reference. Of course, axioms do not constitute reality without what Hilary Putnam calls the "contribution of the environment" ("The Meaning of 'Meaning,'" in *Mind, Language, and Reality: Philosophical Papers,* vol. 2 [Cambridge and New York, 1975], pp. 215-71) on which the trustworthiness of what we say specifically (and not at random) depends. Reality has to "join in": otherwise, language does not work and becomes useless and arbitrary. There is no absolutism of language; it does, however, form a sphere that allows of irreversible coordinations and therefore a definable interconnecting procedure.

A second point of comparison is that axioms are indications that there are obligatory and not purely conventional answers to the questions that are posed. At the outer limit they give us a solid measure of what is unconditional and immovable. They are certainly relative to the reality they depict, but they are absolute for all the statements that are based on them. Axioms allow us to establish that to which other theological statements can (linguistically) refer, and they do so in such a way that other statements can be derived therefrom. To that extent axioms are starting points or points of orientation for arguments that will be both consistent and coherent.

Every science rests on axioms or basic assumptions. Axioms differ essentially from intuitive insights, important as these are as epistemological provocations. The difference is that they make possible a directed nexus of speech. These basic assumptions tell the community of scientists what is irrefutable so far. Along these lines Alfred North Whitehead could even speak of the *dogmas* of physics: "In exactly the same way the dogmas of physical science are the attempts to formulate in precise terms the truths disclosed in the sense-perception of mankind" (*Religion in the Making*, Lowell Lectures 1926, 3rd ed. [New York, 1927], p. 58). Whitehead is showing here how the sciences compare and how they basically differ. Axioms have dogmatic rank insofar as they formulate "truths" (note well, not "the truth" itself!) and thus give a firm foundation to the observations that follow. They can thus be called "dogmas," for real dogmas are not mere assertions that can claim unquestioned validity.

Dogmas and axioms both function equally well in finding the truth (John R. Carnes, *Axiomatics and Dogmatics* [New York, 1982]). Thomas F. Torrance seems to be right, therefore, when he reminds us that the term "dogma," which scientific language mostly despises because of its authoritarianism, in the early church really denotes a "well-grounded and agreed affirmation rather than an arbitrary and individual opinion," and is "opposed to skeptical or merely critical thought" (*Theological Science* [London, New York, and Toronto, 1969], p. 339). This was how the whole church, both East and West, emphasized it. Torrance appeals in this regard to Sextus Empiricus's *Adversus dogmaticos*. As the church fathers saw it, "in the strictest sense the doctrine of the Holy Trinity is *theologia,* that is, theology in the purest form, the pure science of theology, or *episteme dogmatike*" (*The Ground and Grammar of Theology* [Charlottesville, Va., 1980], p. 158).

Today many scientists who are interested in epistemological issues, for example, Michael Polanyi, use religious or quasi-religious terms like "belief" to characterize a kind of basic trust in reality, the reality that prevents scientists from taking control over it instead of letting it also speak to them (*Personal Knowledge: Towards a Post-Critical Philosophy* [Chicago, 1958], p. 271, etc.). Scientists may master their perception of the subject matter, but not the underlying reality.

We have to remember, of course, that the analogy between this confidence and faith is a very broad one. Scientific work does not have religious notes, and faith is more than a confident agreement with the data. The analogy between axiom and dogma finally comes to a point where they are no longer comparable.

In nontheological sciences it is possible to some degree to choose between systems and their axioms. One might decide for a Euclidean or a non-Euclidean geometry. Albert Einstein decided for the second of these, that is, for different axioms of measurement. But his decision did not make the older three-dimensional geometry in everyday use mistaken. Once the decision is made, however, we have to abide by it. If we adopt the axioms of mathematics, we must work with them and not against them. We have to recognize the arrangement of numbers and not begin to probe into the historical roots of the system or how its use was established.

One feature of axioms is that they open up scientific operations. Biology, for example, defines "life" by a set of parameters which are fundamental for planning and realizing experiments in order to acquire empirical observations. Thus they may be corroborated, although it is not possible to verify them by experiments, as noted by the distinguished physiologist Chandler M. Brooks of Brooklyn. A scientist who does not accept the axioms of biology does not make an arbitrary decision, but simply denies the possibility of the scientific investigation of life. There may be reason for such a decision; science may be forced to modify or even to drop axioms. Such a decision, however, does not refute their validity, namely, their validity relative to the knowledge that has been gained with their help. The discovery of axioms is one of the goals of science. Science always has to seek more comprehensive systems of explanation. This is not due to theoretical curiosity. We can think of the shattering that comes when questions have not even been asked, as in early twentieth-century physics.

The field of study can limit the ability to choose axioms. After Einstein, a mathematician can decide for the geometry of Euclid or Riemann. But physicists cannot make choices of this kind. Their task is to describe specific spheres in the world of matter.

Something of the same applies in theology. Some theologians, it is true, do not decide in favor of the doctrine of the Trinity. We often find this to be the case today. But nevertheless this does not imply, however, that their theology becomes "normal science." Quite the contrary! Friedrich Schleiermacher, for example, opted for different axioms. He built upon the constitution of the religious self-consciousness rooted in the "feeling of absolute dependence" analyzed as the constitution of religious subjectivity containing the notion of God. He could deal with the doctrine of the Trinity only in an historical appendix. He used it for historical demonstrations of building up concepts, but it was not theologically basic. In *The Christian Faith* (2nd ed., 1830-31, trans. H. R. Mackintosh and J. S. Stewart [Edinburgh, 1928, reprint 1976]) §§170-72 treats the divine trinity as a combination of various statements about Christian self-consciousness. Traditionally Schleiermacher stayed close to the philosophy of religion. Today many of the principles of predominantly sociological or psychological structures, or a mixture of both, are integrated into theology, mostly without sufficient consideration of this axiomatic shift.

The comparison of sciences in terms of their axioms does not cover the constitution of the axioms, their inner structure. We cannot know these from the historical genesis of certain insights, valid though these may be. In thinking of Christian theology, we might focus on the overwhelming encounter with the person of Jesus of Nazareth who brings God near to us, or on the Easter faith of the disciples which transformed the shattering experience of Golgotha into confidence of a life with God. But we do not learn from these what it means that God became incarnate or that Jesus is one with God. Another example: what the Jews say about God as Deliverer cannot be deduced solely from the experience of the exodus. The exodus and Easter became important data in the history of Israel and the church. They are the starting points of the historical recollection that always has to be made present by retelling. But *what* is really told here? Or, more precisely, about *whom* and *what* do we speak? To reply to these questions we need a depth structure that is certainly contained in the biblical narratives but that has to be made plain as such if we are then to recognize it in other connections.

A new state of affairs has been created: unexpectedly and surprisingly, contingent and not deducible from all former experiences and all of the expectations which arose from these experiences. To articulate such a fact immediately implies talk of God, because such a fact implies God's self-manifestation and self-disclosure. This articulation, therefore, gets a profile and makes it possible to recognize God's action in comparable situations. This is the outer surface of theological thought "in the making": persons are able to talk of God in a more or less different way. Now they call God the Liberator — with respect to the Exodus — and they call upon God who acts in the life, death, and resurrection of Jesus.

It belongs constitutively to what we say of God — this is its inner structure — that all that we say now points to God. We confess that we are not basing all this upon ourselves, not even upon religious experiences which are repeatable. To use the terms of Christian theology, we are bearing witness to the revelation of God, to his self-disclosure as the mystery of human speech. We can speak of this mystery only as a mystery. Even if we talk of it as a mystery, it does not lose its character as a mystery, and as a proclaimed mystery it cannot be absorbed in talking about it. Human talk of God becomes transparent for God's Word. Naturally, we can only repeat what God says, and therefore talk of God. It is very plain, however, that the basis of what we say does not lie in itself but in the mystery of the coming of God within human speech.

Theological statements are grounded in the externality which may be known as the scope of God's action. These statements do not represent God's action, nor the totality of the reasons for it, at any possible instant of statement. They speak instead in faith and in hope. They speak out of a genuine, nonrepresentational recollection and toward a genuine, non-representational expectation.

As rules definitive in dialogue for finding truth, theological axioms demand a discursive presentation. This must be the task of dogmatics. It must open up and play a part in constituting for us the whole sphere of its subject matter, the externality, the being of God, the revelation of God, and the work of God in all its scope. Like any other axiomatics, theological axiomatics has internal assumptions of reality that help to structure its own reality, but these are also dependent on the contribution made by the given reality.

Discursive exposition in the search for truth aims at a genuine concord of theological assurance, namely, at the knowledge of, and agreement with, the will of God in Jesus Christ through Scripture (III.3.1).

A genuine conditioning by time characterizes the subject matter of theology. It is structured by statements made in faith from a specific "past," and with a view to hope in a specific "future." Yet the fact that we cannot formalize these times also characterizes this subject matter. Certain theological statements do not apply at all possible situations in the same sense. They are true, but valid only at specific moments. (We might take as an example the saying that God has done all things well.) We cannot recall or demonstrate such statements. It is thus doubtful whether we can speak of these statements, which we are unable to formalize, as real axioms. Nevertheless, principles that we can develop discursively and with a view to consensus are indispensable in theology if we are to know where to begin our arguments and what are the things that we must never surrender. The axioms of theology help theology not to expect too much of itself, yet also not to demand too little.

According to the physiognomy of Christian theology that we have sketched, we can now make the further point:

50. *Christian theology outlines the event that we know as God's encounter with us, though we cannot foretell this in advance. In this way movements are discernible. Therefore the axioms of theology are constituted dialectically.*

We may start at the innermost core, the possibility of engaging in theological speech. Why should humans talk of God? Because they are no longer able to speak only about themselves if they really want to say who they are:

They are those whom God contradicts, who have broken away from what God is for them and what he wills to be for himself. When we talk of God, we are no longer in harmony with what we really are and can be. This is in keeping with the despairing petition of him from whom Jesus demanded faith, and who thus was carried beyond himself and cried out: "I believe, help thou mine unbelief" (Mark 9:24). Unbelief here is not a subjective impossibility of believing, which implies that we have to risk a leap into faith. It is a shattering recognition of our alienation from God. For this reason talking of God means first dealing with sin and grace, with this dialectic that embraces the mystery of faith: a change of place wrenching us from our terrible self-reference, the shift that comes when we are torn out of ourselves and our hopeless curving in upon ourselves. With dialectical precision Luther formulated the externality of theology as follows: "This is the reason why our theology is certain: it snatches us away from ourselves and places us outside ourselves *(extra nos)*" (I.1.2). The dialectic of faith confronts us with ourselves. We no longer have our basis in ourselves and are without hope. We are directly encountered by the proclamation and the promise of God.

The dialectic of faith prevents us, then, from grounding dogmatics on subjectivism. The "I" of the creed ("I believe") is not a fixed point of reality, or even the center of the universe. At most the "I" can bring to light the inner tensions and moving polarities within which our encounter with reality is apprehended.

Natural scientists and philosophers who have passed through the fire of the scientific criticism of knowledge can hardly follow this movement of the self. In their opinion, "I" and the "world" (to adopt these abbreviations) are dialectically related to each other. This insight is an essential aid in overcoming the Cartesian antithesis of "I" and the "world" that for a long period defined the notion of the subjects of scientific knowledge. But if the act of knowledge is a moment in the flow of the occurrence that we comprehensively try to think of as the "world," it is only approximately and with optical crudeness that we can fix and measure the various parts of this world.

A different kind of dialectic of humanity and the world has a normative role in establishing the basis of the social sciences and political philosophy. We see this especially in the "negative dialectic" of the early Frankfurt School (Max Horkheimer, Theodor W. Adorno). The perplexity that is caused by the conditions of being under which we live is here an aspect of our involvement in history, which is a field of unceasing formation and change. The shaping of the world is thus a process in which humans change as they advance true progress by rejecting anything that does not and may not persist. Dialectic is here a productive struggle with the perversely created world, the perverted world that still has within it the sources of renewal. This view attracts many theologians, for God can be made plausible as the Wholly Other in contrast with this world. Indeed, it appears that God might play a part as a force that moves the world. A knowledge of theological axioms and their constitution has to be on guard at this point.

It is true that this approach leads us far beyond subjectivism and self-referential subjectivity. Nevertheless, it does not adequately delineate the movement of faith. It is bordered and encircled by a broader dialectic, namely, that in Jesus Christ God has assumed a human life and human death. He has come into the world, though he has not been absorbed by it. God manifests himself in the world even though it still differs from him. In so doing he changes it. It can no longer be a self-resting cosmos that moves itself. It is limited by the presence of God in ways that are constantly new as God reveals himself. Yet this revelation is again dialectically characterized by disclosure and concealment in the mystery of his presence. God acts "in his own way." Precisely in his revelation he is always God. "In his own way" he makes himself discernible in contradicting the exposition of the world into which we project ourselves in our efforts to interpret and shape things in time and space. God's contradiction, however, implies the possibility of recognizing God's self-disclosure, and at the same time implies that it is impossible to predict God's encounter.

This dialectic points us to God himself, not to an unceasing tension in God which might offer us the picture of infinite movement, but to the insurmountable dialectic of talk of God that is related to his self-revelation, to his work of judgment and salvation, of salvation through judgment, of judgment as salvation. Here is the extreme dialectic of Christian theology, of what it says about God, the sole and unique God; about the unity of what is irreconcilable, formulated in the biblical predicates of God that we are not able to arrange in a row: power and love, righteousness and mercy, slaying and making alive. This does not mean that God has to be one thing at one time and another at a different time. He acts in various ways in order to lead us to the unity which evades us the moment we experience it as a unity. We do not have here a higher unity or a *complexio oppositorum,* but the suspension of our split world of values. The dialectic of talk of God withstands all attempts to make God into a concept, that is, to think in such a way that he becomes the epitome of all reality. Einstein in his own way, with reference to the ordered enigma of the cosmos, said it well when he stated that "The Lord God is subtle but not underhanded" (written above the fireplace of the lounge of the former Department of Physics at Princeton University).

The dialectical structure of talk of God again brings us back to the starting point, to the question of how we ourselves can talk of God. If we truly try to do this, whether complaining, beseeching, or giving thanks, we are always set in movement toward the coming of God. Our speech of God is not able to represent him, but it can give an outline and point to the traces of God's movements. The dialectic of talking of God becomes a movement of faith so that we reach the point where we have to start. This is a feature of dialectic that distinguishes it from mere circular self-movement.

Here, then, is the extreme dialectic of theology, the dialectic of what we say of God. This dialectic is asymmetrical. It starts with God himself, and our human contribution does not form a counterweight that leads to a dynamic balance. This dialectic is finely stated in Micah 6:8: "it has been said to you . . ." For this reason Karl Barth understood the first commandment as a theological axiom: "I am the Lord, thy God, thou shalt . . ." It sets us in a specific relationship with God. We are made into hearers of God's Word ("Das erste Gebot als theologisches Axiom," in *Theologische Fragen und Antworten* [Zollikon, 1957; 2nd ed., Zurich, 1986]; ET, "The First Commandment as an Axiom of Theology," in *The Way of Theology in Karl Barth: Essays and Comments,* ed. H. Martin Rumscheidt [Allison Park, Pa., 1986], pp. 63-78). We can never see ourselves as participants in a dialogue with God even when we speak to him, and even though we may address God as a friend.

51. Dogmatics has to state what we must say "for God's sake," because we would have to be silent otherwise.

Dogmatics states what we can keep secret only at the high price of the denial of God. It points us then to its own conditions, disclosing these as its axioms or its nexus of axioms. We can discern these axioms in every dogmatic statement, even though they are not expressly mentioned. They help to keep dogmatics to the point. They prevent it from showing false considerations.

In undertaking the task of dogmatics, we accept the status of witnesses. Dogmatics helps us to weigh the price of confessing God or denying him. It must ratify what belongs to faith and also show what faith excludes. It cannot replace the testimony of faith, but it may be helpful if we have to *argue* for the faith. All its knowledge and experience in thinking, acquired and corroborated over the centuries, can help us to articulate the faith and thus enable us to convince others rather than to persuade them.

III.2.3. Subject Matter? A Question with Traps in It

The question of the subject matter of dogmatics is an unproblematic one so long as we see to it that dogmatics maintains its character. Problems arise, however, when we begin to ask whether there really is a true subject, or when concern develops that for many decades dogmatics has had no such subject matter. The question now is not what dogmatics has to say, but whether it has anything to offer at all!

Behind this widespread modern fear there usually stands the idea that the subject matter must be something tangible or demonstrable. If not, there is the assumption that subjective factors hold the field, that is, convictions, untested ideas, or mere feelings. The conclusion is that dogmatics has no real "subject" in a double sense: we cannot lay hold of this subject, and it has no suprapersonal meaning.

This concept of the subject matter arouses false expectations, and sooner or later disillusionment will follow, that is, when it is thought that this subject matter must be something tangible and that it can be understood methodologically with means that are at our own disposal. The subject matter in this case has to be a basic datum upon which all the deductions can be built up once again methodologically. If such a subject matter cannot be found, then dogmatics is thought to be without subject matter and thus superfluous.

This approach puts the question of subject erroneously. It rests on the assumption that reality is absolute and can be described objectively in a single manner of scientific language.

This standard of objectivity is said to be found in modern sciences, but mistakenly so, we might add. The desire to meet this kind of demands of science has never been successful, and indeed it is now anachronistic. It results in shadowboxing even when one is ready to face the question of the subject of dogmatics but searching for a basis free from dogma for dogmatics, when instead a process of dogmatic thinking should be released and its basic principles will then become plain.

It is, of course, understandable that an Archimedean point should be sought from which it would be possible to view the whole world scientifically. But this quest is hopeless. Our interest should be instead in the starting points of sound argumentation.

Those who pursue dogmatics have to be at one with all those who say: "I believe." Their task, however, is different. It is part of their vocation. They are responsible for giving answers to the inevitable questions, and also for showing what answers have to be excluded because they involve self-contradiction.

The question of the subject matter of theology arises at this point. The dogmatic answer is prepared and made possible by the axioms of dogmatics, and in such a way as to follow its dialectical constitution. Therefore, the characterizing of theology is one of the tasks of dogmatics. For this reason I did not strictly differentiate between theology and dogmatics.

Dogmatics has either to tell us what we must say for God's sake or we must be silent. This truth rules out all other definitions. Thus we are not to think that dogmatics can offer explanations of the world and still retain its true character. The fact that people have tried to do this is shown by the history of Christian theology. But at what cost? Again, we must not imagine a theoretical nexus of meaningful experiences and actions that can then be translated into practice. Dogmatic theology, if it is to be true to itself, may not question all the things its dialectic can then interpret as Christian dogmatics relate to the question of meaning that it constructs a theoretical polar tensions or pure connections. Finally, we cannot provide an ultimate rational basis for the statements of dogmatics at the cost of surrendering its character (IV.1). Precisely at this point the axiomatic basis of theology approximates closely to the ongoing debate over theory of science. Theologians can and should take part in this discussion, for vital experiences in thinking have accumulated on this issue in the course of the history of dogmatics.

III.3. Faithfulness to Scripture — Not a Scripture Principle

"Do you stand on Scripture?" This, so we are told, is what Gossler, the Prussian minister for cultural affairs, asked Adolf Schlatter in 1888 when he sought to call him to a chair at the University of Greifswald. The distinguished New Testament scholar, dogmatician, and ethicist is said to have answered, "I stand under Scripture" (*Adolf Schlatters Rückblick auf seine Lebensarbeit*, ed. Theodor Schlatter [Gütersloh, 1952], p. 132).

What is the distinction between standing *upon* the Bible and standing *under* it? People who emphasize standing *upon* the Bible wish to affirm their steadfastness and pious reliability. But the Bible can never be beneath us. That is what Schlatter wanted to say when he turned the secretary's question around and phrased it properly. To place oneself *under* the Bible means, on the contrary, to expose oneself to Scripture and perceive what it has to communicate.

III.3.1. What Does It Mean to Begin with the Bible?

Images of the Bible as a shelter, a bulwark, secure on every side, erected on a rock-solid foundation and therefore rock-solid itself, emerge frequently when we speak of "the principle of Scripture." Since the end of the sixteenth century, Lutheran and Reformed theologians have appealed to the Bible as a theological principle of knowing *(principium cognoscendi)*.[3]

They mean that Scripture is an unconditional prerequisite of theology because God reveals his own self there and has endowed it with his Spirit. God acts in his Word. Therefore Christian doctrine, with which every dogmatician is especially concerned, may not be attributed to any other source. For this reason theology founded upon the Bible considers itself unchangeable and unshakable by anyone or anything.

In the nineteenth century a different, sharper tone was added. The Bible became the "formal principle" which was to characterize Protestantism.

---

3. Carl Heinz Ratschow, *Lutherische Dogmatik zwischen Reformation und Aufklärung,* vol. 1 (Gütersloh, 1964), pp. 71-76. In the first chapter, "De sacrosancta scriptura," of his *Compendium theologiae* (1573; Leipzig, 1587), p. 1, Jacob Heerbrand called Holy Scripture the "universal and indestructible beginning, origin and foundation of all theology" ("commune et irrefragabile principium, origo et fundamentum totius theologiae"). Johann Friedrich König, in *Theologia positiva acroamatica* (1664; Rostock, 1699), p. 79, relates the doctrinal statements of the Bible to the principle of knowing, out of which all theological assertions are in the first place derived and in which these assertions are finally resolved ("e quo omnia in theologia primo deducuntur, et in quod ultimo resolvuntur"). Insofar as they are inspired, they are infallible ("quidquid scriptura sacra docet, divinitus inspiratum adeoquo infallibiliter verum est"). But what human person can determine that? Who is capable of distinguishing the doctrinal assertions of the Bible from the rest of the text? The reference to the inspiration of biblical teaching is subject to a reservation which aims to avoid pronouncing the entire biblical text as inspired and thus infallible. The Calvinist Johannes Wolleb, in *Christianae theologiae compendium* ([Basel, 1626], p. 3), appealed to Scripture, the Word of God, as a "principle of the Christian religion" and applied to it the rule of all scientific discourse, that one who denies the principles is not worth arguing with ("contra negantem principia non disputatur").

The return to the original revelation in Scripture is . . . the *formal princi-ple* of Protestantism which presents itself in application as a critique, seeking to distinguish between those things which have been presented as Christian truth, but are suspected to be human work and therefore polluted by the admixture of human error, from that which is sifted out of Scripture and judged as the unpolluted source of divine revelation (August Detlev Christian Twesten, *Vorlesungen über die Dogmatik der Evangelisch-Lutherischen Kirche, nach dem Compendium des Dr. W. M. L. de Wette,* 2nd ed. [Hamburg, 1829], p. 282).

"Justification by faith alone" was at the same time defined as the "material principle of Protestantism" (pp. 280-81).

The appeal to Scripture, indeed to Scripture alone *(sola scriptura),* can have no other ground than the confession of justification by grace alone *(sola gratia):* God communicates his righteousness by speaking with us. Reading the Bible, like prayer, should be done with the expectation that God desires to give God's own self to us. The two are not to be separated from each other.[4] God's unmerited gift is communicated to us nowhere but in the biblical Word, and conversely, justification by grace and through faith alone *(sola fide)* depends on the expectation of the action of God, an expectation that leads us to Scripture and lets us search in it. We do not search there to find what we already know, what we have been in-formed about for all time through biblical instruction, but rather to come upon Christ in the pages and to hear him alone *(solus Christus)* among all the voices; we encounter him anew time after time. "You search the scrip-tures because you think that in them you have eternal life; and it is they that testify on my behalf" (John 5:39).

The "scripture principle" causes us to think of the Bible as a source which remains clean so long as people do not pollute it. But there is an ele-ment of truth in the idea of "principle" *(archē):*

52. One may not go behind the Bible.

Christian theology begins with the Bible insofar as it seriously takes "the Scripture" (i.e., the canon as the church's confession of God's address to

---

4. This is why Martin Luther takes both together: God's justification in his speaking and our justification. Compare his *Lectures on Romans* (1515-16) 3:24; *WA,* 56:213.13-14; ET, trans. Philip S. Watson, *LW,* 25:198: "Thus also the justification of God in His words is actually our justification; and the judgment or condemnation of Him actually comes upon us."

humankind) to be the place for God's self-communication in Jesus Christ. One cannot get behind the assertion that God has spoken decisively in Jesus Christ, that God has addressed us in him. Whoever pursues Christian theology honestly cannot deny this characteristic of "Holy Scripture" in its unity and wholeness. This certainly does not mean that everything that can be said in Christian faith must always begin with a word from the Bible. But all Christian discourse must be measured by whether it can be cross-referenced to the contingent event of "God coming to speech in Jesus Christ" — or whether it comes from another source.

This event may not be traced back to anything else. What the Bible says can be substantiated neither in a return to historically secured facts, nor in the psychological analysis of the authors of extant texts (certainly not using depth psychology), nor in the sociological reconstruction of circumstances — as informative as all these may be in their place. The Bible is defenseless against such attempts to get to the bottom of its texts, because they intend to use a "foundation other than the one that has been laid; that foundation is Jesus Christ" (1 Cor. 3:11). "To get behind the Bible" commonly denotes other reasons and motives. The reader wants to find the authors out by explaining their unexpressed intentions, their interests, or their reactions to discoverable life situations. Whoever tries to get behind Scripture will usually miss what it itself has to say. So, "to begin with Scripture" means at least "not going behind Scripture," but what else might it mean?

Those who expose themselves to Scripture will discover an entirely different beginning, a new beginning, within it. In Martin Luther's dispute with Erasmus of Rotterdam, the issue at stake was not least centered upon an appeal to the Bible's clarity and its important depth for binding theological language. Nevertheless, Luther referred persistently to a *primum principium*, a "first principle."[5] In so doing he took up a philosophical category that was the unconditioned presupposition of all further argumentation. By "first principle" he meant the "certainty" and perspicuity of Scripture, that is, its unambiguous communication. On the strength of this certainty one can expect clarity on the important life-and-death issues. This he contrasted with laws which only order customs and decide controversies.

---

5. Martin Luther, *On the Bondage of the Will* (1525), *WA*, 18:653.33-35; ET, trans. Philip S. Watson, *LW*, 33:91: ". . . we are obliged to begin by proving even that first principle of ours by which everything else had to be proved — a procedure that among the philosophers would be regarded as absurd and impossible."

The first principle is — God, who steps forth from God's darkness and who encounters us, draws near to us, and deals with us. Stated more precisely, the clarity of Scripture is Christ himself as the light that illumines the darkness, or, better still, that breaks through the darkness, Christ as the truth that is also the life. The reason we cannot get behind Scripture is that in it God makes himself unambiguously clear. Therefore we can begin nowhere else, neither before Scripture was written nor after. If we try to begin elsewhere, we attempt secretly to get behind our trust that it is none other than God who speaks in the Bible. For this reason any truly urgent reading of the Bible, driven by life-and-death issues, begins with the questions, "Who is the God who becomes audible and perceptible in Scripture? Who is the one of whom I read in the Bible?"

III.3.2. Biblical Grounding Also Means Dispute

The exact opposite of the *primum principium* would be to try to affirm one's belief (and certainly to assert one's belief) by using biblical words. It is because of such attempts, however, that the "principle of Scripture" has lost a great deal of vitality. This is an odd irony, yet unfortunately logical. For a long time the Bible was used to challenge ecclesial authorities, who had treated faith as if it were like a door off its hinges, no longer able to swing freely and function properly. The principle of Scripture was used as a kind of Archimedean fulcrum and lever to lift *faith* back to where it belonged. In this way it was hoped that freedom, which ecclesial authority had taken away, could be restored to faith. Since the Enlightenment the Bible itself was classified as being part of the tradition from which enlightened Christians had emancipated themselves, in order to recover Scripture's living foundation in an original and unmediated relationship to God — or so people thought. From this critical point of view, the principle of Scripture was seen as one of the last vestiges of a medieval obeisance to authorities. Though Reformation theology continued to adhere to it, the Enlightenment was the first to cast it off completely. Thereafter the Bible was continually used — and misused — to make obligatory what ought to be *done*, when other motivations were either lacking or too weak to stir people into action.

According to this line of thinking, everything that ought to be done without excuse or complaint must have a biblical "reason." It is striking — even treacherous — that today the Bible is so often "used" as instructions for action. This is not surprising when one considers how much in the

215

field of ethics today is controversial, and how even doing what is most necessary evidently requires stronger motivations than those already present. But it certainly gives one cause to wonder, when biblical precepts or mere motifs taken from the Bible are commonly used — *after the event* — to make obligatory what is already known, that is, to sanction what has already been discussed as a possibility for action. The Bible is then no longer studied to find a biblical direction for action *in the midst* of urgent and necessary decisions. Such direction should not relieve us of a decision, but point us beyond the decision to a view of God's promise. It directs our view to God's act which embraces us, an act which cannot be confused with our goals, regardless of how honorable they may be.

"Biblical grounding" does not therefore consist of a recitation of biblical references, followed by clever ways of bringing them up to date. Insofar as the grounding is the outcome of words and texts, its theological context and connections must be transparent (III.1.1.). This "connectedness" cannot simply be lifted out of the Bible, as a textual structure that can be defined in literary terms. It cannot be established by some sentence removed from its biblical context, or by some single biblical theme or concept, as if this could then be applied as a criterion for other texts. Nonetheless, the clear expression of this "grounding," in all its theological connectedness, cannot be found except by "searching the Scriptures," since this is bound up with the expectation that God speaks the divine judgment there. This judgment not only weighs what we think, do, and say, but also judges what is real: "this is how it is, and there is nothing else." Reality exists first when God comes to us, and tells us who we are. Only then do we discern what is real.

In the to and fro of personal opinion, who can do any more than put a heavy foot down? Who is capable of bringing about a decision in the midst of conflicting points? That is, who is capable of offering a word which really resolves the problem? This question was the starting point for the theologians of the Reformation in their appeal to Scripture, and it was the background of *sola scriptura: Who makes decisions in the church* — as they did at that time, when it is a matter of truth and falsehood, life and death?

53. The appeal to Scripture means to engage in the theological context of justification, perceiving it in the canonical writings and their inner tensions, in short, reading the Bible on the basic assumption that God will intervene here and begin to speak.

This expectation steps out of Scripture toward us, and we perceive it. This is not a circular argument *(petitio principii)*. Rather, the self-reference of

Scripture expresses itself as a living whole, in the same way that every living thing must relate to itself in order to exist. The Bible interprets itself,[6] not in some interminable self-conversation, but through expressing outwardly the way in which it maintains its life. Referring to Scripture therefore means getting involved in the liveliness of the Bible and living with it. In struggling to find a criterion — or, better, an interplay of normative elements — Luther struggles to be directed by God alone, and not by a rigid norm.

If one can speak at all of a "principle" of Scripture in this instance, then it is a *principle of dispute.* Scripture is not to be used to assert oneself during conflicts over claims to validity. On the contrary, referring to the Bible necessitates a conflict of a radical nature. That is, with what do we begin? How do we allow room for God? These basic questions take us beyond the crises of authority into which the principle of Scripture led us, even though the principle was supposed to protect us from such crises.

Dissent in the face of what the Bible says to us — this is the beginning for sola scriptura. When differences of opinion arise in the church over truly fundamental, essential issues, they can only be resolved by a shared listening to Scripture, when everyone places themselves under *God's judgment* and together seeks to hear what is now being said to them in the face of certain tasks, questions, and uncertainties.

54. For Christians, the Word of God perceived through Scripture is the final court of appeal on earth.

The final court of appeal for Christians on earth is not what Christians think or feel about God, nor their inner voice, which might have direct access to God. It is also not the church as God's earthly representative, as a spokesperson for Jesus Christ and the embodiment of God's Spirit. Thus *sola scriptura* proves to be an alternative to a final appeal to the church *(sola ecclesia),* or to one's own conscience *(sola conscientia),* or to reason *(sola ratio),* and especially to one's own good feeling *(solus affectus).*

The 1577 *Formula of Concord* called "the prophetic and apostolic writings of the Old and New Testaments . . . the only true norm according to which all teachers and teachings are to be judged and evaluated" (Solid Declaration, in *The Book of Concord,* ed. Tappert, pp. 503-4). The

---

6. Cf. Luther's *Assertio omnium articulorum* (1520), *WA,* 7:97.23-24, where he speaks of the great certainty and clarity of Scripture as a work that interprets itself *(sui ipsius interpres)* and that can test and judge and illuminate all things.

long and painful formation of consensus that resulted in this formula is itself a normative example of the use of Scripture as a principle of conflict.

The meaning of *sola scriptura* changes fundamentally if everything the church claims as valid has to be *derived* from biblical texts. In cases like this the Bible becomes a "source"; but it is a source in an entirely different sense from the *sola scriptura* of the Reformation, where one, so to speak, searches with all one's might in the wilderness and in the quicksand of human differences of opinion for a source which yields the necessities of life. By contrast, something which is a source from which everything can be derived appears to be a reservoir of historical investigation from which one might draw, or a supply of truths on which one may fall back as needed, or an information desk that can be resorted to. If claim is laid to the Bible in this way, then it becomes a formal principle, an ecclesiastically sealed document of its own self-assertion, rather than the primary proclamation in which God addresses us.[7]

No sentence in the Bible is actually a final court of appeal in and by itself, as if it were a matter of "this is the way it is, just as it says." Only in one place in the Bible is there an explicit appeal to the principle "it is written" — in the story of the temptation of Jesus (Matt. 4:1-11; Luke 4:1-13). Satan, the Bible expert, wants to lead Jesus astray at the beginning of his journey with an "it is written." Jesus retorts with words from the Bible. Looked at superficially, the scene seems to operate as an exchange of blows using biblical quotes — similar to a story told by Johann Peter Hebel:

> A farmer met a schoolmaster in the field. "Were you serious yesterday, schoolmaster, when you interpreted for the children the text 'If anyone strikes you on the right cheek, offer him the other as well'?" "I can neither add to it nor subtract from it," the schoolmaster replied, "It is in the Gospel." Then the farmer slapped the schoolmaster on one cheek, and then the other, for the teacher had annoyed him for a long time. While this was taking place a nobleman and his hunter rode by at a distance. The nobleman said to the hunter, "Joseph, go and see what those

7. Cf. Martin Kähler's discussion of his statement that the Bible "contains the foundational story of the church," and his formulation that the Bible as a whole is "documentation for the performance of the sermon as founding the church." *Der sogenannte historische Jesus und der geschichtliche, biblische Christus,* 2nd ed. [Leipzig, 1896]; ET, *The So-called Historical Jesus and the Historic Biblical Christ,* trans. Carl Braaten (Philadelphia, 1964), pp. 49, 128; cf. 136.

two over there are up to." As Joseph approached, the schoolmaster, a strong man, struck the farmer twice and said, "It is also written, With whatever measure you measure, you too will be measured. A packed down and overflowing measure will be thrown in your lap." Along with this last verse the schoolmaster added a half dozen slaps more. Then Joseph returned to his Lord and said, "It's nothing, my Lord, they are merely interpreting Scripture to each other." (*Schwänke aus dem Rheinländischen Hausfreund [Comic Tales from a Rhinelandish Friend of the Family],* vol. 1 [Stuttgart, 1839; reprint Dortmund, 1979], pp. 87-88)

Boxing with words naturally has nothing to do with the principle of conflict which says "Scripture alone!" That those arguing continue to refer to the gospel only increases the irony of the punchline.

In the temptation narrative the devil puts Jesus to the test by enticing him to reveal what it is that he lives on, puts his trust in, and obeys. Jesus accepts the challenge by appealing three times to the words of the Torah. He does this precisely in order to testify that he desires to obey the explicit will of God. At one point the tempter also cites a scriptural word, a psalm, which he assumes offers the promise that God can be pressed into service. By his own use of Scripture, the tempter calls into question whether the word of Scripture is *God's* explicit will. He whispers that Scripture might be a magical trick, which will help solve all life's problems, or might in the end be the most subtle instrument of domination. By offering the tempter other words from Scripture, Jesus is not trying to outdo him with a greater quantity of quotations or more convincing ones. Rather, he counters Satan's attack with Scripture in order that "it is written" could be heard as "it is said to you, said by God, and therefore it desires only to lead us to God." With this the text unexpectedly changes into a word which addresses and beckons. It is a sign of the devil when one wants to make Scripture into an instrument. Used as a weapon it can only be deadly. But in the mouth of Jesus the word of Scripture shows how alive it is, because it is heard as God's address to us. It is here that the "perspicuity" *(perspicuitas)* of Scripture appears — its clarity, which lets us behold God who now takes hold of the word. Jesus does not seek to demonstrate that he has the right biblical word at his fingertips. His use of Scripture is itself worship of God.

Why do we search the Scriptures? Why do we read the Bible at all? Indeed, why do we not just turn to it now and then, when we need some information, or perhaps even instruction, in order to put pressure on those who are not of our own "Bible-believing" persuasion?

Searching in Scripture is not just looking up quotes to reinforce opinions and prior knowledge, or using it as a book of oracles. Whoever really searches in Scripture hopes that, in the process of searching, God will become audible.

Those who "choose" God's word profess that they are addressed by it in an incomparable way. With this profession they want to confirm what they have already heard in other ways and therefore "know," but now they let it be promised to them anew. In this way they place themselves under the Bible and stay united with it (even if they do not actually express themselves like this) because they want to listen to it. In contrast with much selective listening — not to mention selective exhortation — one must be prepared for surprises if one appeals to the Bible. Thus, placing oneself under the Bible does not just mean to stay put, to persevere by oneself. Those who expect to hear requirements for living in the Bible will also experience their endeavors as being reliable and as keeping faith, encircled as they are by God's promise of faithfulness.

55. The Bible as a whole (as "Scripture") is news of God's faithfulness.

The Old Testament tells of God's faithfulness to God's creation and God's people, who are elected as a promise of blessing for all humanity. God's faithfulness asserts itself time and again against human unfaithfulness, against expectations which falsely understand God's promises because people do not open themselves to God's action but misuse God's promises in order to arrange their lives for their own comfort. In the midst of this human opposition, God expresses his faithfulness. The New Testament testifies similarly to God's faithfulness in the person of Jesus Christ, who secures every promise of God (2 Cor. 1:20) with his death and his life. At the same time this life expresses how, against expectations, even against every hope, people can experience God's faithfulness. In fact they resist God's faithfulness because they think they already know what to expect from good and evil, and this kind of resistance takes place not least in an appeal to "the law and the prophets." Here the words of Scripture have to be interpreted from a very wide scope, and their relation to everyday reality has to be explored extremely carefully because, from this point of view, there is no situation in life which has not already been summed up by Scripture. But in this process the sense of a living claim of God upon us can wither away. Because God demands nothing from the people of God without already taking responsibility for it, God issues his command in order to draw people into God's promise of faithfulness.

Jesus' use of Scripture makes us attentive to this. His words "But I say to you . . ." (Matt. 5:22, 28, 32, 34, 39, 44) strongly oppose the idea that this or that disturbed relationship of life can be put in order, or that even some unacceptable behavior can be avoided, with a mere "it is written." Jesus Christ has the authority to promise a new, immeasurable, and unlimited action of God. The words of Scripture are transparent to this unexpected evidence of faithfulness, and this changes their effects. Those who lock up God's call into an obedience to regulations hold the word of God captive, and go behind Scripture, withdrawing trust in God.

That is why the expression "scriptural faithfulness" has a double ring. In the first place it is the faithfulness *of Scripture itself* in which we trust. Scripture's quality does not depend on our faithfulness, as might be implied — a truly appalling thought! — when someone describes him or her self as "Scripture-faithful," equivalent to the ominous expression "Bible-based." Yet, in the second place, we can remain faithful on the basis of the faithfulness of Scripture — not only in encountering the Bible from our side, but in a reciprocal listening to "what is said to you." The faithfulness we experience makes our faithfulness possible.

Faithfulness is a word for the relationship between persons. When we behave faithfully we show that we rely on the faithfulness of others and others can rely on us. Several things belong to such faithfulness: listening to one another, not cutting the other short or interrupting but letting each other finish speaking in a way that will reveal our identity. These acts of faithfulness also apply to our relationship to the Bible. The Bible witnesses to God's faithfulness, and it does this precisely so that we can put our faith in God. As Michael Beintker aptly comments:

> Faithfulness toward the biblical texts remains because of the basic understanding that, in view of God's relation to us, things really are how the texts themselves try to attest, despite their human brokenness. It is salutary for us to allow their testimony of faithfulness to speak to us. Faithfulness toward scriptural texts thus implies an expectation which is not deterred by ambiguity, or even textual silence. It is an expectation that through the texts we are led to the knowledge and experience of the faithfulness of God, that here there are hidden competencies not at our disposal, indeed that their witness which refers to God's faithfulness is always stronger than their undisputed capacity for error. ("Anmerkungen zur Kategorie der Texttreue" ["Comments about the Category of Faithfulness to the Text"] in *Sola Scriptura*, ed. Hans Heinrich Schmid and Joachim Mehlhausen [Gütersloh, 1991], pp. 281-91; quotation from p. 283)

221

"Scriptural faithfulness" in this double sense — faithfulness *of* Scripture and faithfulness *to* Scripture — is the inner foundation of the biblical canon. With this a "line of sight" has come into being which allows us to perceive the living nature of Scripture together with the horizon of expectation which constitutes it. The horizon of expectation in the Christian canon is the perception of the presence of God and the expectation of Christ in the Spirit. This horizon distinguishes between a faithfulness which would merely preserve the canon of Scripture and place it under its protection, and the actual faithfulness of God by which Scripture lives, and with it all its hearers and readers.

Faithfulness to Scripture takes account of the fact that the church confirmed, in the process of canon formation, what had been impressed upon it — God's faithfulness, disclosed in a *wide variety of perspectives of expectation* in the Scriptures. These perspectives may neither be traced back to one another nor be modelled after one another. They engage with each other in such a way that perception never comes to an end, and is not reducible to a mere sequence of thought.[8] The textual plain contains several vanishing points which draw attention to themselves in such a way that the view is repeatedly directed anew toward other texts, yet without losing the unity of the whole. Consistency and openness here are not mutually exclusive; the perception is neither arbitrary nor fully traced out. Hans Urs von Balthasar, for example, in view of the "four-fold form of the Gospel," inquires whether the "unique, divine plasticity of the living, incarnate Word" could be otherwise attested "than through this system of perspectives which, although it cannot be further synthesized, compensates for this by offering a stereoscopic vista" (*Herrlichkeit. Eine theologische Ästhetik*, vol. 1: *Schau der Gestalt* [Einsiedeln, 1961], p. 29; ET, *The Glory of the Lord*, vol. 1: *Seeing the Form*, trans. Joseph Fessio, John Riches, and Erasmo Leiva-Herikakis [Edinburgh and San Francisco, 1982], p. 32) (III.1).

III.3.3. Dogmatic Rules for Reading the Bible

Our faithfulness to Scripture is dependent on a mixture of consistency and openness which emerges from the biblical texts. Therefore there is a need for reliable aids, such as are provided by Scripture itself. These are rules, bound up with fundamental distinctions, which will enable us to

---

8. Rowan Williams, "The Discipline of Scripture," in *On Christian Theology* (Oxford, 2000), pp. 44-59.

perceive each biblical text as it was intended to be heard. These rules help us not to cut the texts short, not to "harmonize" them arbitrarily, and so to use them appropriately.

56. The dogmatic distinctions "spirit and letter," "law and gospel," and "promise and fulfillment" form a context of perceptions for faithfulness to Scripture.

These theologically shaped distinctions build a structure for perception of biblical texts. They must not be regarded as expository findings. They rest on biblical insights with which the Bible interprets itself. They are rules for dialogue which assist toward a reading which opens the reader for the structure and perspectives of the text. These distinctions disencourage any interpretation which is purportedly greater than that which the texts themselves freely offer, and by which one might read the text differently, more deeply, or with greater consequence.

The term "literal sense" indicates that the stories which we are being told, and the conflicts and irritations which biblical texts direct our attention to, draw us into the very questions and answers which are at stake in them. We have to comprehend their argumentation and not merely to mirror or even to repeat them. Thus today's readers of the Bible are introduced to the different voices which come to speak in Scripture.

The first distinction, between spirit and letter, is the oldest in the history of biblical understanding in the Christian church, and has a really extraordinary story. Origen appropriated two ideas from it. In the first place, and above all, the art of Bible reading is a spiritual perception (*De principiis* I 1:9; IV 4:10; ET, *On First Principles*, ed. G. W. Butterworth [London, 1936], pp. 13, 327-28) requiring prayer (*Epistula ad Gregorium* 3; PG, 11:92A; ET, *A Letter from Origen to Gregory*, ANFa, 4:394). His second idea was fraught with implications for the history of biblical interpretation, and had consequences which were highly problematic: "spirit" was conceived as a human capacity, as a divinely imparted intellectual/spiritual sense which is open to the "upper world" as this has entered the world through Jesus Christ and now fills it. This anthropological allocation is problematic because it gives the appearance that the "spirit" does not belong to all. Despite this misleading, special doctrine of Origen, however, the distinction between spirit and letter helped the early church to read the holy Scriptures of the Jews as a Christian book also. God's Spirit had preceded the law which shaped Jewish history; it is the Spirit which reveals the logical and temporal first sense of each text.

The distinction between letter and spirit goes back to a passage from

223

2 Corinthians 3. Paul stresses its point in 4:5: "For we do not proclaim ourselves; we proclaim Jesus Christ as Lord." This is then worked out in a very condensed and tangled discussion about the Torah and its reception among the devout Jews. The key sentence reads, "For the letter *(gramma)* kills, but the Spirit gives life" (3:6). Both refer to the activity of the Scripture as God's action perceived through God's living word. God is free to act in different ways with the same text: God destroys or revives. But God's freedom is radically different from arbitrariness. God will never refuse what God *has* spoken. God communicates the divine freedom to us and breaks open the walls we have built around ourselves, opening us up to listen to God. In this respect the distinction between letter and spirit should guide every reading of the Bible. It should draw attention to the fact that we only hear and interpret rightly when we hope that God will break us open for God's own self.

The second distinction, between law and gospel, connects with the first and seeks in a particular respect to make it more precise without either superseding or completely replacing it. As a theological (not literary-critical) distinction, it does not seek to separate two sorts of texts from each other, i. e., regulations and words of comfort. It implies rather that every biblical word can encounter us as either law or gospel. In this sense Martin Luther repeatedly called the distinction between law and gospel an art — and it is worth noting in what way he deemed this art to be both indispensable and impossible to achieve.

In a sermon on Galatians 3:23-29 dated January 1, 1532, Luther calls this distinction "the highest knowledge *(maxima scientia)* in Christendom, an art with which we should be acquainted" (*WA*, 36:9.28-29).

> Therefore advance whoever is really good at this art and call him Doctor of Holy Scripture, for without the Holy Spirit this distinction cannot be discerned. I experience in myself and observe daily in others how difficult it is. The Holy Spirit belongs to this distinction. (*WA*, 36:13.22-26)

No one can say that one text is God's word of judgment, and another is God's word of grace. Law is God's sentence of judgment, and gospel is God's sentence of salvation. Both may come upon us with the same word, for one person this way, for another person another way, or for the same person in one way one moment, in another way the next. We can neither determine nor co-determine how or when a text will be law or gospel. What we can "know," however, is that God is judge *and* savior. Those who know the difference between God's judging and saving action — and how else can they know it but through the Bible! — will be able to hear the demand of the law where the sound of the gospel prevails, if God so chooses. Or they will be able to hear the message of the gospel and proclaim it when God places demands on them and others. They will understand the one or the other in its time and place and accept it for themselves. As judge and savior God is one and the same (III.2.3), or, to be exact, it is possible that in the same word God takes a different role at different times with different persons.

The intent of this distinction is to prepare all who are ready to hear the word of the Bible as God's sentence, to expose themselves to the living action of God and to entrust themselves to this action. They should be ready for these things, nothing more and nothing less.

Both of the theological distinctions identified above prepare us to answer the question, "Who is the God about whom we read in the Bible?" God meets us as personal in God's freedom (spirit and letter) and in God's sentencing (law and gospel). That is why it is out of the question to derive one of these distinctions from the other. That would merely encourage a schematization of interpretation, and unfortunately the history of reception of the Bible provides more than enough examples of that!

The third distinction, promise and fulfillment, is especially vulnerable to this danger. It deals with the fact that God promises future action, along with God's future, and even God's own self. Who but God could do that? "The Word of the Lord is truthful, and what he promises he certainly keeps" (Ps. 33:4 in the Luther translation). "For HIS speech is upright, all he does is in faithfulness" (Martin Buber). In speaking God opens up an expanse of time in which God acts, and so makes it possible for those whom God addresses to make sense of events as history. Whatever happens is discerned with expectant mindfulness of the promise.

The time-space conception of "history," however, is especially susceptible to schematization. In an effort to review contexts of events and categorize them for the purposes of historical understanding, persons place themselves in time. They do this by distinguishing everything they can "already" look back upon, from what is "yet" to come.

Such an attempt at classification has also repeatedly been claimed for scriptural interpretation. Above all, it appears suggestive for the relation between "the law and the prophets" on the one hand, and the "gospel and apostolic message" on the other. The so-called "salvation-history" theology, of whatever shade, is built upon such a schematization. It divides the Bible into an expectation section and a fulfillment section, which are interlinked by a wealth of cross-references. Their interrelational richness allows an access to be found to all the information which is important for faith. Johann Albrecht Bengel presents it this way: "Holy Scripture in itself is a *systema historico-dogmaticum*, a *Lagerbuch* of God's people in the Old and New Testaments from the beginning of the world until its end."[9] As bookkeepers, theologians can indicate how far this history has run, and what is yet to come.

In this process the promise of God is transformed into an announcement of future events. Correspondingly, "fulfillment" means that it is possible to ascertain that this prediction has come true. "Promise" and "fulfillment" are then divided into two sorts of textual groups which appear to be contrasted with each other in the course of history.

The theological distinction relates, however, to God's speaking and acting, which cannot be separated cleanly from each other. By fulfilling what God has promised, God displays his promise. Promise and fulfillment form a unity, and this is why we cannot disassemble them. God does not wait for what God says to come true. God acts *in his own way* to fulfill what God promises. Therefore "fulfillment" does not mean the filling of a void, but the penetration of all things by the inexhaustible fullness of God. God keeps what God promises — in just the way that *God himself* promises. God often fulfills his promise differently from the way we expect. Fulfillment does not mean that God checks something off (perhaps a segment of history) and leaves it behind with the stamp of "finished" on it. Promise continues to endure as God's pledge for fulfillment. It does not subsist as a kind of remainder which is still unsettled.

The story of Christ is the quintessential paradigm for the richly diverse unity of promise and fulfillment. In Jesus Christ, God confirms the divine promise in such a way that people, in communion with Christ, may hope in God, may expect God anew, and may expect something new from God. We can only believe as those who hope. To read a biblical text as promise means, therefore, to hear it as God's promise of faithfulness. Thus we become aware that God's faithfulness is not merely a cheque to be paid in the future, but that God has already spoken the divine Yes here and now and we can cling to that Yes. "Scripture gives us the divine promise and because of that we hang fast to it," wrote Adolf Schlatter (*Hülfe in*

9. Oscar Wächter, *Johann Albrecht Bengel. Lebensabriß, Character, Briefe und Aussprüche. Nach handschriftlichen Mittheilungen dargestellt* (Stuttgart, 1865), p. 144. A *Lagerbuch* in Swabian linguistic usage is the "list of all land holdings of a town or region together with their legal standing." It might therefore be translated as meaning, "the sum of everything worth knowing" (Martin Brecht, "Johann Albrecht Bengels Theologie der Schrift," *ZThK* 64 [1967]: 99-120; quotation from p. 117).

Bibelnot, 2nd ed. [Velbert, 1928], p. 19). That is why he said he "stood under the Bible." In this regard the third distinction to be observed in reading the Bible carries the reading of Scripture to a special level, without cancelling out the other two. Only as they are kept in mutual movement can they work together, freeing up new and surprising perspectives on reality and thereby demonstrating together that they are signs of scriptural faithfulness.

IV. Dogmatics in Crisis:
False Trails and Dead Ends

Once we begin to develop dogmatics down a certain path, we need to ask ourselves whether this path is one that furthers dogmatic thought, or one that distracts dogmatics from its proper mode of thinking onto a path that will soon demonstrate itself to be a dead end. Neither should it hinder dogmatics along the way so that it is stopped in its tracks and can only voice its belief from a single standpoint.

IV.1. Dogmatics Suspected of Dogmatism

Dogmatics would hinder itself if it were to claim an epistemological certitude that knows no "ifs" and "buts." Such knowledge would only need to be disseminated widely and must regard itself as demonstratively free from human error. This would be dogmatism. Moreover, dogmatics would also be hindered if it became intimidated by the suspicion of dogmatism.

IV.1.1. Endangered Integrity

When the German Enlightenment went into battle, its point of attack was dogmatism. The accusation of dogmatism was hurled against all standpoints that could be accused of being deduced from principles that defied demonstration. This included every form of metaphysics and all the modes of reflection, including dogmatics, that could be associated with metaphysics (Wolfgang Nieke, "Dogmatismus," in *Historisches Wörterbuch der Philosophie,* vol. 2 [Basel and Stuttgart, 1972], p. 277). Through the "censure of reason," claimed Immanuel Kant in *Critique of Pure Reason* (B 788), dogmatism is shown for what it is. For those in the English-speaking world, the very word "dogmatic" carries with it the implication that its knowledge rests upon a priori and implacable principles. Such knowledge is deductive knowledge rather than inductive or empirical knowledge. In this culture, even among academics, dogmatics is equated with arrogance. If dogmatics implies dogmatism, an encounter with it holds out no prospects! In the nineteenth century, Roman Catholic Neo-Scholasticism laid claim to the label "dogmatism" in its fight against skepticism (Herbert Wackerzapp, "Dogmatismus," in *Lexikon für Theologie und Kirche,* vol. 3, 2nd ed. [Freiburg, 1959], p. 457). This must certainly have strengthened the suspicion that theology, and especially dogmatics, avoided criticism of its principles.

The suspicion of dogmatism can certainly be directed toward the resistance to criticism. Hans Albert, the critical rationalist, states: "Through *dogmatization* we at any point achieve certainty, by *immunizing* any particular component of our convictions *against every possible criticism,* thus *securing it from the risk of failure*" (*Traktat über kritische Vernunft,* 2nd ed. [Tübingen, 1969], p. 30; ET, *Treatise on Critical Reason,* trans. Mary Varney Rorty [Princeton, 1985], p. 40). Dogmatism might ballast itself against external criticism, but should it do so it wastes its resources through constant efforts to confirm itself.

Today the champions of a sociopsychological theory of action, which seeks to unmask authoritarianism, find it easy to speak about dogmatism. Like many theologians, they too readily associate dogmatics with dogmatism. According to Karl-Fritz Daiber and Manfred Josuttis, editors of *Dogmatismus. Studien über den Umgang des Theologen mit Ideologie* ([Munich, 1985], p. 15), Milton Rokeach stated that "a system is dogmatic when its authors set up straw men consisting in barely nuanced convictions designed to contrast with their own convictions. The mark of a dogmatic mood is the belief that one's own convictions are the only correct convictions. These are focused on their own basic convictions. Their underlying authority is also exaggeratedly affirmed."

Dogmatism of this kind always fails. Such a dogmatic mood is perceived to be authoritarian, and consequently rigid, aggressive, arrogant, and incapable of dialogue. Such a diagnosis does nothing to improve the possibility of dialogue. No one wants to be suspected of subscribing to dogmatism. This would be a mortal blow to one's reputation. In turn this leads those accused to accuse their critics of falling into dogmatism by establishing the principle of unceasing criticism. They would accuse them of appealing to principles that stand above criticism, such as rationality, which unites prosecutors, defenders, and judges, but is self-enclosed rationalism in the end.

When the verdict of dogmatism is passed, it usually signals that dialogue is over and that the battle of worldviews has begun. The weapons that will be used here are for the most part the white elephants of earlier controversies. They are blunted weapons, but they can still be quite devastating. A closer investigation discloses that false alternatives will often lead to unbridgeable antitheses. Thus deduction and induction are seen as antithetical procedures. Detailed statements are either deduced from a theory or explained by a theory, or the theory itself is built upon the description of repeated processes and this makes possible further deductions. The truth is that deduction and induction are different ways of describing reality, not different approaches to its understanding. We must decide for ourselves how we use them.

At this critical juncture we should not lose sight of the way dogmatics is constituted. The basic condition of all theological speech is that God has acted by drawing the human race into his will and purpose. Acceptance of what he has done by way of promise, and of what he will do (I.2.1), is constitutive for dogmatic thinking. What dogmatics involves is that we confess ourselves to be hearers and that we thus show that we recognize the presuppositions of what we say (II.4.1). We hold fast to this in seeking the will of God. Any other attempt to provide a basis for theology would misdirect the starting point of theological speech and dogmatic reflection and would fail.

The steps we take in dogmatic thinking point us to the externality, where faith, hope, and love are grounded (I.1.2). Hence dogmatics follows the scope of the work of God. It tries to do this progressively, thus taking into account its linguistic form, the basic theological context of justification (III.1.1). At this point we must discuss the grounding that underlies each dogmatic argument. Upon what does it rely? What can it imply? What does it promise? Such questions help us to formulate theological axioms (III.2.2). The question of the subject matter of dogmatics (III.2.1 and III.2.3) offers us a glimpse of the rich distinctions and the inner differences that have come to light at key points in dogmatic history. Experiences in thinking of this type have also drawn attention to the weighty errors that have been caused by apparently easy solutions, as, for example, when efforts were made to make God the direct theme of dogmatics, or when its immediate theme was sought in the inner world of devout subjectivity. We must find the sphere of dogmatic themes only by referring to the divine activity.

Clarifications of this kind awaken our critical attention to self-enclosed convictions that are also self-based, to strivings for a single certainty, and also to the tendency to create a hothouse for theology where it can develop undisturbed theories about the human heart and fruitful living. We ought to exploit these sources of self-criticism instead of raising false questions and fronts that might block them. The critical ingenuity and potential for openness to far-reaching insights of theology can hardly be surpassed. All depends upon whether we understand clearly what we may talk about and what we may properly discuss. We must not count on openness to dialogue and readiness for revision as virtues in themselves.

The theory of dogmatics that is our present concern might seem to outsiders to be no more than a catalogue of standards of correctness. Yet those who think in terms of these standards will quickly appreciate their depth and sharpness. When speaking in this connection, we will be so involved in the breadth of these statements that it will not be enough to show how logically correct they are. What must be said unconditionally and in all circumstances will be our support in both life and death. It will affect what we do and what we leave undone. Will this really happen? Only God can decide. All our judgments about the soundness of theological statements await the verdict of God. We can offer no human proofs of what we say theologically. We must be aware that we cannot define theological statements as finally true. They are always definitive in dialogue (I.2.2) and are thus reliable enough. Yet they remain open to point and counterpoint. We must put the statements of theologians in the context of the life of the church, of what faith says (I.5), and of what faith discusses (V.3). This will make us aware of the presence of God that encloses us on all sides, so that it cannot be perceived by an individual or individuals alone. All this transcends a dialectical movement between the subject of knowledge and its object. It transcends, too, many of the axioms in the communicative discovery of truth! Every effort to prove unshakable epistemological certainty is absurd.

We no longer need to concern ourselves with the idea of dogmatism as a false intellectual step, nor should we be concerned about self-assertion that is much more rigid and self-assured than the circumstances warrant. Our interest is not in the unmasking of psychological or psychotherapeutical attitudes. The vital question is whether dogmatic statements are based upon dogmatism or not. How are we to decide? Is dogmatism a surrogate or substitute for dogmatics? Is it a sublime threat to speaking in faith and hope and love? Does it pose a risk to dogmatic thinking?

57. Dogmatism can occur as a result of an exaggerated effort to apply dogmatic logic. This can happen when the formation of theological judgment is replaced by a scheme of understanding that interprets everything we encounter in terms of a human reference to God, and consequently claims to know about everything that can happen. Dogmatism is an opponent of theological integrity.

Dogmatism is an accompanying symptom of dogmatic sickness, of a crisis that overtakes dogmatics when it is asked to do what even with the best intentions it is unable to do, or when claims are laid upon it which are of such weight that it loses sight of itself.

This alienation may be imposed by the external pressure of censure, which permits talk only according to an extraneous standard, and not according to the limits of dogmatic self-criticism.[1] Theologians who want to do justice to different norms (e.g., philosophical, sociological, or linguistic) tend to impose this kind of censorship. Their interest is normally in either their academic self-understanding or in the problem of basic communication, not in the question of what can be perceived theologically and brought under discussion as real knowledge. Their concern is not in knowledge for knowledge's sake, but in how to make theology respectable. If a crisis then arises, it will be due to a constitutional weakness, or to a latent sickness that will sooner or later express itself. The crisis can be a help toward healing. But it may also be fatal, leading to asphyxiation. When this happens, all that is left are mummified memories and ideas that have given up the ghost.

Here we are close to a pathology of dogmatics, which can easily develop into a dramatic scenario picturing differing concepts of illness. Dogmatics has, of course, a long, varying, and often conflict-filled history. Its normality is rarely obvious or memorable, especially in comparison to the scurrilous misdirected paths taken, which often evoke fear and perhaps pity as well. To discover living dogmatics in pathological tendencies is a typical example of the crisis of dogmatic thinking. This can be illus-

---

1. For the modern sense of truth as a dogmatic reference point, cf. Emanuel Hirsch, *Leitfaden zur christlichen Lehre* (Tübingen, 1938), and Wolfgang Trillhaas, *Dogmatik* (Göttingen, 1962), pp. 57-68. We might also note contextual theology (IV.2.1) with its demand that theology be socially and politically functional.

trated in a sketch of the doctrine of providence. In doing so we will see the limits of what can be said in faith and hope and love, even though for the good of humanity it might seem to be desirable to say more than can be said and to establish some control over our lives that pass our understanding.

Dogmatism lurks on the far side of these limits. It takes the form of the assertion that all reality can be understood and deciphered as coming from God. Its patterns of interpretation are so self-enclosed that a ready answer can be given to every possible question. Dogmatism, of course, will give the answers only for prepared questions. What it says will be so relentlessly asserted that it is said to be factual. No room is left for openness or flexibility. Dogmatism can only repeat itself. It resists criticism. It has long since immunized itself against any counterquestions.

The doctrine of providence is a good example of the close relationship of dogmatics to dogmatism. Dogmatics can easily slip into dogmatism, but dogmatism can only with great difficulty regain the definition of dogmatics and its preserve.

That God has planned and ordered the world; that in it he follows up his own purposes that with some insight into the course of things we are able to measure, at least insofar as we can adapt them to our own existences and live lives that are pleasing to him: These ideas were adopted by Christian theologians from the practical philosophy of Stoicism in the first century. Stoicism had taught that God planned and gave order to the world, where he accomplishes his purposes. We can gain some insight into the course of things and can measure our wisdom to the extent that we can align ourselves in our existence to God's purposes. Thereby we can live lives pleasing to God. These ideas seemed to fit in with basic biblical insights, namely, that God directs the destinies of those that belong to him and makes known to them his will by interventions in their histories. Has not this will been manifested in a special way that affects the whole world, that is, by the coming of Jesus Christ? The concern of these theologians was to make understandable what God did in and by Jesus Christ, to offer an "apology" for it, an account of what Christians believe that would demonstrate its credibility for those outside. The apologists counted on the fact that their contemporaries would be open to this faith so long as they could provide answers to open-ended questions. These answers were based on notions that Christians shared with non-Christians. The answers, the apologists thought, would also help to answer the questions that were facing the church. Why, for instance, had God sent his Son to redeem the world? Why had he done this at this particular time and place, and not sooner or later, or somewhere else? Why did history have to go on after the resurrection? What change had been brought by the resurrection? How does our present history relate to the time prior to Christ's coming?

The idea of providence, of the saving will and plan of God, seemed to offer a key to answering these questions. It also offered the chance to overcome the rigidity of the Stoic concept of God, claiming that from the very first God ordained that everything that took place in the world would have to follow well-regulated paths. In tracing world occurrence, the idea of providence posited a goal that would reach far into the future. God was working unceasingly to achieve this goal.

What was the relation between this line of thought and faithfulness to Scripture (III.3)? To respond to this question it is not enough simply to mention instances of what is said about God's plans and purposes. We have also to consider how and when it can be said that God directs human destinies and brings to fulfillment what he has willed.

The story of Joseph and his brothers provides an illustration. Genesis 50:20 reads: "Even though you intended to do harm to me, God intended it for good, in order to preserve a numerous people, as he is doing today." The one whom the other brothers had once rejected had now become the one who aided them in their distress, which now threatened to destroy the whole family. God had used the death-dealing goals of individuals as a means to protect them from hunger. The story is, of course, full of twists and turns and dramatic changes, which pose a threat to the final outcome. But God takes up the human designs into his own purpose, so transforming them that when we look back we can see what could not enter into our calculations. Joseph will not exact vengeance. He is not God's representative (v. 19). The brothers need not be afraid. They should fear God in thanking him.

This backward-looking glance should have a place in our thanksgivings. We should be amazed that we are still alive in spite of all that we have done and left undone. But we should also have hope in the promise of blessing, the promise of the future of God's own people, which will be fulfilled in a highly unexpected way that is contrary to their own purposes. To be able to say this, we need figures like Joseph who, for all their own planned and forward-looking activity, cannot take the place of God, but align themselves to his judgment. In doing this, we can attain the wisdom that is denied to those who are concerned only about their own plans and hopes and must then wrestle with the unforeseen consequences.

The story of Joseph points dogmatics in the right direction. We learn here what the result of the events is when it is put in words and concepts. We run the risk, however, of formulating what is not in the story but is suggested by it. Dogmatism does this. It grants autonomy to a specific interpretation, not only of this story, but of every story. This model of interpretation has its own logic which prejudices whatever stories we might study in favor of this understanding. Thomas Mann did this for the story of Joseph in his novel *Joseph and His Brothers* (New York, 1945) where he developed a gripping and tormenting narrative. He depicted Joseph as a man who was so convinced of his own uniqueness that he could control his life in spite of all the blows that fell upon him. From the standpoint of religious psychology, we have here an antithesis to the doctrine of providence.

Another story that leads us in the same direction is that of the conversation of the risen Lord with the two disciples on the way to Emmaus. These disciples could not understand the events of Good Friday and Easter Day. "Did not Christ have to suffer these things in order to enter into the glory of God?" (Luke 24:26). This is the question asked by the unknown person, who puts right the obvious question: "Why did Christ have to suffer?" He is not offering an explanation that will show how plausible was that inconceivably dreadful happening. He does not point, for example, to the concept of a suffering Messiah, or to a redemption that can be attained only through suffering. He teaches them to read the Holy Scriptures with a reference to Christ, who had come to do what God willed. This must be the meaning of Scripture for those Jesus meets on the way. This meaning is very different from that which we find when we ask what is "meaningful" or "meaningless," for in that case we presuppose that we know already what "has meaning" or "makes sense." When we read this story, or when we hear it, we should remember Jesus' prayer in Gethsemane: "Not my will but yours be done" (Luke 22:42). Praying, Jesus seeks the will of God. He does not equate it with what happens but with what takes place for him, with what he lets take place, in expectation of suffering as God has willed. This distinction helps us to separate the doctrine of providence from an explanation of the world that equates the will of God with all that happens, or seeks it in what ought to happen according to the measure of our own knowledge of the will of God. This hairline distinction forms the boundary between dogmatics and dogmatism.

The controlling theological question when we speak about providence (or the meaning of history or of suffering) is this: Does it safeguard the character of dogmatics? Have we considered the cost of the statements we make (III.2.2)? They might cost us our life. Or at least the confidence is shaken that all that happens to us, with us, and through us fits together in an intelligible way. It is possible to speculate and debate engagingly the purposes of God and the order of things, but can we not be responsible for what we think and conclude? Does it make sense? Are we afraid of either saying too much or not being ready to say more? Will what ought to be said in faith and hope and love merely evaporate into a vague adjuration of God and of his unfathomable dominion that differs so much from what we can comprehend that we are left seeking our path in the mists? Statements about God's providence force us to examine ourselves. Do they truly depend on the externality of the promises of God that will give the church its direction even in relation to what lies beyond its boundaries? Are we really aware of how far-reaching is the work of God? How far reaching in time and in space as well, its height and depth, its intensity and extensity?

It is no accident that precisely when he speaks about providence (though using other terms), Paul has these dimensions in view:

> We know that all things work together for the best to those who love God, who are called according to his purpose. For those whom he foreknew he also elected to be conformed to the image of his Son. . . . What are we to say to these things? If God is for us, who shall be against us? He who did not spare his own Son but gave him up for us all, will he not also give us all things in him? . . . For I am certain that neither death nor life, neither angels nor powers, neither things present nor things to come, neither principalities, heights, depths, nor anything else in God's creation, can separate us from the love of God in Jesus Christ our Lord. (Rom. 8:28-29, 31-32, 38-39)

Paul speaks of separation only in relation to the past. The forgiveness of God has erased it.

The apostle offers no positive prognosis here. We cannot measure by our standards of good and ill how everything will be for the best. We do not even know what to pray for (Rom. 8:26)! Being taken up into the will of God is the decisive thing. God has foreseen this. He has not merely foreseen it. He has provided for it. The God of judgment and salvation has acted for us, for guilty and condemned humanity (Luther, cf. III.2.1). God's election does not restrict his providence to a few. It does not exclude all the rest. We must look further afield, first to the groaning creation in its frustration (Rom. 8:20-22), then to the fate of the Jewish people which announces God's coming work (Rom. 9–11), and then to the doxology that "from him and through him and to him are all things" (Rom. 11:36).

Paul's understanding is a fitting development in the basic theological context of justification (III.1.1). It relates the destiny of creation to the inconceivable point at which it was unwillingly plunged into frustration. But it also demonstrates an awareness that the hope of our suffering fellow creatures is part of the hope of the redeemed and that this hope is based only on what God has determined for creation as a whole (Rom. 8:22-25).

What theology can say about providence is marked by a certain imprecision. We are unable to identify the work of God with the actual course of things. Yet God does not do his work above and beyond things. He works in them and with them. At times we can see this work, at other times it is hidden. Faith becomes hope in that it does not try to overcome the resistance of not seeing or knowing, either by evading this resistance or presuming more knowledge than one can have.

58. The specific lack of precision of dogmatic language is due to the way we describe facts in a theological way that seeks to identify them linguistically and conceptually, even though the work of God cannot be pinned down by us. Such judgment is left to God. Therefore dogmatic speech arises within an eschatological perspective.

Consequently Paul speaks confidently — he knows that he can say that hope grows patiently when it is exposed to temptation and suffering (Rom. 5:3-4). This saying, too, characterizes the imprecision that clings to dogmatics. The confidence of faith cannot be a personal possession. It cannot be observed; it is not a human endowment nor an achievement into which we can grow. In the end we must say that we cannot allow talk about providence to use our own destinies, the way things happen to us, as a general standard. When we look at the suffering of others, an even greater uncertainty grips us. We do not know what to pray for (Rom. 8:26). Trust in the providence of God stands closely related to the "we" that is constituted by the blessing of God, the address of the community (II.5), and the recollection of the church (I.5.3 and III.1.2). Faith in providence is also bound up with prayer. In prayer all the others who pray secretly join us, for we all share the language of prayer.

To a large degree the doctrine of providence is implicated in the work of the church. If it is detached, dogmatism creeps in. Providence is then seen as a network of global connections. Much information is fed into the doctrine. The Pauline saying that all things work together for the best is twisted. Either it tells us that we must make the best of things, which is good positive advice but something quite different from the divine promise of provision. Or else it tells us to learn to see that sooner or later something good may come even if it be through pain. If this were so, trust in the providence of God would be a basic insight of universal application. Dogmatic statements would then be changed into interpretations of all reality.

How, then, are we to proceed (III.1.3)? How far can we or should we go? We certainly should not go so far as to think that we can pervert theology into a grandiose coordination strategy which views the course of things in the world as God sees them, or claims to be able to do so.

We think, for instance, of theodicy, a justification of God face-to-face with irrational suffering and inexplicable evil. Destructive natural events make it plain that we are the victims of natural forces, innocently so or not. People also act with such unheard-of cruelty to one another that any assumption of a moral world order is shattered. If we try to trace back these inconceivable things to the purposes of God, and thus to disclose their meaning — for example, that they are instruments of education (sufferings serve a goal) — we will easily fall victim to cynicism. Explaining the suffering of others violates the integrity of that suffering.

Looking at things and explaining them in terms of the will and plan of God does not provide a basis for what must be said in faith and hope and love. We cannot answer the question why things happened as they did. But we can cautiously answer the question why things happened to *me* as they did by trying to put it afresh within the basic theological context of justification.

Should we try to equate this answer with a comprehensive explanation of reality, we will suffer a great loss of theological integrity, which is to be regarded first as the integrity of those about whom and to whom we speak.

59. Theological integrity means not promising more than we can perform, not feigning an insight that cannot properly be attained, not allowing for errors and confusion in thinking or discourse even for the best of purposes.

Theological integrity means not concealing things, not having hidden meanings or reservations, not deceiving either ourselves or others, not saying things that we cannot stand by in the long run, not laying claim to perspectives that can claim to be right only because they are full of loopholes. Theological integrity means not surreptitiously speaking about other things than the real issue; for example, about the general validity of theological statements when we ought to be considering the universality of God. To do this is to confuse two different issues, the validity of theological statements on the one hand, their far-reaching range on the other (II.9.2). Integrity means asking in such a way that real point and counterpoint are possible and dialogue can proceed (Rowan Williams, "Theological Integrity," in *On Christian Theology* [Oxford, 2000], pp. 3-15). Above all, integrity means not becoming mired in self-contradictions. It is a fundamental self-contradiction to posit something at the outset that later has to be retracted — for example, the promise to induce faith.

IV.1.2. The "Doctrine of Principles," "Fundamental Theology," and Encyclopedia as Signs of Crisis

Dogmatics can proceed when it is clear where it is going (III.1), where it starts, and how far it reaches (III.2), also behind what it may not go (III.3).

We are going in the wrong direction as soon as we fail to recognize the point of departure and of reference for dogmatics. We need to ask: What are the criteria for assessing our experiences in theological thinking and how might such an assessment be possible? The false path may at first seem passable, but in time following it will mire us in a thicket in an inaccessible country. Those who wish to follow this path at any cost will easily become nervous as they frantically seek new directions instead of admitting that they had made the wrong decision. They are not really doing dogmatics. They have lost their way. They have deviated not merely from a trail but from the very track.

60. A crisis overtakes dogmatics when theologians are no longer sure where to begin, when they try to find an intelligible basis for theology which will be open to all and which will allow approaches that have general validity, so that the step to faith will come almost as an afterthought.

Crises develop from errors of thought and the miring of discourse that may easily appear. They are rooted complications that are not so easily overcome. When we take a look at the development of dogmatics (III.1), we can see how such a crisis is characterized: as a path to dogmatics that just keeps getting longer and longer. Decked out with references, it promises to introduce more predogmatic foundations that will carry more weight than any of the reasons that dogmatics has thus far proposed. The guides along this path carry the warning sign that we must not begin directly by thinking in dogmatic terms. We must not count on the fact that there is a church, but rather to call it into question in order to discover what its function might be, and then, perhaps, find good reasons for joining it. We should, they think, not try to speak in faith before we have found out what faith means, and how attainable it might be. This would be like staying out of church for a stipulated time or like staying at a calculated distance from joining in its work. Dogmatics is thus put in the sphere of virtual reality, and sooner or later it will prove to be only a castle in the air.

A first crisis is that of making a false beginning. This is called fundamental theology. Roman Catholics gave it its name, and Protestant theologians then adopted it. It might also be called a doctrine of principles, or even prolegomena, that is, what has to be *said first,* before we can take up the themes of dogmatics. This concern to find a stable foundation can take different forms. It cannot be brought under a common denominator, though it always bears the same title. At this point we shall simply describe the symptoms of the crisis.

The aim is to name the presuppositions of faith that all people could share, at least all intelligent people, when they would think along these lines. One such basis could be reason as a human attribute, or our linguistic ability in which reality is disclosed (Gerhard Ebeling), or hope as that with which we stretch out our feelers for the boundless (Wolfhart Pannenberg), or the feeling of co-humanity with which we attain to personhood (Hansjürgen Verweyen). Though there are exceptions that prove the rule — e.g., Wilfried Joest, who limits himself to describing the references of theology — fundamental theology intends to give a foundation that is prior to the grounding of Christian faith and hope. This attempt at providing a foundation is the result of a confusion of the scope of theological statements and the sphere of their validity (II.9.2). General validity is sought according to the assumption that only by doing so can truth-statements about God be demonstrated. The idea is that the deity of God is disrespected if it is only meaningful for believers. But how can fundamental theologians achieve what is of general validity? Only by not initially using theological language. Their contemporaries can thus feel that what they say to them in ordinary terms is addressed to them, especially when they put it also in the terms of proper instruction. What they tell them about the origin and goals of life, if related to the involvement and the future of humanity and other consequent and compelling issues, could carry credibility. And then, so long as they define what they say as one form of a basic religious experience, they can speak to them what seems to be in faith and hope. Does this mean that dogmatics is then given a free passage? Not at all, for the externality of faith and hope is in this case localized in that which transcends human existence and no lon-

241

ger affects us. The surprise of the unquestioned message (II.4.2) is logically overcome in the questionable nature of human existence and the linguistic possibilities this entails.

A second crisis is that of looking at dogmatics from outside in order
to test its effectiveness, its ability to convince the public. A hypothetical
counterpart is constructed which can be observed by a theologian, for the
purpose of gaining greater plausibility. This is an error of thought that
leads to the danger of disputing *about* theology at a descriptive level instead of *presenting* theology. It is also a confusion of discourse.

Behind this effort lies the concern that theology might become a
conversation that is merely of use within the church and thereby understood only there. In order to avoid talking only with those who think as
they do, many theologians prefer to understand theology from the perspective of unbelievers and to abandon the bastions of their collective private language. They want to expose their thinking to the raw winds of
public common sense — not in real dialogue. They want to internalize an
external perspective in order that "believers" may get a better view of
themselves. But a continual squinting at what is outside can easily lead to
a faulty perception of what is really there.

*61. Those who seek to develop a doctrine of theological principles, or a fundamental
theology, seek to inquire into the possibility of a theology founded upon valid
intersubjective and transsubjective principles. The theology they seek is virtually incontestable — even if it is constantly being debated. Faith should be shown to be understandable at the point where it appears to be unbelievable to those using common
sense, adopting only what is generally valid, and who thus cannot make the move to
faith.*

The doctrine of principles, or fundamental theology, rests on false promises even with the best of intentions. This leads to a dead end. What it says
differs widely from the true agenda. It exchanges talk about the grounding of theology with the possibility of making sense of theology. It investi-
gates only what is generally intelligible and makes the problem of communication a criterion of its argumentative ability. To be understood by
others means here to find a common basis, instead of seeking understanding even from those who disagree for different reasons.

We need to be just as sensitive as fundamental theology to the re-
quirement for a groundwork — even more sensitive. Theological statements should be well grounded. They need to be understood on their own
terms. That is why we inquired into their context of justification (III.1),

their axioms (III.2), and their principle (III.3). If, perhaps inquisitorially, we now inquire into the grounding, not merely of detailed dogmatic questions but of theology as a whole, we are challenging theology to validate or defend itself. The question is not what it has to say, but whether it is justified in saying it. Does it do justice to accepted standards? Is it plausible? We must pay strict attention when this type of question is raised.

Today the question of the character of the theological groundwork is hardly raised, especially where cultures have little in common, so that there is no normative validity and we are content so long as different groups live peaceably with one another and do not collide about their convictions, if they so name them. What might be said on a theological basis has in this case no links to the chain of rationality that supposedly unites all humanity, or at least its rational part. Instead, it seems to be enough if a religious fellowship knows the rules of its own linguistic use, if it learns how to express itself correctly. As Hans W. Frei said, "Christian theology is strictly the grammar of faith, a procedure in self-description for which there is no external correlative" (*Types of Christian Theology*, ed. George Hunsinger and William C. Placher [New Haven, 1992], p. 4).

This view restricts the means for grounding theological beliefs to their own arena of validity, and it understands these in principle to be sociolinguistic substrata, factual linguistic usages that groups are taught and pass on (I.5.2). The question of the basis (not the function) of this manner of speech seems to be quite superfluous. In the United States this movement is called anti-foundationalism, a radical opponent to the strategy of foundationalism, and it has both philosophical and theological proponents. (For a survey cf. John F. Thiel, *Nonfoundationalism* [Minneapolis, 1994].)

The groundwork of theology, however, does not arise within inner church reflection, like a family conversation. Dogmatics must stand on guard against this confusion. It must distinguish between the theological context of justification and the church's goal. It must not see itself as a means of steering the church (I.1.1). The theological context of justification points to the externality of God's work (I.1.2). God is calling us into his family. The nexus is thus open to all who can understand it. Dogmatics is concerned with its understandability. The theological context of justification must not be divided into the faith languages of individual churches or religious groups. It points to the *unity* of the church. It thus has an *ecumenical* character.

Against foundationalism we argue that we cannot trace back the theological context of justification to a virtual universality — for example, to the way all people who think rationally converse with one another. Dogmatics must steer a course between the heights of the universalism developed by the philosophy of the European Enlightenment and the depths of what sociologists list as the "worlds" of the languages that groups have constructed for their own particular use. The path of dogmatics has to pass between foundationalism on the one side and anti-foundationalism on the other.

Third, the emancipation of fundamental theology from dogmatics is also a crisis, for it links dogmatics primarily with tradition, and although tradition may be reactivated, it is no longer a living linguistic structure. The starting point of dogmatics, its development, and the question of its credibility all have to be tested and decided outside the field of dogmatics.

Rightly to assess this crisis, we must consider the relation of dogmatics to the rest of theology and therefore look at theology's encyclopedic structure.

The terms "dogmatic theology" and "dogmatics" arose only in the seventeenth century when the academic grouping of theology came under critical scrutiny. The substance of dogmatics had been there already in the early church, but the name was not used (I.1.1). As theology took systematic form, various names were introduced (III.1.3). The heart of theology lay in concern for a true tradition of faith, correct didactic instruction, and authentic reading of the Bible, such as theological judgments have always maintained and the gradual development of the theological context of justification has supported.

In 1659 Lucas Friedrich Reinhart published his *Synopsis Theologiae christianae dogmaticae,* in which it was his aim to offer a full presentation of theology. Reinhart did not use the word "dogmatic" when he listed the different *gradus theologiae:* church theology (didactic and positive, "given" in contrast to the theoretical constructed), exegetical theology, historical theology, and "academic" in relation to polemical theology. "Dogmatics" appears to refer to the whole of theology, so the name does not help us here.

A significant distinction came into play in the outline of theological ethics by Georg Calixtus (1634). Calixtus saw a division between moral theology on the one side and dogmatic theology on the other. Whereas dogmatic theology deals with statements of faith, moral theology deals with traditional values in relation to the universal moral consciousness. It focuses in what all people are supposed to do. Philosophy had previously been responsible for this, but now theology was given the task of universalizing the norms of Christianity. There had already been talk of dogmatic teaching concerning faith and ethical teaching concerning morals. But now the impression was gradually given that teaching concerning faith was a specific field with a different basis and a different claim to validity when compared to ethical teaching. Does dogmatics stand or fall with the claims of church tradition? Does dogmatics depend on the authority of the church, whereas moral theology finds its vitality in exchange with universal moral standards? Are not experts in dogmatic theology challenged in the same way by external pressures? Should not their answers demonstrate the power of the Christian mind to convince?

The express purpose of Calixtus was to include moral theology within theology itself. But the distinction he made plunged dogmatics into a crisis in relation to ethics, no matter whether ethics was seen as a part of theology, or there was fear of the Trojan horse of philosophy, or moral theology was viewed as an opportunity for boundary contacts between the church and society. For now only a limited validity was assigned to the church's tradition, and it was given only a restricted sphere of influence, one that would become more restricted as the church's influence began to dwindle in the public realm. Ethics was now given universal significance, the more so as it came increasingly to represent cultural mores and influential moral opinions. Programmatically from the time of Kant, ethics has sought to be a universal morality. It seeks to forge rules of conduct that are of universal application because they help to promote the unlimited well-being and even the perfection of humanity.

Heinrich Alting worked out a further delimitation. He contrasted dogmatic data (the faith content of church teaching) with historical data, the realities of Christianity that are open to historical investigation (*Theologia Historica, Sive Historici Loci Quatuor,* 1635, Amstelodami 1664, pp. 3-4). Expression was now given to an historical awareness that theology had previously defined. Sooner or later a new basis for theology itself would be demanded. The theological rivalry between an historico-critical method and a dogmatic method was still a long way off. Dogmaticians did not yet have to choose the more modest course of having to claim only an academically nonviable, alien, and even suspect revealed truth. This was the situation as depicted by Ernst Troeltsch in his "Über historische und dogmatische Methode in der Theologie," in *Gesammelte Schriften,* vol. 2 (Tübingen, 1913), pp. 729-53. With the sense of superiority that attached to those who worked in the humanities, Troeltsch's advice to the dogmaticians was that they should come under the protection of the wings of an enlightened philosophy of history that would also have a profound religious basis. Even in Alting an important switch could be seen. Dogmas, the statements of faith formulated and recognized by the councils of the early church, had now become theological data to be described by history. The rise and development of these traditions could now be investigated. How does that relate, both yesterday and today, to what has to be said unconditionally and in all circumstances? Can there even be statements that are valid for all time? The problem of the basis of dogmatic statements is thus raised in its relation to the knowledge of the Christian faith that can be proved historically. This is the wedge that would later threaten to split theology.

Dogmatics indeed became a separate department, a partial discipline of theology. Three questions were bound up with this development. First, can theology claim to be a unity, and what is the nature of this unity? Second, what is meant by theology as compared to research into the history of religion, moral teaching, or social philosophy, and where is the place for Christianity and its churches and groups? Third, what is the grounding of theology?

Theology was not (or not merely) split up into various departments and fields of research in order that its developing tasks might be more effectively distributed. Its different methods and goals do not always lead to fruitful rivalry, but rather consistently to competition. This is especially true when different strategies for foundation intrude into specific disciplines such as the attempt to provide a totally historical explanation (historicism), the attempt to provide a complete interpretation based upon a theory of action, or the attempt to provide a framework for the entirety of theology based on the sociology of religion or the psychology of religion. Each of these efforts contrasts with the effort to exchange insights with other fields of research. Especially critical to the integrity of theology, and even a threat to it, are the claims made by the new theological departments, who want their own specific disciplines to represent theology as a whole. With the introduction of practical theology, for example, its first theoretician, Carl Immanuel Nitzsch, enthroned it with his use of the word "praxis." He defined all theology as a praxis-driven science (*scientia ad praxin*) that would find fulfillment in practical theology (*scientia praxeos*) (*Praktische Theologie*, vol. 1 [Bonn, 1847], p. 5). The tendency to relate all new fields of research to theology as a whole, or at best to use them as a lever for it, is still with us today. We have only to look at feminist theology or liberation theology.

Subsequent attempts to explain the compartmentalization of theology in relation to its unity hardly do justice to the fact that over the last three hundred years theology has not undergone any serious organic development. It has drifted into several fads that have sometimes only been linked to the postulate of a common purpose. Friedrich Schleiermacher saw in church leadership the focal point of theological study (II.8.2). Karl Barth and his companions viewed theological departments as links in the exposition of biblical texts with preaching in view (II.4.1). Tillich's concept of pastoral care helped him promote concentration on the question of meaning (II.6.1). Those who are seeking to recapture the unity of theology today appeal to hermeneutics, the understanding by language, which might open up the meaning of traditions for the present day (Gerhard Ebeling, *Studium der Theologie. Eine enzyklopädische Orientierung* [Tübingen, 1975]). Alternatively, they see this unity in the theologians themselves and their attempt to safeguard their intellectual integrity (Edward Farley, *Theologia: The Fragmentation and Unity of Theological Education* [Philadelphia, 1983]).

The fragmentation takes many different forms in the various books and classes. For students, the compartmentalization of theological disciplines means being bathed in a constant swirl of standpoints differing with the lecture or the book that is being studied. This can strengthen the spirit, but it can also encourage latent unhealthy tendencies.

A division of labor requires not only a common task that brings together the different capabilities but also an interlocking of the capacities. From the standpoint of the practice of dogmatics, historical theology examines the background of what was said and done in the past in order to reconstruct its development. In doing this, it can lay bare its comparability and particularity. It relates the church's historical documents to each situation, and in this way profiles and relativizes these situations. Practical theology takes the form of a theory of the work of the church and must take note of the tension between the fields of action and the inner reasons for it. Dogmatics is dependent on both these areas.

IV.1.3. Self-Correction and Growth in Knowledge

We recall that dogmatics came into being because something new had taken place, the Christ event as the foundation that God himself had laid (1 Cor. 3:11). But what did this foundation say and mean in relation to the promises of God to his people, which the church now saw to be empowered afresh with its inclusion of Gentiles as well as Jews (2 Cor. 1:20; Eph. 2:13)? It no longer followed the line of tradition which would simply attach itself to the Jewish tradition of faith or gradually grow out of it. We had here a new work of God, even though he remained faithful to his promises. He had set up a fellowship which transcended all previous religious, cultural, and social groupings. To perceive, to express, and to reflect upon this extremely tense complexity was and is the task of dogmatics. It has to say unconditionally and in all circumstances who is the God to whose action the existence of the church points, even though its own expressions are so fragmentary and its own actions are so questionable.

Dogmatics has a critical task, for it must make distinctions that are vital for faith — even the distinction between what is given for our talk of God's action and the tradition that has been handed down to us. Dogmatics must examine precisely and give detailed attention to what really has theological status and what does not, if it has a basis and how it is grounded. An essential instrument in this critical work is formed by the question of the principle of theology that will induce faithfulness to Scripture (III.3.1). This instrument is sharpened both by answers that guarantee the art of reading the Bible and by the further and far-reaching questions that these call forth. Self-correction and growth come from attentive reading of the Bible, and they might well be inexhaustible.

Advances in knowledge have been gained through insights into the structure of the world and its temporal course; into the complications of experiences of self, space, and time; and also into the possibilities and difficulties of putting in words that which can neither be mastered nor understood linguistically, that which surpasses our human power of comprehension and which can be imparted only indirectly.

I will mention a few prominent examples. What is the relation between old and new when we refer to the work of God? When we see God retrospectively from his actions, do we not see him as the one who hides himself even as he reveals himself? Is it not a paradox that in the resurrection of the crucified one God has called to his side the one who was rejected by all and even forsaken by God himself? When we proclaim the death of Jesus Christ until he comes, we think of him as the Coming One, but what then is the relation between future, past, and present? How are we to compare or contrast the divine personhood and human personality? What is meant by the finitude of the created world and its temporal span? Hope is confidence, not reaching out into a dubious future that could bring both happiness and terror, yet what about the dramatic antithesis of hoping against hope? And what are we to think about the freedom and bondage of the human will, or the abysses of self-knowledge, or the outer and the inner self, whether it involves division, dualism, or external unity?

The insights that have promoted theology in the course of its history could take it further afield, into philosophy, for example. Conversely, philosophical and other insights initiated, deepened, and expanded theology, putting to it new questions that demanded new answers. So long as theology and philosophy don't restrict themselves in their specific roles in a friendly intellectual rivalry, they can engage in give-and-take. (Cf. Diogenes Allen, *Philosophy for Understanding Theology* [Atlanta, 1985].) We must not distinguish them too rigidly, as though thinking belonged to philosophy alone and faith to theology. Are we not to think in theology? Is there no place for faith in philosophy?

Exchanging philosophical and theological insights, however, is endangered and even made impossible if philosophy is viewed as an advocate of universality and theology is allotted only a specific sphere. This is a modern prejudice which is linked to the growing exclusion of the church from the public forum.

Recourse to universality easily neglects the fact that that on which all our contemporaries, or a representative portion of them, can agree, has itself been culturally imparted. To this many-layered legacy Christianity has contributed many things which we can see now in more generalized form. It would be perverse to say that these at first belonged to Christians and to demand them back. Nevertheless, we can and should ask what is now their context of justification. What can be said on theological grounds is always interwoven with the work of the church. If the link is snapped, this may blossom for a time, but it will surely wither away. For this reason dogmatics does not have to do only with cognitive elements or with a specific manner of speech. It has also to relate these to the spiritual life as a whole, which means to everyday life before God in the boundless fellowship of all who call upon him. Rootage in spirituality does not mean a regression into protected territory. This form of steadfastness allows room for movement into a richer dialogue with others than we might have expected.

If we are looking for a primary form of the doctrine of providence, we shall find it in prayer, in the prayer for patience, for example, the patience to accept the things I cannot change, the courage to change the things I can, and the wisdom to know the difference. The origin of this prayer is not known. A common form of it was handed down by Reinhold Niebuhr, but we find echoes of it in many other writers (Hans-Jürgen Luibl, "Das Gelassenheitsgebet. Anmerkungen zu einer Legende," *EvTh* 54 [1994]: 519-35). Did it even have its origin in the Stoic philosopher Epictetus, who expressed similar thoughts? If so, we should once more stand at the source of the doctrine of providence (IV.1.1). But Epictetus was thinking of the art of distinguishing things that are under our control from those that are not. Reflection can then classify occurrences and give them the appearance of what is incomprehensible and threatening. In prayer, however, those who pray place themselves under the care of God and seek his will, so that the context of what they say is different.

The doctrine of providence can help us to relate our life story, or some part of it, to what can be said theologically. This was depicted by a contemporary writer, John Irving, in his novel *A Prayer for Owen Meany* (New York, 1989).

Owen Meany is a young man who feels that he has been chosen to be an instrument of God. For a moment during a play he caught a glimpse of his own tombstone with the date of his death. From this time onward he attempted to direct his life toward this end, with results that he only partially understood, yet with a full trust in the providence of God of which he had glimpsed the outcome. He could not forge his own plans nor seek the hero's death of which he had dreamed. In trying to harmonize his own plans with the vision of his death, he constantly ran into obstacles. Only at the end did he — and we — acquire the connection. He had been engaged in a training exercise, the details of which seemed to be without weight or meaning. Thanks to this training, however, he could save children from their murderers even at the cost of his own life. He had sought this lacking connection for long enough, and yet it was always there even without his planning, even though he did not realize it. He moved around without any grasp of what was there before him. The meaninglessness itself plays a decisive role.

As we have seen, Owen Meany had an idea of when and how his life would end. But he did not fix on this prognosis even though it constantly affected him. He wanted to believe, to cling fast to God, to seek God's will in all his life plans, not to allow his self-doubt arising inexorably from the circumstances of life to overcome him. We are not told how to assess the experiences he had with others and himself, or what he thought about them, or how he spoke about them. The author succeeds, however, in telling his story without any division of aspects on the one hand, or psychological harmonization on the other. Gaps and inconsistencies stand in the way of any conclusive interpretation. Meany's exaltation might be unmasked as pathological self-centeredness. The author leaves it an open question whether this might at times have been possible. We might also read the story as follows. A typical American awareness of election is awakened by his dreams of happiness, and prepares him to die for others.

"Chosen to suffer" — is this the new and paradoxical message of success? The dying Meany had always wished to be given a medal for bravery. But this was only another indication of the highly developed relation between the personal power of decision and the problematic political destiny that plagued Owen Meany for many a long year.

The inner tension bridging what we can say theologically and what we see before us has developed new insights that can help to solidify new thinking experiences. Alternatively, older insights might be renewed as they say something fresh in different situations.

IV.2. Contextual Theology as a Countermovement to Dogmatics

IV.2.1. Context as a Catchword

Since the 1960s the term "context" has come into worldwide use in theology. Its intent is to place theology on the solid ground of the facts Christianity needs for proving its worth in facing political conflicts, economic confrontations, and various social divisions and oppressions. "Context" refers to the entirety of the given facts. Stemming from the context are the challenges to which theology must respond.

Context is, then, a catchword. It refers to cultural debates that have arisen in the conversation of churches that have developed under differing circumstances, or have taken place between theologians from differing backgrounds. The dependence on background and on one's own living conditions must first be brought to consciousness and clarified so that it can be confronted. This is the challenge of those who rely on "context" for theological clarification. Usually this involves the rejection of European theological traditions. When they explore the context of these traditions, they can see how limited these traditions are. They want to gain a sharper vision of the many theologies that are now possible and necessary, theologies that correspond to the varied cultural life and conditions of our common world.

To this extent the concept of "context" has been given a place that within the characteristics of this arena of speech can properly be characterized as a "context." It is determinative for this arena that the demonstrable conditions under which theology develops have not only formed and provided the external situation for this theology, but determine it fundamentally. If this is so, theology must always be explained in relation to the context which is its home. And then we simply have theologies, and not a single theology. If we have an adequate knowledge of the context of a theology, we can know what it will be, and perhaps we can foresee what will be our attitude toward it.

It might be well to recall that the usage of the term "context" was introduced by Paul L. Lehmann in his *Ethics in a Christian Context* (New York, 1963). Lehmann (1906-94) describes the church as the field of ethical reflection as "context." Ethics is Christian action within the *koinonia* of faith, within the community of Jesus Christ in fellowship with God's work in Jesus Christ and therefore in perception of God's work in the world. To paraphrase the argument of Lehmann, the church points primarily to God's work in the world, which is made known to us through the context of "God's messianic action" (p. 105) in the life, death, resurrection, and ascension of Jesus of Nazareth. This does not mean that we can disclose the work of God by analyzing the cultural, social, and political intermeshing of our own action, nor does it mean that we can perceive the divine direction by looking at the needs and calamities and opportunities around us. For Lehmann this context is always present, but it is not the real context to which our ethical reflection must primarily relate. What we must always critically ask ourselves is this: "What am I, as a believer in Jesus Christ and as a member of his church, to do?" (p. 25).

Precisely at this important point those who now favor the term "context" reject Lehmann's approach. They use the church's empirical and so-called social and cultural context to define the term "church." Here is where it is brought to light. A movement has thus been initiated which opposes Lehmann's orientation regarding Christian ethics. James Cone, a younger colleague of Lehmann at Union Theological Seminary and an advocate of black theology as a theology of liberation, wrote as follows:

> Because a perspective refers to the whole of a man's being in the context of the community, the sources and norm of Black Theology must be consistent with the perspective of the black community. Since white American theologians do not belong to the black community, they cannot relate the gospel to that community. Invariably, when white theologians attempt to speak to the black people about Jesus Christ, the Gospel is presented in the light of the social, political and economic interest of the white majority. (One example of this is the interpretation of Christian love as nonviolence.) Black theologians must work in such a way as to destroy the corruptive influence of white thought by building theology on the sources and norm that are appropriate to the black community. (*A Black Theology of Liberation* [Philadelphia, 1970], p. 53)

The concept of "contextual theology" reflects a momentous shift in direction, a real intellectual turn in thinking. It has affected all branches of theology, especially dogmatics. There are many motives for this turn in thinking. In the English-speaking world, the word "context" has many meanings. It originally denoted a nexus, especially in relation to words — for example, the combination of signs which form a text and without which they cannot be adequately understood. What is meant is a hermeneutical relationship.

The development of linguistics, especially under the influence of the social sciences, expanded this understanding of texts, and even swallowed it, for texts had now to be placed in the flow of preliterary, extraliterary, and prespoken communication. This communication achieved stability in the texts, but only for a time, for the flow constantly swept it onward. We have to decipher the flow as we do a text. It must be legible, or be made legible, as the context of the texts. Context is now the general background of a text, deciphered, of course, by statements which are usually again texts at a second stage, the highly artificial texts of the sciences that have developed these theories, that is, sociology, especially the sociology of science, and linguistics, assisted by psychology and depth psychology.

When we speak of "contextuality," we do not usually have textual hermeneutics in view, except in a figurative sense in which we demand a hermeneutics of a very different, indeed a universal scale. "Context" has now become a term for a universal hermeneutics. Texts are now construed as elements in a functional nexus which will help us to understand them, but often in another meaning that differs from their outspoken message. To make them understandable in relation to their context, or in debate with it, we must often run contrary to the grain, unmasking their concealed character of communication. We have to find out what they mean or try to mean if other aims have suppressed the real sense.

IV.2.2. Context as the Root of Dogmatics?

Another nuance of the term "context" has prepared the way to see "context" as the "environment," in its everyday and undifferentiated sense. Here it is the situation, the state of things, and preferably the network of conditions under which something exists, occurs, is done and discussed.

The first step in this direction seems to be a harmless one. How can one object to shedding light on statements or thoughts by means of the circumstances under which they arose? Will they not be clarified hereby?

Yet when we give an inch to the question for the context, it will take a mile. We are tempted to think: if we have an adequate knowledge of the context, we can explain what is said or thought, or at least make it plausible, if what is said or thought is the product of struggle with the context.

To prove this lies behind the claim that we must resort to contextuality. Contextuality will explain the development of each theology as fully as possible. It will trace back its thinking to the context or to the struggle with the context, that is, to the circumstances under which it arose. "Under which" does not refer to a localized situation only but to the determining material from which it derives its functions. In short, theology becomes explainable in terms of its function. Even if we do not go this far, the idea that we can adequately grasp a context shows an astonishing confidence in our ability to know some section of our world and to see our findings in their relation to the comprehensive nexus of relations that we call our world. What instruments are really at our disposal to view a situation in this way, to penetrate the network of this segment, and finally even to show why people thought and spoke as they did, but without realizing it, because they were imprisoned by their own presuppositions?

Of course, many advocates of contextual theology do not want to go so far. Often they use context in the modest sense of background. Theologians talk of the interplay of biography and theology. Yet here again the methodological problem is no less great. How far and to what extent can that which we know of the life of theologians help us to elucidate what they wrote better even than the writings themselves? The experiences that we can later discover can certainly shed light on many instructive details and bring out the facets of what was stated. But do they really touch on the substance of what was thought and said?

Let us take Dietrich Bonhoeffer as an example. Bonhoeffer's theological thinking was early on related to the church of his time. It was fashioned by the tasks of that time and by the responsibility he shared for making Jesus Christ real in the world. We certainly cannot value too highly the role played by the age and by his life within it, by these exceptional circumstances. Nevertheless, Bonhoeffer himself warned against any attempt to decipher his works biographically. Quite a few modern interpreters might not be too glad about it. Bonhoeffer has indeed become a key figure in the interrelating of biography and theology. The truth is, however, that notwithstanding his insistence on the "concrete," his real background was a christological way of thinking, and Christology was for him much more than a foil for a Christian program of global restructuring or a function for a medley of interests.

We might also use Karl Barth as a prominent illustration. Barth is supposed to have let fall the remark that it might be instructive to make a kind of synopsis of the rise of the bulky volumes of the *Church Dogmatics* on the one hand and political and ecclesiastical developments on the other. This would cover a span of thirty-five years (1932-67), and what turbulent years they were! Barth did not say, of course, what this synopsis would bring to light. Barth took up a vehement position in relation to, for example, the Cold War, but how small a trace of this there is in his doctrine of reconciliation (*Church Dogmatics* IV/1-3). He published this between 1953 and 1959, at the very height of the irreconcilable military and political conflict that had then split Europe and the whole world!

If what has been thought out theologically has really been thought out and is also worthy of thought, it has a dignity all its own. To be sure, it is not independent. It does not lie outside time and space. Yet it demands respect as a theological argument. It must be discussed as such. Goals must not replace argument, reflexes not reflection, reactions to challenges not replace experiences in thinking. Yet always the range of thought is such that no transition has to be made from one context to another as the claim is made for communication even to those who do not have the same background.

Thus far what has been mainly discussed are questions of interpretation and principles of reconstruction which have arisen in the field of a radical historical, sociological, and perhaps psychological form of approach. We have here an older cleavage between historicism (a radical explanation of what is produced in terms of the historical conditions of its development) and systematic theology. This cleavage constantly breaks out like a wound that can become infected. That is why it is so important for the intellectual hygiene of theology that we are to settle on an intellectually and theoretically sound use of the term "context" and not to use it without any concern for its risks and consequences, like a center of disease that we carelessly allow to proliferate.

62. Contextual theology intends to develop theology according to a comprehensive reflection upon actions within historical, social, and cultural reality. Thereby it hopes to demonstrate how theology comes into being. It is so explained as a function of mastering reality that it basically makes theology (i.e., what must be said with a specific commitment to truth-claiming statements) virtually superfluous.

Contextual theology should be talked of only as the attempt to explain theology in terms of its function. This is so because this is the claim that it makes. When we understand it thus, however, it very sensitively touches on the nerve of Christian theology, that is, on Christology.

During recent decades stronger efforts have been made to put contextual questions to Christology and even to make Christology subject to these questions. All this is in the interests of Christian-Jewish dialogue. In this dialogue the context of the person of Jesus is often sought in a direct relationship to Judaism and its historical continuity. The predicate "Christ" then serves as a key to an historical development which through the person of Jesus, the Jew, enables the Gentiles to participate in the work of the God of Israel. Jesus of Nazareth, in virtue of his Jewishness, has always been the link between his own people and the Gentiles. The church can then be reconstructed as a valid branch of Israel, the people of God. The grounding of the confession of Jesus Christ and of the confessional statements of Christology will then depend on the realized coexistence of Jews and Christians. This would be understood only contextually. It alone can allow Christians to speak about God, especially after the Holocaust, for which the church was partly guilty because it had not seen its existence as a "being with Israel," and had thus contributed to the limiting, questioning, and even the fully denying of the right of Jews to exist. The truth, then, of what we say about "God in Christ" no longer derives from the judgment of God that what we may perceive in the person of Jesus, in his life and death, and what we may receive through his gracious presence and on no other basis, is what comes to expression in John 1:17b, 18: "Grace and truth came through Jesus Christ. No one has seen God at any time. The Only Begotten, who is God and sits in the bosom of the Father, he has made him known."

An objection to "classical" Christology is that it does not pay enough attention to the history of Israel as the context of Jesus of Nazareth and of its significance. It thus bears some guilt for the separation from Judaism. The Christological dogma was trying to answer the question: "Who is Jesus Christ, the one whom we proclaim, to whom we pray, and in whom we hope?" The answer was: "Jesus Christ is true God and true humankind" (I.3.2). The criticism is that this is an abstraction, a typical mistake of the generalizing thinking of Greek metaphysics. What should have been said was this: "Jesus Christ was a true Jew." This would have embraced his relationship with God, namely, with the God of Abraham, Isaac, and Jacob. The being of Jesus Christ, his being for us, his significance for humanity, would become apparent only in his participation in the history of Israel, in the history of its suffering, which as the suffering of those who feared God, as Jesus of Nazareth did, would be expressed with confidence in God and in the fulfillment of his promises.

At last the cloven hoof of contextual theology reveals itself. It denies theology's externality, the significance of which in Christology is the coming of Jesus Christ from God, God's work in and through him, and his unity with God. On this basis we know of his true humanity and know that we share in this humanity. We do not know this because he was a Jew, decisive though it was that he, born a Jew, could call upon God as his Father and our Father. It is these theological statements, and the distinctions that are necessary for faith, that form the real context of what we say about Jesus Christ.

IV.2.3. The Context of Discovery and the Context of Justification

63. The primary context of Christian talk is the theological context of justification: all of the dogmatic statements that seek to follow the scope of God's work.

It is a mistake to equate "context" with the totality of the world, that is, to understand from the beginning what holds the world together, in order to arrange all that can be done, said, thought — and all that may be believed and hoped in the world. A consistent contextual theology of this kind would be unbelievably harassing, an instrument of oppression. Is it a mere phantom? Or does it stretch out its totalitarian feelers? Is it the music that accompanies liberation from the fetters of traditional thinking?

If problems arise here, it is as well to make a distinction between the context of discovery and that of justification.

64. The context by which we discover theological statements theoretically covers all the factors that in some way promote insights or contribute to significant findings.

The physicist Werner Heisenberg used to have his best ideas when out walking, especially on rising ground and under shade. Physiologically and for other reasons this is an interesting point. Yet it does not offer any founding for the resulting assertions. It is merely instructive for the conditions of intellectual productivity, like the rotten apple that is supposed to have stimulated Friedrich Schiller when writing poetry, or, at a different level, like the music which Martin Luther occasionally remarked as having a decisive influence upon his thought. We might think, too, of the great medieval theologians and their grandiose systems, to which their contemplative lives in the cloister made no little contribution, the mea-

257

sured rhythm of their daily round, their walks within the monastery courts. Who would not in time become a systematician when everything that he or she did followed a definite and measured course? But what bearing had this on Anselm of Canterbury's demonstration of God or on the insights of Thomas Aquinas? They do not reflect the steps they daily took year by year.

We must also think of the discoveries of Augustine. In his *Confessions* he tries to depict how he became aware of time in his experience, the flow from the not-yet of the future to the no-longer of the past, which is there in the instant of the present but at once disappears in the memory, from whose chamber it may constantly be recalled (*Confessions* 10:8.12-15; NPNF, 5:145-46). This experience of our human sense of time, and not simply of its measurement, is one of the great insights of Christian theology (IV.1.3) that proved to be most significant, especially for psychology and phenomenology in their dealings with inner or experienced time. Yet Augustine did not lose himself in the astonishing achievements of this human experience. What distressed him was that recollection unceasingly grows during our lifetime and that the place for hope naturally seems to dwindle. Nevertheless, hope in God increased for him as he sought to set his life in the context of the work of God that stretches from the creation of the world to the end of all things (*Confessions* 11:13.16–14.17; NPNF, 1:168). Thus he learned to relate his own history afresh to the movement of God's history with humanity, and to derive from this a hope that would reach beyond death. Augustine describes the context of his discovery autobiographically, for the death of a friend had caused him to put this question and awakened interest in himself, causing him to inquire into himself and there to find God. Philosophically we might also mention the influences of Neoplatonism and other movements that had reflected on time. Yet these and other factors did not really offer a basis for what Augustine discovered. We should not isolate his discovery from its real context, that of the *Confessions,* which is embedded in the prayers from which the insights derive and into which they return. The context of theological demonstration gives these insights both their cohesiveness and their references.

The basic theological context of justification (III.1.1) is the context in the strict and precise sense of the linguistic context in which we move. It is an open one, yet it is still coherent and consistent, so much so that it can support individual arguments and allow us to reject anything unsound. In it the theme of Christian theology is stated insofar as we are able to encompass it.

By means of the context of justification into which we grow and with which we advance our theological argumentation, we theologians are protected against looking only at ourselves. This context does indeed tell us that we will be betrayed into a labyrinth of complications if we would see through ourselves. Our theological integrity is at stake precisely at this point. Are we finally going to speak only of ourselves, of our wrestling with the conditions of life, of our social role, of our race and sex? Or will we take the risk of exposing ourselves to others? Their reaction to us will make us aware of where we come from. It will often be truly painful. It will show us how limited our vision is even in the theology in which we were reared. These complications can only be overcome through a shared growing into the theological context of justification (III.1.1). They cannot be overcome by trusting an approach that sufficiently promises to explain how we are "situated" and why.

IV.3. Ethics as a Catalyst for Dogmatics?

Contextual theology seeks to set theological thinking in what it regards as larger contexts. Its aim is to work with like-minded persons outside the Christian fellowship on matters of common concern. A similar view has been present since the Enlightenment, controlling ethical interests within theology and the church. Ethics is viewed here as a transition of the church, a delimited sphere of communication to the public domain. In social, economic, and political matters, and increasingly in those relating to global information, which the mass media direct, Christians, come what may, must live with others, work with others, and arrive at an understanding with others if they are not to retreat into a ghetto, which is, in fact, possible only in part. An overlapping understanding relative to action is an ethical concern. The understanding itself is a highly important task for ethics. Dogmatics can work on it indirectly at best, by reminding ethics of the values and norms of the faith tradition, and by reinforcing the piety that can provide impulses for conduct. From this angle dogmatics may still flourish within the church, with its "internal language," as in a small niche within a biological habitat, which society allows itself in order to offer protection to a variety of convictions.

But only in ethics, we read, does the raw and chilling wind blow that must bring to light the ramifications of faith and hope. Faith and hope will then be seen as the presuppositions on which our lifestyle is based. We always keep these presuppositions at the back of our minds or foster them as motivations in our spiritual economy. Their impact, however, will not extend to actual conduct. When dogmatic maxims are exposed to ethical discourse, then the latter acts as a catalyst. It produces reactions that otherwise would not occur, or would not come so quickly. It will then, we expect, rouse dogmatics from its lethargy. It will subject dogmatic particles to a far-reaching reaction that will partly make dogmatics more serviceable and partly keep its harmful effects, the poisoning of the spiritual atmosphere by rigid convictions, within reasonable bounds.

IV.3.1. The Intersection of Dogmatics and Ethics

If ethics is related to an area of global communication, then we must consider carefully once again the limits of the sphere of validity of theological statements (II.9.2). Along these lines ethics promises access to dogmatics. Such an access may respect the limits of dogmatics, but it also evades its limitedness. What is said dogmatically should be stated plainly in order that comparison may be made with the attitudes of contemporaries who are far off from Christianity. We can then see that it is mainly on the frontiers that aggravating distinctions arise that may be traced back to different motivations or norms. Does this imply, then, that there is a distinctively Christian way of acting and a corresponding Christian ethos? Are not the contours of what is Christian lost precisely in the living of daily life?

This observation finds support in a concern that particularly troubled the Reformation churches and their theology. Can a specific form be given to the Christian life? Is not this life "hidden with Christ in God" (Col. 3:3)? If we were to try to show its hiddenness and intangibility, we should make it manifest by a specific lifestyle. If we try to do this, will we not come close to moralism, the equation of God's will with what *we* do, or do not do, citing this will, in distinction from others? Theology has developed a mortal fear of moralism, of dogmatic instruction on how to live a proper life. There are reasons for this fear. What consequences are revealed when we consider the rigid group morality of, for example, the left wing of the Reformation, or the American Puritans! Their maxims of a life that is pleasing to God persisted for many generations. But the cost was high. Those who thought differently were mercilessly suppressed or excluded, and within their own ranks there arose an ongoing spiritual deformation, scrupulosity, and prejudice which were the product of endless self-scrutiny.

This example, which similar problems might multiply, should direct our attention to the trouble area of morality with a Christian stripe. Theological judgment is replaced by an assessment of what we do or leave undone, and this pushes into the background what needs to be said about the will of God rather than exposing itself to it. The access to dogmatics that moral reflection on the motives for action promises to give proves only to be a dead end. The final upshot is then that we are to trust in ourselves. It does lead us to submit our judgments, whether we want to or not, to the judgment of God. At this point we come upon a very different limit from that envisioned by a comparison of modes of conduct, and even of norms and values.

What, then, is the point of contact between dogmatics and ethics? It is where the classic basic question of ethics, "What is right action?" meeets the perception of God's acting. It is when the question "What shall we do?" forces itself upon us with unexpected urgency. And when the answer is no longer within our range of vision, let alone at hand.

When do people ask: "What shall we do?" — and this not merely because they face a wealth of possibilities or are awakened out of indolence or overconfident negligence? The question "What shall we do?" becomes an unavoidably urgent one when the kingdom of God has drawn near, the end of all things is in sight, and the time of human activity is running down with the coming of God (Luke 3:10). Or perhaps so when the coming of the Spirit of God has brought the history of Jesus so close to home that people are cut to the quick (Acts 2:37ff.). What may so far have been their aim in life is now shattered. The reply to this question, "What shall we do?" is an invitation to baptism. Those who accept baptism are submitted to the will of God. "What shall we do, what can we do?" in expectation of justification, of God's judgment which stands over all that we do or fail to do, and in expectation of the divine sanctification of all our human work, even if it be apparently ineffective.

The invitation to baptism gives an indication of how we may regard God's acting in relation to what we see as our own possibilities or to how we view ourselves as acting subjects. God is not an acting subject competing with all others, a much superior one, of course, who only leaves space for others to act within his own activity. On this view individuals could not be real persons. They would merely have allotted roles, as in Hugo von Hofmannsthal's *Great World Theater*, referring to Pedro Calderon. Theology ruled out the idea of "person" as a "mask," but here social anthropology would reinstate it.

The work of God precedes what we do or leave undone. He makes of us those who do what the Bible calls "good works," the acts that God has prepared for us, so that we slip into them and effortlessly move into their format. "For we are his work, created in Jesus Christ for good works which God has prepared that we should walk in them" (Eph. 2:10). We can preserve God's creation only if we first understand that we are God's creatures. We can establish peace only if we are at peace with God. We can seek after righteousness only as those to whom the righteousness of God has come. No theory of action is needed for this. What we need is the formation of a judgment that can distinguish between what has been done for us, because we could not do it for ourselves, and what it is now given us to do. In achieving this judgment we must follow the distinction that God himself has made, and that we must now try to fathom out afresh in our judgment.

For this reason dogmatic statements cannot be transformed into ethical statements or reinterpret dogmatic concepts as ethical directives. We cannot express God's work in terms of our own reality, for which ethics might construct a theory (cf. Trutz Rendtorff's *Ethik*, 2 vols., ThW 13,1, 2nd ed. [Stuttgart, 1990]; ThW 13,2, 2nd ed. [1991]; ET, *Ethics*, 2 vols., trans. Keith Crim [Philadelphia, 1986-89]). "Atonement" and "reconciliation" might serve as an example. This amazing and incommensurable act, with which God has restored the relation to himself that human guilt had hopelessly shattered, would thus become a divine initiative for global reconciliation and peacemaking that begins with our relationship with God but then finds fulfillment in our reconciliation with others. In this way, unwittingly, the theological concept of "atonement" is altered. What it amounts to now is simply the "reconciliation" of God and humankind, not to say the peaceful coexistence of God and humanity.

65. Theological judgment both distinguishes and connects the work of God and our human work, both the will of God and our human will, both the promises of God and our human goals, both the goodness of God and what we regard as good, both the righteousness of God and our sense of what is right, both his perfection and what is perfect for us.

Defining the relation between dogmatics and ethics must abide by the distinction that dogmatics has to make between the work of God and our human work. Dogmatics cannot speak only of the work of God. Human work does not come within the competence of ethics alone. Rather, dogmatics has to speak of God's acting in such a way that ethics does not stay limited to human action. Distinguishing between what God does and what we do belongs to the doctrine of providence. The two cannot be separated. They also cannot be mixed. Tension arises between the caring foresight of God and our human foresight.

The question of God's will relates both to the will he wants us to do as his will and the will he reserves for himself (Hinrich Stoevesandt, "Deus iustificans gubernator. Notizen zur 'Vorsehungslehre,'" in *Rechtfertigung und Erfahrung,* ed. Michael Beintker, Ernstpeter Maurer, H. Stoevesandt, and Hans G. Ulrich [Gütersloh, 1995], pp. 113-36, esp. pp. 132-33). The distinction is not quantitative, for then we would stand over both. We ask concerning God's will in order that we may accept it. The doctrine of providence is a continual reminder that the will of God is incomparable to any conceivable sum of the will of those who are ready to accept God's will. This distinction restrains our urge always to try to investigate our own possibilities when making a right decision.

Prayer forms the link between the doctrine of providence and ethics. It draws attention to the fact that God's providence is not limited to the maintenance of the creation, but that our will comes up against *God's pronounced will,* which faces us in his *commandment.* The commandment tells us where and how we are embraced by God's acting, full of promise, in what we do and fail to do. And prayer happens because we are embraced by it in such a way. The fact that we pray makes it clear that our human possibilities are limited. When people put ethical questions, they mostly think into the incalculable. They involuntarily reckon with the fact that they have an incalculable amount of time that will allow them to determine the consequences of what they do, and if need be to take corrective action should they have enough knowledge and foresight. The thrust into the incalculable moves in every possible direction. Getting the directions under control can become a burden that overwhelms people, making them incapable of action. The prayer "Your will be done, on earth as it is in heaven" (Matt. 6:10) contains the question of where we may be spared such incalculability. God's will is not an arbitrary or incalculable will, but the will expressed in his works, his promise, and his commandment.

Sound moral judgment is needed when an account must be given of the things we do or fail to do. We might be asked, or we might ask ourselves, why we did this or did not do it, or whether we ought not to have done much more. The stress falls on the "this," on the specific act, not on the "why." The "why" can be a further question in itself. Judgments must be reached when things are unclear, or when things begin to become surprisingly clear but have not yet developed into a judgment, that is, into a distinct perception. This is a perception which is aware of the distinct but does not make distinctions.

IV.3.2. The Formation of Moral Judgment in Theology

How does dogmatics as the formation of theological judgment relate to the formation of moral reflection?

66. Perceiving the work of God, especially in the specific form of the formation of theological judgment, is especially necessary when we have not only to make distinctions and reach decisions, but also to change the form of our perception so as to be able to test the will of God as regards our tasks and opportunities (Rom. 12:2). Training our thinking in dogmatic contexts can be helpful in this respect. The formation of theological and moral judgment provides a test for our action in its response to various demands as to its observance of God's express will.

Dogmatics is concerned with the context of justification of what we say about the will of God, that is, with the providence of him whose faithfulness sustains our lives by keeping them in relation to what he wills. We experience God's providence in his "visitation" of our action or inaction. He grants us freedom to trust in him, to rely upon his promise even in the things we do and the reasons why we do them. But he does not grant freedom to the acts as such. He never lets go of them.

We test the will of God by first asking what his will is for us particularly. What does he want from us? We can assess God's will only when we know how to say what he has done for us, full of promise. This is the point of reference for what we think we ought to do, led by the prayer, "Thy will be done." Testing what is God's declared will and thereupon forming a judgment on what is "good, acceptable, and perfect" (Rom. 12:2): nothing regarding ethics could be more concrete. The will of God in concrete means the coalescing of God's action for us and to us on the one side, and our own possibilities of action on the other. When we test our goals and purposes by the divine concretion, we expose our ethical assessment to the judgment of God, in the expectation that he will place what we do in the context of his action as judge and savior.

The coalescing of God's work and ours gives us no reason to adopt a pious attitude toward the deep-lying religious structure or the ultimate basis of our own activity. Instead, it makes us disturbingly aware that nothing can shake off the work of God. We are never alone in our acts. It might seem that God's acting and the human acts are like two parallel lines that will intersect only in infinity. God's acting seems to run parallel on the far side of our action or inaction; although God is always close by, we can set this aside in our calculations. But God's proximity does not allow itself to be put off, nor to be part of a calculation. If we interpret it as an intervention in our own actions and events, then we are only asking when things occur that we cannot classify, when breaks appear in the otherwise calculable context of actions that accords with God's providence.

In every attempt to relate our experience to the divine action, we must always make their conjunction plain. It is dangerous to do this only schematically, either by linking presuppositions to consequences or by seeing in God's acting an inaudible accompaniment to our vocal earthly music. Yet dogmatics can be of methodological help in the forming of moral judgments by forming unexpected distinctions expressing the mystery of the presence of God (I.2.1). This formation of theological judgments does not only involve moral reflection: this is a sign that we are not acting subjects alone.

67. If dogmatics has to give regard to what must be said under all circumstances, we have to ask in forming a moral judgment about what might be demanded of us in specific and perhaps changing circumstances.

What becomes possible for us when we confront God's acting with all its promise and with all the hope that it gives us?

We must ask how our own activity relates to the work of God, not just in a general way, and certainly not only in the crisis situations just mentioned, but face-to-face with everything that encounters us.

One prayer, for example, puts it thus:

> Lord Christ, since your will is that we should act as your representatives until you come, enable us so to feed the hungry that they seek you as the bread of life, so to care for and support the sick that they learn to look for the greater aid that you alone can give, so to stand by the prisoners and oppressed that they pray to you for liberation. Let us always be there where there is fighting for righteousness, so that your truth may no longer be obscured. Remind us that you are seeking fruit in us. Our desire is not only to cling to you, but also to obey you. (*Neuer Erde Morgenstern. Gebete aus der Hoffnung* [Zurich, 1965], p. 21)

"So" comes again and again in this prayer. This is what we must investigate. It is not a recipe for any one course of action. It does not summon us to immediate readiness. We do not have to do only this if we are truly to meet human needs, give help, and exercise solidarity, and yet at the same time point to God, drawing attention to him as the one who will complete what we have so inadequately begun! Rather, the "so" shows how relative our action is when we assess it in terms of faith and hope and love. It tells us whether and how far it is motivated in express or secret, uncanny opposition to what must be said in expectation of justification and sanctification and in prayer for God's blessing. No correspondence is offered by the "so." It is oriented to the fact that our action is part of God's action, that becomes perspicuous for what God has done and what he has reserved for himself to do.

Contrary to a "Christian ethos" that tries to substitute a distinctive lifestyle for the hiddenness of the Christian life, the life that is "hidden with Christ in God" (Col. 3:3) will get a chance only in the way in which we pray and judge. This is the way it should be in every Christian life. An express presentation will arise only when a full account is demanded by others, or by those who are striving to achieve their own judgment.

A formation of judgment is then necessary that is oriented to this "so" and takes it into account. Ethics must develop it, in the form of a moral judgment. Theology demands this discipline just as it demands theological judgment from dogmatics, which must tell us what we can say in and to faith, ruling out the opposite.

The formation of dogmatic judgment seeks to assess what God does in relation to the action that he prepares for us. It concerns our human search as we think things immeasurable. I have time incalculable, otherwise I could not act responsibly. I must be able to consider the results of my actions and be responsible for them without ever reaching an end. But God's action, on the other hand, sets a limit to our activity, as we learn what we cannot do and judge under any circumstances.

We might illustrate from one of the petitions in the prayer cited above. We fight for righteousness and for the truth of God. The two go together. But how? The real meaning is surely not that a decision is made for the truth of God only where we fight for righteousness. In praying that we may be there where there is fighting for righteousness so that God's truth is not obscured, we open ourselves up to the truth of God, and more especially so when we cannot help taking sides. But what is the relation between our unavoidable partisanship and the truth of God? Is the truth only on the one side? Is it identified with it?

Do we know what we are praying for when we ask for God's assistance, ask for God's blessing, ask for him to work in and along with us?

In theology the formation of ethical judgment helps to clarify requests of this kind. We would deceive ourselves and others if we wished to load our acts with false expectations or exonerate them with false excuses.

266

This kind of clarity has to be achieved from case to case. Individual judgments have to be given. We cannot apply a rule that we know to be permanently valid to each specific instance. New situations create new problems and require their own solutions.

Paul has such judgments in view when he says in Romans 12:2: "Be transformed in your understanding, that you may prove what the will of God is, namely, what is good and acceptable and perfect." He had been writing just before about the gracious acts of God and about the promise that they held out over God's unsearchable ways and purposes. He is now exhorting believers to "sacrifice" their lives, since this grace has come to them along with its promise. Sacrifice here means a full commitment to the reasonable service of God (Rom. 12:1, NRSV: "the worship offered by mind and heart"). Those who thus sacrifice themselves cannot be conformed to the "world." Their minds, their full abilities to understand, will now be transformed and renewed. They will not receive a new disposition. They will not adopt an emotive theory of ethics that treads down all else with radically changed principles. Instead, the form of judgment must change to admit of a new testing and proving, not of this or that possibility of action, but of nothing less than the will of God itself. This will is to be put to the proof so that we can say in each specific instance what action is positively required of us.

What Paul has to say next does not sound at all revolutionary in moral terms. His admonition concerning acts and accountability does not introduce a fundamentally new morality, that is, a new attitude on the part of the acting subject in relation to the time of his acts or the sphere of their possibilities. Instead, Paul tells the recipients repeatedly who they are, namely, creatures of God and redeemed sinners, who no longer live and die to themselves but to Christ (Rom. 14:8). For this reason their acts will always have to be different, or about to be different, especially in comparison with what they formerly used to do or not to do, and with a sidelong glance at others whose conduct is so very different. The comparison with what others do, of course, never plays a leading role in the formation of moral judgments.

This explains why the ethical parts of the NT for the most part fit in with the moral views that were prevalent at the time. The authors accept the valid ethical standards and never promote mere arbitrariness. Early Christianity had no specific morality of its own. It certainly never produced an elitist ethics. Yet a definite switch had been made, and at touchy points changes were visible that would later become permanent. Such a switch does not, however, consist of single new or radicalized regulations, even if something new is said now and then in the "house rules" laid out in the letters of the New Testament. What is decisive, rather, is that the whole of every day life is subjected to God's judgment — and that no attempt is made to transpose God's judgment into everyday life, so that it could be tied up and immobilized morally.

Let us turn to a later example. Luther did not associate the word "vocation" with the summons to a specifically "spiritual" form of life that is meant only for a few. For him a vocation was any activity that serves the common good (Gustaf Wingren, *Luthers Lehre vom Beruf* [Munich, 1952]; ET, *Luther on Vocation,* trans. Carl C. Rasmussen [Philadelphia, 1957]). Any vocation can be a reasonable service of God. But it is not sanctioned as such. It belongs to the specific sphere in which the will of God must be tested and proved. For this reason the perception of vocation calls for the development of judgment. Otherwise there could be no questioning any conscientious discharging of a vocation. It would be "sanctified" already. The earlier understanding of the calling to the monastic life as a "vocation," when contrasted with "secular" activities, did at least show that life is not made up only of labors and perhaps accomplishments. If a wider concept of vocation is to be valid, we must submit each form of it to judgment. Otherwise vocation is in danger of becoming idolatry.

In his own testing Luther developed the judgment of the doctrine of the two kingdoms as an example of the formation of moral judgment. Christians must live in both the world and the church. The world and the church are the intermingled spheres of action in faith and hope. Accepting the gospel, and pursuing what is good for the state, Christians are encompassed by the direction and promise of God. In different ways they experience the unity of God's action. In his own fashion God is at work in both state and church. The world, then, is not a general sphere in which Christians might be seen because of specific actions. The church as a body also belongs to the world, to the world which can resist the will of God, and which God himself must for this reason oppose.

IV.3.3. Active Hope

If we try — mistakenly — to understand the acting of God as the prerequisite of our human acts, ethics would have to go back to the source of our acts and to the motives that lie behind our goals and values. Whenever we consider the promise embedded in the acts of God, and the question relating to the interweaving of our own actions, we are led at once to prayer, whether as complaint, petition, intercession, or thanksgiving (II.3.2). We are summoned to this prayer by proclamation, by pastoral care, by instruction, and by other forms of speech that express faith, hope, and love.

Prayer leads us to grow into a different way of life, in our judgment on what we do and suffer as well: we grow into the life in expectation of God's judgment. Dietrich Bonhoeffer proposed that we should practice such a form by distinguishing between the "ultimate" and "penultimate." God's irreversible word as the justification of the sinner is the final word that is preceded by "penultimate things": "doing, suffering, going, willing, submitting, rising again, praying, and hoping, a serious span of time at the end of which it is to be found" (*Ethik,* ed. Ilse Tödt, Heinz Eduard Tödt, Ernst Feil, and Clifford Green, *DBW* 6 [Munich, 1992], pp. 140-41; my trans.).

This categorization might, of course, result in our thinking that we can make the distinction between the ultimate and the penultimate even from a temporal standpoint, and that would be erroneous and even fatal. We cannot speak any final word, and this ought to make us take note of the limits of our judgment and also direct us to a perception of the express will of God. In such a perception we are led by the Spirit of God (Gal. 5:18). It forms part of living in expectation of the judgment of God in which we have the experience of being guided and letting ourselves be guided.

Bad historical experiences might have made us suspicious of any attempt to work out a "Christian ethos" that would give to the question of how to live aright a different answer from that given by Christians generally. This should not prevent us, however, from asking how we can learn a way of life, knowing as we do that faith and hope and love are not to be taught (II.7) and that the "Christian life" differs from a set of directives. Certainly the history of the church has handed down norms. We must remember these norms. They will help us not to slip into ways of life that are in contradiction with faith and hope and love and that put our fellowship with Jesus Christ at risk. A distinction must be made between the development of norms and moralism. Making this distinction is one of the foremost tasks in the formation of theological judgments in ethics.

Like dogmatics, such a formation of judgment relates primarily to the life of the church as the foremost public sphere of theology and is constantly fed by it. Just as we must not regard dogmatics as the self-steering of the church, we are also not to think of ethics as the theological task of constructing a group morality. When theologians like Stanley Hauerwas (*In Good Company: The Church as Polis* [Notre Dame, Ind., 1995]) develop ethics in relation to the church's ways of life, they never intend to tie ethics to any specific church as an ideal fellowship. They want to open up worship, or liturgical forms, as a means for the learning of lifestyles. Not the least part of the liturgy is the confession of guilt in the prayer for forgiveness, in which we commit our acts and the acting of others to the providence of God.

In the church dogmatics interlocks with ethics when we pause in what we are doing or thinking, or when the question forces itself upon us: "Upon what do we put our trust as we act or fail to act?" When we have to judge between possibilities, and decisions have to be made, then what must happen is that with this judgment we do not make a decision concerning ourselves, concerning our being or nonbeing. This judgment must be formed by the expectation of the judgment of God. This judgment belongs to what is hidden and secret in Christian life, which God alone sees and rewards (Matt. 6:18). And this expectation is especially necessary when we no longer have any further opportunities of acting ourselves, either because the time for acting is irrevocably reaching an end or because the freedom of decision has been taken from us. But our end has not really been reached. We hope against hope. This is the eschatological perspective. It will, we hope, encounter us in its advocate, dogmatics.

V. Dogmatics as Vocation

V.1. Vocational Skills and Occupational Diseases

We find dogmatics in those who think dogmatically or know how to judge theologically, which amounts to the same thing. They might be professional teachers of theology who "do dogmatics." They might work in other fields, in pastoral or academic or other spheres, but dogmatics is so much on their hearts that they cannot function or even exist without it. Dogmatics does not have to be a job. That is secondary. Happily no limits restrict its market. It might play a role only for periods. Dogmatic thinking and evaluating might very well claim a specific amount of time. What counts, however, is whether individuals have learned the basic art of thinking dogmatically, and whether they continue to learn it. They can then economize on time. They can avoid detours. They will not waste time by following false trails or bypaths, no matter how attractive they might at first seem to be.

What do we mean when we call dogmatics a vocation? We shall not look now at methods (I.2), or at basic knowledge (III.1), or at the many tasks (II.1-9), or at the readiness to devote our resources to it without being obsessed by it. Our inquiry concerns the specific vocational characteristics. How are we to judge whether people are experienced in dogmatics or are just playing around with dogmatic concepts that they have acquired? On this might depend whether we encounter true dogmatics or only a caricature, a caricature that would rob us of any pleasure that the learning of dogmatics might afford. Those for whom dogmatics has really become a vocation will be able to help us in our own approach to it. They will at least give us confidence, as experts do in other vocations.

If we must try to sketch some of the features and qualities of this vocation, we must also speak of the typical occupational diseases. There are risks and side effects involved in dogmatics as a vocation. We cannot always avoid these dangers. Some of us are more susceptible to them than others. We need to know and recognize the individual symptoms, not just to be on guard against them, but also not to be confused and thus led into mistakes when we see them in others, possibly so much so that we transfer the symptoms to dogmatics itself, thinking that dogmatics is the cause, and that, since it makes us sick, we do best to avoid it.

The first feature of dogmatics is that it sees theological connections, thinks about them coherently, and achieves an overview of what can be said in this context in order to bring other relationships to light. Dogmatics is a systematic discipline, but there is no pressure for a system (III.1).

In his novel *The Eighth Day,* Thornton Wilder has an engineer say that he had no time to become a systematician. Falsely accused of murder, this engineer is always on the move, fleeing from place to place. Every day that he survives is full of joy. He has no time for retrospective or far-ranging thinking, and least of all for pondering on extraneous connections.

Those who wish to think systematically must have adequate time to reflect, and this not only in theology, though in theology as well. Time is needed to ask whether a thing can be viewed as necessary for faith. We also need to see how it relates to memory and hope, and to its versatility in a theological context. Testing a challenge to act for evidence of God's will cannot be done at once. Otherwise, dealing with dogmatics would merely involve the exploitation of a stock of words and themes, as Johann Wolfgang von Goethe put it in *Faust:* "It's exactly where a thought is lacking / That, just in time, a word shows up instead" (trans. Randall Jarrell [New York, 1976], p. 95). We would thus always have something theological to say about everything and anything. We could always show that in this respect or that we have to do with God and our faith. Dogmatics is often mistaken for some conceptions of systematic theology. Yet it is not just a theoretical structure in which God, the world, humanity, and its history all find their place.

To think dogmatically involves ongoing thought about the scope of the work of God and the connections which are disclosed with it.

Nevertheless, a complication easily arises here. How can we succeed in this ongoing thought without arriving at all too human conclusions? Drawing hasty deductions is one of the risks of all systematic thinking. It is an added risk in dogmatics, for dogmatics uses human speech when it talks about the work of God. For this reason the greatest sensitivity is required when dealing with the linguistic links, with the relation between what is said and what is not said, and with questions to which the answers raise new questions.

Just thinking further can be very dangerous. The development of dogmatics (III.1.3) and the crisis relating to its true beginning (IV.1.2) offer sufficient examples. But when we have trained ourselves in the seeing of connections and the establishing of relations, when we have learned to place details in the context of what must be said unconditionally and under all circumstances in theology, we can then be inclined to pay regard mainly to the consequences of what we reflect and say theologically. And the better we know the history of the church and its theology, the more skilled we will be in detecting dubious deductions and dangerous inferences. Sooner rather than later we will then be warned against such conclusions, and we will strive with all our powers to obstruct them when we see how momentous they are. This is not just understandable psychologically. It also seems to be justified if we observe distinctions that are truly necessary for faith, and if the corresponding discernment has then to be made.

But only if and to the extent that this is true! If we think we can hear grass grow and fleas cough, we are usually out of our mind. If we can only take note of possible conclusions, and use these to write a warning sign on the wall, we might well be led to an overanxiety that will block every venture. We overload the range of systematic thinking, in which dogmatics also has a part.

The prognoses of experts are often upset by the fact that known problems at first appear to be much more powerful than the possibility of hitherto unknown solutions. Why should not dogmaticians be made proof against this type of self-blockade? They can test out unknown and risky theological ideas. They can see if they prove themselves. This is not only legitimate. It is also urgently necessary if we are not to go on repeating what is familiar to us already. It is a venture, because we rightly value tested thinking experiences in dogmatics. And yet both theology and the church need new insights that are neither too lofty nor too traditional, insights that can be revised at the right time and in the right situation.

Let me mention another risk. Many contributions to dogmatics resemble frantic efforts to establish order in the intellectual world, reducing rents and faults and preventing everything from falling apart. This trait can affect body language. Gestures are used to restrain high-flying thoughts, to embrace an otherwise chaotic intellectual world, to restore clarity to it. The hand is used like an axe to mark off divisions and to cut away the phantoms of thought. Alternatively, the hands grasp in the void so as to give emphasis to things that we do not see to be either black or white.

Gestures of this kind merely give evidence of the involvement of dogmaticians in relation to what they are saying. This is why we must understand dogmatics as a vocation, and so describe it. It is not an embodied effort to master problems. It is an activity that demands commitment to objectivity.

Dogmatics does not require us to say the last word. What must be said in all circumstances is *not* the last word by which we stand or fall. We can and should be allowed to make mistakes. We must have the courage to make statements that will need to be revised, the courage not to be prejudiced and block any further advance. This courage frees us from the obligation to get everything right — that is the best experience in dogmatics.

Secondly, dogmatics teaches us to distinguish between true and false theological statements. One of its elementary tasks is to learn the difference between statements that "might be true" and those that are "virtually false." These distinctions allow dogmatics to say what is theologically correct.

This is the core of truth in the term "orthodox." This term frightens people away because it gives force to the objections made against dogmatics. It carries the sense of authoritarian, inflexible, knowing better than anyone else. But the real meaning is "of the true faith." We would perhaps do better to translate it "in accordance with the faith," that is, in accordance with what we can say in faith and hope. We are orthodox if we stay in the faith, if our memory is true, if we are credible in relation to what must be said in all circumstances. The opposite of orthodoxy is heterodoxy. Orthodoxy does not cling to tradition. It inquires into the real tradition. It seeks to follow it. This is an enterprise that needs faith. It calls for a good deal of attentiveness and sagacity.

There are virtuosos among theologians who with anxious haste can always tell us at once what is "orthodox," and even more so what is "heterodox." By the latter they have in view an opinion that differs from their own. Heterodox for them means "unbelieving," "hostile to the faith," or even "of the devil."

Dogmatics is not, of course, about branding people as heretics. Part of its task is to put the right questions and to answer them on a theological basis. We are thus able to differentiate these from false and therefore misleading questions which cost us unnecessary time and trouble. Dogmatics needs time, but protects us from wasting time.

Dogmatics then teaches us, thirdly, to identify theological issues and to make theological judgments. We have used the doctrine of providence as an example of the internal tension this might cause (IV.1.1; IV.1.3; IV.2.2). We must not confuse identification with classification. Classification involves knowing already "what is at issue," so that we can lay our hands upon it as a phenomenon or a construct of thought. Dogmatics is quickly and permanently injured if it becomes a mere matter of themes and associated impressions and broadly meshed analyses that no longer have any real substance.

Knowledge is then cut short by an observation schematism which tosses out information like a coining press that follows a pattern and simply turns out its product. Schematism means the freezing of a schema, that is, of a form of perception. We cannot do without schemata. Otherwise no knowledge would be possible. The basic distinctions of theology provide us with possibilities of perception such as the unity of God and man in Jesus Christ that defines the relation between God and the world. But in a frozen schematism such as "God has come into the world," we simply have a repetition of the same information and find no aid to perception.

People resort to schematism, to the positing of information, far too easily. In so doing they abandon dialogue for the investigation of issues. Putting too high a claim on right insights might be the origin of this occupational diseases, or perhaps a faulty attitude, or simply wear and tear, numbness, or exhaustion. We need to take these with much more essential seriousness than we do such slanders as the defining of "dogmatic" as "immobile," "determined once and for all," or "authoritarian." It is hard to refute these charges, for they rest only on prejudices. Our best rebuttal is to demonstrate that dogmatics is really very different, and will, it is hoped, do much better than people suppose.

V.2. Dogmatics as Diagnosis and Advocacy

In defining the true subject of theology, Luther compared it to medicine and jurisprudence (III.2.1). This was in keeping with the role of theology in the universities. The German university reforms of the nineteenth century described these three faculties as "positive sciences" because they are built upon the investigation and teaching of given data and offer training for vocations which will directly affect people and therefore are in the public interest.

I might venture here to develop this comparison more broadly, not making delimitations as Luther does, but indicating some vocational similarities.

68. Dogmatics should help us to gain a theological knowledge of processes, facts, and expressions, characterizing them diagnostically (with precise distinctions), marking off what they tell us for the dialogue of faith, and yet not always being forced to put this in directly theological concepts.

Is dogmatics really a kind of diagnostics? Yes, for good theologians, when conversing with those who come to them, or with whom they have to do, have a relation with them that is very like that of a good physician or psychologist. They have to identify the issue with the help of everyday words and hints and allusions. They must discover what it is and distinguish it from what it is not. In his work *On the Consolation of Philosophy (Consolatio Philosophiae),* the philosopher Boethius (ca. 480-524) says that philosophy, which is the master of diagnosis, comes to the philosopher and tells him step-by-step where and why he has gone wrong.

When a physician or psychologist wants to recognize an ailment, the memory of the sick person must help him. Certain tests are valuable, but it is by conversing with the person concerned that he or she will find out what is wrong. Outward expressions such as feelings of pain can be localized, and in this way the physicians or psychologists can recognize the causes of the sickness, the accompanying phenomena, and the symptoms (though they could, of course, be attracted to a false track), but they keep the full diagnosis to themselves. They will not impart the full details to the sick person, who would probably not understand them. It will probably be enough to give him or her something helpful to which to cling. A correct and timely diagnosis is, however, vitally necessary. Diagnosis means distinction, and making a differential diagnosis of complex and hardly distinguishable phenomena needs great skill on the part of physicians. Quick conclusions and wholesale explanations might have fatal consequences.

Pastoral ministers are important diagnosticians, precisely when they do not try to use psychological terms for theological issues. Their judgment is nonschematic, because they are good listeners. They have a wide range of theological knowledge. Hoping to give the best form of help, however, they do not exploit this knowledge. If they are to engage in a relevant dialogue, they must be able to know what the problem is.

The point of contact between dogmatics as a vocation and the work of an attorney lies in the representation of others when they run into complications that they are unable to handle, either linguistically or professionally, at the level of decision.

Along these lines Martin Kähler called the dogmatician a theological advocate for the laity ("Jesus und das Alte Testament" [1896] in *Dogmatische Zeitfragen*, vol. 1: *Zur Bibelfrage*, 2nd ed. [1907; reprint, Gütersloh, 1937], p. 117). By laypeople Kähler does not mean only those with no ecclesiastical office, but also those who "are not specialists" ("though perhaps well educated in other fields," p. 117 n. 1). The laity are "lay" not in subjection to the clergy, but as distinct from scholars or specialists. Specialists, Kähler adds, must display their expertise by not meddling in every subject but restricting themselves to those in which they have both experience and competence.

Relating to this expertise, Kähler fixes on the neuralgic point of reading Scripture. Laypeople read the Bible without presuppositions. They do so because they count on it that God will speak to them in and through the Bible. They take seriously the express claim that God will continue to work through human history, through that which we experience as his explicit will. They turn to the dogmatician with the question: Are we really allowed to do this?

Laypeople are summoned to receive God's Word, to live it out, and to impart it. That is why they read the Bible. As Bible readers, they put specific questions to theology, especially the question about the Bible as the basis of the Christian faith. Their faithfulness to Scripture or their doubts concerning it require that theology — notwithstanding its involvement in the development of knowledge — should give an account of the certainty of the knowledge that is achieved with the help of the Bible.

Dogmaticians, then, represent the laity in one of the basic questions of theology. They are better equipped to do this, for they are well acquainted with questions of grounding and justification and are familiar with questions such as that of the starting point and the goal of thought. But of what concern are these and other dogmatic questions to the laity? Have not dogmaticians "fallen into disrepute for entering the fields of theology that are not relevant to the laity" (Kähler, p. 117)? Perhaps for entering into those areas in which historians pursue their excavations and do reconstructions which will simply be disordered by unauthorized hands, or possibly the area of "praxis" which will investigate and give better direction to the vital expressions of piety!

Dogmaticians have to be concerned about theological statements. How did we reach them? What is their basis? They must take up a variety of questions which are beyond the competence of laypeople, even though the latter find them relevant and pursue them. Dogmaticians are experts. They have the appropriate experiences. Yet they are not experts in faith. They cannot tell in advance how people will come to faith or keep the faith.

69. As experts in the problems of theological reasoning, dogmaticians are advocates for the laity when the question of the basis of faith is raised.

Dogmaticians are advocates for the laity when they want to know how to begin to speak about God and humanity. As advocates, dogmaticians in extreme cases will often have to use a different language and bring in other insights from those familiar to the laity. They must speak about that which must be, or become, "self-evident" to the laity.

V.3. Dogmatics as the Form and Forum of the Dialogue of Faith

In terms of form, dogmatics is the structure of the questions and answers that are necessary to faith. Its dialogue is not unlimited and its history is not unending. It shows us where to begin, where to pause, where to advance without ceasing. It helps us to identify the points at which conversations crystallize. These conversations may have many different causes and can often begin with viewpoints that are very distant from one another, but these lead to questions about faith and hope and love. We need to press on to such questions, to break through schemata, to be able to call a halt at the right time and in the right place, to take notice, and to look around, but not into the void. Dogmatics is not a spider's web upon which our questions and we ourselves may remain hanging.

70. Dogmatics is a forum in which the fellowship of faith can engage in dialogue. The dialogue is one of faith. Its form is defined by a common recognition — notwithstanding the situation and its challenges — of what has to be said irreversibly and unconditionally in order not to lose hope for all people.

When do I need dogmatics after university or seminary studies as a minister, in teaching Christian education, or in other professions? When I am alone with a biblical text, for example, and have to prepare a sermon, or when, with ethical responsibility, I have to deliver a judgment. Systematic theology, which offers an outline of a comprehensive view, does not suffice at such points. I need to converse with those who have made the judgments and the distinctions that are vital for faith before me, those who have had and formulated their experiences in thinking. Every contribution to dogmatics that has exercised this perceptive ability brings us into the Christian church's dialogue of faith. We can then experience what it means to have a place in the church, and to be sustained by its thinking experiences, even though we ourselves still have to achieve what constitutes a theological judgment.

Every time we turn to dogmatics, and lay claim to the help it gives, we confront the church itself as one of the themes of dogmatics. That is, we come up against the ongoing dialogue of those who are ready to listen, and to converse, from faith to faith.

Dogmatics deals with the reliable texts of theology. It thus offers us the chance to converse with the "fathers and brethren," the "mothers and sisters." They leap over all temporal and geographical boundaries. The concealed fellowship of theological dialogue is vitally important. Hours of vocational loneliness, when we have to make decisions, make this apparent. None of us stands alone, because we all stand in the presence of God. In its statements and (metatheoretically) in its method of achieving them, dogmatics tries to express this.

Dogmatics points beyond itself, and beyond the church too. In this openness it may not and cannot lose the hope for the salvation of all people. If it is a forum for the dialogue of faith, this means that it does not rely on a set standard of thought or on a set body of information. Good dogmatics is not merely a reference work. It provides arguments for a dialogue of faith that can at times begin with concepts and questions that are not theological at all. Pastoral dialogues that are not planned, and that raise no theological questions, can suddenly become dialogues of faith, perhaps especially when this was not the original intention. If this is to occur, what is needed is a readiness and a mobility of thought within the basic theological context of justification. And this is what the study of dogmatics teaches us. It prepares us for dialogues of faith that pierce through into our own lives and the lives of others.

Dogmatics rests on experiences in theological thinking, not on unchallengeable principles that we can only discuss and develop. Dogmatic statements are statements that are in force until recalled. We can rely on them, continually accept them, and return to them. If we understand dogmatics in this way, we will have to see how broad its material is. Dogmatics does not consist only of dogmatic texts. It writes its own texts. It does so in the context of texts of many different kinds — biblical texts, other literary texts, reference books, hymns, confessions and statements of churches, personal expressions of hope, faith, love, affliction, scepticism, anxiety, and everyday texts. All these can lead us to dogmatics so long as they are transparent to what can be said in faith and hope and love. What, then, is excluded — either at a greater or lesser remove? For this reason dogmatics is not an hermetic affair. Precisely when we pursue it with concentration, it will open up our perceptions to an unsuspected degree.

Appendix I: Theses

The theses are listed here to clarify their interrelationship.

Chapter I

1. Dogmatics resembles a reference system for expressions of faith, showing how these expressions converge.
2. Dogmatics in a truly theological sense says what must be said as credible unconditionally and under all circumstances. God has revealed to us who he is. He has given himself expression by the pledge of his action. This pledge sets free the power of human judgment so that it perceives the reality God has promised. It issues a summons to faith, to faith as the work of God and yet also as human acceptance of what God does. God's promise confronts the church by summoning us to this faith.
3. Dogmatics is built up as a structure of answers to the threefold question concerning why we believe when we believe what we believe.
4. It is the task of dogmatics to express the deep-lying structure and scope of the truth of faith in Jesus Christ, but not in the way that a systematic exposition of Scripture can achieve. Dogmatics opens up a complex nexus of statements of faith, a "context of justification" (*Begründungszusammenhang* — context of validation or substantiation) that relate to one another, illuminate one another, and explain one another.
5. Dogmatics is an attempt to express the finality and fullness of God's

action that does not bring human history to an end but promises it its future, the future of fulfilled fellowship between God and us that is already proclaimed when the Spirit of God links us to God and to one another.

6. Homology tells us what is self-evident according to faith. It thus makes it plain how it can come to a confessing faith. By confessing we unreservedly place ourselves into what God has done and promised. We confess these things because we here find ourselves in the presence of God. To speak homologically is to stand upon what is received through God's action. Homology tells us where to begin when speaking in faith and hope.

7. An exemplarily "thick" statement of faith can be called a dogma. Our appeal to it demonstrates that we may refer to it in all circumstances as we go forward and wait upon God.

8. Dogmatics characterizes the state of theological knowledge that has been provisionally achieved. But it permits theological discourse that can rely but not insist on proven questions and answers, being always ready to prove insights to be grounded in dialogue beyond existing limits, so that growth in faith is possible.

9. Dogmatics starts with necessary distinctions between what must in all circumstances be said in faith and hope, and what must not be said at all.

10. Theological rules of dialogue constitute the core of dogmatics. Their orientation is to faith and hope. They tell us on what we can rely in all circumstances.

11. Dogmatics is formed by the interrelation between all theological statements, which is yet open.

12. Church doctrine expresses what a church lets itself be told unconditionally.

13. Doctrine commits the church to its externality, and its state of knowledge will correspondingly express that which characterizes its power of judgment.

14. A limited text consisting of theological statements will be seen by its reception to have such weight that a church has to confess and proclaim it as its doctrine, showing that it is definitive in dialogue. Doctrine gives unmistakable precision to the language of faith.

15. Doctrine comes into being when dissent is vanquished and consensus is achieved.

16. Dogmatic texts are made up of theological statements. These formulate the contents, in a way that puts the question: Are they true or

false? The significance of a statement does not depend upon those who formulate it, nor is it linked to those who pass it down.

17. Dogmatic statements are necessary because theology is relatively independent in relation to its subjects. They represent the externality of the promises of God. The presence of the Spirit of God is their presupposition. They are unique for this reason.

18. "Faith" stands between the crisis of human self-knowledge and renewed invocation of God.

19. Dogmatics is the aid to memory for the spiritual life; it helps us not to forget essential things.

Chapter II

20. When we ask what is the basis of what the church does, the inner grounding, the answer has to be formulated in the context of theological justification, and hence dogmatically.

21. Dogmatics is directed primarily toward uncertainties and conflicts in the church. It concerns that which is or ought to be debated among Christians when what is at issue is belief or disbelief, talk of God or concealment, discipleship of Jesus Christ or a refusal of discipleship, and in all these things whether the church really becomes the church and continues to be the church.

22. Dogmatics states the inner grounding for what the church does. It is a practice in thinking. It is meaningful in itself. It does not depend on its appropriateness to other things. Therefore it is not a "function" within some superior definition of the church. It thus has what one might call an unrestricted feature, which is a further way of expressing dogmatics as an academic discipline, theology as unconditioned and free from all other presuppositions. It must show the validity of its own grounding. It must not find the grounding elsewhere. It must not let itself be determined by what is thought to be useful or valuable.

23. In confession of sin to God, and in calling upon him for mercy, we can put our trust in the verdict of God. We recognize that we ourselves, and the "things" we have done that now accuse us, stand in need of God's forgiveness. They have become a matter for him alone and are subject to his action.

24. The inner grounding of confession of sin is recollection of the act of God. It is a sign of the beginning of knowledge of God and recognition of the self.

25. Christians can confess their guilt only because they know that all their guilt is borne by Jesus Christ; otherwise they would find it to be intolerable.

26. The rule of faith rests on the rule that prayer follows. Intercession, our prayer for other people, points us to the grounding of prayer which must be the subject of dogmatic reflection.

27. Prayer is the path of consent to the work of God and its dimensions. The forms of prayer denote stages along this path as well as contours in talking of God.

28. The hearing of proclamation is a beginning behind which we cannot go. Therefore all proclamation gives constant life to the question of the commencement of talk about God, no matter what form it takes. The inner grounding of all proclamation is surprise, surprise at the interjection of God that is so full of promise.

29. The promise of proclamation is that God precedes our speaking.

30. Proclamation delivers an unrequested and unexpected message. God has acted and we are now addressed. The promise of his action is pronounced to us. We are thus made aware of the fullness of the presence of God, of his unrecognized nearness.

31. Worship is the form of God's action that directly demands that we should serve God by letting God do his own work with us.

32. The inner grounding of blessing is the pronouncing of God's saving presence.

33. The address that contains the divine greeting constitutes the "we" of the Christian community. Related to this fact is the inclusive language of dogmatics.

34. The inner grounding of pastoral care is the grace of God that orients our human wills to God.

35. Pastoral care can help us expose ourselves to the judgment of God and to accept this judgment.

36. Pastoral care participates in God's setting up of his kingdom and in Christ's victory over the powers of destruction.

37. To be instructed in the faith means to learn that faith cannot be learned. Yet it must be practiced as we learn to formulate all the questions that arise under all circumstances with a reference to the promises of God, and thus to answer them, although not in the sense of giving an answer once and for all.

38. Order in the church rests on the fact that Christians must always be ready to let the decisive thing be said to them, and to hear it also from others, who thereby become their brothers and sisters.

39. Consensus, as agreement in the faith, is an expression of church leadership.

40. Christian mission takes place when, without restriction or limitation, we beseech people to be reconciled with God (2 Cor. 5:20), to let the reconciliation with the world that God has made in Jesus Christ occur for them, to expose themselves to this reconciliation.

41. The range and scope of theological statements is just as unlimited as is God's work of reconciliation. The sphere of validity of theological statements is the church, though this fact does not reduce their scope.

42. Mission takes place when the statements of faith venture out into a sphere of communication in which they are not yet valid but are seeking validity.

Chapter III

43. Theological grounding is linked and interrelated in such a way that it forms the theological context of justification. It unites the basic statements that have been gained from experiences in theological thinking so far.

44. The theological context of justification stands over against the church as a sign of the faithfulness of God, of the breadth of his promises, and of the range of his divine activity.

45. The Christian festivals permit us constantly to begin once again and yet to move forward according to their rhythm, although even step-by-step we can never catch up with the fullness of God.

46. The arrangement of the church year releases us from the hopeless attempt to say everything decisive at once, or always to want to say something completely new.

47. The basic dogmatic knowledge arises out of the interrelating of questions and added questions with which dogmatics starts and to which it constantly refers in seeking the right connection.

48. The physiognomy of theology is characterized by statements about the being of God, the self-manifestation of God, and the action of God — by the theological answers to the questions: "Who is God that we might call upon him?", "How does God address us, how do we encounter God?", and "Who are we in relation to God?"

49. The character of dogmatics is established by basic theological state-

ments that stand in a specific relation to one another, and as thus connected, form a certain structure and context.

50. Christian theology outlines the event that we know as God's encounter with us, though we cannot foretell this in advance. In this way movements are discernible. Therefore the axioms of theology are constituted dialectically.

51. Dogmatics has to state what we must say "for God's sake," because we would have to be silent otherwise.

52. One may not go behind the Bible.

53. The appeal to Scripture means to engage in the theological context of justification, perceiving it in the canonical writings and their inner tensions, in short, reading the Bible on the basic assumption that God will intervene here and begin to speak.

54. For Christians, the Word of God perceived through Scripture is the final court of appeal on earth.

55. The Bible as a whole (as "Scripture") is news of God's faithfulness.

56. The dogmatic distinctions "spirit and letter," "law and gospel," and "promise and fulfillment" form a context of perceptions for faithfulness to Scripture.

Chapter IV

57. Dogmatism can occur as a result of an exaggerated effort to apply dogmatic logic. This can happen when the formation of theological judgment is replaced by a scheme of understanding that interprets everything we encounter in terms of a human reference to God, and consequently claims to know about everything that can happen. Dogmatism is an opponent of theological integrity.

58. The specific lack of precision of dogmatic language is due to the way we describe facts in a theological way that seeks to identify them linguistically and conceptually, even though the work of God cannot be pinned down by us. Such judgment is left to God. Therefore dogmatic speech arises within an eschatological perspective.

59. Theological integrity means not promising more than we can perform, not feigning an insight that cannot properly be attained, not allowing for errors and confusion in thinking or discourse even for the best of purposes.

60. A crisis overtakes dogmatics when theologians are no longer sure where to begin, when they try to find an intelligible basis for theol-

ogy which will be open to all and which will allow approaches that have general validity, so that the step to faith will come almost as an afterthought.

61. Those who seek to develop a doctrine of theological principles, or a fundamental theology, seek to inquire into the possibility of a theology founded upon valid intersubjective and transsubjective principles. The theology they seek is virtually incontestable — even if it is constantly being debated. Faith should be shown to be understandable at the point where it appears to be unbelievable to those using common sense, adopting only what is generally valid, and who thus cannot make the move to faith.

62. Contextual theology intends to develop theology according to a comprehensive reflection upon actions within historical, social, and cultural reality. Thereby it hopes to demonstrate how theology comes into being. It is so explained as a function of mastering reality that it basically makes theology (i.e., what must be said with a specific commitment to truth-claiming statements) virtually superfluous.

63. The primary context of Christian talk is the theological context of justification: all of the dogmatic statements that seek to follow the scope of God's work.

64. The context by which we discover theological statements theoretically covers all the factors that in some way promote insights or contribute to significant findings.

65. Theological judgment both distinguishes and connects the work of God and our human work, both the will of God and our human will, both the promises of God and our human goals, both the goodness of God and what we regard as good, both the righteousness of God and our sense of what is right, both his perfection and what is perfect for us.

66. Perceiving the work of God, especially in the specific form of the formation of theological judgment, is especially necessary when we have not only to make distinctions and reach decisions, but also to change the form of our perception so as to be able to test the will of God as regards our tasks and opportunities (Rom. 12:2). Training our thinking in dogmatic contexts can be helpful in this respect. The formation of theological and moral judgment provides a test for our action in its response to various demands and as to its observance of God's express will.

67. If dogmatics has to give regard to what must be said under all circumstances, we have to ask in forming a moral judgment about

what might be demanded of us in specific and perhaps changing circumstances.

Chapter V

68. Dogmatics should help us to gain a theological knowledge of processes, facts, and expressions, characterizing them diagnostically
(with precise distinctions), marking off what they tell us for the dialogue of faith, and yet not always being forced to put this in directly
theological concepts.
69. As experts in the problems of theological reasoning, dogmaticians
are advocates for the laity when the question of the basis of faith is
raised.
70. Dogmatics is a forum in which the fellowship of faith can engage in
dialogue. The dialogue is one of faith. Its form is defined by a common recognition — notwithstanding the situation and its challenges
— of what has to be said irreversibly and unconditionally in order
not to lose hope for all people.

Appendix II: Preparatory and Supplementary Works by the Author

For the whole work:

Arbeitsweisen Systematischer Theologie. Eine Anleitung (with Alex Stock), 2nd ed. (Munich and Mainz, 1982); "Dogmatik I," *TRE*, 9 (1982), pp. 41-77; "Systematische Theologie/Dogmatik," in *Einführung in das Studium der evangelischen Theologie*, ed. H. Schröer (Gütersloh, 1982), pp. 116-32.

For particular subjects:

I.1

"Dogma — ein eschatologischer Begriff," in *Erwartung und Erfahrung. Predigten, Vorträge und Aufsätze*, TB 47 (Munich, 1972), pp. 16-46; "Dogma, Dogmatik I, evangelische Sicht," in *Ökumene-Lexikon*, ed. H. Krüger, et al. (Frankfurt, 1983; 2nd ed., 1987), pp. 274-76.

I.2 and I.3

Wissenschaftstheoretische Kritik der Theologie. Die Theologie und die neuere wissenschaftstheoretische Diskussion (with J. Courtin, H.-W. Haase, G. König, W. Raddatz, G. Schultzky, and H. G. Ulrich) (Munich, 1973); "Dialogik II. Theologisch," *TRE*, 8 (1981), pp. 703-9.

I.4

"Verbindlichkeit als Lehre?" *GlLern* 3 (1988): 120-30; "Confessio-Konkordie-Consensus. Perspektiven des Augsburger Bekenntnisses für das Bekennen und Lehren der Kirche heute," *EvTh* 40 (1980): 478-94; "Nachwort," in Ernst Wolf, *Barmen. Kirche zwischen Versuchung und Gnade,* BEvTh 27, 3rd ed. (Munich, 1984), pp. 183-84; "Consensus," *TRE,* 8 (1981), pp. 182-89; "Konsens als Ziel und Voraussetzung theologischer Erkenntnis," in *Theologischer Konsens und Kirchenspaltung,* ed. P. Lengsfeld and H.-G. Stobbe (Stuttgart, 1981), pp. 52-63, 162-64; "Konsensus," *Ökumene-Lexikon,* ed. H. Krüger (Frankfurt, 1983; 2nd ed., 1987), pp. 711-13; "Was ist Wahrheit in der Theologie? Wahrheitsfindung und Konsens der Kirche," in *In der Freiheit des Geistes. Theologische Studien* (Göttingen, 1988), pp. 57-82.

I.5

"Spiritualität und Glaube," B. Casper Festschrift (in preparation); "Wozu dogmatische Aussagen?" *ZKTh* 111 (1989): 409-19, identical with "Mit dem Rücken zur Fundamentaltheologie," *Theologische Passagen,* H. Jorissen Festschrift, ed. R. Hoeps and T. Ruster, BDS 10 (Würzburg, 1991), pp. 107-20.

II.1

"Theologie — eine kirchliche Wissenschaft?" in *Jenseits vom Nullpunkt? Christsein im westlichen Deutschland,* K. Scharf Festschrift, ed. R. Weckerling (Stuttgart, 1972), pp. 287-99; "Der Ursprung der Kirche aus Gottes Wort und Gottes Geist," in *Handbuch der Fundamentaltheologie,* vol. 3, ed. W. Kern, H. J. Pottmeier, and M. Seckler, 2nd ed. (Tübingen and Basel, 2000), pp. 147-58; "Die Hoffnung der Kirche in der Dogmatik," in *Gottes Zukunft — Zukunft der Welt,* J. Moltmann Festschrift, ed. H. Deuser, G. M. Martin, K. Stock, and M. Welker (Munich, 1986), pp. 39-47; "Dogmatics in the Church," *PSB* 12 (1991): 9-17.

II.2

"Versöhnung und Vergebung. Die Frage der Schuld im Horizont der Christologie," *EvTh* 36 (1976): 34-52; "'Vergib uns unsere Schuld.' Eine theologische Besinnung auf das Stuttgarter Schuldbekenntnis," in G. Sauter and G. Besier, *Wie Christen ihre Schuld bekennen. Die Stuttgarter Erklärung 1945* (Göttingen, 1985), pp. 63-128; "Schulderkenntnis in der Bitte um Vergebung," *GlLern* 1 (1986): 109-19; "Bekannte Schuld," *EvTh* 50 (1990): 498-511; "Verhängnis der Theologie? Schuldwahrnehmung und Geschichtsanschauungen im deutschen Protestantismus unseres Jahrhunderts," *KZG* 4 (1991): 475-92.

II.3

"Das Gebet als Wurzel des Redens von Gott," *GlLern* 1 (1986): 21-38.

II.4

"Kein Jahr von unserer Zeit entflieht, das dich nicht kommen sieht. Dogmatische Implikationenen des Kirchenjahres," in *In der Schar derer, die da feiern. Feste als Gegenstand praktisch-theologischer Reflexion,* F. Wintzer Festschrift, ed. P. Cornehl, M. Dutzmann, and A. Strauch (Göttingen, 1993), pp. 56-68.

II.6

"Die Sorge um den Menschen in der evangelischen Theologie des 19. und 20. Jahrhunderts," in *Seelsorge und Diakonie in Berlin. Beiträge zum Verhältnis von Kirche und Großstadt im 19. und beginnenden 20. Jahrhundert,* ed. K. Elm and H.-D. Loock (Berlin and New York, 1990), pp. 3-21; "Erkenne, daß du dich nicht erkennen kannst!" in *"Daß allen Menschen geholfen werde . . ." Theologische und anthropologische Beiträge,* M. Seitz Festschrift, ed. R. Landau and G. R. Schmidt (Stuttgart, 1993), pp. 223-38; *"Rechtfertigung" als Grundbegriff evangelischer Theologie,* TB 78 (Munich, 1989), 9-29; "Rechtfertigung IV-VII," *TRE,* 28 (1997), pp. 315-64.

II.7

"Glaube und Lernen. Zeitschrift für theologische Urteilsbildung" (editor's introduction), *GlLern* 1 (1986): 2-11; "Zur theologischen Revision religionspädagogischen Theorien," *EvTh* 46 (1986): 127-48; "Religionspädagogik — eine theologische Disziplin? Rückfragen an Gert Otto," *EvTh* 47 (1987): 360-66; "Kann man Glauben lernen? Glaubenslehre im Religionsunterricht," *EK* 23 (1990): 553-56; "Religiöse Erziehung," in *Pädagogische Grundbegriffe,* vol. 2, ed. D. Lenzen (Reinbek bei Hamburg, 1989), pp. 456-64.

II.8

"Kirchenleitung als Theologie," *GlLern* 2 (1987): 47-60.

II.9

"Versöhnung" als Thema der Theologie, TB 92 (Gütersloh, 1997), pp. 7-47.

III.1

"Theologie aus Glaubenserfahrungen," in *In der Freiheit des Geistes,* pp. 83-94;

"Mensch sein — Mensch bleiben. Anthropologie als theologische Aufgabe," in *Anthropologie als Thema der Theologie,* ed. H. Fischer (Göttingen, 1977), pp. 71-118; "Hope — The Spiritual Dimension of Theological Anthropology," in *Spirituality and Theology,* Essays in Honor of Diogenes Allen, ed. E. O. Springsted (Louisville, 1998), pp. 101-11; *What Dare We Hope? Reconsidering Eschatology* (Harrisburg, Pa., 1999).

III.2

"Der Charakter der Theologie," in *Tragende Tradition,* M. Seils Festschrift, ed. A. Freund, U. Kern, and A. Radler (Frankfurt, 1992), pp. 143-55; "'Einfaches Reden von Gott' als Gegenstand der Dogmatik," in *Einfach von Gott reden. Ein theologischer Diskurs,* F. Mildenberger Festschrift, ed. J. Roloff and H. G. Ulrich (Stuttgart, 1994), pp. 159-71; "Die 'dialektische Theologie' und das Problem der Dialektik in der Theologie," in *Erwartung und Erfahrung,* pp. 108-46; *The Question of Meaning* (ET) (Grand Rapids, 1995); "The True Subject of Christian Theology," in *Theology in the Service of the Church,* Essays in Honor of Thomas W. Gillespie, ed. W. M. Alston, Jr. (Grand Rapids, 2000), pp. 176-87.

III.3

Introduction to James Barr's *Fundamentalismus* (GT) (Munich, 1981), pp. 9-23; "Die Kunst des Bibellesens," *EvTh* 52 (1992): 347-59; "Schrifttreue ist kein 'Schriftprinzip,'" in *Die Zukunft des Schriftprinzips,* ed. R. Ziegert (Stuttgart, 1994), pp. 259-78.

IV.1

Vor einem neuen Methodenstreit in der Theologie? TEH 164 (Munich, 1970); "Wie entsteht Theologie?" *LM* 10 (1971): 533-35; "Die Aufgabe der Theorie in der Theologie," in *Erwartung und Erfahrung,* pp. 179-207; "Die Begründung theologischer Aussagen — wissenschaftstheoretisch gesehen," *ZEE* 15 (1971): 299-308, also in *Erwartung und Erfahrung,* pp. 262-75; "Möglichkeiten der Theoriebildung in der Theologie," in *Die Theologie in der interdisziplinären Forschung,* ed. J. B. Metz and T. Rendtorff (Düsseldorf, 1971), pp. 58-64; *Wissenschaftstheoretische Kritik der Theologie* (Munich, 1973); "Überlegungen zu einem weiteren Gesprächsgang über 'Theologie und Wissenschaftstheorie,'" *EvTh* 40 (1980): 161-68; *Grundlagen der Theologie — Ein Diskurs* (with W. Pannenberg, S. M. Daecke, and H. N. Janowski), UB 603 (Stuttgart, 1974); "Die systematische Theologie," in *Wissenschaftliche Theologie im Überblick,* ed. W. Lohff and F. Hahn, KVR 1402 (Göttingen, 1974), pp. 48-55; "Der Praxisbezug aller theologischen Disziplinen," in *Praktische Theologie heute,* ed. F. Klostermann and R. Zerfass (Mainz and Munich, 1974), pp. 119-31; "Beobachtungen und Vorschläge zum gegenseitigen Verständnis von Praktischer und Systematischer Theologie,"

ThPr 9 (1974): 18-26; "Der Wissenschaftsbegriff der Theologie," *EvTh* 35 (1975): 283-309; "Hermeneutisches und analytisches Denken in der Theologie," in *In der Freiheit des Geistes,* pp. 152-65; "Eschatological Rationality," in *Eschatological Rationality: Theological Issues in Focus* (Grand Rapids, 1996), pp. 171-200; "Fundamentaltheologie — Grundlagenforschung oder Orientierungskrise?" *VF* 35 (1990/91): 30-40.

IV.2

"How Can Theology Derive from Experiences?" in *Eschatological Rationality* (Grand Rapids, 1996), pp. 54-72; "Kontextuelle Theologie als Herausforderung der Dogmatik," in *"Ihr alle aber seid Brüder,"* A. T. Khoury Festschrift, ed. L. Hagemann and E. Pulsfort (Würzburg and Altenberge, 1990), pp. 365-83; "Zum Kontext deutscher evangelischer Theologie in den dreißiger Jahren — und zum Problem seines kontextuellen Verständnisses heute," in *Text und Kontext in Theologie und Kirche,* ed. F. Hauschildt (Hanover, 1989), pp. 64-95; "Die Wahrheit im Kontext des Redens von Gott. Zum Stellenwert von 'Kontexten' in der systematischen Theologie," *ThGl* 86 (1996): 157-66; "Kontextuelle Theologie im 'Kirchenkampf'?" in *Kaum zu glauben. Von der Häresie und dem Umgang mit ihr,* H. Faulenbach Festschrift, ed. A. Lexutt and V. von Bülow (Rheinbach, 1998), pp. 221-39.

IV.3

"Was heißt 'christologische Begründung' christlichen Handelns heute?" in *Evangelische Ethik. Diskussionsbeiträge zu ihrer Grundlegung und ihren Aufgaben,* ed. H. G. Ulrich, TB 83 (Munich, 1990), pp. 98-112; *Zur Zwei-Reiche-Lehre Luthers,* TB 49 (Munich, 1973), pp. vii-xiv.

V

"Der Dogmatiker als Anwalt des Laien in der Theologie," in *Vom Amt des Laien in Kirche und Theologie,* G. Krause Festschrift, ed. H. Schröer and G. Müller (Berlin and New York, 1982), pp. 278-95.

Bibliography

I.1.2

A. Grillmeier, *Christ in Christian Tradition: From the Apostolic Age to Chalcedon (451)*, trans. T. Hainthaler, P. Allen, and J. Cawte (New York, 1965); idem, *Mit ihm und in ihm. Christologische Forschungen und Perspektiven* (Freiburg, Basel, and Vienna, 1975), esp. pp. 528-54; R. W. Jenson, *The Triune Identity: God according to the Gospel* (Philadelphia, 1982); E. Maurer, ed., *Der lebendige Gott. Texte zur Trinitätslehre*, TB 95 (Gütersloh, 1999).

I.1.4

A. M. Ritter, "Glaubensbekenntnis(se), V. Alte Kirche," *TRE*, 13 (1984), pp. 399-412 (rule of faith, pp. 402-5).

I.1.5

Ecumenical aspects: E. Schlink, *Ökumenische Dogmatik. Grundzüge* (Göttingen, 1983; 2nd ed., 1993); W. Pannenberg, *Systematic Theology*, vols. 1-3, trans. Geoffrey W. Bromiley (Grand Rapids, 1991-99); R. W. Jenson, *Systematic Theology*, vol. 1: *The Triune God* (New York and Oxford, 1997), vol. 2: *The Works of God* (1999). The term "dogma": J. Koopmans, *Das altkirchliche Dogma in der Reformation*, BEvTh 22 (Munich, 1955); M. Elze, "Der Begriff des Dogmas in der alten Kirche," *ZThK* 61 (1964): 421-38; H. J. Iwand, "Der moderne Mensch und das Dogma," in *Nachgelassene Werke*, vol. 2: *Vorträge und Aufsätze*, ed. D. Schellong and K. G. Steck (Munich, 1966), pp. 91-105; U. Wickert and C. H. Ratschow, "Dogma," *TRE*, 9 (1982), pp. 26-41.

I.2.1

P. Schaff, *The Creeds of Christendom,* vols. 1-3 (New York, 1877; reprint Grand Rapids, 1985).

I.2.2

W. Kamlah and P. Lorenzen, *Logische Propädeutik. Vorschule des vernünftigen Redens,* BI-Hochschultaschenbücher 227, 2nd ed. (Mannheim, 1973 [1992 impression]); J. Track, *Sprachkritische Untersuchungen zum christlichen Reden von Gott,* FSÖTh 37 (Göttingen, 1977).

I.3.3

A. Jeffner, *Kriterien christlicher Glaubenslehre. Eine prinzipielle Untersuchung heutiger protestantischer Dogmatik im deutschen Sprachbereich,* AUU.SDCU 15 (Uppsala, 1976); G. Sauter and A. Stock, *Arbeitsweisen Systematischer Theologie. Eine Anleitung* (Munich and Mainz, 1976; 2nd ed., 1982). On Wittgenstein: G. Brand, *Die grundlegenden Texte von Ludwig Wittgenstein* (Frankfurt, 1975); F. Kerr, OP, *Theology after Wittgenstein,* 2nd ed. (London, 1997); R. Munz, *Religion als Beispiel. Sprache und Methode bei Ludwig Wittgenstein* (Düsseldorf and Bonn, 1997).

I.4.3

L. Vischer, "Wie lehrt die Kirche heute verbindlich?" *ÖR* 25 (1976): 527-47; *Verbindliches Lehren der Kirche heute,* ÖR.B 33 (Frankfurt, 1978); D. Ritschl, "Lehre," *TRE,* 20 (1990), pp. 608-21; E. Martikainen, *Doctrina. Studien zu Luthers Begriff der Lehre,* SLAG 26 (Helsinki, 1992); R. Hütter, *Suffering Divine Things: Theology as Church Practice,* trans. D. Scott (Grand Rapids, 2000).

I.5.1

O. Bayer, *Promissio. Geschichte der reformatorischen Wende in Luthers Theologie,* FKDG 24 (Göttingen, 1971); idem, *Theologie,* HST 1 (Gütersloh, 1994), esp. pp. 440-42; A. Peters, *Kommentar zu Luthers Katechismen,* ed. G. Seebass, vol. 2: *Der Glaube. Das Apostolikum* (Göttingen, 1991).

I.5.2

G. A. Lindbeck, *The Nature of Doctrine: Religion and Theology in a Postliberal Age* (Philadelphia, 1984); R. Williams, *The Wound of Knowledge: Christian Spirituality from the New Testament to St. John of the Cross* (London, 1979; rev. ed., 1990); L. Boyer, J. Leclerq, and F. Vandenbroucke, *A History of Christian Spirituality,* vols. 1-3 (New York, 1982); G. S. Wakefield, *Dictionary of Christian Spirituality* (Philadelphia and London, 1983; 5th ed., 1993); B. McGinn, J. Meyendorff, and J. Leclerq, eds., *Chris-*

tian Spirituality, vols. 1-3 (London and New York, 1985ff.); C. Jones, G. Wainwright, and E. Yarnold, SJ, eds., *The Study of Spirituality* (London, 1986); G. Ruhbach, *Theologie und Spiritualität* (Göttingen, 1987); D. Allen, *Spiritual Theology: The Theology of Yesterday for Spiritual Help Today* (Boston, 1997).

I.5.3

L. Steiger, *Erschienen in der Zeit. Dogmatik im Kirchenjahr — Epiphanias und Vorpassion* (Kassel, 1982); H. Auf der Maur, *Feiern im Rhythmus der Zeit,* vol. 1: *Herrenfeste in Woche und Jahr: Gottesdienst der Kirche,* Handbuch der Liturgiewissenschaft, vol. 5 (Regensburg, 1983); K.-H. Bieritz, *Das Kirchenjahr. Feste, Gedenk- und Feiertage in Geschichte und Gegenwart* (Munich, 1987; 3rd ed., 1991); H. U. von Balthasar, *Mysterium Paschale: The Mystery of Easter,* trans A. Nichols, OP (Edinburgh, 1990).

II.1

M. Seils, "Die Rolle der Dogmatik in der Praxis der Kirchenleitung," *EvTh* 44 (1984): 2-11; A. Geense, "Kanzel und Katheder: Über den Bezugsrahmen unseres Theologisierens," *KuD* 43 (1997): 124-50; M. Welker, *What Happens in Holy Communion?* trans. J. W. Hoffmeyer (Grand Rapids, 2000); P. J. R. Abbing, "Diakonie II. Theologische Grundprobleme der Diakonie," *TRE,* 8 (1981), pp. 644-56; R. Turre, *Diakonik. Grundlegung und Gestaltung der Diakonie* (Neukirchen-Vluyn, 1991).

II.2.3

Schuld und Vergebung, GlLern 1 (1986); J. Zehner, *Das Forum der Vergebung in der Kirche. Studien zum Verhältnis von Sündenvergebung und Recht,* Öffentliche Theologie 10 (Gütersloh, 1998), pp. 13-51; M. Beintker, *Rechtfertigung in der neuzeitlichen Lebenswelt. Theologische Erkundungen* (Tübingen, 1998).

II.3.2

K. Federer, *Liturgie und Glaube,* Paradosis 4 (Fribourg, 1950); G. S. Henry, "The Life Line of Theology," *PSB* 65 (1972): 22-30; G. Wainwright, *Doxology: The Praise of God in Worship, Doctrine, and Life,* 2nd ed. (New York, 1984), pp. 218-83.

II.4.3

R. Bohren, *Predigtlehre,* 6th ed. (Gütersloh, 1993); R. Lischer, *A Theology of Preaching: The Dynamics of the Gospel* (Nashville, 1981); idem, *Theories of Preaching: Selected Readings in the Homiletical Tradition* (Durham, N.C., 1987); H. Stoevesandt, "Was ist Predigt?" in *Gottes Freiheit und die Grenze der Theologie. Gesammelte Aufsätze,* ed. E. Stoevesandt and G. Sauter (Zurich, 1992), pp. 45-57; K. H. Miskotte, *Das Wagnis der*

Predigt, ed. and trans. H. Braunschweiger and H. Stoevesandt, AzTh 87 (Stuttgart, 1998).

II.5

P. Brunner, *Worship in the Name of Jesus,* trans. M. H. Bertram (St. Louis, 1968); F. Rosenzweig, *The Star of Redemption,* trans. from the 2nd ed. (1930) by W. W. Hallo (Notre Dame, 1985); M. L. Frettlöh, *Theologie des Segens. Biblische und dogmatische Wahrnehmungen* (Gütersloh, 1998).

II.6.4

H. Tacke, *Glaubenshilfe als Lebenshilfe. Probleme und Chancen heutiger Seelsorge,* 2nd ed. (Neukirchen-Vluyn, 1979); P. Bukowski, *Die Bibel ins Gespräch bringen. Erwägungen zu einer Grundfrage der Seelsorge* (Neukirchen-Vluyn, 1994); D. van Deusen Hunsinger, *Theology and Pastoral Counseling: A New Interdisciplinary Approach* (Grand Rapids, 1995).

II.7.2

K. E. Nipkow and F. Schweitzer, *Religionspädagogik. Texte zur evangelischen Erziehungs- und Bildungsverantwortung seit der Reformation,* vol. I, TB 84 (Munich, 1991); vol. II/1, TB 88 (Gütersloh, 1994); vol. II/2, TB 89 (Gütersloh, 1994); H. G. Ulrich, "Was heißt: Von Gott reden lernen?" in *Einfach von Gott reden. Ein theologischer Diskurs,* F. Mildenberger Festschrift, ed. J. Roloff and H. G. Ulrich (Stuttgart, 1994), pp. 172-89.

II.8.3

E. Herms, "Was heißt 'Leitung in der Kirche'?" in *Erfahrbare Kirche. Beiträge zur Ekklesiologie* (Tübingen, 1990), pp. 80-101; G. Müller, "Theorie und Praxis von Kirchenleitung in der Reformation," *KuD* 42 (1996): 154-73.

II.9.3

M. Kähler, *Schriften zu Christologie und Mission,* ed. H. Frohnes, TB 42 (Munich, 1971); G. W. Peters, *A Biblical Theology of Missions* (Chicago, 1972); A. W. Glasser and D. A. McGavran, *Contemporary Theologies of Mission* (Grand Rapids, 1983); D. Senior and C. Stuhlmueller, *The Biblical Foundations for Mission* (Maryknoll, N.Y., 1983); T. Sundermeier, *Theologie der Mission,* in *Konvivenz und Differenz. Studien zu einer verstehenden Missionswissenschaft* (Erlangen, 1995), pp. 15-42; J. A. B. Jongeneel, *Philosophy, Science, and Theology of Mission in the Nineteenth and Twentieth Centuries: A Missiological Encyclopedia,* vol. 2: *Missionary Theology,* SIGC 106 (Frankfurt, 1997).

III.1.3

J. Pelikan, *The Christian Tradition: A History of the Development of Doctrine*, 5 vols. (Chicago and London, 1971-89).

III.2.3

G. Sauter, ed., *Theologie als Wissenschaft. Aufsätze und Thesen*, TB 43 (Munich, 1971); K. N. Micskey, *Die Axiom-Syntax des evangelisch-dogmatischen Denkens. Strukturanalysen des Denkprozesses und des Wahrheitsbegriffs in den Wissenschaftstheorien (Prolegomena) zeitgenössischer systematischer Theologen*, FSÖTh 35 (Göttingen, 1976); H. U. Jones, *Die Logik theologischer Perspektiven. Eine sprachanalytische Untersuchung*, FÖSTh 48 (Göttingen, 1985); D. Ritschl, *The Logic of Theology: A Brief Account of the Relationship between Concepts in Theology*, trans. J. Bowden (Philadelphia, 1987); *Implizite Axiome. Tiefenstrukturen des Denkens und Handelns*, D. Ritschl Festschrift, ed. W. Huber, E. Petzold, and T. Sundermeier (Munich, 1990).

III.3.3

K. Barth, *Evangelical Theology: An Introduction*, trans. G. Foley (Grand Rapids, 1979); D. H. Kelsey, *The Uses of Scripture in Recent Theology* (Philadelphia, 1975); *Scriptural Authority and Narrative Interpretation*, H. W. Frei Festschrift, ed. G. Green (Philadelphia, 1987); W. G. Jeanrond, *Text and Interpretation as Categories of Theological Thinking*, trans. T. J. Wilson (New York, 1988); R. Ziegert, ed., *Die Zukunft des Schriftprinzips*, Bibel im Gespräch 2 (Stuttgart, 1994); H. H. Schmid and J. Mehlhausen, eds., *Sola Scriptura. Das reformatorische Schriftprinzip in der säkularen Welt* (Gütersloh, 1991); F. Mildenberger, *Biblische Dogmatik. Eine Biblische Theologie in dogmatischer Perspektive*, vol. 1: *Prolegomena: Verstehen und Geltung der Bibel* (Stuttgart, 1991); J. Barton and G. Sauter, eds., *Revelation and Story: Narrative Theology and the Centrality of Story* (Aldershot, Hampshire, 2000).

IV.1.3

Fundamental theology: G. Ebeling, "Erwägungen zu einer evangelischen Fundamentaltheologie," *ZThK* 67 (1970): 479-524; idem, "Hermeneutische Theologie?" in *Wort und Glaube*, vol. 2 (Tübingen, 1969), pp. 99-120; idem, "Discussion Theses for a Course of Introductory Lectures on the Study of Theology," in *Word and Faith*, trans. J. W. Leitch (Philadelphia, 1963), pp. 424-33; W. Joest, *Fundamentaltheologie. Theologische Grundlagen- und Methodenprobleme* (Stuttgart, 1974); T. Williams, *Form and Vitality in the World and God: A Christian Perspective* (Oxford, 1985); D. L. Migliore, *Faith Seeking Understanding: An Introduction to Christian Theology* (Grand Rapids, 1991); H. Verweyen, *Gottes letztes Wort. Grundriß einer Fundamentaltheologie* (Düsseldorf, 1991). Encyclopedia: K. Barth, *Evangelical Theol-*

ogy (Grand Rapids, 1979); E. Jüngel, "Das Verhältnis der theologischen Disziplinen untereinander," in *Unterwegs zur Sache*, BEvTh 61 (Munich, 1972), pp. 34-59; B. J. F. Lonergan, *Method in Theology* (New York, 1972, 1973, 1979); F. Mildenberger, *Theorie der Theologie. Enzyklopädie als Methodenlehre* (Stuttgart, 1972); O. Bayer, *Was ist das: Theologie? Eine Skizze* (Stuttgart, 1973); W. Pannenberg, *Jesus — God and Man*, trans. L. L. Wilkins and D. A. Priebe (Philadelphia, 1968); idem, *Theology and the Philosophy of Science*, trans. F. McDonagh (Philadelphia, 1976); G. Ebeling, *The Study of Theology*, trans. D. A. Priebe (Philadelphia, 1978); K. Rahner, *Foundations of Christian Faith: An Introduction to the Idea of Christianity*, trans. W. Dych (New York, 1978); D. Tracy, *The Analogical Imagination: Christian Theology and the Culture of Pluralism* (New York, 1981); *Einführung in das Studium der evangelischen Theologie*, ed. H. Schröer (Gütersloh, 1982); E. Farley, *Theologia: The Fragmentation and Unity of Theological Education* (Philadelphia, 1983); F. Schüssler Fiorenza, *Foundational Theology: Jesus and the Church* (New York, 1984).

IV.2.2

G. Collet, ed., *Theologie der Dritten Welt. EATWOT als Herausforderung christlicher Theologie und Kirche*, NZM.S 37 (Immensee, 1990), esp. pp. 142-61; N. Slenczka, "Kontext und Theologie. Ein kritischer Versuch zum Programm einer 'kontextuellen Theologie,'" *NZSTh* 35 (1993): 303-31.

IV.3.3

K. Barth, *The Christian Life*, trans. J. S. McNab (London, 1930); H.-J. Birkner, "Das Verhältnis von Dogmatik und Ethik," in *Handbuch der christlichen Ethik*, vol. 1, ed. A. Hertz, W. Korff, T. Rendtorff, and H. Ringeling, 2nd ed. (Freiburg and Gütersloh, 1979), pp. 281-96; M. Honecker, *Einführung in die Theologische Ethik* (Berlin and New York, 1990), pp. 20-32; H. G. Ulrich, ed., *Evangelische Ethik. Diskussionsbeiträge zu ihrer Grundlegung und zu ihren Aufgaben*, TB 83 (Munich, 1990); N. J. Duff, *Humanization and the Politics of God: The Koinonia Ethics of Paul Lehmann* (Grand Rapids, 1992); P. L. Lehmann, *The Decalogue and a Human Future: The Meaning of the Commandments for Making and Keeping Human Life Human* (Grand Rapids, 1995); R. Hütter, *Evangelische Ethik als kirchliches Zeugnis*, Evangelium und Ethik 1 (Neukirchen-Vluyn, 1993); B. Wannenwetsch, *Gottesdienst als Lebensform. Ethik für Christenbürger* (Stuttgart, 1997).

V.3

K. H. Miskotte, "Der moderne Dogmatiker als Dilettant und Dirigent," *EvTh* 20 (1960): 245-62; G. Sauter and T. Strohm, *Theologie als Beruf in unserer Gesellschaft*, TEH 189 (Munich, 1976).

Index of Biblical References

Index of Names

Index of Subjects

References characteristic of this book appear in boldface type.